PREPARE
FOR THE COMING OF
MESSIAH

A MESSAGE OF LOVE, RESTORATION, WARNING AND HOPE

BY PERRY ENNIS

PREPARE
FOR THE COMING OF
MESSIAH

By Perry Ennis

ISBN: 978-0-9796887-3-7
Printed in the United States of America
Copyright @ 2007 by Menorah Books

Menorah Books
740 Greenville Blvd.
Greenville, NC 27858-5135 USA
Website: www.MessiahIsComing.net

PREPARE
FOR THE COMING OF
MESSIAH

A Message of Love, Restoration, Warning and Hope

The LORD preserves all who love Him, but all the wicked He will destroy.
Psalm 145:20 (NKJV)

"In that day I will raise up the booth of David that is fallen and repair its breaches, and raise up its ruins, and rebuild it as in the days of old; that they may possess the remnant of Edom and all the nations who are called by my name," says the LORD who does this.
Amos 9:11-12 (RSV)

"And now, friends, I know that you acted in ignorance, as did also your rulers. In this way God fulfilled what he had foretold through all the prophets, that his Messiah would suffer. Repent therefore, and turn to God so that your sins may be wiped out, so that times of refreshing may come from the presence of the Lord, and that he may send the Messiah appointed for you, that is, Jesus, who must remain in heaven until the time of universal restoration that God announced long ago through his holy prophets."
Acts 3:17-21 (NRSV)

Then I saw heaven opened, and there was a white horse! Its rider is called Faithful and True, and in righteousness He judges and makes war. And the armies of heaven, wearing fine linen, white and pure, were following Him on white horses.
Revelation 19:11 & 14 (NRSV)

Thy dead shall live, their bodies shall arise. O dwellers in the dust, awake and sing for joy! Come, my people, enter your chambers, and shut your doors behind you; hide yourselves for a little while until the wrath is passed. For behold, the Lord is coming forth out of His place to punish the inhabitants of the earth for their iniquity, and the earth will disclose the blood shed upon her, and will no more cover her slain.

Isaiah 26:19a, 20-21 (RSV)

Immediately after the tribulation of those days shall the sun be darkened, and the moon shall not give her light, and the stars shall fall from heaven, and the powers of the heavens shall be shaken: and then shall appear the sign of the Son of man in heaven: and then shall all of the tribes of the earth mourn, and they shall see the Son of man coming in the clouds of heaven with power and great glory. And He shall send His angels with a great sound of a trumpet, and they shall gather together His elect from the four winds, from one end of heaven to the other.

Matthew 24:29-31 (KJV)

But we do not want you to be uninformed, brothers and sisters, about those who have died, so that you may not grieve as others do who have no hope. For since we believe that Jesus died and rose again, even so, through Jesus, God will bring with him those who have died. For this we declare to you by the word of the Lord, that we who are alive, who are left until the coming of the Lord, will by no means precede those who have died. For the Lord Himself, with a cry of command, with the archangel's call and with the sound of God's trumpet, will descend from heaven, and the dead in Christ will rise first. Then we who are alive, who are left, will be caught up in the clouds together with them to meet the Lord in the air; and so we will be with the Lord for ever. Therefore encourage one another with these words.

1 Thessalonians 4:13-18 (NRSV)

DEDICATION

To all peoples of all nations and races,
who seek the truth of the one true, living God,
the God of Abraham, Isaac, and Jacob,
and after receiving His truth from His Holy Word,
choose to live it.
To Almighty Yahweh be the praise, honor, and glory
now and forever!

ACKNOWLEDGEMENTS

The writing and publishing of this book would not have been possible without the influence in my life of many men and women of the one true God. Holy Spirit has taught me, from research of the Holy Scriptures, much of what I have typed in this labor of love. I have also learned much from the research of other brothers and sisters in Messiah Jesus who are also diligently seeking revelation from Holy Spirit regarding the prophecies of the last generation that we are living in and how to live according to Almighty Yahweh's Words.

I thank Sid Roth for the inspiration, his love for our Lord Jesus (Yahshua) Messiah, and his powerful ministry of taking the gospel of Messiah to the Jew first and to non-Jews throughout the world. I thank Eddie Chumney, Angus and Batya Wooten, Monte Judah, and many other unnamed inspired authors of our time who are helping many individuals to learn of our Hebraic Roots and how to live in obedience to our Creator's instructions. I thank Edwards Brothers, Inc. for their excellent work-manship in the printing of this book. I offer special thanks to the editor and designer, Nancy Williams, and cover artist, Grace Metzger, for their hard work and expertise. I thank my Heavenly Father Yahweh and praise Him and our Master Yahshua Messiah for my wife, Debbie Ruth, and for her patience, love, and support for me. I am thankful for our daughter, Amanda, her husband, Brad, and our son, Joshua, who are so precious to us. All of my family members have been very supportive throughout this eight-year project.

Thank you for purchasing this book. A large percentage of the monies received from the sales of "Prepare for the Coming of Messiah" are given to end-time evangelism and human relief ministries that are making a difference in people's lives. Shalom!

TABLE OF CONTENTS

TABLE OF CONTENTS

TABLE OF CONTENTS

PREFACE

This is a book of biblical truth, revelation knowledge, and understanding from the Holy Scriptures. You may be a person who is looking for answers to the many questions regarding the injustice, fear, violence, and evil that is in our world today. Your curiosity of the title and the interesting cover may be the reason you purchased this book. If you are a Christian, you may be seeking to learn more about the biblical end-of-time prophecies. You may be a person of Jewish ancestry and desire to know more about the coming of the long-awaited Messiah. Perhaps you are a professing Muslim, Jehovah's Witness, or Bahaist. Your belief system may be that of Mormon, Shaman, or Hindu. You could be into any of the New Age beliefs, Raelian, Wiccan, Buddhist, or a member of one of the hundreds, or even thousands, of other types of religions and belief systems throughout the world today. You may have made the decision to buy this book so you could compare its teachings with those that you hold dear from your beliefs. You may not have a defined belief that offers understanding about the complex questions of life, death, and what is after death. Please don't stop reading. Whatever your reason for purchasing this book, you have made an excellent choice. No matter what your belief or non-belief background is, the biblical Scriptures and messages on these pages are powerful and can be life-changing for you. There is a supernatural power from the one true God that is working in your life, and I believe that power has drawn you to read this material.

There is only one true, living God, our Creator, Who wants to be real in your life and to have a personal relationship with you. He loves you more than you or I will ever be able to comprehend in this life. I encourage you, whether you have prayed before or not, to say a short prayer before you begin to read and ask the one true God, Whose name is Father Yahweh, to help you to understand His Word. It is my prayer that you will read this work with an open mind, seeking the truth.

I appeal to you therefore, brothers and sisters, by the mercies of God, to present your bodies as a living sacrifice, holy and acceptable to God,

which is your spiritual worship. Do not be conformed to this world, but be transformed by the renewing of your minds, so that you may discern what is the will of God—what is good and acceptable and perfect. Romans 12:1-2 (NRSV).

I yearn and weep for the souls
    Of family members, strangers, and friends,

Who are lost in this self-centered world
    Of delusions, deceptions, and sins.

Listen to the call of the Master today,
    For He is faithful, and His words are true.

He and only He your soul can save.
    His name is Jesus, and He truly loves you.

Hear, dear child, created in His own likeness,
    The still voice that is calling to you from within.

Calling to you in your state of spiritual blindness,
    For the turning away from your sins to begin.

Let His Holy Spirit fill you, guide you, empower you,
    And keep you through and through.

Once you have received His gift of life His way,
    You'll be a new person, willing His work to do.

After you die and meet Him, you'll hear Him say,
    "Enter, my servant, the home prepared for you."

                  Perry Ennis
                  November, 2006

INTRODUCTION

W ho I am as the author of this book is not important. The messages in this book, especially the truth that the one true Creator God loves you more than you or I can comprehend, is of paramount importance. I give my Heavenly Father, Yahweh, all of the credit for the revelation of His Holy Word from His Holy Set-apart Spirit because all glory, praise, and honor belong to Him, now and forevermore.

I first began studying the Scriptures of the Holy Bible in the spring of 1972 after I accepted Jesus (Yahshua) Messiah as my Lord (Master) and Savior. God used a young man to literally save my life from a one-way trip of destruction from alcoholism and drug use that would have led to my suicide. I have included my testimony of how God transformed my life in Chapter Three, "Receiving Eternal Life."

The idea for this book of understanding was given to me by the Holy Spirit many years ago.

Hear, O Israel: The LORD our God is one LORD: And thou shalt love the LORD thy God with all thine heart, and with all thy soul, and with all thy might.
Deuteronomy 6:4-5 (KJV)

This book is revelation for you, the reader, from your Creator, Savior, and King eternal, providing you accept Him and live for Him. I am one of His many humble servants whom He is working through during this last generation before His return to earth to reveal very important end-time messages. His Word reveals His great master plan for humanity that includes the end-time prophecies that are presently being fulfilled. The Messiah, King Yahshua (Jesus), is coming back to this planet that He created so long ago to destroy all of His/our enemies, restore His ways among His covenant people, bring His family together with new resurrected bodies, and establish His righteous kingdom on this earth.

There have been many books written on the subjects of the end of the world, Armageddon, last generation Bible prophecy, and the second coming of Messiah, or Christ. Over the past thirty years, I have read a lot of books that expound on those subjects. Each author conveys his or her explanation of these intriguing topics according to his or her own interpretation of the biblical Scriptures as they apply to world events. There is one statement that I can make that I know is 100% accurate: No author or individual has all the answers to all the questions concerning the end of this world as we know it, including yours truly. Like the other authors of these types of books, I will expound upon my interpretation of the Holy Scriptures to the very best of my ability based upon my research of these subjects. More than trying to influence you with my interpretation, I encourage you to think for yourself, with an open mind, as you read the Holy Scriptures and the paraphrasing I have provided, so that you can obtain the best understanding of the most important compiled book of knowledge ever written, the Holy Bible.

This book is more than an explanation of biblical prophecy. It is a concise account of Father Yahweh's plan for us humans that He created on this small planet, which is a tiny speck in His immense and vast universe. Each chapter could easily fill several hundred pages, but for the sake of keeping this book brief and to the point, I've included what I believe to be the most important verses and paraphrasing.

Chapter One will be helpful to you in your understanding of the beginning of God's master plan that runs true throughout the Holy Bible. Chapter Two introduces you to the prophecies of the first coming of Messiah and explains His mission to this planet and the significance of what He accomplished in His life as a human being. Chapter Three, "Receiving Eternal Life," is the most important chapter in this book. Chapter Four provides historical background that exposes how the beliefs of the first century followers of Messiah were changed in the third and fourth century. Chapter Five will help you to understand the significance of the Sabbath and our Creator's appointed Holy Feasts that are symbolic of the millennium rest, and the first and second coming of Messiah. Chapters Six through Ten cover prophecies and understanding of how they relate to the end times. Chapter Eleven gives teaching and instruction from God's Word as to how we should live day to day as followers of Yahshua (Jesus) Messiah and how we are to prepare for His second coming to this earth. Chapter Twelve provides teaching for the followers of Messiah in how to minister to others. I encourage you to read this material slowly and more than once. Let the revelation of the Word from our Creator Yahweh soak into the depths of your being. In doing so, you will be blessed!

I have not seen great visions of revelations or audibly heard God's voice from on high, but I know that there are some modern-day prophets who have. I believe that God has a purpose for each person's life, and a specific work for each person to do. He gives each person talents and abilities to fulfill His will in us. There is no doubt in my mind that one of the works He has for me is the writing, publishing, and distributing of this book to as many people as possible to prepare the way for His coming.

I have not been called to deliver from God any new divine messages directly to individuals, church congregations, peoples in certain geographical locations, or even whole nations as true prophets are sometimes called to do, but I have been chosen to be one of many watchmen of today that God is using to do intercessory prayer, to warn people of the terrible events that will be fulfilled in this generation, and to offer a message of understanding, love, warning, and hope.

As it is written:

The Lord spoke to me. "Mortal man," he said, "tell your people what happens when I bring war to a land. The people of that country choose one of their number to be a watchman. When he sees the enemy approaching, he sounds the alarm to warn everyone. If someone hears it but pays no attention and the enemy comes and kills him, then he is to blame for his own death. His death is his own fault, because he paid no attention to the warning. If he had paid attention, he could have escaped. If, however, the watchman sees the enemy coming and does not sound the alarm, the enemy will come and kill those sinners, but I will hold the watchman responsible for their death."
Ezekiel 33:1-6 (TEV)

The prophetic Scriptures that are included in Chapters Five through Nine are many of the ancient prophecies that God gave to several writers of the Bible. I have expressed in paraphrase how these prophecies relate to current events of our time. Most of the prophecies that the ancient prophets recorded made no sense to them or to the people that have read them over the course of the past two to three thousand years. Many of the prophecies didn't make sense because they could not have applied to any generation except the time that we are living in now and the few years ahead of us. As it is written:

> **"But you, Daniel, shut up the words, and seal the book until the time of the end; many shall run to and fro, and knowledge shall increase."**
> Daniel 12:4 (NKJV)

It is so important that we study, not only the prophecies that apply to our time, but all of God's Word. In doing so, we have a better understanding of Who God really is and what He is about, so we will know how to live our lives in a way that will be pleasing in His sight.

There is a great responsibility associated with the teaching and administering of God's Word. It is very important that apostles, prophets, evangelists, pastors, and teachers communicate God's Word with as much truthfulness, integrity, and compassion as possible.

> **My brothers and sisters, not many of you should become teachers. As you know, we teachers will be judged with greater strictness than others.**
> James 3:1 (TEV).

> **I warn everyone who hears the words of the prophecies of this book: if anyone adds to them, God will add to that person the plagues described in this book; if anyone takes away from the words of the book of this prophecy, God will take away that person's share in the tree of life and in the holy city, which are described in this book.**
> Revelation 22:18-19 (NRSV).

Throughout this book, the word *God* is used, which is a word that is familiar to most people. The word *God* can, and does, have many different meanings to individuals from different backgrounds and life experiences of the world. For clarification, wherever the word *God* is used in this book, unless otherwise explained, it will imply the Hebrew deity title *Elohim* as it is implied in the Holy Bible. *Elohim* is the Hebrew word from which the English word *God* is translated. *Elohim* is a plural noun in form, but is singular in its meaning. The one true and living Supreme Creator of all that is in the universe, as revealed in His Word, is the God of Abraham, Isaac, and Jacob. The evidence in the Holy Bible is that God (Elohim), the Godhead, is One but has expressed Himself in three different ways. There are not three different Gods as is sometimes associated with the Christian faith. The names and titles for God are explained in more detail in Chapter One.

The Hebrew name *Yahshua* (some writers prefer the spelling *Yeshua* or *Yahushua*) and title *Messiah* are interchanged with the name *Jesus* and title *Christ* through the first three chapters of this book. From Chapter Four on, His original Hebrew name *Yahshua* and title *Messiah* will be used in the Scriptures and text. Both names and titles refer to the same person with Whom believers have come to identify, Jesus Christ, as He was referred to during His first coming, from approximately 4 B.C. to A.D. 29. The names and titles also refer to King Yahshua when He returns to earth during His second coming at the end of this age, whenever that takes place. The name *Jesus* and the titles *Lord* and *God* will remain in the Scriptures as referenced in the Bible text. My reason for using the set apart, sanctified, Hebrew names of our Heavenly Father, Yahweh, and His Son, our Savior and Master, Yahshua, is to help restore them, so that believers will be able to understand the truth about their original Hebrew names. Do you prefer to be called and referred to by your real name or by a name that has been translated through three or four languages and sounds nothing like it did in its original form? Our Master's name, *Yahshua*, was translated from Hebrew as *Yehoshua* or *Yahshua* to *Iesous* in the Greek. In the early 1500's, translators of the Scriptures added a tail on the English "i" and created the new letter and sound of "j," and therefore, a new name for Yahshua, *Jesus*. There is no "j" in either the Hebrew or Greek alphabet.

Much of this book is about helping you, the reader, to gain a new and fresh understanding of important truths that Holy Spirit is restoring throughout the earth in this last generation to help us prepare the way for Messiah's coming.

In several places where Scriptures are printed, I have provided my interpretation as a paraphrase in parentheses.

Some of the teaching in this book is to introduce you to our Hebraic roots and giving understanding that clears up much of the confusion that has been taught throughout Christianity and Rabbinical Judaism for the past nineteen hundred years. There is also teaching on how to do Scriptural ministry that will help people to be overcomers of the many challenges that this life presents. Our Creator, Savior, King eternal, Father Yahweh does love us and wants us to believe and accept Him, so that we may have a real personal and power-filled relationship with Him through His Son, Messiah Jesus, and fellowship with Holy Spirit.

The information in this book will help you in many ways if you receive it with the right attitude and apply it to your life. It will also give you insight and prepare you for the terrible and difficult times that are prophesied to happen in this world, or may already be happening as you are reading this. I encourage you to let the truth of the Holy Scriptures help you to accept Yahshua (Jesus) into your heart and to live for Him. The only way we will escape His coming wrath is by learning to love and trust Him with all of our heart and loving and treating all people with whom we come in contact as we would like to be treated.

May Yahshua Messiah (Jesus Christ), King of the Universe, by the power of His Holy Spirit presence, bless your reading and understanding of His Word, to the glory of our Heavenly Father Yahweh forevermore! Amen!

1

GOD'S MASTER PLAN,
IN THE BEGINNING

Understanding God's Master Plan can be accomplished only by studying God's Holy Word that is found in both the old and new covenants, or testaments. You may be asking yourself this very important question. How do I know that God's Word is true?

The two testaments, or covenants, of the Bible were written by a total of 44 authors spanning a time period of approximately 1,600 years. From an historical perspective, the records of ancient historians of the names of people, dates, locations, descriptions of civilizations, and events line up with the Scriptures in the Bible. The discovery of Noah's Ark near the top of Mount Ararat in Turkey, as it is recorded in Genesis 8:4, is one of many proofs that the Scriptures of the Holy Bible are true. Today's archaeologists and historians often go to the Bible first when researching a site or ancient event because it is the most complete collection of ancient history there is, spanning about 5,000 years. Within the sixty-six books of the Bible are the records of the creation of the universe, the great worldwide flood, and the history of the ancient Hebrew, Israelite, Jewish people. The Holy Scriptures reveal God's plan of salvation for mankind, the restoration within His people and the earth of all things that are dear to Him, the prophecies detailing the end of this world as we know it, and the creation by God of a new earth and heaven.

From a prophetic perspective, the hundreds of old covenant prophecies that were written on scrolls about 3,000 years ago were kept under the close protection of the Jewish scribes and priests. During the third century, the old covenant books called the *Torah* and, at that time, the newly written new covenant books began being translated and compiled into one book. The writers of the new covenant books of the Bible had to have been amazed as they witnessed first hand the fulfillment of the very detailed old covenant prophecies as they related to the first coming of the Messiah. All of the old covenant prophecies about the Messiah's first coming to the earth were written approximately 600 to 1,000 years before they came true. The possibility of only one detailed prophecy recorded about an event coming true several hundred years later would be about one in a million odds. The best mathematicians would not be able to calculate the odds of over 100 of these types of prophecies coming true.

From a spiritual perspective, when God's Holy Spirit is working in your life, you are able to comprehend the Scriptures of the Bible and know that God's Word is true. Do you remember in the preface that I asked you to say a short prayer each time before you begin to read material that contains Scriptures of the Bible? God wants very much for you to understand His Word and His Master Plan because you are part of it. When you sincerely pray to God asking for His help, it means that you believe in Him and you truly desire to understand His Word so you can apply it to your life. He will hear and answer your prayer because He is faithful and true.

Here are some verses of Scripture that help us to comprehend the importance of God's Word:

The law *[instruction]* of the Lord is perfect, converting the soul: the testimony of the Lord is sure, making wise the simple. The statutes of the Lord are right, rejoicing the heart: the commandment of the Lord is pure, enlightening the eyes. The fear of the Lord is clean, enduring forever: the judgments of the Lord are true and righteous altogether.
   Psalm 19: 7-9 (KJV). *Bracketed words added for clarity.*

Give ear, O my people, to my law: incline your ears to the words of my mouth. That they might set their hope in God, and not forget the works of God, but keep His commandments: And might not be as their fathers, a stubborn and rebellious generation; a generation that set not their heart aright, and whose spirit was not stedfast with God.
   Psalm 78:1, 7-8 (KJV).

Thy word is a lamp unto my feet, and a light unto my path.
   Psalm 119:105 (KJV).

All Scripture is inspired by God and is useful for teaching , for reproof, for correction, and for training in righteousness, so that everyone who belongs to God may be proficient, equipped for every good work.
2 Timothy 3:16-17 (NRSV).

So we have the prophetic message more fully confirmed. You will do well to be attentive to this as to a lamp shining in a dark place, until the day dawns and the morning star rises in your hearts. First of all you must understand this, that no prophecy of Scripture is a matter of one's own interpretation, because no prophecy ever came by human will, but men and women moved by the Holy Spirit that spoke from God.
2 Peter 1:19-21, (NRSV).

So also no one comprehends the thoughts of God except the Spirit of God. Now we have received not the spirit of the world, but the Spirit which is from God, that we might understand the gifts bestowed on us by God. And we impart this in words not taught by human wisdom but taught by the Spirit, interpreting spiritual truths to those who possess the Spirit.
1 Corinthians 2:11b-13, (RSV).

If you are a person of Jewish ancestry, you may have never read any new covenant Scriptures before reading this book. It's okay to read these verses, no matter what you may have been taught in the past. It is very important that we study from both covenants of God's Word and to have a thorough understanding of key words in the Scriptures. If you are a person who is not from Jewish ancestry and have never read any Scripture before, then it is my prayer that you are having a new revelation of thought and belief. The most important decision for any person reading this book is to think for yourself with your mind open to receiving the truth. You must ask yourself the all-important question: Do I really want to be exposed to truth? If you do, then the Holy Scriptures is the place to find the truth for the many questions about life and the times in which we live.

The focus of the material on these pages is not about converting anyone to anything, but to help you, the reader, have a better understanding of the instructions from the Creator of the universe that are found in His awesome book. The Holy Scriptures enable us to be restored into relationship with Him. Stay with me. I will get to God's plan eventually.

I have included the definitions of a few Hebrew words to help clarify the interpretation of the Scriptures. Incorrect interpretations of Scripture have been the starting point of many false religious cults and much confusion in Christian denominations and in Jewish congregations.

It is important to have some foundational clarity to help us better grasp the big picture. I pray that as you are reading these Scriptures and absorbing the truth in them you will be receptive to God's Holy Spirit imparting the truth into your heart. I know from my own experience that the Scriptures from God's Holy Word are life changing and supernatural.

In Genesis 1:1 it is written: **In the beginning God created the heavens and the earth** (NKJV). The word *God* in this verse and throughout the old covenant is translated into English from Hebrew as one of the two primary titles of the one true Deity. These titles in the original Hebrew are *Elohim* and *Adonai*. The title of God in this verse is *Elohim*. As stated previously at the end of the Introduction, this word is a plural noun in form but is singular in meaning. This means that God, the Creator of the universe, exists as more than one individual being that is one within Himself, but it also means that Elohim is immortal, omnipotent, omniscient, and omnipresent. It is written in Deuteronomy 6:4: **Hear, O Israel: The Lord our God, the Lord is one!** (NKJV). This is an important part of the Jewish *Shema* that is recited as a confession of faith. The *New Jewish Version* adds the words to that verse, "the Lord alone." The Hebrew word for *alone* is *echad*, which means "one, in the sense of one alone, no other." The God of Abraham, Isaac, and Jacob is the one true, living God, and there is no other. The Bible does not contradict itself. It is written in Genesis 1:26 (NKJV): **Then God *Elohim* said, "Let Us make man in Our image, according to Our likeness ..."** From this, we learn that there must be more than one entity of God the Supreme Being, which is clearly one Godhead being. This is something that we cannot possibly comprehend completely. To believe and accept this, we must have faith that it is true.

The second Hebrew title of God is *Adonai*, which means "omnipotent one, having unlimited power and authority." It also implies God's relationship to mankind as being a husband. This name/title was substituted for the proper name of God often by early Jewish scribes because they feared that people would accidentally use the proper name Yahweh in vain, thereby breaking the third commandment. Through the many translations and transliterations from Hebrew to Latin to English, the terms *Lord*, *God*, and *Jehovah* are written in Bibles to identify our Supreme Creator, instead of the Hebrew names *Elohim*, *Yahweh*, and *Adonai*. I have interchanged *Elohim* for "God," *Adonai* for "Lord," and *Yahweh* for the name of God throughout the remainder of this book.

The majority of scholars today agree that the most accurate Hebrew translation for the true name title *God* is *Yahweh*, which is a proper name meaning "I AM WHO I AM." This is the name, as it is written in Exodus 3:13-14, that God told Moses to tell the enslaved Hebrew people if they asked for the name of the Lord God of their fathers. Also, King Yahshua (Jesus) referred to Himself as having been before Abraham and being I AM, as recorded in John 8:56-59. The name *Jehovah* is the name *Yahweh* that has been transliterated from Hebrew into English. *Yahweh* is more accurate since there is no "j" sound or letter equivalent in the Hebrew language. The single most universal and common word in the world is *hallelujah* or *halleluYah*. This Hebrew word that you may be familiar with means "praise God," or originally, "praise Yah," the short form of Yahweh. Our Creator is certainly worthy to be praised for all that He has done, is doing, and will continue to do in our lives.

The best way I know to begin to describe the Master Plan of Father Yahweh is in a parable. A parable is a short story that illustrates a moral truth. I will follow it with a brief study of the fall from eternal life of the first humans, along with references of Scripture from the old and new covenant prophecies that proclaim the Messiah and the necessity of His first-coming mission.

I don't know where this wonderful little parable originated. I heard it one morning at a men's prayer breakfast from a friend who said it had been told to him by a friend. The story goes like this.

There once was an elderly couple that had been married for many years. They lived somewhere in the country of northern rural America. They took care of each other and a few animals they had on their farm. It was a bitter cold day in January. Six inches of fresh snow had fallen the night before on top of the already ice-covered and snow-packed frozen ground. The old man and his wife sat by the oil heater looking out the window at the white barnyard scene, watching as swirling snow blew off the roofs of their home and barn. Suddenly, a flock of small birds flew around the barnyard. As the elderly couple watched, they realized that the birds were frantically looking for shelter from the frigid cold so that they wouldn't die. The little birds darted from the trees to bushes to barn top with no avail. The old man and his wife were sad when they saw the first bird fall to the ground dead. And then another. The old man said to his wife, "I feel so helpless. I don't know what to do. If I go out into the yard, I will scare them away because I'm so much larger than they are. Oh, if only I could become as one of the little birds for a while, then I could lead them and show them the way into the barn where it's warm enough to save them. Inside, there would be plenty of grain that they could eat. I know where there is a small hole in a wall of the barn where a pine knot fell out of a board. It's just big enough for the birds to pass through. Oh, if I could only be one of them for a little while, so I could show them the way that they could be saved and not perish."

This touching story must be similar to what God had on His mind long ago before creation. He must have looked into the future, into the hearts of mankind, and realized how lost and perishable the souls and bodies of humans would become, even before He created them. I encourage you, at this point, to stop and read the record of the creation story and the fall of Adam and Eve as it is written in Genesis Chapters One, Two, and Three. I will continue to paraphrase.

God knew that He must create human beings with their own free will so that they would have the ability to choose and make decisions for themselves. How did and how does God know all of these things? He is omniscient, which means He has total knowledge, knowing everything. When God created plants, they were created not having a conscious mind, or soul, but when He created animals, He created them with a conscious, thinking mind, or soul, that has a personality. Man was created by God in the image, or likeness, of God. As the most intelligent animal that God created, man was and is capable of a much higher thought process than that of animals. Man, in a much lesser way than God, can reason and make decisions.

God did something extra when He created Adam and Eve. In verse seven of Genesis Chapter Two, it is written that God **"breathed into his nostrils the breath of life"** (NKJV). It is implied that God did the same for Eve because it is written in Genesis 1:27, **"... in the image of God He** [Elohim] **created him; male and female He created them,"** (NKJV).

The breath that God blew into them made them living souls, souls that would not die as long as they ate—received their wisdom and knowledge—from the Tree of Life—symbolic of the Torah and Yahshua

Messiah, the living Torah—and did not enter into rebellion. He also knew that, by placing these spirit, soul, and body combinations in a physical environment, they would try and test their being in every possible way. He knew that His human creations would need His help. God perceived that the first humans, and all humans after them, would not be able to withstand the overpowering deception and temptation of the evil one and his huge army of demonic forces. Our Creator (Elohim) knew that, at the right time in history, He would have to intervene with the human race He had created in order to provide a way out of their dilemma. Their dilemma, as well as ours today, is that of separation from God.

The first man and woman, Adam and Eve, had everything provided for them by God while they were living in the Garden of Eden. Their home in nature was surely the most beautiful place that has ever been on this earth. Their spirit/soul/bodies were created in the image of God and were designed to live forever in perfect relationship with Him. Adam and Eve glorified God in their bodies as they communicated and loved their Creator as members of a family. When Father God looked at them, He saw righteousness, purity, holiness, and all of the other wonderful attributes of Himself because they were made in His image. The glory of Adonai Elohim (Lord God) was in them and covered them.

In the middle of the garden where they lived were two trees. One was the Tree of Life and the other was the tree of the knowledge of good and evil. They were doing great until they gave in to the temptation and deception of Satan, the evil one, and made the wrong choice. There are several pages of explanation and Scripture about Satan later in this chapter.

Adam and Eve did not know of nakedness until their eyes were opened to the knowledge of good and evil and the glory of Elohim was removed from them. Father Yahweh had told Adam about the one tree in the garden that he was not to eat from. As it is written:

And the LORD God took man, and put him into the garden of Eden to dress it and to keep it. And the LORD God commanded the man, saying, Of every tree of the garden thou mayest freely eat: but of the tree of the knowledge of good and evil, thou shalt not eat of it: for in the day that thou eatest thereof thou shalt surely die.
Genesis 2:15-17 (KJV)

Their wrong choice changed their whole image, nature, and character.

When they ate the fruit from the tree of the knowledge of good and evil, areas of their minds were expanded, and they were able, like Elohim, to discern good from evil. The overwhelming complication in this for Adam, Eve, and all of their descendants up to us and through to the end of this age is that, in having this knowledge, man must always choose good and never evil in order to be pleasing and acceptable in God's sight. God knew that because of the powerful, deceptive influence of Satan, always choosing good was impossible for Adam and Eve, and it would continue to be impossible on down through the centuries for all of mankind. Adam and Eve had broken the covenant with God. As much as God loved His children, He had to keep His Word, for His Word is faithful and true throughout all eternity.

Adam and Eve were cast out of their garden home, which was the kingdom of the world that God had given them to reign over. They were forced to leave the Tree of Life that had been for their health and well being. The Tree of Life is symbolic of Yahweh's instructions for life, which if followed, provide blessings and protection from curses. The Tree of Life is Father Yahweh's Holy Word which became flesh nearly 4,000 years after the creation of Adam and Eve. Adam and Eve were driven out of the garden and forbidden to eat from the Tree of Life because it was not in Father Yahweh's Master Plan for His newly created human beings to live eternally in a fallen state. As a result of their fallen state, their status had changed; physical death came and also the horrible separation of relationship with Almighty Yah.

Adonai cursed the earth and drove them into the barren land of Satan's domain to do hard labor in order to earn their existence. The fullness of the reality of their punishment for disobedience was their death sentence. Within this sentence, there are two types of deaths that were allotted upon mankind. One is that, through Adam, God enforced a spiritual death of their souls. It was not a complete destruction, but an eternal separation between Himself and mankind. You may be saying to yourself, "Man, this is really getting deep, and how could God do that?" When God looked at Adam and Eve after their fall, what He saw was the new image they had taken on—the image of the devil, which is self-centered, arrogant, vile, lustful, hateful, unrighteous, lying, unholy, and the list could go on. They had crossed over from the protection and provision of God in His domain to the curse, influence, and punishment of Satan's domain.

The other death is the one we are more familiar with. After their fall, their immortal bodies, which had been in the likeness of Elohim's, were changed. With this change, their bodies became susceptible to the attacks of the evil one that brings disease, deterioration, and death of the human body just as it happens to our bodies today. With the death of the human body comes the separation of the soul from the body. The soul lives forever, but in the fallen state of mankind, the soul is separated from God. So, you see, there has existed this most serious dilemma between humanity and our Creator. It is extremely important that we fully understand our dilemma and the solution that God has provided.

God (Elohim) knew this terrible separation would happen. The most significant part of His plan was creating a way for fallen mankind to be able to come back to Himself. There had to be a way to restore the relationship with humanity that God deeply desired and mankind desperately needed.

The following are old covenant Scriptures that clarify God's plan and man's needs. Our Heavenly Father loves all of mankind and desires that all individuals should be able to live their lives being blessed by Him. These verses are quoted from *Today's English Version* (TEV).

You will show me the path that leads to life; your presence fills me with joy and brings me pleasure forever.
   Psalm 16:11

LORD, your constant love reaches the heavens; your faithfulness extends to the skies. Your righteousness is towering like the mountains; your justice is like the depths of the sea. Men and animals are in your care. How precious, O God, is your constant love! We find protection under the shadow of your wings. We feast on the abundant food you provide; you let us drink from the river of your goodness. You are the source of all life, and because of your light we see the light.
   Psalm 36: 5-9

Do not be afraid—I am with you! I am your God—let nothing terrify you. I will make you strong and help you; I will protect you and save you.
   Isaiah 41:10

Mankind has been separated from God because of disobedience, rebellion, and sin. We cannot help it because we all have inherited our sinful natures from our ancient parents, Adam and Eve.

> The fool has said in his heart, *"There is* no God." They are corrupt, and have done abominable iniquity; *There is* none who does good. God looks down from heaven upon the children of men, to see if there are *any* who understand, who seek God.
>   Psalm 53:1-2 (NKJV)

> For *there is* not a just man on earth who does good and does not sin.
>   Ecclesiastes 7:20 (NKJV)

> But we are all like an unclean *thing,* and all our righteousnesses *are* like filthy rags; we all fade as a leaf, and our iniquities, like the wind, have taken us away. And *there is* no one who calls on Your name, who stirs himself up to take hold of You; for You have hidden Your face from us, and have consumed us because of our iniquities. But now, O LORD, You *are* our Father; we *are* the clay, and You our potter; and all we *are* the work of Your hand.
>   Isaiah 64:6-8 (NKJV)

As I stated earlier, spiritual death is the result of our sin and produces separation from God.

> There is a way which seemeth right unto a man, but the end thereof are the ways of death.
>   Proverbs 14:12 (KJV)

> Behold, the LORD's hand is not shortened, that it cannot save; neither His ear heavy, that it cannot hear: But your iniquities have separated between you and your God, and your sins have hid His face from you, that He will not hear.
>   Isaiah 59:1-2 (KJV)

There is no possible way that mankind can reestablish a relationship with the Creator by man's own actions. A person can never redeem himself; he cannot pay God the price for his life because the payment for a human life is too great. What he could pay would never be enough to keep him from the grave, to let him live forever.

Those who trust in their wealth and boast in the multitude of their riches, none *of them* can by any means redeem *his* brother, nor give to God a ransom for him—for the redemption of their souls *is* costly, and it shall cease forever—that he should continue to live eternally, *and* not see the Pit.
     Psalm 49:6-9 (NKJV)

Can anyone really say that his conscience is clear, that he has gotten rid of his sin?

Who can say, "I have made my heart clean, I am pure from my sin"?
     Proverbs 20:9 (NKJV)

God, with His infinite love and mercy for us, has provided a way in His plan to bring us back into relationship with Him. He has provided a way for our sins to be blotted out and for the powerful nature of the evil one's influence that we are born into to be controlled and overcome. Almighty Yahweh initiated the custom of sacrificing animals to offer their blood for the atonement of the people's sins with Moses and the Hebrew people during the great exodus from their slavery in Egypt. The life of every living thing is in the blood, and that is why the Lord commanded that blood be poured out on the altar to be an atonement for the people's sins. The word *atonement* means: "amends or reparation (something paid) made for an injury or wrong." According to Yahweh's Holy Word, blood, which is life, is sacrificed in order to make amends for human beings' sins, which is not keeping His Torah instructions.

For the life of the flesh *is* in the blood, and I have given it to you upon the altar to make atonement for your souls; for it *is* the blood *that* makes atonement for the soul.
     Leviticus 17:11 (NKJV)

But God will redeem my soul from the power of the grave, for He shall receive me. Selah.
     Psalm 49:15 (NKJV)

From the new covenant it is written:

For when every commandment had been told to all the people by Moses in accordance with the law, he took the blood of calves and goats, with water and scarlet wool and hyssop, and sprinkled both the scroll itself and all the people, saying, "This is the blood of the covenant that God has ordained for you." ... and without the shedding of blood, there is no forgiveness of sins.
Hebrews 9:19-20, 22b (NRSV)

So, what do we do now that no animals are being sacrificed and no blood is being sprinkled on us to take away our sins. How will God accept us without the atonement? God's plan was to work with the Hebrew people using the blood of animals as an acceptable, but not permanent, sacrifice for many centuries. During these centuries, He would empower certain men and women to be His prophets. The prophets would proclaim and record approximately three hundred different prophecies that would serve to point people to a new way of dealing with their sins.

Yahweh would make the next phase of His plan available, not only to the nation of Israel, but also to the entire human race. The new covenant that God would establish would be accomplished through the fulfillment of the many old covenant prophecies concerning the life of the Messiah at His first coming to earth. The Messiah was to leave His home in heaven and come to this earth to complete the mission that Father Yahweh sent Him out to do.

Messiah, or *Mashiah* in Hebrew, means "anointed liberator." The great master plan of Holy Father Yahweh is revealed in the symbolism of His weekly Sabbath and the feast days that the Word, His Son Yahshua Messiah, gave to the great prophet Moses as it is recorded in the books of Exodus and Leviticus in the old covenant. You will be able to read more about the description of these very important feast days of Father Yahweh and the symbolism of each feast in Chapter Four of this book.

Our Savior fulfilled in detail all of the symbolism of the spring feast in His first coming to this world. He will fulfill in detail all of the symbolism of the fall feast when He comes to this world the second and final time to destroy Satan's kingdom and establish His kingdom here as it is in heaven. Our Creator, Savior, and King gave us the instruction in His Holy, set-apart Word to keep and observe His Sabbath and appointed feasts. In doing so, our relationship with Him is enriched, and we have a clearer understanding of His master plan because these special times of the week and year are prophetic. The Scriptures teach us that they are shadows of things to come. It is written,

> **Therefore do not let anyone condemn you in matters of food and drink or of observing festivals, new moons, or sabbaths. These are only a shadow** *(symbolic of important prophetic events that are to be fulfilled)* **of what is to come, but the substance belongs to** *(our focus in all our ways is to be in and on)* **Christ.**
> Colossians 2: 16-17 (NRSV). *Bracketed words added for clarity.*

I pray that these powerful Scriptures from God's Word are helping you to have a clearer understanding of our Heavenly Father's plan. In the next chapter, you will learn about the prophecies of the coming of Messiah and how His coming is such an important part of God's master plan. I feel that before you leave this chapter, it is important to have an understanding and foundation of who the evil one is and what he does.

You may find this shocking and hard to grasp, but Satan—the devil— is real. He and his millions of followers, called fallen angels and demons, operate in another dimension that we cannot see or audibly hear. Satan is the creator of all lies. Thus saith the Lord,

> **He** *[Satan the devil]* **was a murderer from the beginning, and has nothing to do with the truth, because there is no truth in him. When he lies, he speaks according to his own nature, for he is a liar and the father of lies.**
> John 8: 44b-45 (RSV). *Bracketed words added for clarity.*

Satan is angry with Elohim, knowing that the worship and glory he has gained for himself through the sins of mankind as a result of his lies and deception over a few thousand years will soon come to and end. He is determined to steal as many souls from Father Yahweh as he can. That is his mission, and all of his fallen angel demons must obey him, deceiving humans to fulfill his mission. It is written:

> **Be sober, be vigilant; because your adversary the devil walks about like a roaring lion, seeking whom he may devour.**
> 1 Peter 5:8 (NKJV)

The thief comes only to steal and kill and destroy. I came that they may have life, and have it abundantly.

John 10:10 (NRSV)

We realize the terrible manifestations of the spirits of evil as we witness the terrible behavior of people doing bad things to other people and living self-serving lives.

Satan—the devil—and his great army of demons and fallen angels are beings that long ago were part of God's kingdom in heaven. When the devil was part of God's kingdom, his name was Lucifer (which means "bearer of light"), and he was a cherub. A cherub is an angel with one of the highest positions in God's kingdom. When Satan was Lucifer, before he was cast out of God's kingdom in heaven, he was a powerful, supremely intelligent, and beautiful being. He still has these capabilities and attributes today.

I believe that when Satan was Lucifer, he was the closest created being to Elohim's throne and that he was the leader in charge of worship. I believe he became jealous of the worship Elohim received and began to change in his thinking to covet and desire to have all the power and worship of the universe that our Creator has and is due. The following Scripture from the NKJV, goes beyond describing the King of Tyre to describing Satan before and after his fall. Satan is the unseen ruler of all self-centeredness and arrogance and the instigator of all false belief systems. I have included only the most relevant verses.

... "You *were* the seal of perfection, full of wisdom and perfect in beauty. You were in Eden, the garden of God; every precious stone *was* your covering ... The workmanship of your timbrels and pipes was prepared for you on the day you were created. You were the anointed cherub who covers; I established you; you were on the holy mountain of God; you walked back and forth in the midst of fiery stones *[planets]*. **You *were* perfect in your ways from the day you were created, till iniquity was found in you. By the abundance of your trading** *[merchandise]* **you became filled with violence within, and you sinned; therefore I cast you as a profane thing out of the mountain of God; and I destroyed you , O covering cherub, from the midst of the fiery stones** *[planets]*. **Your heart was lifted up because of your beauty; you corrupted your wisdom for the sake of your splendor ...**

Ezekiel 28:12-17 (NKJV). *Bracketed words added for clarity.*

I believe the fiery stones that Ezekiel is referring to are the planets God created in our solar system that can be seen at night as they reflect the light from the sun. There is much more on this topic in Chapter Nine.

Lucifer, with his band of millions of angels, was delegated by God to be the overseer of the planets. He was created, like everything else that Elohim created, to glorify God and to assist God in managing the creation. Lucifer pleased God until he began to covet God's power and authority. His nature changed, and the evil rebellion began. God, Who is holy and righteous, could not tolerate the evil that Lucifer had become. He and his great army of followers, approximately one third of all the angels God created, were driven out of the heavenly realm were Elohim lives.

The following is another account of the fall of Lucifer.

"How you are fallen from heaven, O Lucifer, son of the morning [dawning]**!** *How* **you are cut down to the ground, you who weakened the nations! For you have said in your heart: 'I will ascend into heaven, I will exalt my throne above the stars of God; I will also sit on the mount of the congregation on the farthest sides of the north; I will ascend above the heights of the clouds, I will be like the Most High.' Yet you shall be brought down to Sheol, to the lowest depths of the pit. ..."**
Isaiah 14:12-15 (NKJV). *Bracketed words added for clarity.*

Sheol is the Hebrew word for hell, meaning "a place of separation from God, with sorrows and torment." This last verse is a prophecy that is yet to be fulfilled; it describes the devil—Satan—being cast into hell when the Messiah returns to earth.

Satan and his millions of demons are not in hell now. Satan's throne is in the second heaven where he still has access to the throne of God (third heaven), to accuse people before God. As it is written:

Now war arose in heaven, Michael and his angels fighting against the dragon [Satan]**; and the dragon and his angels fought, but they were defeated and there was no longer any place for them in heaven. And the great dragon was thrown down, that ancient serpent, who is called the Devil and Satan, the deceiver of the whole world—he was thrown down to the earth** [this hasn't happened yet, but does during the tribulation period]**, and his angels were thrown down with him. And I heard a loud voice in heaven,**

saying, "Now the salvation and the power and the kingdom of our God and the authority of His Christ have come, for the accuser of our brethren has been thrown down, who accuses them day and night before our God *[at His heavenly throne]*. And they have conquered him by the blood of the Lamb and by the word of their testimony, for they loved not their lives even unto death *[this speaks of tribulation events]*. Rejoice then, O heaven and you that dwell therein! But woe to you, O earth and sea, for the devil has come down to you in great wrath, because he knows that his time is short."
    Revelation 12: 7-12 (RSV)

Satan and his host of demons are presently operating out of a domain in the atmosphere above the earth and below God's throne that I believe is way out from the North Pole in space. They will be forced out of their present domain down to the earth during the great tribulation that is coming. Satan will come with greater deception and power to perform miracles to deceive and pull even more people into his traps.

Satan and his demons have been deceiving humanity for the past 6,000 years of recorded biblical history, since the creation of Adam and Eve. In the third chapter of Genesis, which I hope you have already read, it is written that the serpent (translated from the Hebrew word *Nachash*, meaning "shining one") deceived Eve because it was more cunning than any other beast. It was not a writhing reptile as we relate to the word *serpent*, but a very beautiful, shrewd, and manipulative creature that Satan spoke through. Satan can transform himself into an angel of light in order to accomplish his deception. **For Satan himself transforms himself into an angel of light** (2 Corinthians. 11:14 NKJV). This is how he has been successful in creating, though human beings, all of the false belief systems of the world.

    Satan trains his demons to be very subtle in their attack on the minds and bodies of humans. Demons operate in other dimensions in the air around us that we cannot see or hear.

And you He made alive, when you were dead through the trespasses and sins in which you once walked, following the course of this world, following the prince of the power of the air, the spirit that is now at work in the sons of disobedience. Among these we all once lived in the passions of our flesh, following the desires of body and mind, and so we were by nature children of wrath, like the rest of mankind.
    Ephesians 2:1-3 (RSV)

For we are not contending against flesh and blood, but against the principalities, against the powers, against the world rulers of this present darkness, against the spiritual hosts of wickedness in the heavenly places.
Ephesians 6:12 (RSV)

Although Satan knew that God would have a plan to redeem mankind after the fall of humanity through the disobedience of Adam and Eve, he didn't know the exact details of the plan. As it is recorded in Genesis 3:14-15, God curses the serpent, causing the beautiful creature to become a slithering reptile, and then God proclaims the first prophecy of His plan to defeat and destroy Satan through the human lineage of Adam and Eve.

So the LORD God said to the serpent: ... "I will put enmity [hatred] **between you** [Satan] **and the woman, and between your seed and her Seed; He** [Messiah] **shall bruise your head, and you shall bruise His heel."**
Genesis 3:14-15 (NKJV). *Bracketed words added for clarity.*

The bruising of the heel means the temporary sufferings associated with the death of Messiah. The bruising of the head is referring to the complete destruction of Satan and his works forever by the perfect life, sacrifice, the atonement by the perfect blood of Messiah, and the resurrection of the Messiah's dead body, overcoming the power of death from Satan. As it is written:

Since therefore the children share in flesh and blood, He Himself likewise partook of the same nature, that through death he might destroy him who has the power of death, that is, the devil, and deliver all those who through fear of death were subject to lifelong bondage.
Hebrews 2:14-15 (RSV)

Whoever continues to sin belongs to the Devil, because the Devil has sinned from the very beginning. The Son of God appeared for this very reason, to destroy what the Devil had done.
1 John 3:8 (TEV)

The devil has tried to destroy God's plan and all mankind in every way he can conceive and initiate, within the realms that God allows him to operate. He knew that God would one day send a powerful Deliverer to be born as a human. So Satan sent his fallen angels to earth and instructed them to mate with human women to create mutated humans, believing that the human race would become so evil that God would give up on humanity and destroy the part of His creation that was, and is, so dear to His heart. I know this may be hard to grasp, but it is important to understand. It is written:

> **When men began to multiply on the face of the ground, and daughters were born to them, the sons of God** *[fallen angels]* **saw that the daughters of men were fair; and they took to wife such of them as they chose.**

> **The Nephilim were on the earth in those days, and also afterward, when the sons of God came in to** *[bred]* **the daughters of men, and they bore children to them. These** *[gaints]* **were the mighty men of old, the men of renown** *[the Titans and gods of Greek and Roman mythology who were deceived, evil and ripe for Elohim's judgment].* **The Lord saw that the wickedness of man was great in the earth, and that every imagination of the thoughts of his heart was only evil continually. And the Lord was sorry that He had made man on the earth, and it grieved Him to His heart. So the Lord said, "I will blot out man whom I have created from the face of the ground, man and beast and creeping things and birds of the air, for I am sorry that I have made them." But Noah found favor in the eyes of the Lord;**
> Genesis 6:1-2, 4-8 (RSV)

In the *Septuagint*, which is the original translation of the old covenant into Greek, all of the verses of Scripture that include "the sons of God" refer to angels, whether of God's kingdom or Satan's. The previous verses are describing Satan's fallen angels (demons) transforming themselves into physical bodies, taking human wives, impregnating them, and creating a mutated race of giants with the intent of ultimately taking control of the earth. In verse 4 of the *King James Version*, the word *giant* is used in place of *Nephilim*. *Nephilim* is the Hebrew word meaning "fallen ones," taken from the word *naphal*, "to fall."

The world became so evil that God did destroy all people except Noah and his family. Satan had been outsmarted by Father Yahweh. The promise of the coming of the Messiah, the anointed Liberator, was intact through the lineage of Noah. I encourage you to read the account of Noah and the great, world-wide flood as it is written in Genesis Chapters Six, Seven, and Eight.

Let's review the material that has been covered in this first chapter:

- There is a lot of proof that the Scriptures of the Holy Bible are true.
- All Scripture was inspired or breathed into the writers of the Bible by God's Holy Spirit.
- We need God's Holy Spirit to understand the Scriptures that God inspired.
- There is only one true creator God—the God of Abraham, Isaac, and Jacob, Who has revealed and manifested Himself to humankind in three ways.
- There is a real devil named Satan. He is a very powerful fallen angel that leads many millions of other fallen angels and demons.
- Satan, his fallen angels, and demons do not live in hell somewhere down in the earth, but in the air in another dimension around humans, having access to the thought process in people's minds.
- Adam and Eve were the first humans that Elohim created. They fell prey to the deception of Satan and chose to disobey God. The result was their taking on the sinful nature of the devil. God cast them out of the garden and separated them from Himself, which began the separation of man from Adonai.
- At some point in time after Adam and Eve were expelled from the garden of Eden, Satan sent his fallen angels to breed and impregnate human women to create a mutant race of evil giants.
- The human race had become so evil that it grieved God, and He decided to destroy it all except for Noah, his family, and a male and female pair of all of the animals, and seven pairs of the clean animals that were to be used as sacrifices for blood atonement.
- God kept the blood line of Adam and Eve intact, so that the promise of the Messiah would be fulfilled.
- Almighty Yah loves us and desires that we be restored and have relationship with Him. Our sinful nature separates us from Him. We need forgiveness of our sins.
- Our sins can be forgiven and blotted out only by the shedding of the blood from a perfect sacrifice before God.

2

THE FIRST COMING OF
MESSIAH, LAMB OF GOD

In chapter one, I'm sure you remember the short story (parable) of the old man who wanted to become a little bird for a while in order to show the other little birds the way into the barn, so they would live and not die. I believe it is a simple parable of the kind of solution that God had in mind long before He created anything on the earth. He knew mankind would fall to the deception of Satan, who was and is a much more powerful being than we humans when we are operating with only our own resources. So God, Elohim, made arrangements to manifest Himself and be born as the Son from a human mother and Himself as the Holy Father of a human being of His divine seed. He planned and carried this out in order for the human race to have the choice of believing the truth about the birth, life, death, and resurrection of His Messiah, His Chosen One that He would send. He chose prophets who lived many hundreds of years before the correct timing of the birth of Yahweh's divine Son. These great prophets of Elohim wrote down and spoke the words that He gave to them so the people of their day would have hope and so there would be a record of the prophecies from God. These prophecies would be very important in helping the people who would be alive at the correct time of the birth, life, death, and resurrection of the Messiah, in proving that the Messiah was true and not some false imitator.

Father Yahweh also chose to give great power to His Anointed One, His Son, the Messiah, so that He could perform miracles. The performing of the miracles would convince many people in all walks of life that the Messiah was Who He claimed to be. The Messiah is the One Who has come forth from Yahweh's bosom, not created, but supernaturally expressed as the divine fullness of His Father Yahweh, the great I AM That I AM. He loves all humanity, and wants to set everyone free from the bondage and deceptions of Satan. Messiah came forth to speak the complete, inerrant Holy Word from the Almighty Father and to show mankind the correct way to have relationship with His and our Heavenly Father and with our fellow man.

The following are some powerful Scriptures that give descriptions of the great Anointed One from Elohim.

> **Before the world was created, the Word already existed; He was with God, and He was the same as God. From the very beginning the Word was with God. Through Him God made all things; not one thing in all creation was made without Him. The Word was the source of life, and this life brought light to mankind. The light shines in the darkness, and the darkness has never put it out.**
> John 1:1-5 (TEV)

> **Christ** [Messiah] **is the visible likeness of the invisible God. He is the first-born Son, superior to all created things. For through Him God created everything in heaven and on earth, the seen and the unseen things, including spiritual powers, lords, rulers, and authorities. God created the whole universe through Him and for Him. Christ** [Messiah] **existed before all things, and in union with Him all things have their proper place. He is the head of His body, the church; He is the source of the body's life. He is the first-born Son, Who was raised from death, in order that He alone might have the first place in all things. For it was by God's own decision that the Son has in Himself the full nature of God. Through the Son, then, God decided to bring the whole universe back to Himself. God made peace** [with humanity] **through His Son's sacrificial death on the cross and so brought back to himself all things, both on earth and in heaven.**
> Colossians 1:15-20 (TEV). *Bracketed words added for clarity.*

The main theme of the Bible is the one true Creator, Yahweh, and how He has revealed Himself to His created humanity.

> **... God was manifested in the flesh, justified in the Spirit, seen by angels, preached among the Gentiles** [and the House of Israel]**, believed on in the world, received up in glory.**
> 1 Timothy 3:16 (NKJV). *Bracketed words added for clarity.*

Much of the new covenant Scripture is a written account of the fulfillment of an event or events that were prophesied and recorded in the old covenant Scriptures and prophecies. But who is this One that was with God from the beginning, that is the very image of God, that through Him all things have been created, that is called the Word and the Son in whom God is pleased to reconcile all things unto Himself and is the first-born from the dead? Who is this amazing being or person? The name or title *Messiah* is a word of Hebrew origin that means, "the Anointed Liberator and King of the Jews."

There are more than one hundred prophecies of the *Tenach* (old covenant) that foretold significant aspects of the Messiah's birth, life of ministry, death, and the resurrection of His dead body. The *Brit Chadashah* (new testament) records the prophesied events as each actually took place. All of the prophecies are like pieces of a large puzzle showing us how God has worked and is working out His great plan for humanity. By understanding the prophecies, we have the proof of the life and first mission of the Messiah. With the understanding of the prophecies that apply to His second coming mission and the relevance of the prophecies to events of our time, we can determine approximately where we are in history and what is in store for this world in future years.

The fact which is so amazing is that the old covenant prophecies were written on parchment scrolls hundreds and, in some cases, over a thousand years before the events actually happened. The odds of even one of the prophecies about the Messiah being fulfilled would have been slim, but for over one hundred to have come true, it would be impossible to calculate the odds.

How are you receiving this information so far? Are you beginning to see a glimpse of the big picture yet? Are you beginning to believe that there really is a God Who created the universe and really loves and cares for you? If you have already been a believer, are you beginning to have a better understanding of Who God really is, and what He is all about? I sure hope and pray that God's big Words and my little words are helping you. Please continue reading. The text will continue to become more real to you as the Holy Spirit opens up your heart and mind to God's truth.

The next section of this chapter includes a requirement of the true Messiah that is underlined and in italics, followed by an old covenant prophecy about the Messiah as it relates to His first mission to earth. The old covenant prophecy is then followed by the fulfillment of the prophecy as it is recorded in the renewed covenant or *Brit Chadashah*. At the end of each verse after the type of translation is stated in parenthesis, there will be given an approximate historical date of when the old covenant prophecy was given, and then from the renewed covenant (New Testament), the approximate historical date of the fulfillment of the prophecy as it is recorded. I have paraphrased some of the verses because of their importance and relationship to other verses in the following chapters. My paraphrase is in brackets and non-bold, italic type.

OLD COVENANT PROPHECIES OF MESSIAH AND THEIR FULFILLMENT

- *The Messiah would be a descendant from Abraham.*

   "By Myself I have sworn says the LORD, because you have done this thing, and have not withheld your son, your only *son*—blessing I will bless you, and multiplying I will multiply your descendants as the stars of the heaven and as the sand which *is* on the seashore; and your descendants shall possess the gate of their enemies. In your seed *[Messiah]* all nations of the earth shall be blessed, because you have obeyed My voice."
   Genesis 22:16-18 (NKJV); 1420 B.C. *Bracketed words added for clarity.*

   Now to Abraham and his Seed were the promises made. He does not say, "And to seeds," as of many, but as of one, *"And to your Seed,"* Who is Christ *[Messiah]*.
   Galatians 3:16 (NKJV); A.D. 49. *Bracketed words added for clarity.*

- *The Messiah would be the greatest of the prophets speaking the words of Father Yahweh.*

   And the Lord said to me ... "I will raise up for them a prophet like you *[Moses]* from among their brethren; and I will put My words in His mouth, and he shall speak to them all that I command Him *[Messiah would be the living Torah, the living Word of Yahweh]* And whoever will not give heed to My words which He shall speak in My name, I Myself will require it of him.
   Deuteronomy 18:17-19 (RSV); 1408 B.C. *Bracketed words added for clarity.*

"... He who believes in Me, believes not in Me but in Him who sent Me. ... He who rejects Me, and does not receive My words, has that which judges him—the word that I have spoken will judge him in the last day. For I have not spoken on My *authority*; but the Father who sent Me gave Me a command, what I should say and what I should speak. ... Most assuredly, I say to you, before Abraham was, I AM."
John 12:44, 48-49; 8:58 (NKJV); A.D. 85.

- *The Messiah would be born in the family lineage of King David.*

The LORD says, "The time is coming when I will choose as king a righteous descendant of David. That king will rule wisely and do what is right and just throughout the land. When He is king, the people of Judah will be safe, and the people of Israel will live in peace. He will be called, 'The LORD Our Salvation.' "
Jeremiah 23:5-6 (TEV); 477 B.C.

This is the list of the ancestors of Jesus Christ, a descendant of David, who was a descendant of Abraham.
Matthew 1:1 (TEV); A.D. 50.

Yahshua is the true Hebrew name that the Messiah's mother, Mary (Miriam), was instructed to name her Son by the angel Gabriel as it is recorded in the book of Luke 1:26-31. The name *Yeshua* is Aramaic and means "salvation." The name *Jesus* was first printed in the late 1500s when scribes were creating the King James Version of the Bible from the older English version. The English version did not have the letter "J" in it because it had not been used prior. I prefer *Yahshua* because proper names should not be translated like regular text, but should be transliterated, so that the closest rendering of the correct pronunciation remains intact. Again, for clarification: properly using the name *Jesus* does not diminish the power that manifest from Holy Spirit in ministry. Holy Spirit knows when we are sincere, the intents of our hearts, and Who we mean when we call upon the Son of Almighty Yahweh.

And when He had removed him *[Saul]*, He raised up for them David as king, to whom also He gave testimony and said, *"I have found David the son* of Jesse, *a man after My own heart, who will do all My will."*

From this man's seed, according to *the* **promise, God raised up for Israel a Savior—Jesus ...**
Acts 13:22-23 (NKJV); A.D. 60. *Bracketed words added for clarity.*

Yahshua fulfilled this prophecy when He came to this world as the Holy Lamb of God and sacrificed His life for our sins in order to provide a way for our salvation from God's judgment. Yahshua is King of the Universe but has not established His kingdom and rule upon this earth yet. That will take place when He returns to this earth, coming in the clouds as the Lion of Judah. He has and is establishing His spiritual kingdom in the hearts of His born-again believers. Is His Kingdom established within you?

- *The Messiah would be conceived in and born of a virgin as a sign to the world.*

   Therefore the Lord Himself will give you a sign: Behold, the virgin shall conceive and bear a Son, and shall call His name Immanuel. *[El is the short form of* **Elohim;** *Immanuel means "God," or "El with us."]*
   Isaiah 7:14 (NKJV); 633 B.C. *Bracketed words added for clarity.*

   Now all this happened in order to make come true what the Lord had said through the prophet, "A virgin will become pregnant and have a son, and he will be called Immanuel" (which means, "God is with us").
   Matthew 1:22-23; (TEV); A.D. 50.

- *The Messiah would live during a certain time in history before the destruction of the second Jewish temple.*

   "Seven times seventy years *[490 years]* **is the length of time God has set for freeing your people and your holy city from sin and evil. Sin will be forgiven and eternal justice established, so that the vision and the prophecy will come true, and the holy Temple will be rededicated. Note this and understand it: From the time the command is given to rebuild Jerusalem until God's chosen leader** *[Messiah]* **comes, seven times seven** *[49]* **years will pass. Jerusalem will be rebuilt with streets and strong defenses, and will stand for seven times sixty-two** *[434]* **years, but this will be a time of troubles. And at the end of that time God's chosen**

leader [Messiah] **will be killed unjustly.**
   Daniel 9:24-26 (TEV); 426 B.C. *Bracketed words added for clarity.*

The prophecies in this group are some of the most important in the old covenant (Tenach). At the age of 16, the prophet Daniel was taken into captivity by the Babylonians, along with the majority of the people of Israel. It was during the 70 years of captivity that Daniel was given many visions and prophecies by God. Some pertained to his captors, and some described future events of the people of Israel and Messiah.

In verse 24, the original translation says that "seventy weeks of years are determined," which means seventy times seven (70 x 7), or 490 years, would be the total number of years required to fulfill the events described in verses 24 through 27 but not the total number of years from the beginning of the first event until the end of the last event. The events in verses 24 through 26 have already taken place. The last week, or final seven years, has not yet begun as of this writing. There will be much more about the final seven-year period later in this book.

The first block of time in verse 25 is seven times seven (7 x 7) years, or 49 years, from the time of the command to go and begin building Jerusalem until it was finished. The Babylonians were overtaken by the Persians, who then ruled over the Israelites. As recorded in history and the old covenant, during the year 454 B.C., the Persian king named Artaxerxes gave the decree, or command, allowing a group of Israelites to return to Jerusalem to rebuild the walls and finish the temple. In the year 405 B.C., 49 years later, the temple was finished and dedicated, thus completing the project and fulfilling the prophecy.

In verse 26 of Daniel 9 (KJV), it is written: **"And after three score and two weeks shall Messiah be cut off, but not for Himself ..."** This second block of time is seven times sixty-two (7 x 62) years, or 434 years, which began in the year 405 B.C. and was completed in the year A.D. 29, the year that the Messiah was crucified on the cross by the Romans. That event completed the prophesied 483 years.

However, the prophecy continues with more detailed information as it states, **"... and the people of the prince** [General Titus and the Roman army] **that shall come shall destroy the city** [Jerusalem] **and the sanctuary** [temple]; **and the end thereof shall be with a flood** [great army], **and unto the end of the war desolations are determined** [the whole city would be destroyed and left a wasteland.]**"** The Messiah was to fulfill His mission before the second temple and the city of Jerusalem were destroyed in A.D. 70.

During the early years of the third millennium of the Hebrew calendar (years A.D. 1 thru A.D. 30), the religious leaders and those who studied the old covenant prophecies concerning the first coming of the Messiah would have been able to calculate the birth date of Yahshua after He began His ministry in approximately A.D. 25. The amazing miracles that Yahshua performed during His ministry confirmed that He was the true Messiah.

> **But when the right time** *[in human history when the good roads for travel throughout the Roman Empire were in place]* **finally came, God sent His own Son** *[into the world to conquer Satan, hell, and the grave].* **He came as the son of a human mother and lived under the Jewish Law** *[He lived in a predominately Jewish society that followed the Torah instructions],* **to redeem those who were under the Law** *[of sin and death],* **so that we might become God's sons.**
> Galatians 4:4-5 (TEV); A.D. 49. *Bracketed words added for clarity.*

Daniel 9:27 refers to the events of the third block of time, which will be the final seven years of this age and will include the short rule of the anti-messiah (the Antichrist). Those years will be very significant because all of the prophecies that relate to the Messiah's second coming will be fulfilled then. I believe that those final seven years will be in this generation that we are now experiencing. More on this later.

- *The Messiah would be born in a town called Bethlehem.*

> **But thou, Bethlehem** *[means house of bread]* **Ephratah,** *though* **thou be little among the thousands of Judah,** *yet* **out of thee shall He come forth unto Me** *that is* **to be ruler in Israel; whose goings forth** *have been* **from of old, from everlasting.**
> Micah 5:2 (KJV); 620 B.C. *Bracketed words added for clarity.*

> **Jesus was born in the town of Bethlehem in Judea, during the time when Herod was king.**
> Matthew 2:1a (TEV); A.D. 50.

- *The Messiah would be taken to Egypt by His family to protect His life.*

When Israel *[Yahshua]* **was a child, I loved Him, and out of Egypt I** *[Father Yahweh]* **called my Son.**
Hosea 11:1 (NKJV); 625 B.C. *Bracketed words added for clarity.*

When he *[Joseph]* **arose, he took the young Child** *[Jesus]* **and His mother by night and departed for Egypt, and was there until the death of Herod, that it might be fulfilled which was spoken by the Lord through the prophet, saying, "Out of Egypt I called My Son."**
Matthew 2:14-15 (NKJV); A.D. 50. *Bracketed words added for clarity.*

- *The Messiah would be preceded by one announcing His coming.*

Behold, I send My messenger, and he will prepare the way before Me.
π   Malachi 3:1a (NKJV); 480 B.C.

The voice of him that crieth in the wilderness, Prepare ye the way of the LORD, make straight in the desert a highway for our God.
Isaiah 40:3 (KJV); 633 B.C.

In those days John the Baptist came preaching in the wilderness of Judea, and saying, "Repent, for the kingdom of heaven is at hand!" For this is he who was spoken of by the prophet Isaiah ... "I indeed baptize you with water unto repentance, but He who is coming after me is mightier that I, whose sandals I am not worthy to carry. He will baptize you with the Holy Spirit and fire."
Matthew 3:1-3, 11 (NKJV); A.D. 50.

- *The Messiah would be blessed with a special anointing of the Spirit of God.*

The Sovereign LORD has filled me with His Spirit. He has chosen me and sent me to bring good news to the poor, to heal the brokenhearted, to announce release to captives and freedom to those in prison.
Isaiah 61:1 (TEV); 633 B.C.

And when Jesus, was baptized, He went up immediately from the water, and behold, the heavens were opened and He saw the Spirit of God

descending like a dove, and alighting on Him; and lo, a voice from heaven, saying, "This is my beloved Son, with whom I am well pleased."
   Matthew 3:16-17 (RSV); A.D. 50.

- *The Messiah was and is God's Son.*

   Who has ever mastered heavenly knowledge? Who has ever caught the wind in his hand? Or wrapped up water in a piece of cloth? Or fixed the boundaries of the earth? Who is he, if you know? Who is his son?
      Proverbs 30:4 (TEV); 965 B.C.

   "I will declare the decree: The LORD *[YAHWEH]* has said to Me *[Yahshua]*, 'You *are* My Son, today I have begotten You. Ask of Me, and I will give *You* the nations *for* Your inheritance, and the ends of the earth *for* Your possession. ...' "
      Psalm 2:7-8 (NKJV); 980 B.C. *Bracketed words added for clarity.*

   And Simon Peter answered and said, Thou art the Christ *[Messiah]*, the Son of the living God.
      Matthew 16:16 (KJV); A.D. 50. *Bracketed words added for clarity.*

- *The Messiah would die for the forgiveness of humanity's sins and be beaten to bring the healing of diseases.*

   Who hath believed our report? and to whom is the arm of the LORD revealed? For he shall grow up before him as a tender plant, and as a root out of a dry ground: he hath no form nor comeliness; and when we shall see him, there is no beauty that we should desire him. He is despised and rejected of men; a man of sorrows, and acquainted with grief: and we hid as it were our faces from him; he was despised, and we esteemed him not. Surely he hath borne our griefs, and carried our sorrows: yet we did esteem him stricken, smitten of God, and afflicted. But he was wounded for our transgressions, he was bruised for our iniquities: the chastisement of our peace was upon him; and with his stripes we are healed.
      Isaiah 53:1-5 (KJV); 633 B.C.

Bless the LORD, O my soul, and forget not all His benefits: Who forgives all your iniquities, Who heals all your diseases, Who redeems your life from destruction ...

Psalm 103:2-4a (NKJV); 980 B.C.

For to this you have been called, because Christ also suffered for you, leaving you an example, so that you should follow in His steps. "He committed no sin, and no deceit was found in His mouth." When he was abused, He did not return abuse; when He suffered, He did not threaten; but He entrusted Himself to the One Who judges justly. He Himself bore our sins in His body on the cross *[tree],* so that, free from sins, we might live for righteousness; by His wounds you have been healed. For you were going astray like sheep, but now you have returned to the shepherd and guardian of your souls.

1 Peter 2:21-25 (NRSV); A.D. 60. *Bracketed words added for clarity.*

- *The Messiah would make His final and triumphant entry in Jerusalem as a humble king, the Prince of Peace.*

Rejoice greatly, O daughter of Zion! Shout, O daughter of Jerusalem! Behold, you King is coming to you; He *is* just and having salvation, lowly and riding on a donkey, a colt, the foal of a donkey.

Zechariah 9:9 (NKJV); 408 B.C.

Then a great many of the Jews knew that He *[Yahshua]* was there; and they came , not for Jesus' sake only, but that they might also see Lazarus, whom He had raised from the dead. The next day a great multitude that had come to the feast *[Passover],* when they heard that Jesus was coming to Jerusalem, took branches of palm trees and went out to meet Him, and cried out: "Hosanna! *'Blessed is He who comes in the name of the Lord!'* The King of Israel!" Then Jesus, when He had found a young donkey, sat on it; as it is written: *"Fear not, daughter of Zion; behold, your King is coming, sitting on a donkey's colt."* His disciples did not understand these things at first; but when Jesus was glorified, then they remembered that these things were written about Him and *that* they had done these things to Him. Therefore the people, who were with Him when He called Lazarus out of the tomb and raised him from the dead, bore witness. For this reason the people also met Him, because they heard that He had done this sign.

John 12:9, 12-18 (NKJV); A.D. 85. *Bracketed words added for clarity.*

- *The Messiah would die by crucifixion, with His hands and feet pierced.*

   The congregation of the wicked has enclosed Me. They pierced My hands and My feet.
      Psalm 22:16b (NKJV); 980 BC.

   And I will pour out on the House of David and the inhabitants of Jerusalem a spirit of compassion and supplication, so that, when they look on Him whom they have pierced, they shall mourn for Him , as one mourns for an only child, and weep bitterly over Him, as one weeps over a first-born. *[The fullness of this happens at the end of the tribulation period when King Yahshua returns to earth in the air. Many Jews in and around Jerusalem see Him, and their eyes are opened to Who He really is.]*
      Zechariah 12:10 (RSV); 515 B.C. *Bracketed words added for clarity.*

   So they took Jesus, and He went out, bearing His own cross, to the place called the place of a skull, which is called in Hebrew Golgotha. There they crucified Him ...
      John 19:17-18 (RSV); A.D. 85.

   [After His resurrection] But Thomas, one the twelve, called Didymus, was not with them when Jesus came. The other disciples therefore said unto them, "We have seen the Lord." But he *[Thomas]* said unto them, "Except I shall see in His hands the print of the nails, and put my finger into the print of the nails, and thrust my hand into His side, I will not believe." After eight days again His disciples were within, and Thomas with them: then came Jesus, the doors being shut, and stood in the midst, and said, "Peace be unto you." Then saith He to Thomas, "Reach hither thy finger, and behold My hands; and reach hither thy hand, and thrust it into my side: and be not faithless, but believing." And Thomas answered and said unto Him, "My LORD and my God." Jesus saith unto him, "Thomas, because thou hast seen Me, thou hast believed: blessed are they that have not seen, and yet have believed."
      John 20:24-29 (KJV); A.D. 85. *Bracketed words added for clarity.*

When King David wrote in Psalm 22:16, **"They pierced my hands and my feet,"** execution by crucifixion was being revealed to him by the Holy Spirit, and he spoke the prophecy as if he were Yahshua the Messiah. Approximately 700 years would pass before the Romans would invent the cruel execution process called crucifixion.

- *The Messiah would be buried in a rich man's tomb.*

> **And they made His grave with the wicked—** *[the plan of the Jewish leaders was to bury Jesus in a separate part of the Jewish cemetery that was set apart for criminals]* **but with the rich in His death,** *[the plan changed when a rich Jewish leader came forth to give Jesus a proper burial in his own tomb]* **because He had done no violence, nor was any deceit in His mouth.**
> Isaiah 53:9 (NKJV); 633 B.C. *Bracketed words added for clarity.*

> **Now when evening had come, there came a rich man from Arimathea, named Joseph, who himself had also become a disciple of Jesus. This man went to Pilate and asked for the body of Jesus. Then Pilate commanded the body to be given to him. When Joseph had taken the body, he wrapped it in a clean linen cloth, and laid it in his new tomb which he had hewn out of the rock; and he rolled a large stone against the door of the tomb, and departed.**
> Matthew 27:57-60 (NKJV); A.D. 50.

- *The Messiah would die for the sins of all mankind and does on-going intercession for humans, so that a relationship between God and man would be restored.*

> **He is despised and rejected by men, a man of sorrows and acquainted with grief. And we hid, as it were,** *our* **faces from Him; He was despised, and we did not esteem Him. Surely He has borne our grief and carried our sorrows; yet we esteemed Him stricken, smitten by God, and afflicted. But He** *was* **wounded for our transgressions,** *He was* **bruised for our iniquities; the chastisement for our peace** *was* **upon Him, and by His stripes we are healed. All we like sheep have turned astray; we have turned, every one, to his own way; and the LORD has laid on Him the iniquity of us all.**
> Isaiah 53:3-6 (NKJV); 633 B.C.

> **Christ** *[Messiah]* **was without sin, but for our sake God made Him share our sin in order that in union with Him we might share the righteousness of God.**
> 2 Corinthians 5:21 (TEV); A.D. 57. *Bracketed words added for clarity.*

Previously saying, *"Sacrifice and offering, burnt offerings, and offerings for sin You did not desire, nor had pleasure in them"* (which are offered according to the law), then He said, *"Behold, I have come to do Your will, O God".* He takes away the first that He may establish the second. By that will we have been sanctified through the offering of the body of Jesus Christ once for all.

Hebrews 10:8-10 (NKJV); A.D. 68.

Also there were many priests, because they were prevented by death from continuing. But He, because He continues forever, has an unchangeable priesthood. Therefore He is also able to save to the uttermost those who come to God through Him, since He always lives to make intercession for them [us]. For such a High Priest was [is] fitting for us, who is holy, harmless, undefiled, separate from sinners, and has become higher than the heavens; who does not need daily, as those high priests, [former] to offer up sacrifices, first for His own sins and then for the people's, for this He [Yahshua] did once for all when He offered up Himself.

Hebrew 7:23-27 (NKJV); A.D. 68. *Bracketed words added for clarity.*

- **_The Messiah would be resurrected from the dead, ascend into heaven where He sits at the right hand of God the Father, and would send life-changing power in the person Holy Spirit._**

And so I [Yahshua as prophesied by David speaking for Him] am thankful and glad, and I feel completely secure, because you protect me from the power of death. I have served you faithfully, and you will not abandon me to the world of the dead.

Psalm 16:9-10 (TEV); 980 B.C. *Bracketed words added for clarity.*

The Lord says to my Lord, "Sit at my right hand, till I make your enemies your foot stool."

Psalm 110:1 (RSV); 980 B.C.

"My brothers, I must speak to you plainly about our famous ancestor King David. He died and was buried, and his grave is here with us to this very day. He was a prophet, and he knew what God had promised him: God had made a vow that He would make one of David's descendants a king, just as David was. David saw what God was going to do in the future, and so he spoke about the resurrection of the Messiah when he said, 'He was not abandoned in the world of the dead; His body did not rot in the grave.' God has raised this very Jesus from death, and we are all witnesses to this fact. For it was not David who went up into heaven; rather he said, 'The Lord says to my Lord: Sit here at my right side until I put your enemies as a footstool under your feet.' All the people of Israel, then, are to know for sure that this Jesus, whom you crucified, is the one that God has made Lord and Messiah!"

Acts 2:29-32, 34-36 (TEV); A.D. 60.

"… But when the Holy Spirit comes upon you, you will be filled with power, and you will be witnesses for me in Jerusalem, in all of Judea and Samaria, and to the ends of the earth." After saying this, He was taken up to heaven as they watched Him, and a cloud hid Him from their sight. They still had their eyes fixed on the sky as He went away, when two men dressed in white suddenly stood beside them and said, "Galileans , why are you standing there looking up at the sky? This Jesus, who was taken from you into heaven, will come back in the same way that you saw Him go to heaven." *[This is a prophecy of His second coming to establish His Kingdom on this earth.]*

Acts 1:8-11 (TEV); A.D. 60. *Bracketed words added for clarity.*

Who *is* he *[Satan]* who condemns? *It is* Christ who died, and furthermore is also risen, who is even at the right hand of God, who also makes intercession for us.

Romans 8:34 (NKJV); A.D. 57. *Bracketed words added for clarity.*

I hope you have thoroughly read these powerful Scriptures of God's Word that detail in prophecy form the mission of God's Holy Son, Yahshua Messiah, Jesus the Christ, when He came to this earth the first time as the Holy Lamb of God. All of the prophecies that were written down, recorded on scrolls hundreds of years before, have actually taken place. Following the events of the Messiah's life, they were recorded by His followers, the disciples, so that people all through the centuries for nearly 2,000 years would be able to read or hear the Gospel, or good news, of God's plan of salvation for humanity. God instructed four different men to give their own account of the events of the Life of the Messiah. That is why we have what is called the four Gospels found in the new covenant, or testament. Each account is accurate, having some details that are unique, and many that are recorded in the other accounts.

I encourage you to continue reading, not only this little book, but also more of God's Holy Word. It is a lamp unto our feet and a light unto our path (Psalm 119:105).

Let's review briefly what we have learned in Chapter Two:

• Through the reading and understanding of God's Holy Word, we see God carrying out His plan to make a way for His created human being to have a relationship with Him once more through the life, death, and resurrection of His only Son, King Jesus, the Messiah.

• God's plan included the giving and recording of prophecies by a few chosen men and women who were to live hundreds of years before the birth of the Messiah. These prophecies are proof that Yahshua was from Yahweh our Heavenly Father. All that He did was for the benefit of all peoples, and all that He said was and is true forevermore.

• What Jesus the Messiah did on the cruel cross of the Roman crucifixion was to become a curse for us. He took all of the sins of the world onto Himself and paid the penalty of our sin debt with the shedding of His holy and precious blood. The perfect blood sacrifice was acceptable to God (Yahweh), our Heavenly Father, for all people, once, forever. Yahshua Messiah fulfilled all of the righteous requirements of the Law.

• After His resurrection from the dead, our Savior, King Yahshua, returned to heaven and sat down at the right hand of Father Yahweh to intercede on our behalf. He confirmed our Heavenly Father's promise that after He ascended to His heavenly throne, Father Yahweh would send the manifestation of the person of *Ruach Ha Kodesh*, which is Hebrew and means "Spirit of Holiness." Holy Spirit comes in the Name of Jesus and desires to have a personal relationship with us.

• As the apostles of King Yahshua were watching Him ascend into heaven, two angels of God appeared and told them that King Jesus would return from heaven one day, coming through the sky as they had seen Him leave through the sky.

ﷺ

3

RECEIVING
ETERNAL LIFE

T he first two chapters of this book gave you a condensed, scriptural background that explains Who God is and an overview of His-story of His interaction with a few members of the human race, from Adam and Abraham, on through to His Son, Jesus, and His disciples. If we believe that God's (Elohim's) Word is true, then we cannot help being in awe of His magnificence, His compassion and willingness to fulfill the most important part of His master plan by coming to a planet He created and being born a human, just so He could die and make a way for us to be able to be in relationship with Him forever. That is truly amazing to me, and I hope and pray that it is amazing to you as well.

Now that you have absorbed this awesome information, are you processing it and applying it to your life now? Do you believe the truth of these Holy verses that are alive and from God? Are you allowing Holy Spirit to begin to work on the inside of you so that you can be set free from the entrapment and suffering of sin? Do you realize that you and all of mankind have sinned against God and fall short of what He requires? As it is written;

But now, apart from the law, the righteousness of God has been disclosed, and is attested by the law and the prophets, the righteousness of God through faith in Jesus Christ for all who believe. For there is no distinction, since all have sinned and fall short of the glory of God; they [we] are now justified by His grace as a gift, through the redemption that is in Christ Jesus, whom God put forward as a sacrifice of atonement by His blood, effective through faith.

Romans 3:21-25 (NRSV). *Bracketed words added for clarity.*

By reading the Scripture verses of God's Holy Word and believing they are true, you have activated Holy Spirit. Holy Spirit is a very real, personal, invisible, supernatural, powerful part of God (Elohim), whose mission is to search out the hearts of all people looking for the opportunity to be invited into a person to help them. Holy Spirit begins to draw us to the heart of God when we begin to open our hearts up to the truth of God found only in His Word. In doing so, we receive a very important gift from God called faith.

For by grace you have been saved through faith, and this is not your own doing; it is the gift of God—not the result of works, so that no one may boast. For we are what He has made us, created in Christ Jesus for good works, which God prepared beforehand to be our way of life.
 Ephesians 2:8-10 (NRSV)

Now faith is the substance of things hoped for, the evidence of things not seen.
 Hebrews 11:1 (NKJV)

Faith is God's precious gift to us. It is received once we comprehend God's words of truth and believe them, no matter what the teachers of false doctrines and religions of this world say or do to convince us otherwise. Once we have faith that Yahshua was (is) the Messiah Who died for us to save us from our sins, then Holy Spirit begins nudging us to be invited in. He is received by faith and comes into our very inner being when we ask Him into our hearts.

Our Master Yahshua redeemed us from the curse of the law by becoming a curse for us; for it is written:

If a man has committed a sin deserving of death, and he is put to death, and you hang him [by the neck] **on a tree, his body shall not remain overnight on the tree, but you shall surely bury him that day, so that you do not defile the land which the LORD your God is giving you as an inheritance; for he who is hanged is accursed of God.**
 Deuteronomy 21:22-23 (NKJV). *Bracketed words added for clarity.*

... in Christ Jesus the blessing of Abraham might come to the Gentiles, so that we might receive the promise of the Spirit through faith.
 Galatians 3:14 (NRSV)

For there is one God, and there is one who brings God and mankind together, the man Christ Jesus, who gave Himself to redeem all mankind. That was the proof at the right time that God wants everyone to be saved …
  1 Timothy 2:5-6 (TEV)

MY TESTIMONY OF THE LIFE-CHANGING POWER OF GOD

I now want to share with you how it is that I know that God (Almighty Yah) is real and how I know that Jesus, the Messiah, has saved me. This is my testimony to the awesome, life-changing power of God working in people's lives on this earth. I am a living miracle.

I was raised in a Christian home by a loving family in a small rural town in North Carolina. In 1968, I was a junior in high school and began to rebel against everything I had been taught. I began to drink alcohol and partied a lot with many friends. I became caught up in the anti-Vietnam war movement and was intrigued by the hippie lifestyle.

After I graduated from high school, I rambled around for a while and became frustrated with trying to figure out what college was all about. So, I decided to jump head first into the American revolution of the sixties and early seventies and pursue all that being a hippie could offer. That lifestyle was my excuse and justification to party and be rebellious.

One weekend, after 18 months of the highs and the lows, a set of circumstances brought my situation to a critical crossroads. I had not seen my parents in about six months and decided that I should make the effort. I had sold the motor cycle and van that I had worked and saved for in order to continue the shameful lifestyle I was living at that time without working. With no transportation of my own, I did what many young people did during that tragic time in our country's history; I hitchhiked to my hometown.

As I walked up the driveway on that spring afternoon in April of 1972, my father saw me and began walking to meet me. He had been mowing his lawn. He met me in the driveway and said, "I don't allow hippies on my property. You will have to leave now." As he firmly spoke those hard words, tears were streaming down his face. I didn't realize at that moment how much I had been hurting my mother and father. I didn't have a clue how bad I looked and stunk due to the terrible state of degradation I was caught up in. My hair was very long, and I had lost down to about 120 pounds.

My father had rejected me, but he knew he had to administer tough love and take a stand to get my attention. I felt hurt and rejected. It was past time for me to feel something other than artificial bliss. It was time for me begin thinking again.

Well, that day being a Thursday afternoon, I decided to head out to nearby Raleigh, North Carolina, and call on some friends to help bring me up from my, as we called it, "bummer state of mind." They welcomed me in, and the party was on.

By Sunday noon, I was ready to return to Greenville, North Carolina, where I had been living. After catching rides into town, I stumbled up to the house that seven friends and I were renting in a hippie village called "positively Fourth Street." I felt the worst I had ever felt. I hadn't eaten in three days. I was terribly hung over from alcohol and strung out from drugs.

As I was walking up the steps to the house, I began reading a large cardboard sign that had been tacked on the front door. It said, "Keep out. This house has just been busted."

My heart sank lower than it already was. I went in and found my room had been turned upside down. I hit rock bottom, knowing the police had probably found some evidence that could have been used against me and were, no doubt, looking for me. I later found out that all seven of my friends and housemates were in jail and that the police had been looking for me.

The hard reality of my destitute life hit me between the eyes like a sledge hammer. I had no job, no ambition, no possessions, no money, no real friends, no belief in anything except the next party and, at that point, no hope. I had studied a variety of different Eastern religions, be-your-own-god philosophies, and had practiced yoga meditations in my constant search to be happy and fulfilled. There just wasn't a "real" god in my perspective at that time in my life. I had reached such a confused and depressed state of mind that I was ready to end my life.

I sat down on the railroad tracks beside the dilapidated house I had been living in. Tears were streaming down my face, and I felt this heavy, heavy weight pressing on my chest. I wanted a train to run over me. I was so lost and strung out from all the alcohol and drugs I had consumed for years that my brain was fried. I knew my parents loved me, but I was so ashamed of how I had thrown my life away and wasted the time I should have been in college. Negative thoughts of how I could put an end to the hell of emptiness and depression that I was experiencing kept flooding my mind. As I stated earlier, I had run out of everything, including hope.

Hope is the one thing a person can't be without for long and have any chance of surviving.

As I was sitting there on the tracks thinking of different options for taking my life, I felt a hand on my shoulder. I looked up and recognized a guy that I had met at a party a few months back. We could not remember each other's name, so we introduced ourselves. Then he said, "Man, you look terrible; what's wrong?" I explained with an awful stutter what had developed a few months back, how messed up my life was, and that I just wanted to give up and end it.

Jim sat down with me on the tracks and proceeded to tell me how he had gone through pretty much the same experience a couple of months before. He said, "Yea, I was ready to end it all when this guy I didn't really know came along and helped me to understand that there was a whole lot more to life that what I had been experiencing." He then helped me up and said something like, "I don't want you to harm yourself. Come on with me. I'll hide you from the police and help you through this rough time you are having."

With tears streaming down both our faces, we walked the half mile to his apartment. He fed me and provided a small room with a mattress on the floor for me to use. He gave me some clothes. The clothes I was wearing were the only ones I had, and they were filthy. He encouraged me, prayed with me, cried with me, laughed with me, and loved me as a lost brother who had been found.

Jim shared with me about how dramatically his life had been changed when he had accepted the Lord Jesus into his life. I wanted what Jim had—peace down in my soul and assurance that I could be forgiven for the self-serving, sinful lifestyle I had been living.

I began going with Jim to a Bible study and worship service that was held in someone's home. All of the people there were compassionate and happy. I knew that they really cared about me. They helped me to understand the Scriptures and to realize how much I needed the one true living God in my life. I believed the words I was being taught. I saw the need to repent, to turn away from the sins of my past. I cried out to God with all my heart and accepted Jesus, the Messiah, as my Lord and Savior.

The man named Jim was truly a good Samaritan. God used him to save me literally from the jaws of death and a sentence of eternal damnation. He is a dear brother in Jesus, and I will always love him for allowing God to use him to help me up when I was at the lowest point of my life. Jim's loving assistance gave me the opportunity to choose to come before the Creator of the Universe just as I was, so that I could ask our dear Savior and Friend to forgive me and come into my life. HalleluYah!!!

I tell you, dear reader, the one true God of Abraham, Isaac, and Jacob is real, and He makes Himself known to us through His written Word that gives us all of the details about the Son of the Living God, King Yahshua, the Messiah, and by the presence and anointing of His Holy Spirit.

God (Elohim) also reveals Himself though the awesome power of His Holy Spirit Who comes to help us in the powerful name of His Son, Jesus, or Yahshua. Holy Spirit is a gentleman and will not force Himself on you. He supernaturally enters your heart only when you cry out to Him in repentance with godly sorrow, asking for forgiveness, and inviting Him into your heart. As I stated earlier, there is only one Creator God, and He has revealed Himself to mankind in three different ways: Father, Son, and Holy Spirit.

I encourage you, please don't try to play games with Almighty Yah. He knows when you are sincere and when you are playing games and are not willing to submit to His will in your life. Be sincere and transparent with our Heavenly Father's Holy Spirit and our Savior, Yahshua, recognizing that you and I, and all people, need to be forgiven and need to have His peace in our lives. Only the one true God—the God of Abraham, Isaac, and Jacob—can forgive us and give us His peace that the world cannot give or understand.

If you have accepted King Yahshua as your Savior and Master eternal, then His powerful Agent—Holy Spirit—is already working in your life and is in the process of transforming your mind. The following are a couple of verses of Scripture from the book of Romans, that really ministered to me after I became born of Yah's Holy Spirit in 1972.

> **So then, my brothers, because of God's great mercy to us I appeal to you: Offer yourselves as a living sacrifice to God, dedicated to His service and pleasing to Him. This is the true worship that you should offer. Do not conform yourselves to the standards of this world, but let God transform you inwardly by a complete change of your mind. Then you will be able to know the will of God—what is good and is pleasing to Him and is perfect.**
> Romans 12:1-2 (TEV)

These powerful words still help me today as they did many years ago. I know that they will help you, too!

The power of Holy Spirit healed me of the stuttering problem I had and gave me new hope in the life that God had given to me. After being saved, my health was restored. I began to see life from a whole new perspective. Nature was more colorful. The sound of birds was more beautiful. I had a new respect for people. I no longer was oppressed and depressed. I felt real peace, love, and joy in my heart for the first time since I was a child. I was in awe that Father God loved me, and all people, so much that He was willing to temporarily give up His only Son, King Jesus Messiah, and that King Jesus was willing to temporarily give up His place of great authority in heaven in order to come to this earth to be born as a human being, to suffer so much, and die for us. He knew that His precious blood would be for our forgiveness and a redemption from the death penalty for our sins. The most awesome news I can share with you or anyone is that you, too, can experience the love and peace of knowing your sins are forgiven and that you are part of our Creator's family.

A short time after I asked Jesus to come into my heart, I desired to receive the baptism by fire. He blessed me with the manifestation of what is known as speaking in tongues, or in a heavenly language. Wow, what an experience to be able to communicate supernaturally with the One Who created me, you, and the universe. There is more on this subject in the last chapter that explains the manifestations of Holy Spirit.

Do you remember the story I shared with you about the old man and the little birds that were perishing? Father Yahweh loves you, me, and all people so much that when He puts His love in us, we just can't bear knowing that someone we love is not born of His Spirit and is lost, perishing in this world. If you have accepted our Lord Jesus into your heart, then you know what I'm talking about. It is for this very reason and purpose that, with the Holy Spirit's help, I have written this book, praying that you and everyone else who reads this book will be saved and not perish.

Dear reader, there is no way for you or me to be saved from our sins and receive God's gift of eternal life after this life unless we accept what the Messiah Jesus has done for us and are born of His Holy Spirit. These are the words of our Master Yahshua:

"Very truly, I tell you, no one can see the Kingdom of God without being born from above. Very truly. I tell you, no one can enter the Kingdom

of God without being born of water and Spirit. What is born of the flesh is flesh, and what is born of the Spirit is spirit. Do not be astonished that I say to you, 'You must be born from above.' "

John 3:3, 5-6 (NRSV)

"If you love me, you will obey my commandments. I will ask the Father, and He will give you another Helper, who will stay with you forever. He is the Spirit, who reveals the truth about God. The world cannot receive Him, because it cannot see Him or know Him. But you know Him, because He remains with you and is in you."

John 14:15-17 (TEV)

"But the Helper, the Holy Spirit, whom the Father will send in my name, He will teach you all things ..."

John 14:26 (NKJV)

Life is an invisible spiritual battle for your soul. God has made a way for us to overcome the influence of the evil one and the sin of this lost and deceived world through the blood of Jesus and the power of His Holy Spirit, but we must be willing to believe that God's Word is the truth. We must be willing to accept His gift of faith, and then invite His Holy Spirit to come into us to clean us up. When we receive Father Yah's Personal Representative, Holy Spirit, He empowers us to live for the one true God, to have a change of status and turn away from our sinful ways to be His witnesses. Do you feel the nudging of Holy Spirit on your heart, your innermost being? As it is written;

Listen, I am standing at the door *[of your heart]*, **knocking; if you hear my voice and open the door, I will come in to you and eat with you, and you with me.**

Revelation 3:20 (NRSV). *Bracketed words added for clarity.*

I ask you now, have you realized your sin and your need for forgiveness? Have you humbled yourself before the Almighty Creator of this universe to ask Him to forgive you through the precious blood of the Messiah Yahshua? Have you asked our Lord Jesus to come into your life with His Holy Spirit, to help you turn from your sins and begin to take on His perfect and Holy nature? If you have not, dear friend, please do so now. Prayer is simply talking to Almighty Yah—our Heavenly Father, Creator, and Savior. To be fulfilled in God and receive eternal life, just be sincere and pray a simple prayer like this:

Dear Lord Jesus *(or if you are Jewish, you may want to begin with,* Dear Yahshua Messiah*)*, I know that I am a sinner and need your forgiveness. I believe by Your Holy Word that You died for my sins. I am asking now for Your help so I can turn away from my sins. I invite You to come into my heart and live in me that I may be a new person in You. Help me to trust and follow You as my Lord and Savior all the days of my life. This I pray in Yahshua's name. Amen.

This is God's assurance from His Holy Word:

... if you confess with your lips that Jesus is Lord and believe in your heart that God raised Him from the dead, you will be saved. For man believes with his heart and so is justified, and he confesses with his lips and so is saved. The Scripture says, "No one who believes in Him will be put to shame." For there is no distinction between Jew and Greek; the same Lord is Lord of all and bestows His riches upon all who call upon Him. For, "everyone who calls upon the name of the Lord will be saved."
Romans 10:9-13 (RSV)

If you prayed that simple prayer and were sincere, then the Holy Spirit of the living God is now living in you and working to make you a new creation in Him. Give our Lord Jesus a praise, for He desires the fruit of our lips, and He inhabits all those who love Him and praise Him. You are born of God's Holy Spirit, fulfilled and saved by His amazing grace. It does not matter how much of a sinner you have been, God loves you and rejoices with all of His angels in heaven when one sinner receives His gift of eternal life.

Now that you are born of God's Spirit, you will see life from a whole new perspective. Your thinking will be different. If you cursed before, you should be ashamed and repent from that. If you have been a liar, a thief, a murderer, or full of pride, you should repent from those sins. If you ever desired (coveted) what others have, or have ever been caught up in any of the sexual sins, such as adultery, homosexuality, fornication, masturbation, or pornography, you must repent from those habits and lifestyles. If you have been greedy, worshipping money, materialism, and power, then repent and turn away from that lifestyle. If you have been a member of a false religion, which is every belief system apart from a relationship with the one true God, then turn away from those ways of this world.

Know this: The power of Father Yah's Holy Spirit is greater than the power of any sin in your life. I encourage you to humble yourself and speak to our Father God, our Lord Jesus, ask Him to help you to be delivered from every single sin. You may be under the control and influence of a demonic spirit. The power of Holy Spirit can and will deliver you from all evil spirits that bind you to sin in this life, including those that bring disease and infirmaries. There will be more on this subject in the final chapter of this book, "Ministry of the Bride of Messiah."

If you are a Jewish person, then praise Yahshua Messiah and thank Him for allowing you to be born into the great race of the Jewish people, and for saving you to make you complete in Him. Jewish people are Jewish because they are able to trace their family lineage on their mother's side all the way back to their ancestors of the tribes of Judah, Benjamin, and Levi. These were the tribes of the southern kingdom of Israel after the nation was divided in 880 B.C. These tribes were three of the twelve original tribes that were named after the twelve sons of Jacob. Jacob was the son of Isaac, who was the son of Abraham, the great patriarch with whom God made the covenant.

If you are a member of a Jewish congregation, I encourage you to continue to worship in the rich tradition of the Jewish faith. If you are the only Messianic Jew in your congregation, then you should pray and ask Father Yahweh for wisdom, courage, and the right timing and opportunities to share your good news with your family and friends. Remember this, after you are born of God's Holy Spirit, you will never be the same again, and Satan—the devil—will try to tear you down and turn others against you. Often when a Jew becomes a born again believer in Yahshua, they are ostracized by their family, which is very sad and can cause a lot of problems and strife. If you are reading this book and this applies to you, I encourage you to get on the internet and seek out a Messianic congregation or fellowship in your area. Two very good places to check out are Messianic Israel Alliance at: http://www.mim.net/front.html and Eddie Chumney's web site at: http://www.hebroots.org/.

Have faith and courage, my friend, for the Savior of your soul is with you and will never leave you. As it is written:

Let your conduct be without covetousness; *be* content with such things as you have. For He Himself has said, *"I will never leave you nor forsake you."* So we may boldly say: *"The LORD is my helper; I will not fear. What can man do to me?"*
Hebrews 13:5-6 (NKJV)

But you belong to God, my children, and have defeated the false prophets, because the Spirit who is in you is more powerful than the spirit in those who belong to this world.
1 John 4:4 (TEV)

"If you love Me, keep My commandments. And I will pray the Father, and He will give you another Helper, that He may abide with you forever—the Spirit of truth, whom the world cannot receive, because it neither sees Him nor knows Him, but you know Him, for He dwells with you and will be in you.
John 14:15-17 (NKJV)

What are God's commandments? You may have heard of them, or you may have actually read them, but have you ever meditated on them? All of the verses of the Holy Bible were written down by men and women as God gave them the correct message of instruction or information that He wanted the writer or group of people to have. The truths and doctrines that God gave to the people to record are timeless, meaning they were beneficial to the people that were alive when they were recorded and taught, and they are beneficial down through every generation to our time and beyond. The ten commands were written by God, in stone, by His finger. That makes them very powerful and special. As it is written:

And when He (YAHWEH) had made an end of speaking with him (Moses) on Mount Sinai, He gave Moses two tablets of the Testimony, tablets of stone, written with the finger of God.
Exodus 31:18 (NKJV)

And the Lord (YAHWEH) said to Moses, "Cut two tablets of stone like the first ones, and I will write on these tablets the words that were on the first tablets which you broke."
Exodus 33:1 (NKJV)

These are the Ten Commandments that our Creator wrote down for humanity to live by. I encourage you to meditate on these words.

> **"I *am* the LORD your God, who brought you out of the land of Egypt, out of the house of bondage. You shall have no other gods before Me.**
>
> **"You shall not make for yourself a carved image—any likeness of *any-thing* that *is* in heaven above, or that is in the earth beneath, or that is in the water under the earth; you shall not bow down to them nor serve them. For I, the LORD your God, *am* a jealous God, visiting the iniquity of the fathers upon the children to the third and fourth *generations* of those who hate Me, but showing mercy to thousands, to those who love Me and keep My commandments.**
>
> **"You shall not take the name of the LORD your God in vain, for the LORD will not hold him guiltless who takes His name in vain.**
>
> **"Remember the Sabbath day, to keep it holy. Six days you shall labor and do all your work, but the seventh day *is* the Sabbath of the LORD your God. *In it* you shall do no work: you, nor your son, nor your daughter, nor your male servant, nor your female servant, nor your cattle, nor your stranger who *is* within your gates. For *in* six days the LORD made the heavens and the earth, the sea, and all that *is* in them, and rested the seventh day. Therefore the LORD blessed the Sabbath day and hallowed it.**
>
> **"Honor your father and your mother, that your days may be long upon the land which the LORD your God is giving you.**
>
> **"You shall not murder.**
>
> **"You shall not commit adultery.**
>
> **"You shall not steal.**
>
> **"You shall not bear false witness against your neighbor.**
>
> **"You shall not covet your neighbor's house; you shall not covet your neighbor's wife, nor his male servant, nor his female servant, nor his ox, nor his donkey, nor anything that *is* your neighbor's."**
>
> Exodus 20:2-17 (NKJV)

Our Savior and Master, Jesus, summed up the ten commands into two commandments. And it is written:

> **When the Pharisees heard that He had silenced the Sadducees, they gathered together, and one of them, a lawyer, asked Him a question to**

test Him. "Teacher, which commandment in the law is the greatest?" He said to him, " 'You shall love the Lord your God with all your heart, and with all your soul, and with all your mind.' This is the greatest and first commandment. And a second is like it: 'You shall love your neighbor as yourself.' On these two commandments hang all the law and the prophets."

Matthew 22:34-40 (NRSV)

Pure love of God (Elohim) and pure love of any and every person throughout the world, both around us and distant from us, is what being born of God's Holy Spirit is all about.

I conclude this chapter with a poem and the words to a very familiar hymn.

"I will sing of my Redeemer and
  His wondrous love to me;
On the cruel cross He suffered,
  from the curse to set me free,
Sing, O sing of my Redeemer,
  with His blood He purchased me;
On the cross He sealed my pardon,
  paid the debt and made me free."
—James Rowe

The following song lyrics are from, no doubt, the most popular Christian gospel song that has ever been written. John Newton, who wrote the song in 1779, was a shipping merchant of the high seas, buying goods on one continent, transporting them across the ocean, and selling them to people on another continent. The goods that this man bought, transported across the ocean on a trip that took many weeks by ship, and then sold in America were human beings—slaves from Africa. After years of doing this evil, God convicted him of his terrible sins. John Newton repented and lived the rest of his days in England, blessing generations of people with the beautiful and powerful words of his hymns and other written works. I pray these moving words will be a blessing to you as they have for millions of people all over this world. These words really say it all.

Amazing grace! How sweet the sound,
　　that saved a wretch like me!
I once was lost, but now am found;
　　was blind, but now I see.

'Twas grace that taught my heart to fear,
　　and grace my fears relieved.
How precious did that grace appear,
　　the hour I first believed.

The Lord has promised good to me;
　　His word my hope secures.
His will my shield and portion be,
　　as long as life endures.

Thro' many dangers, toils and snares,
　　I have already come.
His grace hath brought me safe thus far,
　　and His grace will lead me home.

When we've been there ten thousand years,
　　bright shining as the sun;
We've no less days to sing God's praise,
　　than when we'd first begun.

Amazing grace! How sweet the sound,
　　that saved a wretch like me!
I once was lost, but now am found;
　　was blind, but now I see.

HalleluYah! To our Creator, Heavenly Father, Master, Savior, Judge, Friend, and King eternal, be the glory and praise forever and ever. Amen.

4

SATAN'S PLAN OF DECEPTION AFTER MESSIAH'S FIRST COMING

From the beginning of the creation of humanity in the Garden of Eden and throughout the inspired writings of His Word, Father Yahweh has given instruction to His created children to choose life and not death. Incorrect translation and teaching of the original Hebrew Scriptures has caused 1,900 years of deception, false teaching, and strife among believers. This becomes clear when you realize that there are over 1,600 different denominations throughout the world today that make up what is known as Christianity. This fragmentation has been a part of the plan of Satan, the father of all lies, to hinder the called-out ones from loving and serving Yahweh with all of their hearts in spirit and in truth.

Satan knew that his doom was certain and that his defeat was confirmed when Master Yahshua lived as a person and overcame Satan's influence to sin by living a sinless life. Satan knew after the 120 believers were filled with the Holy Spirit during the Feast of *Shavuot* (Pentecost) that he had to work hard and fast to attempt to destroy the great move of Yahweh to draw people to eternal life by putting their faith and trust in Yahshua. The early apostles remained true to living their lives the way their Master, Yahshua, had taught them. Most of them died as martyrs because they would not give in to the pressure from the Roman government and the hierarchy of the Jewish temple priests to renounce their risen King. Satan tried in every way he could to rub out the first-century followers of Yahshua.

HalleluYah, he was unable because Holy Spirit was in them and with them, even unto torturous deaths. Father Yahweh's plan of establishing His kingdom on earth in living temples was working and spreading.

By the time the four Gospel books and the letters that make up the

New Covenant were written, apostasy (turning away from the truth) and false teaching were infiltrating into the congregations, and many were turning away from the truth the Apostles taught and lived. Satan's plan of driving a wedge between the true followers of Messiah—those who were predominantly Jewish and the masses of new Gentile believers—was successful.

King Yahshua destroyed the wall of separation between Jew and Gentile by His own blood atonement for the salvation of everyone who accepts Him. In order to draw the masses of new believers in the Roman Empire away from understanding Father Yahweh's instructions for life in His *Torah*, Satan's deceptions in the minds of religious leaders initiated a different belief system and way of life than that of Yahshua and His apostles. A new wall of separation between Jew and Gentile began to be established in the societies of people.

A part of this wall of separation and deception was the introduction of Gnosticism from Greek influence. The Greeks were famous for being great thinkers and philosophers who established doctrine with logical and rational deduction. From the influence of the Greeks to place great emphasis in the power of human intellect, the teaching of the first-century disciples became more and more watered down. The truth of the all important gift of faith and the importance of praying for the gifts of the Spirit and operating in the flow of the manifestations of the power of Holy Spirit became lost in human intellect and self recognition as the hierarchy of the Church of Rome began to grow its roots. The apostles Paul and Peter had divine understanding of what was beginning to happen in their day and knew that apostasy would progress much worse after they were gone. It is written:

> **In the presence of God and of Christ Jesus, who is to judge the living and the dead, and in view of his appearing and his kingdom, I solemnly urge you: proclaim the message; be persistent whether the time is favorable or unfavorable; convince, rebuke, and encourage, with the utmost patience in teaching. For the time is coming when people will not put up with sound doctrine, but having itching ears, they will accumulate for themselves teachers to suit their own desires, and will turn away from listening to the truth and wander away to myths.**
>
> 2 Timothy 4:1-4 (NRSV)

But false prophets also arose among the people, just as there will be false teachers among you, who will secretly bring in destructive opinions. They will even deny the Master who bought them—bringing swift destruction on themselves. Even so, many will follow their licentious ways, and because of these teachers the way of truth will be maligned. And in their greed they will exploit you with deceptive words. Their condemnation, pronounced against them long ago, has not been idle, and their destruction is not asleep.
  2 Peter 2:1-3 (NRSV)

The following is a summary of what happened in history that caused the masses of new believers not to be taught the significance of the Biblical Sabbath, the Holy Feasts, and dietary instructions that our Heavenly Father Yahweh initiated and instructed us to keep according to His *Torah*. These basic truths were replaced by the traditions of men, with a sprinkling of gospel truth, and promoted as being acceptable though Elohim's grace. The premise was that the whole law given to Moses was presumably nailed to the cross with our Savior Yahshua. I'll address that doctrine a little farther along.

By studying the history of the early Christian church, we have a better understanding as to why the modern day Christian church is so different in the observance of Holy days (holidays), of rest and worship, and in practice of ministry to the congregation. After the destruction of Jerusalem by the Roman army in A.D. 70, the surviving non-believing Jews, Messianic Jews, and Gentile believers had to flee and hide to escape persecution. The presence of Father Yah's Holy Spirit in us bares witness to the truth, so there was no stopping the good news message of salvation from one's sins, eternal life through the acceptance of Yahshua, all that He had accomplished on the cross, and of being born of His Spirit.

Semitic refers to a group of Afro-Asiatic languages, such as Arabic and Hebrew. So the term *anti-Semitic* refers to anyone who is hostile to the peoples of any of these native languages and, most often, in reference to Jews. Anti-Semitism was birthed out of the desire of many Gentile new believers to escape the on-going pressure from the Caesar of the day to wipe out anything Jewish, Messianic or not. That mindset then and now is the breeding ground to encourage separation from anything Jewish. At some point in the early church, the lies of apostasy surfaced that the Jews were responsible for putting Yahshua to death and, because of that, all people of their generations should suffer. This propaganda produced more justification to separate from anything Jewish. Can you see how Satan, our adversary, was successful in watering down the foundation that King Yahshua had laid and on which the Apostles had built? It is written:

For no other foundation can anyone lay than that which is laid, which is Jesus Christ.
1 Corinthians 3:11 (NKJV)

Now, therefore, you are no longer strangers and foreigners, but fellow citizens with the saints and members of the household of God, having been built on the foundation of the apostles and prophets, Jesus Christ Himself being the chief cornerstone.
Ephesians 2:19-20 (NKJV)

During the time when the Holy Spirit came to the 120 believers in Jerusalem and the early called-out ones began to spread the Gospel, the mainstream people of the Roman Empire had been indoctrinated with several hundred years of Greek philosophy and pagan belief systems. The history and understanding of these ancient belief systems is very deep and wide. I am going to give you only the high points that apply to the great deception that has been affecting humanity for the past 5,000 years or so.

THE ORIGIN OF FALSE RELIGIONS AND BELIEF SYSTEMS

The following is a summary of the Roman god system, which was a carryover of the Greek god system, which was a carryover of the ancient Babylonian/Assyrian god system. The historical facts that I have included in this summary can be found in any of the following three books. The books are: *Christianity: New Religion or Sect of Biblical Judaism?* by Robert and Remy Koch, published by Messenger Media; *The Truth About Reformation* by Rabbi Jeffery Weiss, published by For The Glory of Yahshuah Ministries; and *Fossilized Customs* by Lew White. I will also include Scripture as it applies.

In Chapter One of this book, I covered the account of Noah and the great flood that Elohim brought on the earth because the human race had become so full of evil. After the flood, Noah and his family procreated to repopulate the earth. One of Noah's great-grandsons was a very rebellious man named Nimrod. Nimrod did not desire to follow the ways of Father Yahweh. He chose to pursue the way of humanism and the deception of the fallen angel Lucifer, who is Satan, the devil. Nimrod's name, from the Hebrew name *Marad*, meaning "to rebel."

As Nimrod became mighty in the world, he became the leader of rebellion, initiating the building of the Tower of Babel. Standing several hundred feet high, the tower was built so that Nimrod and his priest could worship the sun, moon, planets, and constellations. By not worshipping Yahweh, he opened himself up to the deception of the power of the air, Satan, and the fallen angels.

Nimrod and his wife, Semiramis, followed the same path as Adam and Eve—believing Lucifer that they could become gods by eating of the tree of the knowledge of good and evil. Wealth, power, and humanistic ego took over, resulting in Nimrod and Semiramis requiring their subjects to worship them. This set the stage for the beginnings of all deity worship, astrology, and the beginnings of all of the false pagan belief systems that have come down through the centuries.

Elohim saw how successful the perversion of Nimrod had become, so He confused the one language of the human race at that time, which I believe was Hebrew, and created many dialects. That is the reason the tower that Nimrod built is called Babel, and the city he built is called Babylon. *Babel* is a Hebrew word that means "confusion." The record of the Tower of Babel is found in Genesis Chapter Eleven.

Babylonian history reveals that Nimrod and Semiramis added to their false belief system by giving each other god names with meanings for themselves. Nimrod became known as Kronos, Bel, and Baal. His most significant god title from the Persian language was Zoroaster, which means "woman's promised seed." It was taught from this title and meaning that Nimrod was to be the god-man savior who was to give his life for humanity, and he would crush the head of the serpent, the adversary. As the false belief system developed, it was taught that Nimrod was to be a sacrifice for the sins of the people. This false teaching was perverted from the truth about the prophesied promised coming of the true Messiah. Thus, Nimrod became the first anti-Messiah.

After Nimrod's death, Semiramis further elevated the worship of Nimrod as the sun god, declaring that he had ascended into heaven and would supernaturally impregnate her. Is this starting to sound familiar? Semiramis gave birth to a son whom she named Tammuz. He became known as the son of "the sun god" and the reincarnation of his father, Nimrod. He was born on the day of the celebration of the winter solstice. This day was called *Saternalia*, the high holy day of the year for sun worship that was celebrated on what is known today as December 25. Tammuz was given deity status and, with his mother, was worshiped as a god. This is the origin of mother and child worship that found its way into many cults down to our present day, including the belief system of the universal organized church of the Roman Empire in the fourth century.

Nimrod died at the age of forty from a hunting accident by being gored to death by a wild boar. After his death, his subjects who worshipped him wept bitterly for him and began to worship his son as "the son of the sun god." A new tradition was initiated by them in which each year the people would weep for forty days for Nimrod, one day for each year of his life. During the forty days, his worshippers would grieve and deny themselves one worldly pleasure which they believed would be for his pleasure where he was in the afterlife. He had such a god status that people made idols of him and continued the manmade tradition of worshipping him and grieving over his death. As time went by, the son, Tammuz, became the focus of worship. We have proof of this from the writings of the prophet Ezekiel that even the women of the nation of Israel had fallen into this type of idolatry. As it is written:

> **And He said to me, "Turn again, *and* you will see greater abominations that they are doing." So He brought me to the door of the north gate of the LORD's house; and to my dismay, women were sitting there weeping for Tammuz.**
> Ezekiel 8:13-14 (NKJV)

The mother of Tammuz, Semiramis, was worshipped in Babylon as Rhea and Ashtarte, or Ishtar. The name *Ashtarte* means "woman that made towers." Her goddess name began to carry with it the title, "Queen of Heaven." The false belief system of the sun god, Nimrod, with his different names and titles; Semiramis, with her different names; and their re-incarnated son of the sun god, Tammuz, with his different names and titles, transcended languages and cultures. In Assyria, these false deities were known as Cybele, with wife Ishtar, and son Ninus. In Egypt, father deity was known as Osiris, with wife Isis, and son Horus. Later, in India, the sun god was worshipped as Iswara, with wife Isi, and son Vishnu. Later still, in Greece, they were known by the name Bacchus, with wife Irene, or Diana, with son Plutus. Then in pagan Rome, they were known as Juniper, with the mother goddess wife Fortuna, and son deity Bacchus. Some of the other names of mother goddess that spun off of these in the Greek and Roman cultures were Venus, Athena, and Aphrodite. In each of these false belief systems, there were manmade rituals, customs, initiations, and traditions designed to help the individual who accepts the beliefs to atone for their sins.

In Persia, the male false deity became known as Mithra, the Lord of the Covenant. He was taught as being the mediator between man and his supreme creator in heaven. He was given the title Adonis, which is the equivalent of the Hebrew title Adonai, or in English, Lord. This particular false god and false belief system developed into what is known as Mithraism. Mithraism was the universal State religion of the Roman Empire during the life of Yahshua and for 300 years after His death and resurrection. This pagan belief system was centered on the worship of the sun. Throughout the empire, the day that was set aside as the day to cease from work and to worship the sun was the first day of the week, called Sunday.

TRANSITION FROM MESSIANIC JUDAISM TO THE NEW RELIGION OF THE ROMAN EMPIRE

Earlier in this section I explained that Satan influenced Nimrod to rebel against the worship of the true God of his grandfather Noah in order to worship Satan (Lucifer, the light bearer) by worshipping the sun, moon, planets, and constellations. Two thousand years later, Satan's plan of deception was working very well as the false belief system of worshipping the sun was entrenched in the pagan society of the Roman Empire during the time of the life of Messiah Yahshua.

When the 120 followers of Yahshua received the promised Holy Spirit while in Jerusalem during the Feast of Shavuot (Pentecost), they went out and taught the truth of the Creator Yahweh's plan of salvation from sins through the atoning blood of Yahshua. They taught the promise of His return to establish His Kingdom on earth and experienced many miracles of healing and deliverance by the power of Holy Spirit. This awesome, life-changing message that introduced people to the power and authority of Holy Spirit spread like wildfire throughout the empire. The emperors were not pleased with this new belief system that had a Judeo/Hebraic foundation, with the added teaching of the King of the Jews Who was raised from the dead, and in Whom was found forgiveness of sins and eternal life. Satan worked through the emperors to try to wipe out all of the followers of Yahshua of Nazareth, the risen King, by intense persecution. The early congregations of the called-out ones were known as *The Way* and the *Nazarene Israelites*. These brave men and women were persecuted not only by the Roman Empire, but by the orthodox Jews who were attempting to wipe out the new belief system that came from their Hebraic roots. In order to survive, the true first-century followers of Yahshua had to go underground.

After Jerusalem was destroyed by the Romans in A.D. 70, the persecution of the Jews intensified. Throughout the second and third centuries, as the spreading of the good news of the risen Messiah Yahshua spread, the apostasy that the Apostle Paul taught about in his second letter to the Thessalonians had begun. As it is written,

> **Let no one deceive you in any way; for that day** *[the second coming of Messiah]* **will not come, unless the rebellion** *[apostasy]* **comes first ...**
> 2 Thessalonians 2:3a (RSV). *Bracketed words added for clarity.*

As stated previously, *apostasy* means "to forsake" or "to fall away from the truth." As the good news spread into the non-Jewish communities, the new Gentile believers began to gradually disassociate themselves from their Jewish counterparts in order to escape the heavy persecution of the Jews. The trend of forsaking the Israelite customs continued and increased, even though they were based on instructions from the *Torah*. By the early years of the fourth century, nearly half of the people of the Roman Empire were believers in the risen Messiah Yahshua, but only a small percentage were true followers.

The fast-growing religion called *Christianity* presented a large challenge for the Emperor Constantine who knew he could not kill off so many people in the empire. We thank Yahweh that he brought an end to the persecution of the Christians and the sport deaths in the coliseums.

Economically, Constantine needed to keep the tax base as large as possible to fund his greed. Militarily, he needed a vast numbers of men to supply the huge army used to defend his empire. Politically, he was constantly being challenged by Caesar wannabees who would rally armies to come against him.

Constantine needed to do something to unite the two sprawling regions of the empire, with the western capital in Rome, Italy, and the eastern capital in Constantinople, Turkey. It was about this time that he was away with his army defending the northern part of the empire when he had to return to Italy to meet an old foe named Maxentius, who had raised a large army and was preparing to take control of the empire by subduing Rome.

Before the battle, either while he was sleeping or as seen in the sky, Constantine reportedly had a vision of a cross that came to be identified with Christ. With the vision and dream, he saw the words, *In Hoc Signo Vinces*, "In this sign conquer." He believed this was a true sign from the gods, so he placed the sign of the cross at the top of his standard and on the shields of his men and won the battle of Milvian Bridge outside of Rome in 312. *[Reference: Wikipedia, encyclopedia.]*

Constantine became intrigued by the cross and began to study Christianity. From his studies, he devised a brilliant plan. He decided to use the belief of the followers of the risen Jewish Yahshua of Nazareth and blend it with the State religion of Mithreism to create a new State religion called Roman Catholicism (which means *universal*.)

In the year A.D. 313, Constantine made the belief system of Christianity the official religion of his empire. He initiated a series of councils to give State organization and authority to his new religion. During the following 130 years, the councils would be attended by the most wealthy, influential, and power-hungry leaders of the empire to set policy and establish the foundational doctrines for the newly founded belief system that had its true roots in paganism.

In A.D. 325, the most famous council, the Council of Nicea, brought forth the most significant changes from that of the first century followers of Yahshua. The bishops of the cities of Rome, Alexandria, and Antioch were appointed to be the supreme leaders during the council. Previously, in A.D. 96, leaders from these same cities had petitioned the Emperor to completely separate from the Jews—either Messianic or non-Messianic—and their beliefs.

The Nicean council proposed to make the official day of weekly worship for the newly formed Roman Catholic Church to be the same as the long-established pagan day of worship of the sun god. It just made sense because, for centuries, the majority of the people of the empire had been worshiping the sun god on Sunday, the first day of the week.

Soon after Constantine pretended to accept Christianity, he had his wife and child beheaded. Later, he had coins minted with the stamp *Sol Invictus Mithras,* which means "Invincible God of the Sun." The people of the Roman Empire had been deeply devoted to Mithraism for several hundred years because it was law, and they were afraid to not give complete loyalty to the Caesar, who was revered as a god.

Within this pagan belief system, they were required to worship the Caesar as the representative of the sun god, just as Nimrod, and later his son Tammuz, had been worshiped. Because it was Jewish, the leaders of the councils saw no need to honor the true Sabbath day of worship that Yahweh had given to the Israelites as a set-apart day to be kept holy unto the God of Abraham, Isaac, and Jacob. They certainly had no interest in keeping the feasts of Yahweh as holidays, so they elected to continue with the established pagan feasts. They knew they had to create a new religion for the empire that would retain worship of the emperor in order to have his approval. Instead of recognizing the pagan gods, they would use parts of the historical accounts of the birth, crucifixion, and resurrection of Yahshua as recorded in the four Gospels of the new covenant in order to build the new Christian theology.

The Council of Laodicea, in 336, made Sunday the official day of worship throughout the empire. Along with this sweeping legislation, the leaders made it law that Christians could not abstain from work to observe Saturday, the Sabbath, as the day of worship as instructed by the Torah.

A few years later in A.D. 341 at the Council of Antioch, a law was passed prohibiting the Christians throughout the empire from celebrating the Feast of Passover with any Jews or Nazarene Jews—those believers of Yahshua who continued to follow the Torah as did Jesus and His first followers.

These councils and the men who became known as the early church fathers, created a huge chasm between the newly formed belief system called Roman Universal (Catholic) Church and that of Messianic and non-Messianic Judaism. By the fourth century, the Nazarenes, both Jew and non-Jew believers who were keepers of Torah, were meeting and worshiping underground in order to survive.

The manmade holiday of Christmas was initiated into practice during the Council of Nicea in A.D. 325 and was officially made into law. December 25 had been celebrated in the empire for centuries as

Saturnalia, the birthday of the sun god—Nimrod's son, Tammuz. This high holy day in the pagan belief system of Mithraism was celebrated during the winter solstice.

Down through the false belief systems, that I covered a few pages back, originating from Nimrod's Baal worship, the traditional customs for celebrating the birth of the sun god were assimilated in with the good news of salvation from the Jewish Messiah Yahshua. The Yule log symbolized the stump of Nimrod that was cut down. Out of his stump would be his rebirth, the birth of his son Tammuz who would be symbolized by the evergreen tree that was to be cut and decorated. The leaders of the Council of Nicea decided they could substitute the birth of the Messiah Yahshua for the birth of the sun god and continue the celebration of Saturnlia on the 25th of December.

Dear reader, please understand that our Savior Yahshua was not born in December. There is absolutely no reason to celebrate His birthday then when the truth is known. There is substantial evidence that He was born in either late September or early October during the Feast of Tabernacles. That is the time to celebrate His birth. Celebrating on December 25 is a thoroughly man-made holiday that was originally known as the Mass of Christ, later being changed to Christmas.

Here is a strong word from Yahweh through the prophet Jeremiah addressing man's customs and traditions.

> **Thus saith the LORD, Learn not the way of the heathen, and be not dismayed at the signs of heaven; for the heathen are dismayed at them. For the customs of the people are vain: for one cutteth a tree out of the forest, the work of the hands of the workman, with the axe. They deck it with silver and with gold; they fasten it with nails and with hammers, that it move not. They are upright as the palm tree, but speak not: they must needs be borne, because they cannot go. Be not afraid of them; for they cannot do evil, neither also is it in them to do good.**
> Jeremiah 10:2-5 (KJV)

The custom of cutting trees and decorating them for the pagan high holy day of Saturnalia, had been a tradition among people of the different empires for approximately 2,300 years before the mass of Christ was created. Now granted, these verses are describing the making of decorated idols that people were to hold in awe, but isn't that what decorating a tree during the Christmas holiday is about? It is both that and a type of materialism worship of a mountain of presents. It is simply not instruction from our Heavenly Father and Creator. It must grieve His heart when He sees that His children have turned away from His Holy Sabbath and appointed times, His feasts.

We have much to un-learn that is of the adversary's world, so we can learn afresh the things of Father Yahweh. I know this is a hard pill for you to swallow if you are a modern-day Christian. Being a good mommy or daddy and putting up and decorating a Christmas tree to put presents under each year is a family tradition that you have probably experienced all of your life. I can relate because that is my background.

But dear reader, please hear me. We are near the end of the last generation, and we must get our relationship with our coming King Yahshua right according to His instructions. In all things, our Creator tests us to determine our loyalty and commitment to love Him and seek Him first in all that we do. It only gets more challenging as we understand the revealed truth about the origins of Easter.

As the new belief system called *Christianity* was being formed by the early bishops who were establishing the Roman Catholic Church, the push was on to remove everything Jewish/Hebraic from the holy days and replace them with pagan customs and traditions. There is no support for anything called *Easter* in the Scriptures.

Easter is an English word translated from the name *Ashtarte* or *Ishtar*. These were the goddess names of worship for Nimrod's wife Seriramis. After Seriramis died, the pagan cult that she and Nimrod created continued on in the hearts of their followers and was passed down to their children.

The ancient legend is that Semiramis, being the mother of the sun god, was sent back to earth after her death and was re-born as the spring fertility goddess named Ishtar. She was depicted as a well-endowed, bare-breasted queen of sexual desire, from which the goddess Aphrodite in the Greek culture originated. The belief was passed down that Ishtar had emerged from a giant egg that had landed in the Euphrates River at sunrise on the day of sun worship—Sunday—that followed the day of the spring equinox. In order to promote her divinity, it was taught that she changed a bird into an egg-laying rabbit, which proliferated the fertility season.

From this, the pagan cult progressed deeply into evil. The priest of

Ishtar initiated the doctrine that they should impregnate young virgins on the altar of the goddess of fertility at sunrise on Ishtar Sunday. One year later, and on a different altar, the priest would sacrifice the three-month-old infants to Ishtar and her son Tammuz, the sun god. The priest would take the blood of the murdered infants and use the blood to dye eggs in honor of Ishtar. The ceremony of impregnating young virgins took place at one end of the pagan temple, and the sacrificing of the babies from the previous year's virgins took place at the other end of the temple. How horrible! Now we know where the four-thousand-year-old tradition of dying Easter eggs came from.

A few pages back is the information of how the people who worshipped Nimrod wept for him for forty days, one day for each year of his life, and continued on after his son Tammuz died. The forty days of weeping and morning the death of the sun god Nimrod became known as Lent and was to begin forty days before the Ishtar (Easter) fertility celebration.

During the forty days of Lent, the people of the pagan cultures were to abstain from some worldly pleasure, thinking their sun god would be able to experience and benefit from what they had abstained from having. Ceremonies and rituals were added and practiced as the worshippers prepared for the great day celebrating the rebirth of their savior, the sun god, and the celebration of Ishtar, their mother goddess of fertility.

The Ishtar fertility goddess and sun god worship services began with the priest of Easter and worshipers facing the sun at sunrise on Sunday. Then came the sex orgies, the sacrificing of the babies, and the dying of eggs. The pagan services finished up with a feast of prepared wild boar to honor Nimrod, their sun god sin bearer. They probably invented the pig-picking concept.

Centuries later, the sex orgies and sacrificing of infants had been removed from the false religion, but some new customs were added. The worship of the Philistine, and later Phoenician, god Dagon was incorporated into the pagan world of gods. Dagon was portrayed as half man and half fish. This god was worshiped on Friday, which was called "Good Friday," and was celebrated with a feast of fish. This practice rolled over into Constantine's new Roman religion and was a good fit for the false teaching that Yahshua was crucified on a Friday.

Are you beginning to see clearly the picture of how the early founders of the Roman Catholic Church conveniently incorporated some teachings about the life, death, and resurrection of Jesus the Christ into an already established heathen belief system? Constantine was very successful in pulling off his plan to keep unity in the empire by keeping his pagan belief systems alive. Those belief systems kept him as the object of religious veneration. With the help of his cohorts and by blending in some truth with the deception and falsehood of Mithraism, he was able to elevate himself as the spokesman of god. That would lay the foundation for establishing the highest office of the State church, the Pope.

In A.D. 445, the emperor declared the Bishop of Rome to be "the venerable man, the Pope of the Eternal City." The position of the Pope became even more powerful than that of the Emperor. By the fifth century, the Roman Empire was fading into history, but the powerful Roman Catholic Church, with the popes at the head was taking control of as much of the world as it could. The longest running empire in the history of the world was now able to institute a new universal religion that was committed to removing everything Jewish from its doctrines and observances.

The leaders of the new Roman Catholic Church seized the opportunity to elevate themselves to positions of power, and the hierarchy of the Pope and the Church government system was formed. The early Bishops accomplished great successes in their indoctrination of the people of the empire by taking some truth from the account of the birth and death of King Yahshua Messiah and conforming these events to mesh with the already highly accepted pagan god holidays of the Roman Empire. In doing so, the great wall of separation between Christianity and Orthodox Judaism, including Messianic Judaism, was well established.

THE CHANGING OF THE BIBLICAL SABBATH

Today, throughout the world, many of these pagan customs that have been passed down through both the Roman Catholic Church and Protestant churches and are still practiced out of ignorance of the truth. The following are historical statements that are relevant to this teaching.

"They (the Catholics) allege the Sabbath change into Sunday, the Lord's day, contrary to the Decalogue (Ten Commandments) as it appears; neither is there any example more boasted of than the changing of the Sabbath day. Great, say they, is the power and authority of the church, since it dispensed with one of the ten commandments." *Augsburg*

Confession, Article 28 written by Melanchton, 1530.

"The Catholic Church of its own infallible authority created Sunday a holy day to take the place of the Sabbath of the old law." *Kansas City Catholic*, February 9, 1893.

"Sunday is a Catholic institution, and its claims to observance can be defended only on Catholic principles. From beginning to end of Scripture there is not a single passage that warrants the transfer of weekly public worship from the last day of the week to the first." *Catholic Press*, Sydney Australia; August 25, 1900.

"You may read the Bible from Genesis to Revelation, and you will not find a single line authorizing the sanctification of Sunday. The Scriptures enforce the religious observance of Saturday, a day which we never sanctify." Cardinal Gibbons, "The Faith of Our Fathers," page 111, 1892.

"Of course, I quite well know that Sunday did come into use in early Christian history. But what a pity it comes branded with the mark of paganism, and christened with the name of the sun god, adopted and sanctioned by the papal apostasy, and bequeathed as a sacred legacy to Protestantism!" Dr. Edward T. Hiscox, November 13, 1893 edition of the *New York Examiner*.

"The festival of Sunday, like all other festivals, was always only a human ordinance, and it was far from the intentions of the apostles to establish a Divine command in this respect; far from them, and from the early apostolic Church, to transfer the laws of the Sabbath to Sunday." Dr. Augustus Neander, *The History of Christian Religion and Church*, page 186, 1843.

"The Sabbath was binding in Eden, and it has been in force ever since. The fourth commandment begins with the word 'remember,' showing that the Sabbath already existed when God wrote the law on the tablets of stone at Sinai. How can men claim that this one commandment has been done away with when they will admit that the other nine are still binding?" Dwight L. Moody, *Weighed and Wanting*, pp. 47, 48.

"The Sabbath is a part of the Ten Commandments. This alone forever settles the question as to the perpetuity of the institution. Until, therefore, it can be shown that the whole moral law has been repealed, the Sabbath will stand. The teaching of Christ confirms the perpetuity of the Sabbath." Presbyterian T.C. Blake, D.D., *Theology Condensed*, pp. 474, 475.

"But, say some, it was changed from the seventh to the first day.

Where, when, and by whom? No man can tell. No, it never was changed, nor could it be, unless creation was to be gone through again. It is all old wives fables to talk of the change of the Sabbath from the seventh to the first day. If it be changed, it was that august personage changed it who changes times and laws *ex officio*. I think his name is Doctor Antichrist." Alexander Campbell, *The Christian Baptist*, February 2, 1842, vol. 1, no. 7, page 164.

It is written:

He shall speak words against the Most High, and shall wear out the saints of the Most High, and shall think to change the times and the law; and they shall be given into his hand for a time, two times, and half a time.
Daniel 7:25 (RSV)

Take heed to all that I have said to you; and make no mention of the names of other gods, nor let such be heard out of your mouth.
Exodus 23:13 (RSV)

... take heed that you be not ensnared to follow them, after they have been destroyed before you, and that you do not inquire about their gods, saying, "How did these nations serve their gods?—that I also may do likewise."
Deuteronomy 12:30 (RSV)

My people are destroyed for lack of knowledge; because you have rejected knowledge, I reject you from being a priest to me. And since you have forgotten the law of your God, I also will forget your children.
Hosea 4:6 (RSV)

I once heard a recorded sermon about the keeping of the Sabbath, the fourth Commandment, that was given by a Protestant preacher. In his opening remarks, he stated for justification purposes that the keeping and observing of the biblical Sabbath, Saturday, the seventh day of the week, was changed to Sunday, called the Lord's Day, by the second generation of Apostles in the latter part of the first century and early part of the second century. He further stated that the proof of this change was from the authentic ancient letter called the "Didache" that is believed to have been written around the time of the Apostle John's death. In the correct translation of the original Greek there is nowhere to be found the word *day* in a proper context that can be used to substantiate the early Christian church worshiping on Sunday, the first day of the week. In the fourteenth paragraph of this famous letter is the statement where the 18th century Protestant scholar translators by the last names of Lake and Hall/Napier, and Lightfoot, translated some words incorrectly. The following is evidence of the mistranslation.

In the *Didache*, the Greek expression normally translated by 19th century Protestant scholars as "On the Lord's day" should have been correctly translated, "As the Lord's way," (*The Didache*. Verse 14. In: Holmes M. *The Apostolic Fathers—Greek Text and English Translations*, 3rd printing 2004, pp. 266-267) which literally means, "According to the Lord's way, even the Lord's," and the context appears to actually be referring to the Christian Passover (which the Protestant scholars did not observe; hence, this may explain why they did not translate it literally). Thus, this passage does not in any way support the idea that Christians observed Sunday. The other early text often cited by Sunday supporters is from Ignatius' *Letter to the Magnesians*. However, the terms for *Sun* or *day* are also not in the text. In Ignatius' *Letter to the Magnesians*, like in the *Didache*, *kupiak* (*koine*) would be better translated as "Lord's way" or, combined with the Greek word that follows it, *zontes,* "Lord's way of life" or "Lord's living." This is also consistent with what Paul wrote: "Imitate me, just as I also imitate Christ" (1 Cor. 11:1). It was the custom of Jesus (e.g. Luke 4:16) and Paul to regularly keep the Sabbath (Acts 17:2). The Sabbath was part of the Lord's way of life, and Paul imitated Christ that way. It is sad that these translators, all born in the 19th century, all decided to selectively change the meaning of the Greek word *koine* from *way* to *day* (Ignatius. *Letter to the Magnesians*. Verse 8. In: Holmes M. *The Apostolic Fathers—Greek Text and English Translations*, 3rd printing 2004, p. 154). These references can be found on the web site address: www.cogwriter.com.

Another false teaching that has been handed down through the centuries to justify changing the biblical Sabbath from Saturday to Sunday says that the Apostles and first-century congregations made the change because our Master Yahshua was resurrected on a Sunday morning. Because Mary went running to spread the good news that He is risen, this false teaching says that the new day to assemble to worship, study the Word, pray and do ministry was assumed to have been changed to Sunday.

The Scriptures clearly teach that Yahshua was resurrected on Saturday afternoon, the Sabbath.

I will keep this short. Yahshua said Himself that, like the example of Jonah in the belly of the great fish, he would remain in the tomb for three days and three nights (Matthew 12: 40). He died at three o'clock P.M. as the priests were killing the lambs for the Passover meal that evening that began the first day of the high holy Sabbath of the Feast of Unleavened Bread. Since He was placed in the tomb soon after His death and before sunset and the beginning of this very sacred feast time, then He would be resurrected with His new body exactly 72 hours later, which could not have been on a Sunday morning, the first day of the week when His tomb was found empty (Matthew 28: 1-8). By counting backwards 72 hours from late Saturday afternoon, we arrive at Wednesday afternoon as the time of His crucifixion. Toward the end of that awesome Sabbath after He had rested, the pre-appointed time came for Him to rise up and proclaim His, and our, victory over Satan, sin, death, hell, and the grave. He made it clear that He is Master of the Sabbath, the time that He initiated to meet with His followers to enter into His rest. And oh, what a sweet rest it is. It is written:

> Therefore, since a promise remains of entering His rest, let us fear lest any of you seem to have come short of it. For indeed the gospel was preached to us as well as to them; but the word which they heard did not profit them, not being mixed with faith in those who heard *it.* For we who have believed do enter that rest, as He has said: *"So I swore in My wrath, 'They shall not enter My rest,'"* although the works were finished from the foundation of the world. For He has spoken in a certain place of the seventh *day* in this way: *"And God rested on the seventh day from all His works"*; And again in this place: *"They shall not enter My rest."* Since therefore it remains that some *must* enter it, and those to whom it was first preached did not enter because of dis-obedience, again He designates a certain day, saying in David, *"Today,"* after such a long time, as it has been said: *"Today, if you will hear His voice, Do not harden your hearts."* For if Joshua had given them rest, then He would not afterward have spoken of another day. There remains therefore a rest for the people of God. For he who has entered His rest has himself also ceased from his works as God *did* from His. Let us therefore be diligent to enter that rest, lest anyone fall according to

the same example of disobedience. For the word of God *is* living and powerful, and sharper than any two-edged sword, piercing even to the division of soul and spirit, and of joints and marrow, and is a discerner of the thoughts and intents of the heart.

Hebrews 4:1-12 (NKJV)

When we come to realize that we need a relationship with our Creator, Savior, and King eternal and are born of His Holy Spirit, we then begin our faith journey. We learn to love Him and please Him not only by our belief and faith in Him, but by how we follow His instructions and live our lives following the example of Yahshua Messiah. This is why the body of Messiah is portrayed symbolically as the Bride. We are to be submissive to His will because we love Him. As we grow in understanding of the truth contained in His Holy Word, we desire to be obedient and to follow His written instructions because we want to please Him; He is the holy Living Word of Father Yahweh. We please Him by putting our complete faith and trust in Yahshua. As we learn the truth from His Word, we are to come out of falsehood, no matter how challenging it may be. It is written:

My little children, I am writing these things to you so that you may not sin. But if anyone does sin, we have an advocate with the Father, Jesus Christ the righteous; and he is the atoning sacrifice for our sins, and not for ours only but also for the sins of the whole world. Now by this we may be sure that we know him, if we obey his commandments. Whoever says, "I have come to know him," but does not obey his commandments, is a liar, and in such a person the truth does not exist; but whoever obeys his word, truly in this person the love of God has reached perfection. By this we may be sure that we are in him: whoever says, "I abide in him," ought to walk just as he walked.

1 John 2:1-6 (NRSV)

5

THE SIGNIFICANCE
OF THE SABBATH AND
THE HOLY FEAST DAYS

THE SABBATH, DAY OF REST

As you are starting this chapter, you may be asking yourself some very good questions, such as, "Aren't the keeping of the Sabbath on Saturday and observing the seven biblical Feasts Jewish stuff?" If you are a believer in Yahshua and have been born of His Spirit, you may be thinking that this teaching is legalistic. Well, I'm going to break it down for you because it is important to understand the revelation truth from Yahweh's Word and how to apply the truth to our lives, especially in this last generation. That is what this book is all about. Please continue reading. You have made a good choice.

Our Creator Elohim's master plan for humanity on this earth before He creates a new earth is a 7,000 year plan. As it is written in the Holy Scriptures,

> **But, beloved, be not ignorant of this one thing, that one day is with the Lord** [Adonai] **as a thousand years, and a thousand years as one day.**
> 2 Peter 3:8 (KJV). *Bracketed words added for clarity.*

There is great symbolism in Elohim's six-day creation of the universe and the seventh day of rest.

God (Elohim) created the sun not only to heat the earth for raising food and making it possible for planet earth to be a habitat for life, but also, with the moon and stars, a way to tell time.

Then God *[Elohim]* **said, "Let there be lights in the firmament of the heavens to divide the day from the night; and let them be for signs** *[prophecy in the constellations]* **and seasons, and for days and years; and let them be for lights in the firmament of the heavens to give light on the earth"; and it was so. Then God made two great lights: the greater light to rule the day, and the lesser light to rule the night.** *He made* **the stars also. God set them in the firmament of the heavens to give light on the earth, and to rule over the day and over the night, and to divide the light from the darkness. And God** *[Elohim]* **saw that** *it was* **good. So the evening and the morning were the fourth day.**

     Genesis 1:14-19 (NKJV). *Bracketed words added for clarity.*

It is clear from the wording in the first chapter of Genesis that the creation process was done in six 24-hour time periods. God's timetable for a 24-hour day begins at twilight—just after the sun sets and just before the darkness of the night begins—and ends 24 hours later at sunset. In this passage of Scripture, following the description of what was created during the course of each day, God clearly defines "the evening and the morning" were the first day, second day, etc. At the end of the sixth 24-hour day, Elohim rested from His achievements and labor.

Thus the heavens and the earth, and all the host of them, were finished. And on the seventh day God *[Elohim]* **ended His work which He had done, and He rested on the seventh day from all His work which He had done. Then God** *[Elohim]* **blessed the seventh day and sanctified it, because in it He rested from all His work which God** *[Elohim]* **had created and made.**

     Genesis 2:1-3 (NKJV). *Bracketed words added for clarity.*

This was the beginning of the institution of the seventh day as the day of rest.

The instruction for mankind to set the seventh day apart as a special day for rest from our physical work was given by Elohim to Moses on Mount Sinai as the fourth commandment. Almighty Yah wrote His Ten Commandments in stone with His finger two different times. Moses destroyed the first set of stone tablets when he threw them down in his rage at seeing the golden calf idol that the Israelites had constructed and were worshiping.

The two events of Moses receiving the Ten Commandments are recorded in the old covenant in Exodus 20:2-17 and in Chapter 34. Moses brought the Ten Commandments (instructions of how to live) to the attention of the second generation of Israelites after the exodus from Egypt, as they are recorded again in Deuteronomy 5:1-21.

Moses wrote the first five books of the old covenant called the Torah. In his recording of the events of Deuteronomy 5, he knew he was about to die and that the younger generation would soon be entering into the Promised Land. He knew they needed to have a clear understanding of how Elohim expected them to live. The fourth commandment is:

> **"Remember the Sabbath day, to the keep it holy. Six days you shall labor and do all your work, but the seventh day *is* the Sabbath of the LORD your God** *[Yahweh, your Elohim]*. **In it you shall do no work: you, nor your son, nor your daughter, nor your male servant, nor your female servant, nor your cattle, nor your stranger who *is* within your gates. For *in* six days the LORD** *[Yahweh]* **made the heavens and the earth, the sea, and all that *is* in them, and rested the seventh day. Therefore the LORD** *[Yahweh]* **blessed the Sabbath day and hallowed it** *[set it apart as special]***."**
>
> Exodus 20:8-11 (NKJV). *Bracketed words added for clarity.*

A few more chapters over in Exodus, Yahweh gave the instruction that all generations of the Israelites are to keep the Sabbath, for, in doing so, it was, is, and will continue to be a sign that we are the Lord's set-apart people. It is written,

> **"Therefore the children of Israel shall keep the Sabbath, to observe the Sabbath throughout their generations *as* a perpetual** *[continuous, on-going]* **covenant. It *is* a sign between Me and the children of Israel forever; for *in* six days the LORD** *[Yahweh]* **made the heavens and the earth, and on the seventh day He rested and was refreshed."**
>
> Exodus 31:16-17 (NKJV). *Bracketed words added for clarity.*

The significance of the seventh day (Sabbath) rest is that it is to be forever a day of memorial for remembering the awesomeness of our Creator. The day is set apart as a time to give special honor and praise to Him. In the context of our Father Yahweh's master plan, the seventh day represents and points us to the one thousand years of what is called the millennium. Prior to the millennium, at the end of the time called the great tribulation, the Messiah will come to establish His kingdom of government, peace, and rest for the earth and its inhabitants.

Understanding the meaning and symbolism of the Sabbath and the feast days of Yahweh helps us to be focused on our Creator, Savior, and King eternal, and on His master plan. The Sabbath and the feast days are blocks of time that Elohim initiated as instructions to help us learn more about Him and His master plan of events of enormous scale. When we learn the significance of these set-apart times, we come to appreciate the infinite love and mercy that our Heavenly Father has for us in the working of His great plan for humanity.

There are more Scriptures and teachings of how to have relationship with our Creator on a daily basis and the keeping of the Sabbath and His appointed Feasts in the Eleventh chapter, "How Do We Prepare for the Coming of Messiah?"

Our Creator has allowed mankind, by free will and choice, to establish all kinds of governments, empires, nations, cultures, societies, religions, traditions, customs, holidays, etc., during the past 6,000 years since the creation of Adam and Eve. To some degree, all have been influenced by deception from Satan and human self-interest. The Holy Spirit of Elohim gave the inspired Word from Elohim in order that we, the humans He created, would have proper instructions for how to live in relationship with Almighty Yah and each other. As stated in Chapter One, the Hebrew word *Torah*, the first five books of the first covenant (testament), means "instruction." When we love the Lord (Adonai) our God (Elohim) with all of our heart, then we will want to do His will by following His instructions.

At the end of this generation, Almighty Elohim, through His Messiah Yahshua, will bring to an end Satan's domination of humanity and life on planet earth as we know it. A whole new and wonderful reality is coming during the millennium after we pass through the very difficult time of the great tribulation at the end of this age. Holy Spirit *(Ruach haKodesh)* is preparing a called, separated people to prepare for the events at the end of this last generation that we are in. Are you among those whom He is calling to be prepared?

THE SEVEN HOLY FEASTS OF YAHWEH

The appointed Feasts, or Holy Convocations, of our Creator are also referred to in the Scriptures as appointed seasons and Sabbaths. The instructions and descriptions of the feasts are found in Leviticus 23:1-44. The word *feast* is translated from the Hebrew word *moed*, which means "an appointment, or fixed time." In the feasts, our Heavenly Father reveals His amazing love, grace, blessing, preservation, promises, and fulfillment for the human race He created—in essence, His Master Plan. All of the feasts are significant and were instituted by Father Yahweh as types of annual rehearsals and memorials that were designed to point us to the reality of His Son, Yahshua, the Messiah, and with all that He would accomplish in His first coming as the Lamb of God and in His second coming as the Lion of Judah.

The keeping of the Sabbath and the appointed feast times were not just for the Hebrew nation that Adonai Elohim led out of Egypt. We, in all generations, have been instructed to keep the Sabbath and the holy feasts to help us remember the mighty acts of Elohim in creation and all that He has accomplished thus far in working out His Master Plan. The Sabbath and Yahweh's holy feasts help us to look forward to all that He is going to accomplish in the major events of the end of this age. It is written:

And the LORD spoke to Moses, saying, "Speak to the children of Israel, and say to them: 'The feasts of the LORD, which you shall proclaim *to be* holy convocations, these *are* My feasts ...' "
Leviticus 23:1-2 (NKJV)

At the end of verses 14, 21, 31, and 41, Father Yahweh instructs Moses that the feasts "shall be a statute forever throughout your generations." Our Savior and King eternal kept the Sabbath and all of the feasts during His life.

If you keep my commandments, you will abide in my love, just as I have kept my Father's commandments and abide in His love.
John 15:10 (NRSV)

Father Yahweh has already accomplished all of the significant events in His master plan that were associated with the first four feasts. As of the publishing of this book, the events relating to the foreshadowing of the Fall Feast have not been fulfilled. These great, holy, appointed times of our Creator, Savior, and King are important to understand, remember, and observe as we see the end of this age approaching very quickly.

Father Yahweh gave the instructions regarding the observing of the feasts to Moses, so that Moses could instruct the Israelites. The feasts were to be known as the Lord's Feasts. The Sabbath and the feasts, or "Holy Days," were to be a special sign between Adonai Elohim and His people.

Thus saith the Lord:

> **Moreover I also gave them My Sabbaths** *[the weekly day of rest and the Holy feast times of the year]*, **to be a sign between them and Me, that they might know that I am the Lord who sanctifies them** *[sets them apart]*.
> Ezekiel 20:12 (NKJV). *Bracketed words added for clarity.*

The apostle Paul in his letter to the congregation in Colossia explains to them, and to us, that we are not to be concerned by what people outside of the Body of Messiah say about following Father Yahweh's instructions *(Torah)* regarding dietary rules, the observing of the Sabbath, the seven Holy festivals, and observing the new moons, which determine the timing of the festivals.

> **Therefore do let anyone condemn you in matters of food and drink or of observing festivals, new moons, or sabbaths. These are only a shadow** *[preview]* **of what is to come, but the substance** *[the solid facts concerning the reality of the first and second coming of Yahshua]* **belongs to Christ.**
> Colossians 2:16-17 (NRSV). *Bracketed words added for clarity.*

The seven appointed holy feasts are divided into three seasons. The first three feasts, or convocations, are continuous days and take place in early spring. They are called Passover, The Days of Unleavened Bread, and the Day of First Fruits. The fourth is Pentecost, which takes place in late spring. The last three are in early fall and are called The Feast of Trumpets, The Day of Atonement, and The Feast of Tabernacles.

The timing of the feasts are associated with the agricultural season of the farmers in the northern hemisphere, specifically, the crop-growing area around Jerusalem, Israel. As long as there was a temple in Jerusalem, the members of all twelve tribes were commanded by Elohim to gather in Jerusalem three times a year to celebrate the festivals of Passover, Pentecost, and Tabernacles. These coincided with the harvest of barley in early spring, wheat in late spring, and fruits in early fall. The description and how to determine the timing of the Feasts of the Lord (Yahweh) are found in the old covenant (*Torah*) in Leviticus Chapter 23.

The Hebraic scriptural calendar of our Creator is based on the beginning of a month falling on the first day phase of a new moon starting the Spring with the month of Nisan (or Abib). The timing of all of the feast days are counted from the first day of the new moon, except the Feast of Trumpets (*Teruah*), that begins on the actual first day of the seventh month (September or October). The new moon was/is determined by seeing the first slither of light reflected from the moon the day after the new moon, or absence of reflected light, which indicates the first day after the new moon.

The Israelites of the old covenant (testament) used a calendar consisting of twelve months as we do today, except the months were consistently twenty-eight days per the moon's cycle. About every three and one-half years, a thirteenth month was added to their calendar, based on the cycle of the moon around the earth, in order to keep the numbers of the years correct. The same principal is applied to adjust our modern-day calendar that is based on the cycle of the earth revolving around the sun with the adding of a day every fourth year as leap year.

I feel I need to offer the following clarification in order to explain the Jewish calendar system because it can be very confusing. Since the beginning of the Rabbinic order that began after the destruction of the great temple in Jerusalem in A.D. 70, Judaism has followed a civil calendar for government, business, commerce, etc., which begins in the Fall of the year. Depending on the day of the month when the new moon falls, the first month of the Jewish new year is called *Tishri,* beginning in late September or early October. The name for the Jewish new year day and celebration is called *Rosh HaShana,* which means "head of the year." It has been passed down through the Jewish faith that this day is associated with the creation of Adam. Devout Jewish people have also kept the religious calendar of the *Torah* (Yahweh's Teaching), which begins in the spring of the year. Depending again on the cycle of the moon, the first month, called *Abib,* begins in March or April and is determined by the inspection of the grain heads on the barley crop. *Abib* is the Hebrew word that means "green ear month," referring to mature grain. If the grain heads of the barley are ripe by the new moon in March, then the new religious calendar begins on that day of the new moon. Passover is determined by counting fourteen days from the new moon. If the grain heads are ripe after the new moon in March, then the new moon in April begins the new religious calendar and the proper count to determine Passover and the timing of the six other appointed feasts.

Today, Sabbath- and Feast-observing Jews and most born-again Messianic Israelites follow the set Jewish calendar that was established in the fourth century by a Jewish Rabbi named Hillel II. He determined a fixed calendar based on mathematical and astronomical calculations. This calendar, still in use, standardized the length of months and the addition of months over the course of a 19-year cycle, so that the lunar calendar realigns with the solar years. By Hillel's calendar, the time of the Feasts are the same each year, based on the cycle of the moon, but actually fall on days of the Gregorian calendar from year to year.

It is important that we learn the meaning of these set-apart times that our Creator, Savior, and King Eternal has appointed, as these are His convocations for us to observe. The keeping of the weekly Sabbath and the Holy Feasts of Father Yahweh enrich our relationship with Him, give us a clear picture of His master plan, and prepare us for the coming of King Yahshua to establish His will and Kingdom here on earth.

PASSOVER *(PESACH)*

Passover is the first of the three great feasts taking place in the spring of the year in the month of *Abib*. Passover *(Pesach)* has great significance in Elohim's master plan for humanity. He established this memorial so the Israelites would remember His awesome power that was displayed when He delivered them from 400 years of slavery under the control of the Egyptian Pharaohs.

The whole incredible account of the events was written down by Moses and has been passed down to us in the book of Exodus. In Chapters Eleven through Twelve of Exodus, we learn that the Lord God (Adonai Elohim) was preparing the Israelites for the tenth and final plague that was to be poured out on the Pharaoh's family and the Egyptian people.

Yahweh spoke to Moses and his brother Aaron, as it is recorded in the beginning of Chapter Twelve. He gave them instruction that the time (the first day of the new moon in the month of *Abib*) they were in was to be established as the beginning of the religious year and that they were to lead the Israelites to follow all of His instructions for the Passover.

The significance of Passover is about the preparation of the lamb sacrifice that would be provided for their protection from death and enable them to leave their state of bondage and move into freedom where they could worship Yahweh as He desired. Our Heavenly Father had heard the cries of the Israelites during their 400 years of bondage and slavery to the Egyptian government. Pharaoh would not allow the Israelites to assemble and worship the one true, living God—the God of their fathers, Abraham, Isaac, and Jacob. Yahweh made a promise to those Israelites that He kept. Passover was to be remembered with a simple ceremony each year on the anniversary date of when God defeated the mighty world-dominant army of Pharaoh and lead the chosen people of Israel to the promised land.

After nine terrible plagues that Yahweh had poured out on the Egyptians, the Pharaoh still refused to let the Israelite people leave his nation of bondage. Yahweh revealed to Moses that the tenth plague would be death passing through the land of Egypt, and that the firstborn of all human families and animal families would be killed, unless they were under Yahweh's protection. The instruction given to Moses and Aaron was to tell all of the Israelites to select a lamb from their herds. The lamb could be either from the sheep or from the goats, approximately one year old, and without blemish. I will continue the historical account with the Scriptures. Notice the timing of the killing of the lambs. Thus saith the Lord:

> **Your lamb shall be without blemish, a male of the first year: ye shall take it out from the sheep, or from the goats: And ye shall keep it up until the fourteenth day of the same month** *[first month of* Nisan, *also called* Abib]**; and the whole assembly of the congregation of Israel shall kill it in the evening** *[mid afternoon at 3:00 before sunset to allow time for cleaning the carcass before cooking]*. **And they shall take of the blood, and strike it on the two side posts and on the upper door post of the houses, wherein they shall eat it.**
>
> Exodus 12:5-7 (KJV). *Bracketed words added for clarity.*

Verses eight through eleven describe how the lamb was to be cooked and eaten. Now continuing in verse 12:

> **For I will pass through the land of Egypt this night, and will smite all the firstborn in the land of Egypt, both man and beast; and against all the gods of Egypt I will execute judgment: I am the LORD. And the blood shall be to you for a token** [sign] **upon the houses where ye are: and when I see the blood, I will pass over you, and the plague shall not be upon you to destroy you, when I smite the land of Egypt. And this day shall be unto you for a memorial; and ye shall keep it a feast to the LORD** [Yahweh] **throughout your generations; ye shall keep it a feast by an ordinance for ever.**
>
> Exodus 12:12-14 (KJV). *Bracketed words added for clarity.*

The importance of observing this set-apart spring feast each year is in the remembering of the mighty acts of Yahweh before and during that first Passover that convinced the Pharaoh to set the Israelite nation free from slavery. The important symbolism that Passover had from the Exodus in 1491 B.C. until the death and resurrection of Messiah in the year A.D. 29 was that the event of Passover also pointed to the coming of the Messiah. As a result of having all of the Scriptures of teaching, we know that the slaying of the Passover lamb gives the picture of the sacrifice of Messiah that He fulfilled completely in His first coming. As it is written:

> **The next day John** [the baptizer] **seeth Jesus coming unto him, and saith, Behold the Lamb of God, which taketh away the sin of the world.**
>
> John 1: 29 (KJV). *Bracketed words added for clarity.*

> **Therefore, purge out the old leaven** [sin in our lives], **that you may be a new lump** [new person born of the Holy Spirit], **since you truly are unleavened. For indeed Christ** [Messiah], **our Passover, was sacrificed for us.**
>
> 1 Corinthians 5:7 (NKJV). *Bracketed words added for clarity.*

This helps us to further understand that we have forgiveness of our sins and acceptance by our Heavenly Father Yahweh when we believe in and accept Yahshua and what He did for us by being the ultimate blood sacrifice. He died on the cross (Roman stake, often a tree on the side of a road) on the Day of Preparation of the Passover lambs at three o'clock in the afternoon (the ninth hour as recorded in Matthew 27:46), which was the same time of day that the priest killed the lambs to prepare them for the evening *seder*, the Passover meal.

You may be asking yourself why this guy is explaining these aspects of Hebraic history with such detail? It is because we are all called by our Master Yahshua to follow in His footsteps when we accept Him and learn the truth from His Word about having relationship with Him and doing His will. As it is written,

For to this you were called, because Christ also suffered for us, leaving us an example, that you should follow His steps: ...
1 Peter 2:21 (NKJV)

You may be called of Messiah Yahshua to be a priest or one of the 144,000 during the thousand-year millennium, and you will need to know these details in order to keep this important scriptural tradition of Elohim and to be able to teach these truths to people who make it through the tribulation. Hang in there mate; there is much to learn.

It is important that we learn the chronological timing of the last days of Yahshua Messiah's life before He was murdered by the Roman Empire's government in the region that they named Palestine. This information applies to the Sabbath and instruction in Elohim's Word.

Based on my research, no one has broken down the timing of the events of the six days prior to the crucifixion of Messiah better than Dr. E.W. Bullinger, 1837-1913, Editor of the *Companion Bible*.

Our Redeemer Yahshua had to have been crucified on a Wednesday of His last week on this earth and not on the traditional Friday of Roman Catholicism and Protestantism. The truth of this is revealed in His Holy Word in the account of the Gospels found in the chapters of Matthew 27-29, Mark 15-16, Luke 23-24, and John 2-21. He gave an important prophecy when pressed by the scribes and Pharisees to show them a sign.

But He answered and said to them, "An evil and adulterous generation seeks after a sign, and no sign will be given to it except the sign of the prophet Jonah. For as Jonah was three days and three nights in the belly

of the great fish, so will the Son of Man be three days and three nights in the heart of the earth. ..."
Matthew 12:39-40 (NKJV)

King Yahshua was hurriedly removed from the cross, his Body cleaned, prepared, and placed in a newly hewn tomb of the rich man before the High Sabbath day, the first day of the Feast of Unleavened Bread, was to begin. This would have been around six to seven o'clock in the evening, as people began to eat the prepared Passover meal. Our Savior, Yahshua, did not eat the traditional Passover meal with His disciples because His last supper with them took place the night before on the eve of Passover, which is called the "day of preparation."

Seventy-two hours after our Lord Jesus physically died on Wednesday would have been Saturday at approximately three o'clock in the afternoon, toward the end of the weekly Sabbath. This means that He received His new resurrected body after three completed 24-hour days following His death. According to Scripture, Mary and the other women went to the tomb on Sunday morning, but He had already passed through the stone tomb several hours before when the huge tombstone was rolled away by the angel.

You may be asking yourself what difference days and hours make. The significance of this revelation of what really happened is that King Yahshua did not instruct His disciples to change the weekly Sabbath from Saturday to Sunday in order to celebrate His resurrection that actually took place on a Saturday afternoon. He did not instruct His disciples to do away with observing the Holy Feast Days of Father Yahweh, nor to start observing new man-instituted holidays called Good Friday, Easter Sunday, and the Mass of Christ (Christmas).

The previous chapter was a summary of the history of this great deception that reveals how most of us in the Christian faith have been lead astray by man-made traditions for the past 1,665 years. This has been a very successful plan of Satan to be a stumbling block that has separated Christian believers and Jews and has kept many Jews from accepting Yahshua as their Redeemer.

In this, the last generation, our loving Creator, Savior, and King Eternal is pouring out His Spirit of truth to call His elect into the restoration worship and work of the followers of Messiah to the former state of the first-century apostles. In this awesome time that we live in, Father

Yahweh is restoring the Two Houses of Israel (the born again believing Jews of the house of Judah and the born again *Torah*-observant followers of Messiah of the House of Ephraim as recorded in Ezekiel 37). I believe this awesome coming together in unity is what is referred to in Ephesians 2:14-16 as the "One New Man in Messiah." There will be more on this important subject in the last two chapters.

FEAST OF UNLEAVENED BREAD *(HAG HAMATZAH)*

The Feast of Unleavened Bread (*Hag HaMatzah*) is recognized as the second of the holy convocations of Father Yahweh, which begins in conjunction with Passover.

The Passover lamb was killed at three o'clock on the afternoon of the fourteenth day of the month of *Abib*. Sunset began the fifteenth of *Abib* and the beginning of the memorial of the seven-day Feast of Unleavened Bread. This feast points us toward repentance for all that we have done or not done that is not in Heavenly Father's will and our coming out of sin.

Remember that the three early spring feasts are interconnected. Passover reminds us of the lamb that was slain, the blood that was applied, the meal eaten in hast, and the night the angel of death passed over.

The sunrise after that first Passover night brought the day that the Pharaoh released the nation of Israel to begin their journey out of Egypt, which is symbolic of leaving sin. The instructions for the Passover were for the Israelites to eat bread made without leaven with the roasted lamb and bitter herbs, and to continue to eat unleavened bread for seven more days. It is written:

> **Then they shall eat the flesh on that night** *[beginning of the 15th]*; **roasted in fire, with unleavened bread *and* with bitter *herbs* they shall eat it. Seven days you shall eat unleavened bread. On the first day you shall remove leaven from your houses. For whoever eats leavened bread from the first day until the seventh day, that person shall be cut off from Israel. On the first day *there shall be* a holy convocation, and on the seventh day there shall be a holy convocation for you. No manner of work** *[except in the preparation of enough food for everyone]* **shall be done on them; but *that* which that which everyone must eat—that only may be prepared by you. So you shall observe *the Feast of* Unleavened**

Bread, for on this same day I will have brought your armies out of the land of Egypt. Therefore you shall observe this day throughout your generations as an everlasting ordinance.

Exodus 12:8, 15-17 (NKJV). *Bracketed words added for clarity.*

Matzah, the Hebrew name for unleavened bread, is made without leavening or fermenting agents, such as yeast, baking soda, or baking powder. The symbolism that our Lord was and is teaching in this feast is that Egypt represents our sinful nature of worshiping false gods, traditions, fulfilling the lust of our flesh, etc.

After we have accepted Yahshua (the Lamb of God) as our Lord and Savior and have applied His blood to wash away our sins, we are to come out of our sinful nature and ways. Leaven represents sin, so we are to remove from our house—our life—all of the leavening agents of sin.

This feast is symbolic of the constant and ongoing process of repenting of our sins, removing all sin from our lives, and being filled up with the presence of Yahshua through the indwelling of Holy Spirit.

The Apostle Paul gives us instruction on keeping this feast in the right spirit and living by the truth it represents.

Your glorying *is* not good. Do you not know that a little leaven *[yeast; sin]* **leavens** *[ferments; blemishes our whole being before a righteous and holy Creator, Savior, and Judge]* **the whole lump? Therefore purge out the old leaven, that you may be a new lump, since you truly are unleavened** *[after being born of the Holy Spirit]*. **For indeed Christ, our Passover, was sacrificed for us. Therefore let us keep the feast, not with old leaven, nor with the leaven of malice and wickedness, but with the unleavened *bread* of sincerity and truth.**

1 Corinthians 5:6-8 (NKJV). *Bracketed words added for clarity.*

Now this I affirm and insist on in the Lord: you must no longer live as the Gentiles *[the unsaved, uncommitted to Yahshua]* **live, in the futility of their minds. They are darkened in their understanding, alienated from the life of God because of their ignorance and hardness of heart. They have lost all sensitivity and have abandoned themselves to licentiousness, greedy to practice every kind of impurity. That is not the way you learned Christ** *[Messiah]***! For surely you have heard about Him and were taught in Him, as truth is in Jesus. You were taught to put away**

your former way of life, your old self, corrupt and deluded by its lusts, and to be renewed in the spirit of your minds, and to clothe yourselves with the new self, created according to the likeness of God *[Elohim]* **in true righteousness and holiness. So then, putting away falsehood, let all of us speak the truth to our neighbors, for we are members of one another.**

Ephesians 4:17-25 (NRSV). *Bracketed words added for clarity.*

I am excited about being a new lump, aren't you? I pray this revelation is a blessing to you and your family. Keeping the holy convocations of our Creator is part of our new life in Him. Along with most of you reading this book, I was not taught these important truths. Instead, like most people who are reading this book who are probably believers from a Christian background, I was taught Constantine Christianity observances that long ago became the traditional holidays of the Roman Catholic Church and later found their way into the Protestant churches. Our Bridegroom is calling us back to the foundational truths that He laid down long ago. Do you hear Him calling you?

THE FEAST OF FIRST FRUITS *(BIKKURIM)*

The Feast of First Fruits is the third and final of the three early spring holy feasts that are part of the Passover season and is an inner part of the early spring Feast of Unleavened Bread. It is not recognized in most Jewish congregations but is usually celebrated as a sunrise service by most Christian congregations. First Fruits is an important part of the Passover season and should be taught and understood.

The Hebrew name for this festival is *Bikkurim*. This holy day will always fall on Sunday, the first day after the Sabbath of the week of the Feast of Unleavened Bread. The year that our Savior Yahshua died on the cross for our sins, there were three complete days between the observance of Passover and the observance of First Fruits, just as He said that He would be in the tomb three complete days, as stated previously. The year that He was crucified, He was resurrected from the dead mid afternoon of the Sabbath, Saturday of that week, and fulfilled the Feast of First Fruits as being the first of the first fruits.

The instructions of the Holy Convocation, First Fruits, was that

Adonai Elohim told Moses to initiate this feast after the Israelites were established in the promised land of Israel. This observance was to take place during the Feast of Unleavened Bread when the early grain crops were beginning to have heads of grain and were nearing the time of harvest. Remember, the month in the spring that Passover is determined coincides with the early grain harvest. In ancient times the early grain crop was primarily barley, but in modern times the grain is primary hybrids of spring wheat.

The ceremony on the Day of Preparation, the 14th of *Abib*, began when a chosen landowner was sent out into a field of barley near the tabernacle (later, the temple) and tied together a sheaf (a small bundle) of early ripening grain. The Hebrew word for sheaf is *Omer*. Near the end of the Sabbath after Passover, before the beginning of the first day of the week, three men were sent out to cut down the standing secured sheaf that had been previously identified and tied with a strip of cloth. The sheaf, or *Omer*, was brought to the priest who would then take it into the tabernacle or temple and wave it before the Lord as the first fruits offering. After the waving of the sheaf, the priest was to offer a yearling lamb without blemish, a prepared cooked grain offering, and a drink offering of wine. The description of this feast day is recorded in the book of Leviticus.

And the LORD spoke to Moses, saying, "Speak to the children of Israel, and say to them: 'When you come into the land which I give to you, and reap its harvest, then you shall bring a sheaf of the firstfruits of your harvest to the priest. He shall wave the sheaf before the LORD, to be accepted on your behalf; on the day after the Sabbath the priest shall wave it. ...' "
Leviticus 23:9-11 (NKJV)

Our Heavenly Father instituted the appointed times of His feast days to coincide with the timing of the agriculture harvest in and around Jerusalem. The significance of the waving of the first fruits of the early spring grain harvest is that our Savior Jesus was and is the first of many of a great harvest of souls throughout the history of mankind that will make up the eternal Kingdom of Father Yahweh. Our King Yahshua was the first to be raised from the dead with a new resurrected body that He, as our great High Priest, presented to our Heavenly Father three days after He was put to death. Remember, He was raised from the dead with

His new resurrected body in the late evening toward the end of the Sabbath after Passover. The sheaf of the firstfruits grain was waved before Adoni Elohim at the end of the weekly Sabbath during the Feast of Unleavened Bread, and beginning of the next day (Sunday).

After presenting Himself at His Father's throne, King Yahshua came back to earth to reveal Himself to His closest followers after the sun had risen on the first day of the week, Sunday. He was the unique, completely sinless, human sacrifice that was acceptable to His and our Heavenly Father for the atonement for our sins. He freely lay down His life so that we would be able to have life in Him and a restored relationship with Father Yahweh. The Holy Feast of First Fruits points us to our Savior Yahshua and all that He accomplished for us when He was chosen, bound, cut down, and died for us. He bore our curses, sicknesses, and sins. He is the first fruits of the great harvest in our Father's Master Plan and has made the way for us to follow.

The celebration of First Fruits was and is also associated with the tribes of Israel dedicating the first fruits and best portions of their harvests unto Elohim (God). In ancient times, each family would give the first tenth of any and all of their harvest of grain crops, fruits harvest, wine, and the animals to the priest of the temple for the offering of cooked sacrifices unto the one true God (Elohim) of Abraham, Isaac, and Jacob. Some of the food was provided for the many priests who worked in service in the temple, some was sold later in the open market to raise money for the work in the temple, and some was given to the poor for their aid.

Our example to learn from the offering of first fruits is that we should give the very best we have to our Creator, Savior, and King Eternal. We should give Him the very best in our worship of Him from our hearts. We should express our true love for Him for Who He is and for all that He has done for us, all that He is doing for us presently, and all that He has promised He will do for us throughout all eternity. We should give Him the best that we can in doing the work of service He has called us to do in fulfilling the great commission of making disciples and building up His body of believers as we are lead. We should also give to Him, by supporting His work in the world, our very best financial gifts, the fruit of our hands, to assist those who are hungry and suffering from lack of basic necessities, as well as those who are hungry for the truth found in Yahweh's Holy Word. There will be more coverage regarding these areas of relationship with our Master in the last two chapters, "How Do We Prepare for the Coming of Messiah" and "The Ministry of the Bride of Messiah."

The appointed time of the Feast of First Fruits is often overlooked, but it is a very significant teaching from the inspired Word of God. It reveals to us that King Jesus Messiah is the Beginning—the Ruler, the Source—of the creation of Almighty Elohim, the first fruits of many people and according to Scripture, in Him we will receive our resurrection. As it is written:

"And to the angel of the church of the Laodiceans write, 'These things says the Amen, the Faithful and True Witness, the Beginning of the creation of God [Elohim]**: …' "**
Revelation 3:14 (NKJV). *Bracketed words added for clarity.*

We know that in all things Elohim [God] **works for good with those who love Him, those whom He has called according to His purpose. Those whom God** [Elohim] **had already chosen He also set apart to become like His Son, so that the Son would be the first among many brothers** [and sisters].
Romans 8:28-29 (TEV). *Bracketed words added for clarity.*

But in fact Christ has been raised from the dead, the first fruits of those who have died. For since death came through a human being, the resurrection of the dead has also come through a human being; for as all die in Adam, so all [those who accept Jesus and are born of His Spirit] **will be made alive in Christ** [Messiah]**. But each in his on order: Christ** [Messiah] **the first fruits, then at His coming those who belong to Christ. Then comes the end, when He hands over the kingdom to God** [Yahweh] **the Father, after He** [King Yahshua] **has destroyed every ruler and every authority and power** [all of Satan's kingdom and influence].
1 Corinthians 15:20-24 (NRSV). *Bracketed words added for clarity.*

First Fruits points us to the future and our hope of glory, the coming of our Messiah, King Yahshua, the Lion of Judah, when He ushers in His Father's Kingdom on earth and blesses His Body of saved ones with new resurrected bodies. HalleluYah! After much travail in the world, what a truly awesome experience that day will be for all who have accepted Jesus as their Savior and are been born of His spirit.

Dear reader, have you asked Him to forgive you of your sins and bless you with His Holy Spirit to dwell in you? If you have, give Him praise, for He alone is worthy. If you haven't, please do it, and don't put it off any longer. He desires more that we can comprehend to reveal His love for us and to have fellowship with us.

First Fruits also leads us into the fourth of the spring feasts called Pentecost, which is calculated by counting from the day of waving the first fruits sheaf offering before Father Yahweh on the first Sunday after the weekly Sabbath during Feast of Unleavened Bread. This calculating is called the "counting of the Omer."

THE FEAST OF PENTECOST *(SHAVUOT)*

The Feast of Pentecost is the fourth of the seven holy feasts of Yahweh. For the ancient Israelites, this was the second season of grain harvest (wheat) in which the Israelites were required to go up to Jerusalem to celebrate the blessing of Yahweh and to bring their grain offerings and gifts to the temple altar. *Pentecost* is the Greek word that is translated from the Hebrew word *Shavuot*, which means "fifty," or "counting fifty." Pentecost, or *Shavuot,* has no predetermined calendar date as it is determined by the counting of fifty days from the day after the weekly Sabbath that falls after the Feast of Firstfruits and Unleavened Bread. Pentecost will always fall on a Sunday, the day after the seventh Sabbath. As it is written:

> **"Speak to the children of Israel, and say to them: 'When you come into the land which I give to you, and reap its harvest, then you shall bring a sheaf of the firstfruits of your harvest to the priest. He shall wave the sheaf before the LORD, to be accepted on your behalf; on the day after the Sabbath the priest shall wave it. And you shall count for yourselves from the day after the Sabbath, from the day you brought the sheaf of the wave offering: sevens Sabbaths shall be completed. Count fifty days to the day after the seventh Sabbath; then you shall offer a new grain offering to the LORD. You shall bring from your dwellings two wave *loaves* of two-tenths of *an ephah* [about one gallon dry weight of flour]. They shall be of fine flour; they shall be baked with leaven. *They are* the firstfruits to the LORD.**
>
> Leviticus 23:10-11; 16-17 (NKJV). *Bracketed words added for clarity.*

The significance of *Shavuot* (Pentecost) is that from ancient Israelites and Jewish Rabbis it has been passed down that *Shavuot*, or Feast of Weeks, is associated as "the season of the Giving of the Law, or instructions." It is not known for sure if the Ten Commandments were given to Moses and the Israelites in oral form exactly fifty days after Passover, but it was certainly approximately fifty days. As it is written:

In the third month after the children of Israel had gone out of the land of Egypt, on the same day, they came *to* the Wilderness of Sinai. ... So Israel camped there before the mountain *[Sinai]*. **Then the LORD said to Moses, "Go to the people and consecrate them today and tomorrow, and let them wash their clothes. And let them be ready for the third day. For on the third day the LORD will come down upon Mount Sinai in the sight of all the people.**

Exodus 19:1-2b, 10-11 (NKJV). *Bracketed words added for clarity.*

It is important to understand the richness of the depth of meaning in this feast. Our Messiah, Yahshua, fulfilled the Feast of Passover by laying down His life, and freely pouring out His blood as being the ultimate and final sacrifice for our sins. He calls us to repent and come out of our sins with the symbolism of the Feast of Unleavened Bread. He fulfilled the Feast of the First Fruits when he was resurrected from the dead on the third day, as He became the firstfruits of many to come throughout the many generations since then.

When our Lord Jesus died on the cross, the sun had been darkened for three hours. At the moment of his death, several things happened. There was an earthquake in Jerusalem; the graves were opened, from which many bodies were raised from the dead like Lazarus; and the great curtain veil in the temple was torn from the top to the bottom, revealing the Holy of Holies. Our Creator Yahweh, was making it clear that we would no longer be required to go through traditional ceremonies and a human priest in order to communicate with Him. We can go directly into His presence after we have repented of our sins, accepted His Son Yahshua, and have been born of His Holy Spirit.

The English word *law*, which is translated from the Hebrew word *Torah*, does not really mean "law." *Torah* means "instruction or teaching." Elohim wrote with His finger into two tablets of stone the Ten Commandments (instructions for life) and gave them to His servant Moses. Later, the two tablets were placed into the Ark of the Covenant and carried with the Israelites as they traveled. When they set up camp, they placed the Ark of the Covenant inside the Holy of Holies part of the tent, which was a portable temple. That temple is where the Holy Spirit of Yahweh dwelt. Later, the same Ark was placed in the Holy of Holies of the two great temples that were built in Jerusalem on the temple mount at two different times.

The children of Israel were very afraid when they were gathered at the base of Mount Sinai as Moses received the Law up on the mountain. The mountain was covered in a cloud of smoke. There were flashes of lightning and long, loud trumpet sounds. The mountain shook. The Almighty, Adonai Elohim, was doing something powerful and supernatural. When our blessed Savior Yahshua suffered from the agony of pain all over His tortured body and from the immense heaviness of bearing the incomprehensible burden of all of the sins of all human beings throughout all generations, something powerful and supernatural was happening. The sun was darkened for three hours in the middle of the day, and the earth shook. As it is written:

And Jesus cried out again with a loud voice, and yielded up His Spirit. Then, behold, the veil of the temple was torn in two from top to bottom; and the earth quaked, and the rocks were split, and the graves were opened; and many bodies of the saints who had fallen asleep were raised; and coming out of the graves after His resurrection, they went into the holy city and appeared to many. So when the centurion and those with him, who were guarding Jesus, saw the earthquake and the things that had happened, they feared greatly, saying, "Truly this was the Son of God!"
Matthew 27:50-54 (NKJV)

Three days after His death, our Master Yahshua presented Himself before His Father and our Father, Yahweh, as the first fruits offering. He was accepted because He had successfully completed the amazing work that Father Yahweh had sent Him to do. Yahshua came to earth, was born of a virgin, and lived a sinless life, even under the influence of Satan's powers. He was anointed from Father Yahweh, received power from Holy Spirit, and went forth preaching the Gospel of the coming Kingdom of God, casting out demon spirits, healing people, and loving everyone He came in contact with. He completely defeated Satan, Satan's kingdom, and Satan's power of authority over the flesh of mankind. Yahshua restored man's ability to have relationship with our Heavenly Father that had been taken away by Adam's fall. He was with His disciples for forty days after His resurrection, giving encouragement and final teaching before He ascended back to His home in heaven. He had given them instructions about another supernatural move of Adonai Elohim that was soon to take place.

A short time before Jesus Messiah was arrested and taken to the cross to die for our sins, He told His followers that Father Yahweh would send a Comforter to help them and all others who followed Messiah. It is written;

> **Judas (not Iscariot) said to Him, "Lord, how is it that You will manifest Yourself to us, and not to the world?" Jesus answered and said to him, "If anyone loves Me, he will keep My Word; and My Father will love him, and We will come to him and make Our home with him. He who does not love Me does not keep My words; and the word which you hear is not Mine but the Father's who sent Me. These things I have spoken to you while being present with you. But the Helper, the Holy Spirit, whom the Father will send in My name, He will teach you all things, and bring to your remembrance all things that I said to you. ..."**
>
> John 14:22-26 (NKJV)

> **And being assembled together with *them*, He commanded them not to depart from Jerusalem, but to wait for the Promise of the Father, "which," He *said*, "you have heard from Me; for John truly baptized with water, but you shall be baptized with the Holy Spirit not many days from now."**
>
> Acts 1:4-5 (NKJV)

In speaking the words recorded in these verses, our Lord Jesus gave a very profound prophecy: Our heavenly Father would send to live in all believers the same Holy Spirit (*Ruach HaKodesh*) that lived in Messiah Yahshua. HalleluYah!!!

The following is the recorded evidence of the fulfilling of the prophecy. As you read Acts Chapter One, you learn that there were about 120 believers who had gathered to pray. They were lead by Peter and were there also to seek the Lord for a replacement for Judas, the disciple who had betrayed the Lord and hung himself afterwards.

When the Day of Pentecost *[Feast of Shavuot]* **had fully come, they were all with one accord in one place. And suddenly there came a sound from heaven, as of a rushing mighty wind, and it filled the whole house where they were sitting. Then there appeared to them divided tongues, as of fire, and** *one* *[flame]* **sat upon each of them** *[above their heads]*. **And they were all filled with the Holy Spirit and began to speak with other tongues, as the Spirit gave them utterance. And there were dwelling in Jerusalem Jews, devout men, from every nation under heaven** *[they had made the pilgrimage to Jerusalem for the Feast of Shavuot to celebrate the giving of the Torah at Mount Sinai]*. **And when this sound occurred, the multitude came together, and were confused, because everyone heard them speak in his own language. Then they were all amazed and marveled, saying to one another, "Look, are not all these who speak Galileans? And how** *is it* **that we hear, each in our own language in which we were born? ..."**

Acts 2:1-8 (NKJV). *Bracketed words added for clarity.*

I encourage you to read thoroughly all of Acts Chapter Two. The meeting place of the 120 had to be near the great temple in order for the multitude of worshippers at the temple to hear the supernatural sound of the mighty rushing wind from heaven, and for there to be a place nearby for the many baptisms. The temple worshippers were drawn to the location of the 120 believers and then began to hear them speaking in eighteen different languages realizing that the believers were local, uneducated people.

After they were assembled, the apostle Peter had their attention and delivered a powerful sermon that convicted the hearts of the hearers. Here is the result:

Then Peter said to them, "Repent, and let every one of you be baptized *[receive a* mikva, *which shows a change of status]* **in the name of Jesus Christ for the remission of sins; and you shall receive the gift of the Holy Spirit. For the promise is to you and to your children, and to all who are afar off, as many as the Lord our God will call." And with many other words he testified and exhorted them, saying, "Be saved from this perverse generation." Then those who gladly received his word were baptized; and that day about three thousand souls were added** *to them* *[the first century congregation—*Kehilat *in Hebrew and* Ekklesia *in Greek, which means "the called out ones"—of followers of Messiah]*.

Acts 2:38-41 (NKJV). *Bracketed words added for clarity.*

Long before Messiah Yahshua came to earth, lived and died as a man, and was resurrected from the dead, *Shavuot* was celebrated by the Israelites in honor of Adonai Elohim (Lord God) for giving the *Torah* to Moses and establishing His covenant with the people forever. This observance was a foreshadow of the time to come when Father Yahweh would send His Holy Spirit to humanity after the death and resurrection of His only Son, Yahshua, Who was manifest from His spiritual inner being. Our Heavenly Father no longer requires that there be a temple built with a section called the Holy of Holies for Him to dwell in because He has sent His Holy Spirit to dwell inside of our bodies, our temples. It is written:

> **Or do you not know that your body is a temple of the Holy Spirit within you, which you have from God, and that you are not your own? For you were bought with a price; therefore glorify God in your body.**
> 1 Corinthians 6:19-20 (NRSV)

When the Israelite children were assembled at the base of Mount Sinai, they were in unity. They were instructed to wash their clothes and be prepared to have an encounter with the one true, living Creator God. Washing their clothes is symbolic of repenting of sin and being cleansed of all unrighteousness, as we are taught in observing the Feast of Unleavened Bread—getting rid of sin. Just as the Israelite children received the instructions from Father Yahweh written on tablets of stone, we are to receive our comforter, Holy Spirit in Jesus' Name, so that He may write our Father Yahweh's instructions on our hearts. It is written:

> **"Behold, the days are coming, says the LORD, when I will make a new covenant with the house of Israel and the house of Judah, not like the covenant which I made with their fathers when I took them by the hand to bring them out of the land of Egypt, my covenant which they broke, though I was their husband, says the Lord. But this is the covenant which I will make with the house of Israel after those days, says the Lord: I will put my law within them, and I will write it upon their hearts** [*minds*]**; and I will be their God, and they shall be my people.**
> Jeremiah 31:31-33 (RSV). *Bracketed words added for clarity.*

Dear reader, it is so important that each one of us accepts Yahshua as our Savior and makes Him Master of our life. In doing so, we are to invite

Holy Spirit into us that we may be born anew with Father Yahweh's Spirit living in us. Have you accepted Yahshua as your Savior and asked Him to forgive you of all of your sins? Have you asked Him to bless you with *Ruach HaKodesh,* the Spirit of Holiness Who comes from Father Yahweh in the Name of Yahshua? If you haven't, please don't delay any longer. Do it now, and be blessed of the Lord. When Holy Spirit takes up residency within our earthly bodies, our temples, He begins to draw us to the truth in God's Word so that we can know what our heavenly Father's instructions are. Holy Spirit also empowers us to have the ability to walk in victory over our defeated enemy, Satan, and his kingdom. Our Creator, Savior, and King eternal desires to work within us to do work for the building of His kingdom and to be a blessing to others. After we have accepted Yahshua, repented of our sins, and been blessed with the sealing and indwelling of Holy Spirit, we are to be a witness to others of the miracle transformation that has taken place in our lives. Our family members, friends. and acquaintances will know that there has been a significant change in our lives because we act differently. Our Lord said that we would be able to identify a tree by the type of fruit it bears. People will be able to know if we are living for Jesus by the way we treat others and our approach to the many challenges of life. We are instructed by our Creator to have a love for one another that is pure and does not expect anything in return. We are also to live and teach His instructions that He writes on our hearts when we submit our will completely to Him.

In the first section of this teaching on the Feast of Pentecost, I used the Scripture from Leviticus 23:17. This was instruction from our Lord to Moses to bring two wave loaves that were baked with leaven, which as we have learned represents sin. What does this mean?

As I have clarified in earlier sections of this book, I believe our Creator God is restoring the two Houses of Israel in this last generation before King Yahshua returns to earth to establish His Kingdom. I believe the two wave loaves represent the great harvest of souls throughout the generations through the last generation, which will be the time of the greatest harvest of souls. Via satellite and great missionary efforts, the preaching of the Gospel of repentance and salvation is being delivered throughout the world like never before.

I believe the two loaves also represent the many believers who make up the House of Israel who are the true followers of Messiah in the Christian church, and the House of Judah that are the true followers of

Messiah that are in the Jewish synagogues. Though these two people groups are presented before Father Yahweh with leaven, or sin, in them, Holy Spirit is doing the work of cleansing them (us), by washing our clothes, and bringing us together in Jesus as the one prepared body—the bride of Messiah. HalleluYah!

You will find in the last two chapters of this book much more teaching expressed from the Scriptures about the gifts of Holy Spirit and the work that He has for each of us in these end times.

THE FEAST OF TRUMPETS
(YOM TERUAH OR ROSH HASHANA)

The meanings of the seven feast times, or holy convocations, given by Almighty Yah to all people for all times are very rich in teaching for us. The feasts give us insight into our Creator's master plan and, along with other truths from the Scriptures, give us instruction as to how to live and have relationship with Him. These feasts, or appointed and set apart times, were to the people, then and now, part of the covenant that Father Yahweh had made with Abraham and his descendants.

Let's recap briefly our understanding of the spring feasts. We celebrate Passover as a memorial to Elohim's deliverance of the Israelite people from the curses that God brought against the Egyptian nation when the Pharaoh would not let the Israelite people go free from his bondage of slavery to be able to go out and worship Yahweh, the great I AM that I AM. The firstborn of the Israelites were protected because the people followed the instructions that were given to them, which was to apply the blood of the lamb to the top and side doorposts of their homes, so the angel of death would pass over them.

The four holy feast times of the spring of the year give us a summary of all that Father Yahweh accomplished in the deliverance of the nation of Israel from Egypt and the giving of His instructions (Ten Commandments) at Mt. Sinai during the time He established as the *Shavout*, the Feast of Weeks.

Approximately 1,490 years later, Father Yahweh continued His master plan with the first coming of His Son, Yahshua Messiah. The feast of Passover pointed the people to the great blessing of Messiah Ben Joseph (Yahshua), the suffering servant that would come through the bloodline of Abraham, Isaac, Jacob, Judah, and then all of the descendants of Judah to His mother, Mary (Miriam), who was betrothed to Joseph (Yosef; there isn't a "J" in the Hebrew alphabet). We are to apply His blood to the door-post of our hearts so that our sins will be completely forgiven, and so that we will receive eternal life, not eternal death and separation from our loving Creator, Savior. and King.

The Feast of Passover speaks to us of our Creator's peace that He makes with us and that we make with Him, when we have accepted his gift, His Son Yahshua. Yahshua paid our sin debt, our death penalty, so we could be restored to a peaceful relationship with Almighty Yah, our God. When we humble ourselves before Him, and ask Him into our hearts, He blesses us with the birthing of His Holy Spirit in us. We have died with Him in His crucifixion and are now born with Him in His lresurrection. HallelluYah!!!

The Feast of Unleavened Bread speaks to us of repentance by identifying our sin and asking our Heavenly Father Yahweh's forgiveness. The coming out of our old ways is our deliverance and being set free. We are to come out of the bondage of the world's systems of deceptive teaching and lifestyles and enter into the freedom that comes from putting our faith in Yahshua to be overcomers in this life.

The Feast of First Fruits speaks to us of our consecration of ourselves to honor our Creator, Savior, and King Eternal by giving Him the very best of all we have and all that we put our hands to do. Our Father Yahweh sent His only begotten Son, His very best, to be born into humanity to confirm His instructions in His *Torah* and to voluntarily lay down His life and die that we may believe and live. Yahshua came as Yahweh manifested in the flesh, and after He was in the tomb three days and three nights, He was then resurrected to life with a new immortal body. He went to our Heavenly Father and presented Himself as the first fruits wave offering for all that He had accomplished in His life, death, and resurrection on earth. He was and is found to be worthy and acceptable, and the first of many that will follow in the ongoing harvest of human souls that will conclude when we also receive our new resurrected bodies at Yahshua's second coming. That event will be the consummation of our betrothal to Him as we are married in the air. HalleluYah!!!

The Feast of Pentecost speaks to us of power from the indwelling of *Ruach HaKodesh*, Spirit of Holiness. This is the manifestation of Father Yahweh's Holy Spirit in us as we are baptized by fire in the name of

Jesus—for those of us before we came to know His Hebrew name, Yahshua—and receive the gifts of the Spirit. His gifts empower us from on high to accomplish Yah's will and purpose for our lives. Each of the nine gifts has a different application to enable us to minister to one another and in our supernatural communication to our Creator. We are to ask Father Yahweh to bless us with the gifts He has for us to enable us to be a blessing to hurting people around us who have not come to their Passover experience with Master Yahshua and are being deceived and abused by the adversary. We are to always walk in the Spirit and administer our spiritual gifts with much prayer and love.

All of the Spring Feasts and the last of the Fall Feasts—Tabernacles, or *Sukkot*—are happy celebrations because of the great and marvelous things that our Creator, Savior, and King eternal has accomplished in the past 4,000 years of His great master plan, and all that He is presently doing by the power of Holy Spirit working in millions of people's lives today.

The observance of the first two fall feasts, *Yom Teruah (Rosh HaShana)* and *Yom Kippur* are different. These feasts are foreshadows of difficult times that are coming and, in many ways, are already here. In our personal application, they are to be a time of serious reflection on one's life; a call to sound the alarm for everyone everywhere to wake up, repent, and prepare, for the coming of our Bridegroom, Great King, and Judge is at hand. These two feasts are to be identified with the second coming of Messiah Yahshua, Who comes as Messiah Ben David, the Lion of Judah.

The Feast of Trumpets is different in that when the events that this feast symbolizes begin to take place, it will be the turning point in history. I believe *Yom Teruah* heralds the beginning of the seventh week that the prophet Daniel wrote about in the book of the Bible that bears his name. Later, in Chapters Six and Seven, there is more detail about the end-time events and of our King Yahshua coming back to this earth to completely destroy the kingdom of Satan, the false prophet, the Antichrist, and all of the people who have accepted the mark of the beast.

Yom Teruah, commonly known by believers as the Feast of Trumpets, begins on the first day of the seventh Biblical month called *Tishri*. Remember, the number seven is a number of completion. Father Yahweh will bring about the completion of His Master Plan with the end-time events associated with the seventh month of His Biblical calendar. Only He knows the exact year, day, and hour of the coming of King Yahshua, but He has given clues in His Holy Word that will help us to discern the times as we continue into them. Elohim's Word bears witness to how our Master Yahshua fulfilled the prophecies of His first coming in detail and as symbolized in the spring feasts. King Yahshua will do likewise in the fulfillment of His second coming mission according to the prophecy Scriptures and symbolism associated with the fall feasts.

Does this mean that Father Yah will fulfill all of the prophecies of the second coming of Messiah during the three feasts of the seventh month of some year in the future? No. I believe the seven-year countdown for the coming of King Yahshua will be preceded with the coming of the anti-Messiah who will cause the signing of a peace treaty with Israel that will enable them to rebuild the third temple. This will fulfill the seventieth week prophecies as recorded in the ninth chapter of Daniel and will happen some future year on or about the day of the Feast of Trumpets. Then begins the seven-year countdown. I believe that three and one half years (possibly on Passover) after the signing of the temporary peace treaty, the anti-Messiah will reveal his true identity. This will take place when he takes control of the third rebuilt temple, stops the reinstated animal sacrifices by the Levite priest, and sets up his own altar to sacrifice swine in honor of his father Satan. Three and a half years after the stopping of the daily sacrifices brings us to the final year of the fall Feasts and the coming of Messiah. I believe this pattern will follow closely to that of Antiochus Epiphanes, the tyrant Syrian leader who took control of Jerusalem and the temple in 168 B.C. He proclaimed himself to be god almighty. Anyone who did not bow down and acknowledge him as god was murdered. We would do well to study and understand the history and symbolism of the Feast of the Dedication of Light known as *Hanukkah*.

The time of year for observing *Yom Teruah* on the Gregorian calendar is either late September or early October. In Hebrew, *Yom* means "day," and *Teruah* means "blowing, or shouting." What is significant is that this is the only feast that begins on the first day of a Biblical month. That makes it difficult to tell when it will start because it requires visually sighting the first sliver of the new moon of the seventh month. This is the time of the month when there is the least amount of light from the moon in the night sky. As it is written:

And the LORD said to Moses, "Say to the people of Israel, In the seventh month, on the first day of the month, you shall observe a day of solemn rest, a memorial proclaimed with the blast of trumpets, a holy convo-

cation. You shall do no laborious work; and you shall present an offering by fire to the LORD."

Leviticus 23:23-24 (RSV)

The Feast of Trumpets, for the follower of Messiah, is to be observed as a time to rededicate ourselves to the work our Lord has called us to do —to fulfill the Great Commission of making disciples and giving a wake-up call to those who are lost in this world. We must have the conviction and compassion to approach people with the good news of salvation in Yahshua and the urgency to repent of sin. None of us has a clue as to how long we are going to live before we expire from this life and pass into eternity, which includes giving an account of our lives before our Creator, Savior, King, and Judge. As we are led, we are also to help people understand the importance of our Hebraic roots in the keeping of the Biblical Sabbath, the Holy Feast Days, and the instructions of *Torah* as best we can in following in the footsteps of Messiah Yahshua.

The Feast of Trumpets comes suddenly at the end of the summer months with the blasts of shofars, silver trumpets, and loud human shouts from all who celebrate the feast. I believe that just as the Feast of Pentecost is a memorial of when Adonai Elohim (Lord God) gave the ten instructions to Moses and the Israelites at Mount Sinai, and the gift of Holy Spirit was given to the 120 in Jerusalem, that Yahweh's coming down to meet with Moses and the congregation is symbolic and connected to warnings associated with the Feast of Trumpets and the second coming of Messiah. I see some contextual parallels between the following account of what was happening at the Mount Sinai encounter and what will be happening to the worldwide congregation of called-out ones during and at the end of the tribulation, as recorded in the book of Exodus. As it is written:

> **And Moses went up to God, and the LORD called to him from the mountain, saying, "Thus you shall say to the house of Jacob, and tell the children of Israel: 'You have seen what I did to the Egyptians, and *how* I bore you on eagles' wings, and brought you to Myself. Now therefore, if you will indeed obey My voice and keep My covenant, then you shall be a special treasure to Me above all people; for all the earth is Mine. And you shall be to Me a kingdom of priests and a holy nation.' ... And the LORD said to Moses, "Behold, I come to you in the thick cloud, that**

**the people may hear when I speak with you, and believe you forever."
So Moses told the words of the people to the LORD. Then the LORD said
unto Moses, "Go to the people, and consecrate them today and tomorrow, and let them wash their clothes. And let them be ready for the third
day. For on the third day the LORD will come down upon Mount Sinai
in the sight of all the people. ... Then it came to pass on the third day,
in the morning, that there were thunderings and lightnings, and a thick
cloud on the mountain; and the sound of the trumpet was very loud, so
that all the people who *were* in the camp trembled. And Moses brought
the people out of the camp to meet with God, and they stood at the foot
of the mountain. Now Mount Sinai *was* completely in smoke, because
the LORD descended upon it in fire. Its smoke ascended like the smoke
of a furnace, and the whole mount quaked greatly. ... Now all the
people witnessed the thunderings, the lightning flashes, the sound of the
trumpet, and the mountain smoking; and when the people saw *it*, they
trembled and stood afar off. Then they said to Moses, "You speak with
us, and we will hear; but let not God speak with us, lest we die." And
Moses said to the people, "Do not fear; for God has come to test you,
and that His fear may be before you, so that you may not sin."**
Exodus 19:3-6a, 9-11, 16-18; 20:18-20 (NKJV)

In Chapter Seven of this book, there is a thorough study of world conditions and events that I have paraphrased from the fourteen visions that
the Apostle John was given by our Master Yahshua as recorded in the
Book of the Revelation of his coming. The seven seals are outline head-
ings with the seven trumpets and seven vials being the details. Many of
the details of plagues and catastrophes are very similar to the plagues that
Father Yahweh allowed to come upon the Egyptians for not allowing the
Israelites be set free so they could gather to worship Him. Throughout all
of the plagues, none of them affected the Israelites where they lived in
Goshen. Just as they were protected from the Egyptians during their
exodus, I truly believe, according to His Word, that there will be a
remnant of end-time Israelites that Father Yahweh will protect and
sustain through the tribulation period until the coming of His mighty warrior Son, Yahshua, the Lion of Judah. I also believe that many believers
will be required by our Master to lay down their/our lives because of our
love for Him and by not bowing to the adversary's puppet rule.

If you are from Jewish ancestry, you may be saying to yourself that you have always been taught that Messiah has not yet come, and we are still looking for the one that will establish peace in Israel. The Scriptures and historical records bear witness that Messiah has already come in the man of Yahshua. He fulfilled perfectly all of the prophecies that relate to His first coming. Please understand that if you are looking for the Messiah to come as a man, you will be deceived by Satan into putting your confidence in Satan's son, the anti-messiah who brings a short peace for Israel so the third temple can be rebuilt.

If you are a believer and love Yahshua, then you are probably wondering about my position on the timing of the rapture teaching. I have written a thorough account from many hours of research detailing the resurrection of the saints in Chapter Eight of this book. I cannot support from Scripture but one timing of the resurrection of the saints to receive our new, immortal bodies, likened unto our Savior's. As revealed in the Scriptures, the timing of that most awesome of events of the saved is at the end of the great tribulation.

There is not anything secret or mysterious about the coming of the King of the Universe. I believe the Feast of Trumpets and the Day of Atonement point us to the fulfillment of our Lord's second coming prophecies and the events described in the Book of Revelation and other Scriptures of Yah's Word. These events describe Israel, made up of Jew and non-Jew believers who are pregnant with hope and in much labor pain and will be yearning for the birth of the coming of Messiah, our Bridegroom.

I believe the Feast of Trumpets speaks to us, the body of Messiah in this incredible last generation before the millennium, to wake us up and to pray for discernment. Our Master Yahshua gave the following response to His disciples when they asked what would be the sign of His return to this planet and the end of the age.

And Jesus answered and said to them: "Take heed that no one deceives you. For many will come in My name, saying, 'I am the Christ,' and will deceive many. ..."
Matthew 24:4-5 (NKJV)

We need to take seriously the realization that this generation we are living in represents our Creator bringing to completion the first six thousand years of His master plan and the beginning of the next one thousand year plan. With each *Yom Teruah* that passes by, we know that we are one year closer to the coming of the great King of the Universe and His wrath upon a world that does not know and love Him. For those of us who do know and love Him, it will be the most challenging and glorious time for ministry in all of the history of mankind. Hang with me through the next couple of pages as I present some of the history of the origin of *Rosh HaShana*. This will help us to have a better understanding of what most Jewish people believe about this season of the year.

As I stated earlier in this chapter, ancient Israel's calendar was establish around the agriculture seasons of planting and harvesting during their growing season. Adonai Elohim gave them the weekly Sabbaths and the seven feasts and times of determining them by the moon, so they would have a way of tracking time. More importantly, these were ways for the chosen people, the descendants of Abraham's seed, to be able to stay in relationship with Father Yahweh.

Many changes took place when the nation of Israel split into two separate nations during the year 880 B.C. A condensed history of this is found in Chapter Five of this book. The northern ten tribes called "Israel" were taken into captivity in the year 611 B.C. They became known as the "House of Israel," or *Ephraim*. After their Diaspora—the scattering to countries outside of Palestine—they were called "the lost tribes of Israel."

The southern kingdom was known as the "House of Judah." They were taken captive by the Babylonians in the year 478 B.C. During their captivity, they were without their temple and did not have any structured worship. The Babylonians began their calendar year during the time of the fall harvest and the time of *Yom Teruah*. It is believed by some history scholars that it was during this time of captivity that the Rabbis began to initiate the oral *Torah* and changed the ceremonial calendar. In doing so, it was decided that the new year was to begin on the first day of the seventh month of *Tishri* and was to be call *Rosh HaShana*.

The following are some quotes from author Nathan Ausubel's book titled, *Book of Jewish Knowledge* (Bantum Books, 1982). "Rosh HaShana is called the Jewish New Year." "Its institution showed no concern with the calendar (ceremonial or Biblical.)" "It occurs, not as one would expect, on the first day of the first month of the Hebrew month of *Nissan* (the Babylonian name for the month of *Abib*.)" "The Babylonians considered it (they called the Day of Judgment) to be their new year. They believed that on that day there took place an awesome convocation of all their deities (false gods) in the great temple of Marduk, the chief god of Babylon." "They assembled there on every New Year to renew the world and to pass judgment on human beings, and then inscribed the fate of each individual for the ensuing year on a tablet of destiny."

"The name *Rosh HaShanah* was not originally used to designate this day." "The first mention of *Rosh HaShana* is found in the *Mishnah*, the code of the Oral Tradition which was first compiled in the second century. It seems that as the early Rabbis began to write down their teachings of commentary on the law in the book called the *Talmud*, they believed that *Rosh HaShanah* represented a time when Adonai Elohim, rather than the false pagan gods, would actually require each person to pass before Him on the day of His judgment of them." Thus *Rosh HaShana* is also associated with the time of The Day of Judgment. As taught in the *Talmud*, there will be three classes of people who will pass before the great Almighty Judge. The classes of people are recorded in His three books called the "book of the righteous," the "book of the wicked," and the "book of remembrance." The basis for this traditional Jewish teaching is taken from the book of Daniel. As it is written:

A fiery stream issued and came forth from before Him *[Father Yahweh].* **A thousand thousands ministered to Him; ten thousand times ten thousand stood before Him. The court was seated, and the books were opened.**
Daniel 7:10 NKJV. *Bracketed words added for clarity.*

In Hebrew, *Rosh* means "head of or chief of something." *Ha*, means "the," and *Shanah* means "year." The Rabbis justified the change of the first month of the Biblical year by proclaiming that the new moon of *Tishri* was when they believed that Elohim created Adam.

Along with this change within the Oral Tradition, the Rabbis initiated the forty-day season called *Teshuvah*, which in Hebrew means "to repent." This season begins on the first day of *Elul* (the month before *Tishri*), continues through the month for thirty days, and ends on the tenth day of *Tishri*, which is *Yom Kippur*.

The Feast of Trumpets (*Yom Teruah*) on the first day of *Tishri*, signals the beginning of the last ten days of the forty days that are known by the Jewish people as the High Holy Days, or "the ten days of awe," or "awesome days." Each morning of the thirty days of the month of *Elul*, shofars are blown in Jewish synagogues to symbolically call people to repentance before *Rosh HaShana*. The Oral Tradition teaches that if a person has followed the *Torah* to the best of their ability, done good deeds, and repented from the previous year's sins, that they would be recorded in the *Book of the Righteous*, also called *The Book of Life*. This means they are sealed for the life to come. This is to be done prior to, or during, the thirty days of *Elul* before *Rosh HaShanah* begins on the first day of the month of *Tisri*.

Those individuals who are completely rebellious by doing evil, not repenting, and not following *Torah* are recorded in the book of the wicked, which means they are destined for perdition and our Creator's wrath. It is believed by most Jewish people that the vast majority of the Jewish people are in the third category of those that are hanging in the balance and waiting until after *Rosh HaShana* begins to get serious about their relationship with Elohim (God Almighty).

It is believed by the Jewish people who embrace this doctrine, that the names of those in this group are written in the book of remembrance and are called "intermediates." The people who feel they are in this group have the ten-day period called, "The Days of Awe" to repent and seek Yahweh, the God of Abraham, Isaac, and Jacob, and do good works. This is so that when they are examined at the end of the ten days on *Yom Kippur*, they will be found acceptable to be written down in *The Book of Life*. One of the most common greetings among the Jewish people during *Rosh HaShanah* is, "May you be inscribed in the *Book of Life.*"

Dear reader, can you see and understand the importance of comprehending the truth from all of God's Holy Word to believe and apply in your life? This is very important to understand. We can't be written into Father Yahweh's *Book of Life* (saved from eternal separation from Him) because of our good works. We can only become complete and spared from God's judgment of our sins by putting our complete faith and trust in Yahweh's Messiah and Son, Yahshua, Whom He sent forth into the world to give His holy life as the final blood atonement sacrifice for the sins of humanity. As it is written:

> **For by grace you have been saved through faith; and this is not your own doing, it is the gift of God** *[Elohim]*—**not because of works, lest any man should boast. For we are His workmanship, created in Christ** *[Messiah]* **Jesus for good works, which God** *[Elohim]* **prepared beforehand, that we should walk in them.**

Ephesians 2:8-10 (RSV). *Bracketed words added for clarity.*

Good works are the fruit that we bear after we have accepted Yahshua and have been born of His Holy Spirit. This doesn't mean that we haven't been doing good works before accepting Yahshua as our Savior and Messiah, but that we don't put our faith in the works. Our good works can't remove our sins and the death sentence that goes with our sin. Only the <u>blood</u> of Yahshua can do that. Holy Spirit works in us, transforming us into the likeness of Messiah so that He can bless us with the gifts of the Spirit to bear good fruit and be a blessing to others. There will be much more teaching on this subject in the last chapter of this book.

As we learn of the Feast of Trumpets and, if so lead, celebrate them, we gain insight into the seven angels' mighty trumpet blasts that are described in the book of Revelation. Those of us living at that time may or may not actually hear real supernatural blasts from heaven, but either way, according to the Scripture, the blasts signal the release of the many disastrous tribulation events that reveal the destruction of the anti-Messiah's world empire, and the coming of King Yahshua to save and resurrect His people. I am confident that you, dear reader, and many others who have pressed into our Father Yahweh by placing their complete trust in our Master Yahshua and have followed His instructions will be protected and provided for during the difficult tribulation time, as were the Israelites during their deliverance from Egypt. His actual coming in the clouds back to planet earth is signaled by a loud trumpet blast. As it is written:

> **Then the seventh angel blew his trumpet, and there were loud voices in heaven, saying, "The kingdom of the world has become the kingdom of our Lord and his Messiah, and he will reign forever and ever."**
> Revelation 11:15 (NRSV)

The great tribulation events and coming of King Yahshua to resurrect His saved ones, are covered in Chapters Six through Eight of this book.

DAY OF ATONEMENT (YOM KIPPUR)

Yom Kippur was (is) the feast day that is to be observed on the tenth day of the seventh month of the Jewish calendar called *Tishri*. The Day of Atonement is the last day of a forty-day time period that begins on the first day of the ninth month called *Elul*. This forty-day period is a time in which the Jewish people (and then ancient Israelites), and us now when we come to the truth from the Scriptures, are to self-examine our lives before Father Yahweh, repenting of any sins, and reconciling with God and fellow man. As it is written:

> **And the LORD spoke to Moses, saying: "Also the tenth *day* of the this seventh month *shall be* the Day of Atonement. It shall be a holy convocation for you; you shall afflict your souls, and offer an offering made by fire to the LORD. And you shall do no work on that same day, for it *is* the Day of Atonement, to make atonement for you before the LORD your God. ..."**
> Leviticus 23:26-28 (KJV)

As stated earlier, the last ten days of the forty-day period are called "the days of awe." I believe that the ten days of awe beginning with the Feast of Trumpets are symbolic of the time of the great tribulation in which Elohim will be bringing His last judgments upon the earth. I also believe that *Yom Kippur* and the days leading up to it teach us that we are to come together as the faithful body of Messiah and reconcile our differences in order to love one another as our Master Yahshua has instructed. Before we can be reconciled to Father Yahweh, we must first be reconciled to all people whom we have wronged, or who have wronged us. Thus saith the Lord:

> **For if you forgive others their trespasses, your Heavenly Father will also forgive you; but if you do not forgive others, neither will your Father forgive your trespasses.**
> Matthew 6:14-15 (NRSV)

The complete account of what Almighty Yah required of the high priest and the Israelites on the Day of Atonement is recorded in the sixteenth chapter of Leviticus.

In summary, during the days of animal sacrifices in the temple in Jerusalem, *Yom Kippur* was the only day of the year when the high priest could enter the holiest place within the temple called the Holy of Holies. Behind the large curtain veil that went from the ceiling to the floor was where the Ark (gold-covered box) of the Covenant (Ten Commandments) was placed. On top of the ark was a gold-covered mercy seat with two carved, gold-covered cherub angles with wings outstretched toward the middle of the seat. The Day of Atonement was a day of fasting and affliction of one's soul before the Adonai Elohim Almighty Yah. Almighty Yah would manifest in a cloud of smoke above the mercy seat and there meet and communicate with the high priest. The Day of Atonement is also called the Day of Meeting.

For the high priest selected to perform the many complex rituals, it was a very intense day. The high priest would enter into the holy place with the blood of a bull without blemish for the purification of the holy place. He would later enter again with the blood of a goat without blemish for the atonement of the sins of the high priest and all of the people of the nation of Israel. The Holy Spirit of Father Yahweh would meet with the high priest and communicate with him above the mercy seat and between the two cherubim. The high priest would intercede on behalf of the people, petitioning Almighty Yah for the forgiveness of their sins for the past year. The high priest would sprinkle the blood from the bull first over the mercy seat and other places in the room. Then he would do the same with the blood from the goat. The sprinkled blood would be for the covering and atonement of the sins of the people, himself, and the nation as a whole.

Earlier in this chapter, I stated that I believed Moses and the Israelites received the oral commandments from God as they were camped at the base of Mt. Sinai in the third month, about the time of the Feast of Pentecost. If you have studied the whole account from Exodus Chapters 19 through 34, you will be able to determine that Moses made six trips up and down the mountain. It was on his forth and sixth trips that he brought the Ten Commandments written on the stone tablets down to the people.

Moses was given a lot of information to write down as instructions that were to be carried out, other than the Ten Commandments. I believe that his fifth trip was during the Ten Days of Awe at the beginning of the seventh month when he made intercession for the Israelites who had sinned against Yahweh by worshipping the golden calf. I also believe that a few days later the descent of Moses' sixth trip was on the Day of Atonement.

Toward the end of the ministry and life of our dear Savior Yahshua, it was prophesied by the high priest in the temple of Jerusalem that one man should die for the nation. The high priest did not realize that he was stating part of Yahweh's great plan to save not only those believers in Israel, but also believers throughout the world through all generations after Messiah's death. As it is written:

> **So the chief priest and the Pharisees called a meeting of the council, and said, "What are we to do? This man** *[Yahshua]* **is performing many signs. If we let Him go on like this, everyone will believe in Him, and the Romans will come and destroy both our holy place and our nation." But one of them, Caiaphas, who was high priest that year, said to them, "You know nothing at all! You do not understand that it is better for you to have one man die for the people than to have the whole nation destroyed." He did not say this on his own, but being high priest that year he prophesied that Jesus was about to die for the nation, and not for the nation only, but to gather into one the dispersed children of God. So from that day on they planned to put to him** *[Messiah]* **to death.**
> John 11:47-52 (NRSV). *Bracketed words added for clarity.*

What does the Day of Atonement mean to us now, approximately 1,930 years after the animals were last sacrificed and the rituals carried out in the temple before it was destroyed? There are three revelations from the Scriptures that I believe answer this question.

First, we look back in time and see how Father Yahweh helped the Israelites understand that they had personal and corporate sin that had to be dealt with. By initiating the rituals that were performed by the high priest during this feast, the people realized, then as well as now, that we must depend completely on our Creator to make a provision to save us from our sins. The blood of bulls and goats could only provide a covering of the people's sins and could not provide permanent removal, so the process had to be repeated each year. This feast pointed the people to the prophecies of the coming of Yahweh's ultimate sacrifice, His only Son Yahshua Messiah. In Him would dwell the full manifestation of the Father's love and provision for the complete removal of our sins once and for all. By placing our complete faith and trust in Yahshua, we have complete redemption from Satan the adversary because we have been purchased with the blood of Yahshua. The righteous judgment of Father Yahweh is transformed into mercy by the atoning blood of Yahshua because no one can keep Elohim's instructions (Ten Commandments) perfectly except His Son Yahshua.

When Yahshua freely gave His life for us by being crucified on the tree during the preparation day for Passover, the total requirement for the penalty of breaking the law (sinning) by all people was completely, and forever, satisfied. HallelluYah!!! As it is written:

> But now, apart from the law, the righteousness of God has been disclosed, and is attested by the law and the prophets, the righteousness of God through faith in Jesus Christ for all who believe. For there is no distinction *[between Jew and non-Jew]*, since all have sinned and fall short of the glory of God; they are now justified by His grace as a gift, through the redemption that is in Christ Jesus *[Messiah Yahshua]*, Whom God put forward as a sacrifice of atonement by His blood, effective through faith. He did this to show His righteousness, because in His divine forbearance He had passed over the sins previously committed; It was to prove at the present time that He Himself is righteous and that He justifies the one who has faith in Jesus.
>
> Romans 3: 21-26 (NRSV). *Bracketed words added for clarity.*

The second important answer to understanding what the Day of Atonement means to us now is that after King Yahshau was raised from the dead with a new resurrected body and ascended to heaven where He sits at the right hand of Almighty Father Yahweh (they are One in Spirit), He makes intercession for us as our high priest. As it is written:

> What then shall we say to these things? If God *is* for us, who *can be* against us? He who did not spare His own Son, but delivered Him up for us all, how shall He not with Him also freely give us all things? Who shall bring a charge against God's elect? It *is* God who justifies. Who *is* he who condemns? *[The answer is Satan our adversary.]* It *is* Christ who died, and furthermore is also risen, who is even at the right hand of God, who makes intercession for us.
>
> Romans 8:31-34 (NKJV). *Bracketed words added for clarity.*

> ... for others who became priests took their office without an oath, but this one *[Yahshua, the Messiah]* became a priest with an oath, because of the one *[Father Yahweh]* who said to Him, "The Lord has sworn and will not change His mind, 'You are a priest forever' "—accordingly Jesus has also become the guarantee of a better covenant. Furthermore, the

former priests were many in number, because they were prevented by death from continuing in office; but He [Yahshua] **holds His priesthood permanently, because He continues forever. Consequently He is able for all time to save those who approach God** [Father Yahweh] **through Him, since He always lives to make intercession for them. For it was fitting that we should have such a high priest, holy, blameless, undefiled, separated from sinners, and exalted above the heavens. Unlike the other high priests, He has no need to offer sacrifices day after day, first for His own sins, and then for those of the people; this He did once for all when He offered Himself.**

Hebrews 7:20-27 (NRSV). *Bracketed words added for clarity.*

The third important answer to understanding what the Day of Atonement means to us now, I believe, is that it symbolizes the actual timing of the coming of our High Priest and risen King, Yahshua Messiah. His return to planet earth in great power and glory will, at that time, usher in a whole new reality for everyone, which will be the end of history as humanity has known it. At the time appointed by Father Yahweh, King Yahshua will leave His place as our great Intercessor and High Priest, and bring His army of warrior angels, along with the untold millions of human spirits that have died in Him, to make their journey to this world. Thus saith the Lord:

"Immediately after the tribulation [persecution] **of those days** [the last half of the seventh week of Daniel] **the sun will be darkened, and the moon will not give its light, and the stars will fall from heaven, and the powers of the heavens will be shaken; then will appear the sign of the Son of man in heaven, and then all of the tribes** [those with the mark of the beast] **of the earth will mourn** [be afraid]**, and they will see the Son of man coming on the clouds of heaven with power and great glory; and He** [King Yahshua] **will send out His angels with a loud trumpet call, and they will gather** [rapture, or first resurrection] **His elect** [all the overcomers; dead and alive] **from the four winds** [the whole world over]**, from one end of heaven to the other** [the soul/spirits of the elect who will have been saved by putting their trust in Yahshua, that have deceased and are in heaven at that time, will be brought with the angels to receive their new resurrected bodies with those alive on the earth at that time that are resurrected afterward]**."**

Matthew 24:29-31 (RSV). *Bracketed words added for clarity.*

When King Yahshua arrives on planet earth, one of His first orders of change will be the binding and removal of the source of sin, who is Satan, mankind's oldest adversary. Satan is guilty of inspiring the sins of mankind and must bear his own guilt. Neither Satan nor any of the other demon angels who fell from heaven are offered salvation through Yahshua, and they refuse to repent. The Levitical ritual of the high priest laying his hands on the azazel goat's head and confessing the sins of the people is symbolic of Satan's future judgment when all of those sins are placed back on his head where they belong. The azazel goat, bearing those sins, was then driven into the wilderness alive. I believe the binding and removal of the azazel goat is symbolic of this awesome future event when this great source of sin is removed from man's presence and is bound for 1,000 years. As it is written:

> **Then the seventh angel blew his trumpet, and there were loud voices in heaven, saying, "The kingdom of the world has become the kingdom of our Lord and of His Messiah, and He will reign forever and ever." Then the twenty- four elders who sit on their thrones before God fell on their faces and worshiped God, singing, "We give you thanks, Lord God Almighty, who are and who were, for you have taken your great power and begun to reign. The nations raged, but your wrath has come, and the time for judging the dead, for rewarding your servants, the prophets and saints and all who fear Your name, both small and great, and for destroying those who destroy the earth."**
> Revelation 11:15-18 (NRSV)

It is my belief that, when King Yahshua is approaching earth, every eye shall see Him and that this will be the time of the first resurrection in which we receive our new dwelling places, our resurrected bodies that will be like His.

When the Romans destroyed the temple in A.D. 70, the surviving Rabbinical priesthood had to find another means for the people to atone for their sins. Their teaching was to pray often for repentance and to do good works. Since that time, and in our present generation, Jewish people who have not accepted Yahshua as their Messiah spend the Day of Atonement in the synagogue. They enter sincerely in repentance, fasting and praying so that, by observing this high holy day, and by doing good works, confessing their sins, and casting bread upon the water, they believe their name will be written in the Book of Life another year.

Dear reader, it doesn't matter if you are of Jewish ancestry or not, for Elohim is not a respecter of persons; to Him, we are all equal. We will not have forgiveness from our sins and be written in the Lamb's Book of Life no matter how much we pray and do good works. The only way that we can have atonement with our Creator and Heavenly Father Yahweh is to accept His Son Yahshua's blood sacrifice for our sins and be born of His Holy Spirit. Then we can truly have our names written and kept in His Book of Life and be led by His Spirit in us forever. It is written:

> **He who overcomes shall be clothed in white garments, and I will not blot out his name from the Book of Life; but I will confess his name before My Father and before His angels.**
> Revelation 3:5 (NKJV)

I believe that Almighty Yah will make a provision for all those who have left this life and never had opportunity to have the truth about Yahshua explained to them so they could make the right choice to accept Him, because He is the Way the Truth and the Life that Father Yahweh has provided for humanity. I believe they will be given that opportunity after the second resurrection. There is more on this subject later.

I pray, now that you have read this summary of the feast of *Yom Kippur*, that you have a greater appreciation of why this day is the most important day of the year for Jewish people and one of the most important for believers, too, who understand it.

THE FEAST OF TABERNACLES *(SUKKOT)*

The Feast of Tabernacles is the last of the seven annual feasts of Yahweh. This feast follows the Day of Atonement in the seventh Biblical month of *Tishrei*. As it is written:

> **Then the LORD spoke to Moses, saying, "Speak to the children of Israel, saying: 'The fifteen day of this seventh month** [*five days after the Day of Atonement*] **shall be the Feast of Tabernacles for seven days to the LORD. ... You shall keep it as a feast to the LORD for seven days in the year. It shall be a statue forever in your generations. You shall celebrate**

it in the seventh month. You shall dwell in booths for seven days. All who are native Israelites shall dwell in booths, that your generations may know that I made the children of Israel dwell in booths when I brought them out of the land of Egypt: I am the LORD your God.' " So Moses declared to the children of Israel the feasts of the LORD.

Leviticus 23:33-34; 41-44 (NKJV). *Bracketed words added for clarity.*

This feast is known by several different names. One is the name *Sukkot* or *Succot*, which in Hebrew means "booths," or "temporary dwelling places." Almighty Yah performed incredible miracles to set the Israelites free from the bondage of the Egyptians in order to bring them into the wilderness en route to the Promised Land (the area of the present day nation of Israel and some areas along the borders). Father Yahweh desires to dwell close to His chosen people, so He instructed them not only to make temporary tents and dwelling places for themselves, but to also make a temporary dwelling place for His Holy Spirit and the implements and furnishings that were to be used in the large tent of meeting. The Hebrew word for the movable tabernacle is *mishkan*.

All the families of the twelve tribes would set up their tents in groups of three tribes around the large tabernacle tent in the center. The tribes were arranged in the four directions of the compass from the large *mishkan* tent. The Israelites set their tents for as long as Yahweh's presence was in and above the *mishkan*.

The large movable tabernacle tent was furnished and set up much like the first and second temples that were built in Jerusalem and included a room called the Holy of Holies. In the Holy of Holies, above the Ark of the Covenant, rested the Shekinah glory of Elohim, the presence of the Almighty that was near to His people.

Almighty Yah manifested as a visible pillar of cloud by day and a pillar of fire by night that led the Israelites. Yahweh did this also to witness to the other nations that He was and is the one true, living, Creator God and His hand of protection was upon His people, the Israelites. As it is written:

And the LORD went before them by day in a pillar of cloud to lead them along the way, and by night in a pillar of fire to give them light, that they might travel by day and by night; the pillar of cloud by day and the pillar of fire by night did not depart from before the people.

Exodus 13:21-22 (RSV)

This great feast is also known as the Feast of Ingathering and the Season of our Joy. The fall feasts of the seventh month, *Tishrei*, start out with trumpets *(Yom Teruah)* calling all people to wake up, be serious—reflect upon your life and your relationship with your Creator. *Yom Kippur* is very solemn, as each person is to confess their sins before Father Yahweh and apply the blood of our Savior Yahshua for the forgiveness of their sins. The Feast of Tabernacles shifts to a time of great celebration and joy.

After the Israelites were established in the Promised Land of Israel, they farmed and raised herds of animals. The seventh month of *Tishrei* will always be in the early fall of the year in the Middle East. This is when the people would have harvested the crops and brought their tithes and offerings to the temple and storehouses. As it is written:

> **"You shall observe the Feast of Tabernacles seven days, when you have gathered from your threshing floor and from your winepress. And you shall rejoice in your feast, you and your son and your daughter, your male servant and your female servant and the Levite, the stranger and the fatherless and widow, who *are* within your gates. Seven days you shall keep a sacred feast to the LORD your God in the place which the LORD chooses, because the LORD your God will bless you in all your produce and in all the work of your hands, so that you surely rejoice."**
> Deuteronomy 16:13-15 (NKJV)

What does the Feast of Tabernacles and Ingathering mean for us today in the 21st century? It points us back to all that Father Yahweh accomplished with the Israelites, His chosen people, as he miraculously led them out of Egypt, which symbolizes sin. The Feast reveals to us how our Creator, Savior, and King eternal loved those people, and us, because He saved them, provided for them, dwelt with them, and protected them. He desires to do the same for you and me today, if we will trust and obey Him. The Israelites brought in a tenth—the tithe—of their harvest, plus extra offerings, given unto the Lord for provision so there would be food for the poor and the priest. He requires the same from us, and we should give with a cheerful heart because we love Him.

The *sukkots*, or temporary dwelling places, are symbolic of our physical bodies, bodies that we know are temporary. Our Master Yahshua was, is, and will always be the Living Word, or *Torah*, that will never change.

He came to earth and lived with human beings as a human in order to complete His awesome mission. It is written:

And the Word was made flesh, and dwelt *[tabernacled]* **among us, (and we beheld his glory, the glory as of the only begotten of the Father,) full of grace and truth.**
John 1:14 (KJV). *Bracketed words added for clarity.*

We look forward to receiving our new resurrected body, just as King Yahshua received when He was resurrected from the dead. It is written,

For we know that if the earthly tent we live in is destroyed, we have a build-ing from God, a house not made with hands, eternal in the heavens. Here indeed we groan, and long to put on our heavenly dwelling, so that by putting it on we may not be found naked. For while we are still in this tent, we sigh with anxiety; not that we would be unclothed, but that we would be further clothed, so that what is mortal may be swallowed up by life. He who has prepared us for this very thing is God, Who has given us the Spirit *[His Holy Spirit when we are born again]* **as a guarantee** *[down payment].*
2 Corinthians 5:1-5 (RSV). *Bracketed words added for clarity.*

I personally believe that the dwelling places referred to in the Gospel of John are our new resurrected bodies that King Yahshua provides for us at His second coming. I also believe that He will provide physical dwelling places for us after He establishes His kingdom here on earth. Thus says the Lord:

"Do not let your hearts be troubled. Believe in God, believe also in me. In my Father's house there are many dwelling places. If it were not so, would I have told you that I go to prepare a place for you? And if I go and prepare a place for you, I will come again and will take you to myself, so that where I am, there you may be also."
John 14:1-3 (NRSV)

This great feast that our Father Yahweh initiated points us to the ingathering harvest of millions of souls throughout the centuries, but especially during this last generation. The marvels of technology have made it possible for hundreds of millions of people each day to be exposed to the hearing of the good news that Messiah has already come as Yahshua, or Jesus, and died for our sins. We must believe this and invite Him into our hearts so that He can birth His Holy Spirit inside of us, and we can be empowered to turn away from our sins. This assures us of being written in His Book of Life.

King Yahshua, in His first coming to earth, fulfilled all that is symbolized in the spring feasts, right down to the minute He died, which was the very time the priest killed the Passover lambs. In His second coming to earth, He will also fulfill all that is symbolized in the fall feasts, right down to the time that His feet touch down on the Mount of Olives. No one knows for sure the year, but I believe His return to this planet as the Lion of Judah will be after the seventh angel blows his trumpet in heaven signaling the final catastrophes that will be playing out on earth at that time.

During *Yom Kippur* of that final year of this generation, the masses of Jews who have not accepted Yahshua and are living under the oppression of the anti-Messiah will see Him coming in the heavens and mourn and weep, realizing Who He is. Thus says the Lord:

And on that day that I will seek to destroy all the nations that come against Jerusalem. And I will pour on the house of David *[descendants of the tribe of Judah, Jews]* **and the inhabitants** *[others that have not accepted the mark of the beast and are seeking the one true Messiah]* **of Jerusalem a spirit of compassion and supplication, so that, when they** *[we are all guilty and responsible for His death]* **look on Him whom they have pierced, they shall mourn for Him, as one mourns for an only child, and weep bitterly over Him, as one weeps over a first-born.**
Zechariah 12:9-10 (RSV). *Bracketed words added for clarity.*

When our mighty Warrior, King Yahshua, returns to this earth, He will destroy Satan's anti-Christ system and all of the armies that have gathered to destroy Jerusalem. He will then establish His kingdom on earth for a thousand years, during which time he truly dwells and tabernacles with us, not in spirit only, but in His resurrected body. The promise of our resurrected body is covered in detail in Chapter Seven.

Elohim's Word teaches us that, each year during the Millennium, all of the surviving people of the nations who gathered to attempt to destroy Jerusalem will be required to travel to Jerusalem to worship King Yahshua and keep the Feast of Tabernacles. As it is written:

And it shall come to pass *that* **everyone who is left of all the nations which came against Jerusalem shall go up from year to year to worship the King, the LORD of hosts, and to keep the Feast of Tabernacles.**
Zechariah 14:16 (NKJV)

We should desire to keep all of our Creator's appointed times because He initiated and sanctified them (set them apart) to be special times of fellowship with Him. He adores us as His beloved bride. We are to freely adore Him as our husband to be, looking forward to the time when He will come to earth to make the marriage complete and dwell (tabernacle) with us forevermore.

The eighth day immediately following the seven-day Feast of Tabernacles is the celebration called the "Last Great Day." The understanding of the Last Great Day points us to the time at the end of the thousand-year Millennium when our great Savior, King, and righteous Judge will initiate the beginning of the Great White Throne Judgment and the judgment of the fallen angels. A thorough rendering of those events are covered in Chapter Eight.

In the Gospel of John, it is recorded that Messiah Yahshua gave a profound invitation to all people to come to Him with the promise that they would be blessed. It is written:

On the last day, that great *day* **of the feast, Jesus stood and cried out, saying, "If anyone thirsts** *after truth and righteousness]*, **let him come to Me and drink** *[receive my Holy Spirit]*. **He who believes in Me, as the Scripture has said, out of his heart** *[inner spirit person]* **will flow rivers of living water** *[the truth and righteousness from Yahshua Who is the Living* Torah, *the Living Word from Yahweh Almighty]*.**"
John 7:37-38 (NKJV). *Bracketed words added for clarity.*

The reason that followers of Messiah celebrate the day after the end of Tabernacles is that we have no fear of King Yahshua's judgment. We know that He is for us and not against. Holy Spirit is wooing us to accept Jesus as our Savior and accept Him as Lord of our life by living according to His instructions found in His Holy Word. When we completely put our faith and trust in Him, He will lead us out of our sinful nature, replacing it with His holy nature. Holy Spirit in us overcomes all fear. As it is written:

... for God [Elohim] did not give us a spirit of cowardice [fear], but rather a spirit of power and of love and of self-discipline [sound mind].
2 Timothy 1:7 (NRSV). *Bracketed words added for clarity.*

The following article was written by a dear brother in Messiah, David Prichard, who gave me permission to include it in this book. This excellent article helps us to understand that we have Hebraic roots and that, when we accept Yahshua as our Messiah, we then become part of the Israelite family of Almighty Yah. I pray David's writing will be a blessing to you as it has been for me.

WHY WE OBSERVE GOD'S APPOINTED TIMES

1. The Eternal Covenant(s)

On the day when Moses delivered the message that we call the book of Deuteronomy, he prophesied to the entire nation of Israel—all twelve tribes—BOTH those standing there that day, AND to the many more who would be <u>born into</u>, <u>adopted into</u>, or <u>"grafted" into Israel in the future</u>:

> "Ye stand this day all of you before the LORD your God ... That thou shouldest enter into covenant with the LORD thy God, and into His oath, which the LORD thy God maketh with thee this day: That He may establish thee to day for a people unto himself, and that He may be unto thee a God, as He hath said unto thee, and as He hath sworn unto thy fathers, to Abraham, to Isaac, and to Jacob. <u>Neither with you only</u> do I make this covenant and this oath; but with him that standeth here with us this day before the LORD our God, and <u>also with him that is not here with us this day</u>: ..."
> Deuteronomy 29:10a, 12-15 (KJV)

And we know that the covenant which the LORD made with Israel in that day was not complete in itself unto eternity—for the "covenants of promise" (Ephesians 2:12) would not be complete without another, "new" (or "renewed") covenant, carried out by the authority of an Eternal Priesthood. (Isaiah 55:1-3, Jeremiah 31:31, Ezekiel 16:59-63, Hosea 1:10-11 & 2:18-23, Hebrews 7:11-28 & 8:6-13). Yet we also know that in His great Faithfulness, YHVH did not sweep away the promises of the covenants of old, which He made with Noah, with Abraham, with Moses and the children of Israel, and with David. For when the Most High gives His Word, it stands forever. Thus, the psalmist writes:

> **He hath remembered His covenant for ever, the word which He commanded to a thousand generations. Which covenant He made with Abraham, and His oath unto Isaac; and confirmed the same unto Jacob for a law, and to Israel for an <u>everlasting covenant</u> ...**
> Psalm 105:8-10

In fact, the Holy Scriptures refer to each one of the holy covenants—individually and collectively, as an "Everlasting Covenant". (Genesis 9:16 & 17:7, 2 Samuel 23:5, 1 Chronicles 16:17, Isaiah 24:5) And the LORD in His Integrity has always kept His Word even when only a small remnant remained faithful in their hearts to their part of the agreement. In fact, He determined to fulfill those covenants despite the fact that "all we like sheep have gone astray". But the method that He used to fulfill His Word has often come in a more complicated way than it had to—or than the original hearers imagined.

Now the promises of land and of heritage and of long life and blessing were made to Abraham and to his seed, to Moses and the nation of Israel, through covenants that were inferior to the one made by the Blood of the Lamb; that is, through covenants that did not <u>secure Eternal Life</u> to the one entering the covenant. For example, the promise that Abraham sought, of a "city which hath foundations, whose Builder and Maker is God" (Hebrews 11:10), was not secured until the Messianic Covenant was made through the Blood of the Lamb of God. For the Scripture testifies of our forefathers in the faith, that "these all, having obtained a good report through faith, received not the promise" (that is, in their lifetime). (11:39)

For even though the promise of Eternal Life was made before the world began (Titus 1:2), that promise was not made available to us as long as we remained trapped in the earthly realm of our death sentence, inherited from Adam. Only the Atoning Blood of Yahshua of Nazareth, the Son of the Living God, could ultimately save us and bring us into right relationship with the One True God. (John 6:47-58, John 17:2-3, Romans 5:9-21) Therefore the prophets called the promised new covenant by the same title: "Everlasting Covenant" (Isaiah 24:5, 55:3 & 61:8, Jeremiah 32:40, 16:60 & 37:26, Hebrews

13:20), for the superior covenant could hardly be called by an inferior adjective. Writing to the Corinthians, Paul contrasts the administration of Torah with the Messianic Covenant this way:

But if the ministry of death, written *and* engraved on stones, was glorious, so that the children of Israel could not look steadily at the face of Moses because of the glory of his countenance, which *glory* was passing away, how will the ministry of the Spirit not be more glorious?
2 Corinthians 3:7-8 (NKJV)

And the writer of the epistle to the Hebrews states very plainly:

But now hath He obtained a more excellent ministry, by how much also He is the mediator of a better covenant, which was established upon better promises.
Hebrews 8:6 (KJV)

Therefore any discussion concerning observance of the Feasts of the LORD, or Sabbaths, or circumcision, etc., must begin with the foundation that the ministry of Jesus Christ—Yahshua haMashiach—in the earth today is based on the True, Eternal Pattern of Heaven itself. And the covenants that YHVH made with Abraham and with Moses cannot stand independent from that Eternal Pattern. (Hebrews 9:23-24, 10:1-9) In fact, clearly that portion of the Mosaic Covenant that had merely stood temporarily "in the place" of Jesus' Priesthood—that is, the Levitical priesthood—has been "taken away", or "annulled"; at least from the perspective of Eternity. (Hebrews 10:9) Yet the entire Mosaic Covenant has not been annulled even to this day, or else it could never have been called "eternal"! Jesus did not come to start a new religion, but to set right that which, "being weak through the flesh" (Romans 8:3), was being "hi-jacked" and used for evil. This is why He made the statement:

And from the days of John the Baptist until now the kingdom of heaven suffereth violence, and the violent take it by force.
Matthew 11:12 (KJV)

Therefore the legitimate debate is in regard to this: Which other commandments—besides those directly concerning the priesthood and the altar service—were done away with, or transformed in some way; and which commandments were meant to remain even to this day, for proper training in holiness, and to preserve the prophetic patterns for understanding these "end times"?

The answers to these questions are found, not just in the New Testament, but in the Old Testament as well. And there is fair room for prayer, meditation, discussion, and some differences of opinion.

2. The Law "transformed"?

Now, since even the inferior covenants are also called Everlasting, then in some way each of these covenants stands as a pillar upon the Foundation that is Christ, the Messiah—Who Alone secured for us the ultimate "everlasting" promises. (For these could not be everlasting without the "Eternal Life" that He secured for us.) And so the Apostle John calls Him "the Lamb slain from the foundation of the world" (Rev 13:8)—for the essence of Eternal Covenant was determined and settled within the heart and mind of YHVH before the world was made.

And just as Paul points out that God's covenant with Abraham could not be nullified by the *Torah* of Moses (Galatians 3:17), that same standard applies "across the board". In other words, the covenant that God made with Moses was not nullified by the Messianic Covenant. For otherwise, Paul could not assert, <u>after</u> the Resurrection of his Messiah, that "the law is holy, and the commandment holy, and just, and good". (Romans 7:12) How could it still be "good" if it was annulled? It was merely <u>incomplete</u> until it could be <u>renewed</u> unto an *Eternal Priesthood*. (Acts 7:37-38; Isaiah 40:3-8,21&31; 2 John 1:5-6; Rev 1:8) This is a major scriptural theme, but it has to be assembled through Bible study.

Paul ***never*** taught that we are to ***break*** the Law. He ***kept*** the Law to the best of his understanding! He even used a *Torah* instruction as seemingly obscure as the one (in Numbers 6) for sanctification through a Nazarite vow (shaving the head, etc.)—as mentioned in Acts 18:18. And after laying down his "righteousness which is in the law" (Philip 3:6), he did not count it completely evil—but counted it "loss for Christ". In other words, he gladly laid down ***even everything he ever did right*** as he followed the Pharisaical interpretation of the Law—which was a lot! He proved his zeal, and he got the Father's attention! He laid it down for "the excellency of the knowledge of Christ Jesus". (Philip 3:7-9) So the Law of Moses itself is not evil, but attempting to find Eternal Life by following the "works of the Law" (Galatians 3:10) is heresy. (John 5:39-47)

The apostle John testified that "sin is the transgression of the law" (1 John 3:4), and he taught us to "keep His commandments". (1 John 5:2) Jesus Himself said, **"If ye love Me, keep My commandments"**. And if Jesus was the One, as Stephen asserted (Acts 7:37-38), Who delivered the "Living Oracles" at Mount Sinai, then He could hardly show up In Person 1500 years later and say, **"Never mind that I punished you severely for the past 15 centuries because you didn't keep My Laws – I was just showing you that you could never do it right anyway. You can forget all those harsh commandments now."** No—those commandments were "everlasting", and this is no contradiction as we come to understand the spiritual nature of "the Law". What, then, was "nailed to the cross"? It was "the handwriting of ordinances that were against us" (Colossians 2:14). Paul explains more about these ordinances in Ephesians 2:12-15:

> **"That at that time** [prior to the advent of the new covenant] **ye were ... aliens from the commonwealth of Israel, and strangers from the covenants of promise ...** [because as "lost sheep", the house of Israel was divorced by God, their Husband, and then scattered among the Gentiles who themselves were also strangers from His covenants] (more about the "lost sheep" and the "house of Israel" in part 3)**: But now in Christ Jesus ye ... are made nigh by the Blood of Christ. For He is our peace, Who hath made both one,** [that is, joined Jews and Israelites (new covenant converts) back together] **and hath broken down the middle wall of partition between us;** [the "wall of partition" existed because: 1. the two Kingdoms were split after Solomon died, and: 2. Israel effectively became "Gentile" and considered the Jews and Torah "strange" Hosea 8:8-12] **Having abolished in His flesh the enmity, even the law of commandments contained in ordinances; ...**
>
> Ephesians 2:12-15 (KJV). *Bracketed words added for clarity.*

What ordinances? The ones that sentenced Israel to servitude to foreign nations and gods: **for to make in Himself of twain one new man, so making peace ..."** In other words, the lost sheep of the house of Israel were supposed to convert and return to their brother, Judah—and the Jews were supposed to rejoice that their Messiah had come and led their prodigal brother back home! But we're STILL waiting for THAT to be completed!

Therefore those who were made "aliens from the commonwealth of Israel" (Ephesians 2:12) because they were cut off from the Mosaic Covenant, have gained access again to the "covenants of promise". So it is not the Mosaic Law that they are free of, but "the curse of the law" (Galatians 3:13). For many aspects of the Law of Moses still have application today. For every principle laid by the former covenants still stands eternal. Yet it may not stand as it was originally given, because some aspects of the Old Testament commandments have been transformed to a higher level by the new covenant in the Blood of our Messiah. This is why the writer of the epistle to the Hebrews writes:

For the priesthood being changed, there is made of necessity a change also of the law *[Torah].*
Hebrews 7:12 (KJV). *Bracketed words added for clarity.*

But as a renewal took place in the Cohen-hood *[Priesthood],* **so a renewal also took place in the Torah.**
Hebrews 7:12 (Hebraic Roots Version NT)

Therefore it is logical that there would be a debate afoot in this "end time" concerning the *nature* of this "change...of the *Torah*". For there are those who will acknowledge only the Ten Commandments and whatever laws and precepts from the New Testament that happen to be obvious to them from their English text, and teach that all the rest of the "law" was "nailed to the Cross". And there are others who would attempt to take away the predominant place of the Spirit of Grace, and reinstate the "ministry of death" (2 Corinthians 3:7). But the Truth is somewhere in between.

For the prophets made it plain that at the time of the birthpangs, the "sons of God" would be manifest (Romans 8:19-22), and the LORD would raise up a remnant of BOTH HOUSES—the Jews AND the 10 tribes of Israel (who are commonly called prophetically by the name of their largest tribe, "Ephraim"). (Ezekiel 37:15-28, Revelation 7:1-8) This remnant will prepare the way for Messiah to return by restoring the ancient paths without getting bogged down again in "works of the law". (Isaiah 58:12-14, 66:8-9; Jeremiah 30:6-9, 31:18-37; Ezekiel 36:22-28, 37:15-28; Daniel 11:32-35; Joel 2:28-32, 3:1-21 Matthew 10:18-20, 10:40-42; 1 Thessalonians 5:3-5; Revelation 11:3-6, 12:14-17)

3. Israel, Judah, and the Gentiles

The Everlasting Covenant was (and is) made for BOTH non-Israelite Gentiles (who are not descended from one of the twelve tribes) AND the scattered, "ten lost tribes" of the house of Israel, who were divorced by YHVH. (Jeremiah 3:8-18, 31:32; Hosea 1:6-2:7, Isaiah 54:5) These "lost" Israelites were sent to live among the Gentile nations until the time of the end. (Dueteronomy 30:3-6, Isaiah 10:20-27, Jeremiah 31:10 & 33:7, Micah 5:7-15, Romans 11:25-26a) Because the nation of Israel did not willingly develop itself according to God's original plan to make them "a kingdom of priests"

(Exodus 19:6), the LORD used one of His many back-up plans. He scattered the majority of them throughout the nations to become the evangelists of the world. (Jeremiah 50:4-7; Ezekiel 22:15-16, 36:16-38, 37:16-25; Hosea 8:8-9; Zephaniah 3:8-20; Zechariah 8:23; Matthew 4:23-25, 10:5-6, 15:24; John 7:35; Romans 11:24-32, and much more).

Of course the Jews also (the house of Judah), who were never divorced from the covenants of promise, nevertheless had just as much need for the foundational covenant as anyone else, for "God hath concluded them all in unbelief" (Romans 3:23, 9:1-4, 11:32). (For YHVH specifically witnessed of the Jews, that after witnessing the whoredoms and judgments of her "sister" – Ephraim, the house of Israel – that rather than repenting, the house of Judah 'followed suit' and became more adulterous than Israel had!)

The thing that sets the Jews apart from all others – even from their brethren, the house of Israel, who basically became "Gentiles" culturally – is that the Jews were reserved by God to be entrusted with "the oracles of God"; that is, the Hebrew scriptures. (Romans 3:2; Acts 7:38) Furthermore, the Jews have preserved priceless knowledge of the Hebrew language, and of ancient traditions that always pointed to our Messiah. Therefore Paul writes:

What advantage then hath the Jew? or what profit is there of circumcision? Much every way: chiefly, because that unto them were committed the oracles of God.
Romans 3:1-2 (KJV)

It is through a small but faithful remnant of Jews, followed by some good Christian and Messianic scholars, through which the LORD at this time is beginning to fulfill the prophecy of Zephaniah:

For then I will restore to the peoples a pure language, that they may call on the name of the LORD (lit.: YHVH), to serve Him with one accord.
Zephaniah 3:9 (NKJV)

We do not know, ultimately, what heavenly language we will be speaking in Eternity, but the first step in restoring a "pure language" <u>here in the earth</u>, is understanding Hebrew. This is becoming popular among many Christians at this "end-time", and by the implication of Zephaniah it will accelerate right into the Millennial Reign of Christ. For whereas the foundational *covenant* is expounded upon in the New Testament, the foundational *Scriptures* are found in the Old Testament, *written in Hebrew!* Thus we find another curious prophecy, written by the prophet Zechariah:

> **... In those days it shall come to pass, that <u>ten men</u> shall take hold out of all languages of the nations, even shall take hold of the skirt of him that is a Jew, saying, We will go with you: for we have heard that God is with you.**
> Zechariah 8:23 (KJV)

The "ten men" here represent the ten tribes of the house of Israel who at this point in history stand on the verge of fulfilling their prophetic destiny. Huge numbers of them are <u>*us*</u>—Christians and Messianic believers who are not Jews! In the prophetic books of the Bible, we are usually called "Ephraim" or "Israel". Other descendants of these ten tribes are already aligned in their hearts with the Anti-Christ, and being positioned to receive the judgments prophesied against the house of Israel at the end-times.

Of course, we need not concern ourselves at this point with whether or not we are physical descendants of Israel—because to be a "true" Christian means to be grafted into the <u>Covenants of Israel</u>. For who did Jesus say He came for?

> **I am not sent but unto the lost sheep of the house of Israel.**
> Matthew 15:24 (KJV)

And to whom did He send His disciples?

> **Go not into the way of the Gentiles, and into any city of the Samaritans enter ye not: but go rather to the lost sheep of the house of Israel.**
> Matthew 10:5-6 (KJV)

Now, the term "house of Israel" (in the New Testament, especially) is sometimes used to include the whole nation of Israel—both houses. But it is important to understand that He spent very little time, proportionately, ministering in Judea where the most "pure" Jewish population of Israel was concentrated. Instead, **He lived and ministered primarily among Greek-influenced descendants of both houses that were considered to be inferior Israelites by the elite Jewish leaders.** (Matthew 4:23-25, Luke 4:43,44) It was only after His resurrection that He commissioned the disciples to go to Samaria (who were primarily Assyrians) and Judea and "the nations". (Matthew 24:19,20; Mark 16:15) The Hebrew word for "nations" (*goyim*) is also translated "Gentiles", so what He was telling them to do was to get ready to preach a worldwide message—because the rest of "Israel" was scattered throughout all the nations as the prophets had declared! And along the way, of course, plenty of non-Israelite Gentiles would join them. (By the way, if you look at a globe, you'll notice that North and South America are "the uttermost part of the earth" (Acts 1:8) from the land of Israel.)

4. The Feasts of the LORD

Once we understand: 1) that the covenants of old were Everlasting Covenants; and: 2) that as Christians we are no longer merely "Gentiles", but literally citizens of the spiritual nation of Israel—then it's all the more clear that we are brothers with those who are "true" Jews (Romans 2:28,29), and we tend to regard Moses and the Prophets in a different "Light". Jesus Himself said that He did not come to "abolish" (or "destroy") the law (*Torah*), but to "fulfill" it. (Matthew 5:17). Then He went on to say:

> **For verily I say unto you, Till heaven and earth pass, one jot or one tittle shall in no wise pass from the law, till all be fulfilled. Whosoever therefore shall break one of these least commandments, and shall teach men so, he shall be called least in the kingdom of heaven: but whosoever shall do and teach them, the same shall be called great in the kingdom of heaven.**
> Matthew 5:18-19 (KJV)

This is a serious statement that deserves our prayer and meditation. The "heaven and earth" of this physical universe are not scheduled to "pass" away and become new for over one thousand years. (Rev 20:1-3) Then will come the *final* "Renewal" of all things. (Isaiah 66:22; 2 Peter 3:8-13; Hebrews 8:13 & 11:10; Rev 21:1-22:5) So Jesus was actually predicting that before His Return, men would be teaching us to break commandments that we should be keeping.

This is not a Salvation issue—but it is an issue of "calling". ("…and thou shalt be called, The repairer of the breach…" Isaiah 58:12) We are called to take "the ministry of reconciliation" that He has given to us (2 Corinthians 5:18), and apply it "to the Jew first, and also to the Gentile". (Luke 24:37, Romans 1:16 & 2:10, 1 Corinthians 10:32) With what's going on in Israel and the world today, we stand on the precipice of the worst wave of Jewish persecution of all time. And if we consider it our end-time assignment to help reconcile the Jews to their Messiah, we must first reconcile ourselves unto the Jews. For if we present to the Jews a Savior Who goes back on His Word by refusing to honor His Own Commandments, we are in danger of teaching men to break God's commandments. But if we recognize the validity of the Mosaic Law to instruct us and lead us to YHVH, yet hold fast to His Atoning Blood and standing in the Liberty that ONLY the Son of God can secure—then we are ready to be "imitators of Christ".

Therefore, since we are free from bondage to sin, and no longer "under the law", but "justified by faith", then we are reconciled to the Father to follow His teachings and instructions throughout _all_ of the Holy Scriptures as appropriate, out of free will. And if God has given grace to Christians for centuries, to celebrate holidays with pagan origins (and mixed with pagan symbolism), shall He not celebrate with His Beloved those holidays ("holy-days") that He originated Himself? Therefore Paul writes to the Colossians:

Let no man therefore judge you in meat, or in drink, or in respect of an holyday, or of the new moon, or of the sabbath days: Which are a shadow of things to come ...
Colossians 2:16-17 (KJV)

For it was not the feasts, of themselves, that God came to despise in the days of old, but the arrogant religious spirit that predominated their celebration. For after the pronouncement, "your appointed feasts my soul hateth" (Isaiah 1:14), still the Son of God kept each "appointment", as an obedient son. And "the Feasts of the LORD" (Leviticus 23:2,4,37,44; 2 Chronicles 2:4, Ezra 3:5) only became "the Feasts of the Jews" (John 5:1 & 6:4) because the rest of the Israel was scattered and took on Gentile customs. So it was part of their _punishment_ that they would forget their rightful heritage of righteous laws and customs "which if a man do, he shall even live", (Ezekiel 20:11) and be turned over to laws and customs that do not have the Life-flow of the Most High God working in them.

And now we find ourselves at "the end of the age", in a Christianized culture that is rapidly losing its Judeo-Christian values and the cultural cohesiveness that they bring. And our God is calling out to His Two Anointed Ones in the earth—the house of Israel and the house of Judah—saying, "House of Judah, can you not recognize the Priestly Anointing on your brother, Ephraim? Put aside your doubts, and know that I have called him to join you at this 'time of Jacob's trouble'." 1 Chronicles 5:2; Isaiah 26:15-21, 54:1-10 & 60:1-11; Jeremiah 16:19-21 & 31:9; Micah 5:8; Zechariah 3:1-10 & 10:6-8) "House of Israel, known to the world as Christians, can you recognize the Kingly Anointing on your brothers, the Jews? Come to Me and learn about the errors in your _own_ traditions. _Then_ you will see clearly to help your brother get free from his own erroneous traditions." (Gen 49:10; Dueteronomy 33:7; Jeremiah 16:19; Hosea 1:7; Zechariah 9:13, 10:6 & 14:21; John 4:22, 1 Corinthians 9:20)

These two witnesses in the earth must be joined together! Therefore PLEASE do not accuse anyone of "trampling on God's Grace", who merely desires to follow more closely to God's commandments. Rather, the Holy Spirit is leading us all forward, unfolding the mysteries of the Kingdom. And neither can we allow ourselves to lose balance, and fall prey to modern

"Judaizers" – or even worse, to forsake the New Testament scriptures. We must recognize that with every new move of the Spirit there are those who go to extremes, and so pray for discernment without judging others.

Did you know that the Puritans came to America seeking freedom to worship God on the seventh day (Sabbath), and to observe the Feasts of the LORD? They were a group of English who set out to return to the "purity" of the Biblical "appointed times". They studied their scriptures, and read the words of God, saying,

> **"The feasts of the LORD, which you shall proclaim *to be* holy convocations, these *are* My feasts."**
> Leviticus 23:2 (NKJV)

Then they studied their New Testament, and could find no place where they were instructed to stop observing them. Every year Americans celebrate Thanksgiving, oblivious that its origin was the Feast of Succot, observed by the Puritans. (Ever heard of a vegetable mixture called "<u>succ</u>otash"?) Thanksgiving used to be celebrated in October because it was timed to one of the Feasts of the LORD, called the Feast of Succot. But in the mid-1900's our government changed it to the end of November. This is all true, documented history that you can verify in any good library. But they didn't teach us these things in grade school, nor did our preachers learn them in Theology School.

How *quickly* one generation loses the knowledge of their fathers! And the Father cries out through the ages: "My people are destroyed for lack of knowledge!" (Hosea 4:6) Paul recognized the holy days as "shadows of things to come". Some deeply significant prophetic events have been occurring on significant dates of the Hebrew calendar ever since 1993, but most Christians today are neither aware of the events nor the dates, because the world has a tendency to lull us asleep. But that is about to change.

As Christians, we are on the verge of a wonderful move of the Holy Spirit. Hearts will be touched – especially among many young people. Many believers will be blessed. But if all we do is soak up the "warm, cozy feeling" of the Holy Spirit, and neglect the serious Bible study and Truth-searching that God is calling many of us to, we will do a great disservice to ourselves and others.

The Feasts of the LORD are *shadows of things to come*. Paul wrote this AFTER Jesus' resurrection, which means these feasts are STILL good "for doctrine, for reproof, for correction, for instruction in righteousness". (In fact, the "all Scripture given by inspiration of God" he referred to, here in 2 Timothy 3:16, were all Old Testament scriptures. There *was* no New

Testament at that time!) The spirit of the anti-Christ, however, wants to divert us from understanding the patterns of the times we live in, which understanding God promises to release to those obedient ones who seek His knowledge. For Daniel warned us about the "little horn" that shall "think to change times and laws" (Daniel 7:25) – and the spirit that drives the anti-Christ has been operating for many centuries. Daniel also warned us that many of God's people "shall fall by the sword, and by flame, by captivity, and by spoil, many days". (11:33) But "the wise shall understand". (Daniel 12:10)

Therefore, as for me and my household, we will seek the God of Israel at His "appointed times", out of a spirit of Freedom and with joy! We believe that if Jesus were among us today, "in cognito", He would set aside whatever was on His schedule and take the time to observe His Appointed Sabbaths and Feasts. We don't do these things to earn brownie points with God. We recognize His Grace upon millions of believers who do not observe Passover, and we do not judge them. We do not follow "the letter" of Torah ourselves; we are still "in process" of "coming home" to the blessings which the Biblical Sabbath schedule permits. Also, we do not consider Jewish tradition to carry nearly the same authority as the Holy Scriptures. Yet Jewish traditions are rich in godly teaching and prophetic insight, and they help to "fill in" the very basic structure given in Scripture for how to celebrate the feasts.

Above all, we observe Passover because YHVH has ***called and instructed us to do so***, by His Spirit. It is a sign to Jews and to Christians alike, that Ephraim, the house of Israel, is "studying to show himself approved", and is doing his part to prepare for "reunion" with his brother, Judah, that we may fight the end-time battle before us as "one new man". And it is a sign to all who will receive it, that we are living in the last days before the Return of the Son of God – the Messiah of Israel – to rule and reign in the earth for one thousand years. Hallelujah!

That is a really good article by Brother David. I agree with all that he has stated, and I will add that another reason we should keep the feasts of Father Yahweh and follow all of His *Torah* instructions, especially in these last years of this last generation. In doing so, we position ourselves to become part of His second greater Exodus people. I will reveal this in detail in Chapter Eleven in the section of the letter to the Church of Philadelphia.

6

PROOF WE ARE IN THE LAST GENERATION

I hope you are not upset with me for using end-time Bible prophecy as a lure for you to purchase this book. This book of media evangelism was written primarily to help you understand Father Yahweh's plan of salvation for all who are willing to accept His gift, His Son Yahshua. I encourage you to do what is required by a holy and righteous God to be redeemed into His Kingdom from Satan's kingdom.

The single most important decision that you will make in this life is your decision to accept Yahshua Messiah as your savior, put your complete faith and trust in Him and to commit yourself to follow Him. Accepting Yahshua guarantees your completeness and happiness in this life. You have the peace and assurance that after death, throughout all eternity, you will be with, and not separated from, Almighty Yah, your family members and friends that are saved. So, if you are not sure you have been born of Yah's Holy Spirit, I encourage you to go back and read Chapter Three again and pray.

What is the proof that we are living in the last generation of this age, just prior to the beginning of the millennial age? We must comprehend prophecy and relate it to the events that have been happening in our world for the past fifty or so years in order to have the answers. Bible prophecy always relates to Israel in some way, and from Israel as a point of reference.

Almighty Yahweh gave the land of present day Israel (and a good bit more) to Abraham and his descendants.

On the same day, the LORD made a covenant with Abram, saying: "To your descendants I have given this land, from the river of Egypt [*not the Nile, but a small river south of Gaza called Wadi el*] **to the great river,**

the River Euphrates *[Iraq]— ..."*
Genesis 15:18 (NKJV). *Bracketed words added for clarity.*

This covenant that Yahweh made with Abraham and his descendants was given approximately 3,400 years ago. Abraham, his son Isaac, his grandson Jacob, with all of their family members, servants, and animals occupied parts of the land until a great famine occurred in all the lands. By this time, Abraham and Isaac had passed on, and Jacob, with his eleven sons and descendants, were in the land of Canaan. Jacob had heard that there was grain in Egypt, so he sent his ten eldest sons to go there and buy grain. The older sons had sold their younger brother, Joseph, into Egyptian slavery many years before because they were jealous of him. They had lied to their father, Jacob, telling him that a lion had eaten their brother.

Joseph spent many years in Pharaoh's dungeon where he had interpreted dreams for both Pharaoh's butler and his baker. Both interpretations happened as he said. Two full years later, when Pharaoh needed someone to interpret his troubling dreams, the butler remembered Joseph in the dungeon. Joseph was summoned, cleaned up, and taken to Pharaoh to interpret his dreams. Joseph told Pharaoh that Yahweh had shown Pharaoh what He was about to do. Joseph interpreted the dreams as seven years of plenty followed by seven years of severe famine; he then told Pharaoh what he must do in preparation.

The advice was good in Pharaoh's eyes, and Joseph found great favor because of his Holy Spirit-given wisdom and ability to interpret Pharaoh's dreams. Joseph was appointed second in command over all of Egypt. During the seven years of plenty, he gathered up grain from all of Egypt and stored it in every city for the coming famine until the amount was immeasurable. Joseph was reunited with his father, Jacob, and his eleven brothers after many years when they came to buy much-needed food. This great story in Hebrew history is found in Chapters 37 through 50 of the book of Genesis.

As a result of the family reunion and the famine, Jacob (Almighty Yah had changed his name to Israel several years before) and all of his clan moved from the land that Yahweh had given them into the land of Egypt. The population of the twelve family clans greatly increased; they were fruitful and grew exceedingly strong. After Joseph died, another Pharaoh ruled who did not know Joseph, nor was he favorable to Joseph's family. He made slaves of them because he feared their great number.

After 400 hundred years of slavery and crying out to Yahweh for help, our Heavenly Father heard their prayers. He sent Moses, the deliverer, with the command to Pharaoh, "Let My people go, that they may hold a feast to Me in the wilderness." With God's assistance and many great and awesome miracles, the estimated two million people of the Hebrew nation of Israel were delivered from the land of Egypt and began the long journey northeastward toward the Promised Land.

It was during this incredible journey of great challenges and dependence on Almighty Yah's provision that He presented to Moses His Royal Law—the Ten Commandants—for His chosen people. Soon thereafter, Almighty Yah revealed His requirements of animal sacrifices, which made up the ceremonial law, including the seven annual. Then there were the much-needed civil, dietary, and health laws. The laws were, and are, actually instructions for life that began the core of Israelite guidance called the *Torah*. We should desire to observe and keep all of the instructions of *Torah*, with the exception of animal sacrifices, not out of legalistic works for salvation, but because we love our Creator, Savior, and King Eternal with all of our hearts, and desire to please him. He knows what is best for us.

The Hebrew people had made great progress in their journey by the time they reached the land of Canaan. Although Yahweh assured them that He would continue to assist them in taking the land from the idolizing, heathen tribes who had settled there during their four hundred years of enslavement in Egypt, the Hebrew people were still afraid to go into the land because the scouts reported that there were giants in the land. The people did not trust Almighty Yah to help them even after all of the amazing miracles that He had performed to sustain them. As a result of their unbelief, Yahweh sent them back into the desert to wander for forty years until that generation of doubters had died out.

With Almighty Yah's help, Joshua led the great nation of people and livestock into the Promised Land. With Yah's help, his great army of approximately six hundred thousand warriors from the twelve tribes conquered over thirty kingdoms of idol worshipers and settled in the land. This was the second occupation of the land of Israel and began about 1,400 B.C.

I am now including some more biblical history because it is helpful in understanding what is taking place now in the land of Israel in order to lay a foundation for understanding the important prophecies for our time.

For approximately 800 years after the Hebrew nation settled in Israel, there was a constant challenge of Yahweh's closest followers and prophets engaged in trying to keep the people from falling into the idolatry of the surrounding nations. It was during this time that the people of the nation of Israel demanded to have their own king because the surrounding nations had kings. Almighty Yah appeased them and selected the three men who were kings during the golden years of the great empire of Israel. The kings were Saul, David, and one of David's sons, Solomon.

It was also during this important time that Yahweh sent the great prophets to warn the people. These men of Yah were called to deliver prophecies from Yahweh concerning the consequences that would befall the people of Israel if they did not turn away from worshiping false gods and become faithful to the one true living Elohim by worshiping Him and keeping His commandments.

Toward the end of King Solomon's reign, it was obvious that the golden era of Israel was coming to an end. The ten tribes in the northern part of Israel, identified as Ephraim and sometimes Israel, decided to become independent from the three southern tribes of Judah, Benjamin, and Levi. The people of both of these separated kingdoms had fallen into idolatry. Yahweh sent His prophets Isaiah, Jeremiah, Micah, Zephaniah, and Habakkuk to warn the House of Judah—the southern kingdom. He sent Hosea and Amos to warn the people of Israel—the northern kingdom.

The Israelites were warned not to mix the truth from Yahweh with the falsehood of the peoples of the other nations. As a result of the Israelite men marrying the women from the pagan nations and being influenced by their beliefs, the king of the northern tribes, Jeroboam, elected his own priest to perform the worship services. He also made a mandate forbidding the people of the ten northern tribes from going to Jerusalem to celebrate the feasts, and he had the times for keeping the feasts changed to other months.

The people were foolish and did not heed the warnings from the many prophets, so the northern kingdom was captured and taken away by the Assyrians in 722-721 B.C. As a result, they lost the identity of who they were in Yahweh and became blended into the peoples throughout the earth. This nation became known as the ten lost tribes of Israel because, after they survived the Assyrian enslavement, they migrated to the north and northwest toward what is now known as Europe. There is strong biblical and historical evidence that some of the descendants of the tribes of Ephraim, Manasseh, Asher, and Dan, of the northern tribes, settled in the British Isles and later into America.

The House of Judah, the southern kingdom, fell to the Babylonians in 586 B.C., and the great temple that King Solomon built, which was the first Jewish temple, was destroyed. The Jewish people, especially the smartest and most able-bodied, along with the beautiful temple vessels, were taken away to the evil kingdom of Babylon.

It was during this time that the great prophet Daniel lived and prophesied. He was called on several occasions by the king of Babylon to interpret his dreams. One of the dreams Daniel interpreted revealed the conquering of Babylon by the Mede and Persian empires. Daniel went on to describe all of the major world empires, including the final one at the end of the age. I will share more on this later.

After the Medes and Persians conquered the Babylonians, King Cyrus issued a decree that any of the Jewish people who so desired could return to Israel. A group of those who were devoted to Yahweh and focused on His ways returned to the original land of Israel. They were committed to rebuilding the second temple, defense wall, and their city of Jerusalem that had been plowed under. This was the third occupation of the Promised Land.

After many hard years of work, the temple was finally finished and dedicated around 500 B.C. During the almost fifty years it took to build the temple, Almighty Yah sent the prophets Haggai and Zechariah. Approximately 450 years after the second temple was completed, King Herod did a major renovation and addition to the temple that took over twenty years. The interior of the temple had an enormous amount of inlaid gold, even in the joints of the large granite stones of the foundation and the walls.

This second temple was where Yahshua Messiah taught and performed miracles of healing. A few days before our Master Yahshua was crucified, as He was making His triumphant entry into Jerusalem, He gave a significant prophecy about the destruction of the great temple and the city of Jerusalem. He wept for the people of this great city of Yahweh because He could see the great suffering that was to come to the people at the hands of the Roman army. As it is written:

Now as He drew near, He saw the city and wept over it, saying, "If you had known, even you, especially in this your day, the things *that make for* your peace! But now they are hidden from your eyes. For days will come upon you when your enemies will build an embankment around you, surround you and close you in on every side, and level you, and your chil-

dren within you, to the ground; and they will not leave in you one stone upon another, because you did not know the time of your visitation."
Luke 19:41-44 (NKJV)

This prophecy was fulfilled to the letter in the year A.D. 70 when the Roman General Titus and his army captured Jerusalem.

The following account is from the great Roman historian, Josephus. The war on the city of Jerusalem lasted about three years. It is estimated that nearly one million Jews were trapped inside the walls of the city. General Titus and his men tried many different tactics to convince the Jewish people trapped inside to surrender, but they would not. General Titus grew weary of the Jews not surrendering, so he ordered his men to begin crucifying some of the Jews who had been captured outside of the city. The Roman soldiers nailed men to crosses and literally to trees on high ground near the walls of the city so the people inside could see them and hear them cry out. At one point, the Romans were crucifying 500 men per day along the walls. The Jewish people still refused to surrender. This brought on the most horrible of all evil during the terrible conquest. Titus ordered his men to gather many of the young Jewish children who had been captured outside of the city and to crucify them. How cruel and devastating this had to have been to witness.

These events took place after the Apostle Paul had written his letter to the congregation in Rome as recorded in the Scriptures below. I believe that he had a dream or vision that revealed the horrible crucifixion of the Jews before it actually happened. After it happened, as people studied the eleventh chapter of Romans, they would be able to make the connection and realize what an incredible price was paid so that we non-Jews could be grafted in by the mercy of Almighty Yahweh through the shed blood of His Son, Yahshua. I believe the Apostle Paul was referring to those dear Jewish men, women, and children who were crucified outside the city as he wrote Romans Eleven about the branches of the Olive tree being broken off. It is written:

Now I am speaking to you Gentiles. Inasmuch then as I am an apostle to the Gentiles, I magnify my ministry in order to make my fellow Jews jealous, and thus save some of them. For if their rejection means the reconciliation of the world, what will their acceptance mean but life from the dead? If the dough offered as first fruits is holy, so is the whole

lump; and if the root is holy, so are the branches. But if some of the branches were broken off *[for you and me]*, and you, a wild olive shoot, were grafted in their place to share the richness of the olive tree, do not boast over the branches. If you do boast, remember it is not you that support the root, but the root that supports you. You will say, "Branches were broken off so that I might be grafted in." That is true. They were broken off because of their unbelief, but you stand fast only through faith. So do not become proud, but stand in awe. ... And even the others *[Jewish peoples]*, if they do not persist in their unbelief, will be grafted in *[by accepting Yahshua as their Messiah and applying His blood for the redemption of their sins]*, for God has the power to graft them in again. ... Lest you be wise in your own conceits, I want you to understand this mystery, brethren: a hardening has come upon part of Israel *[the part here is referring to Jews who have rejected the Gospel message about Jesus Christ (Yahshua Messiah) being the true Messiah because it has been presented incorrectly by people who do not keep the Sabbath and Torah and because they have been taught by the teachers of Rabbinical Judaism to not believe that Jesus or Yahshua was/is the true Messiah]*, until the full number of the Gentiles come in *[meaning all non Jews who accept Yahshua as their Savior become part of Israel]*, and so all Israel will be saved; as it is written, "The Deliverer will come from Zion, He will banish *[turn away]* ungodliness from Jacob; and this will be my covenant with them when I take away their sins."

Romans 11:13-20; 23, 25-27 (RSV). *Bracketed words added for clarity.*

Concerning the gospel *they* are enemies for your sake, but concerning election *they are* beloved for the sake of the fathers. For the gifts and the calling of God *are* irrevocable. For as you were once disobedient to God, yet have now obtained mercy through their disobedience, even so these *[modern day Jewish people]* also have now been disobedient, that through the mercy shown you they also may obtain mercy *[by the properly witnessing to them with the love of Yahshua in our hearts]*.

Romans 11:28-31 (NKJV). *Bracketed words added for clarity.*

After the army of General Titus captured Jerusalem, the great temple and the city were completely leveled and literally plowed under to be left as a desolate wasteland, just as King Jesus had prophesied. The few tens of thousands of the Jewish people who survived the Roman siege were in the hill country outside of Jerusalem and throughout the land of Israel. They were Messianic Jews and non-Jews who had accepted Yahshua as their Redeemer and had believed His Word regarding the coming destruction. They were watching for the signs of the coming of the devastation and they knew to escape. So they fled for their lives and were ultimately scattered throughout the whole world.

This fleeing of the Jewish people from the land of Israel has been called the *Diaspora*. The following prophecy written by Moses in approximately 1,420 B.C., describes Almighty Yah dealing with the rebellion of the chosen people of the tribe of Judah once more. Thus saith Yahweh:

> **"... You shall be left few in number, whereas you were as the stars of heaven in multitude, because you would not obey the voice of the LORD your God." ... "Then the LORD will scatter you among all peoples, from one end of the earth to the other, and there you shall serve other gods, which neither you nor your fathers have known— wood and stone. And among those nations you shall find no rest, nor shall the sole of your foot have a resting place; but there the LORD will give you a trembling heart, failing eyes, and anguish of soul. ..."**
> Deuteronomy 28:62, 64-65 (NKJV)

This prophecy was ongoing from A.D. 70 until A.D. 1948 when the United Nations voted to accept Israel as a nation of the modern world.

The significance of all of the prophets is that they all gave prophecies that applied to their own time, and what would be the future consequences of their people if they did not change the way they lived and believed. We can certainly apply the sound advice and warnings from the prophets of old to our lives today. What is most important for us today is that mixed in with the prophecies of their era are many prophecies that are for this, the last generation, and the second coming of the Messiah. Having a brief understanding of what has been happening to Yahweh's chosen people for the past 3,800 years, will help us to better understand the events that are happening now, in the future in Israel, and the world as a whole.

The Jewish race of people has suffered immensely for the past 1,900-plus years in many countries where they have settled to make their homes. Until 1948, they truly did not have a place to rest the soles of their feet and have experienced much anguish. They have often been the scapegoats in many societies where the economies were failing. This happened in Germany in the 1930s as Nazism began to rule and rise in power, and I believe it will happen again in this last generation. The anti-Semitic rationale and evil justification for mistreatment has been that the Jews must be blamed for crucifying Yahshua, the Messiah. *This is so wrong.* All of us who are not Jews must repent and seek God's forgiveness for these sins that we and our ancestors may have committed in the name of Christianity with false claims and persecutions.

Throughout the past thirty-five centuries of the repeated cycles of being captured and taken away, experiencing persecution, and being brought back into the Promised Land, Almighty Yah has kept the Jewish people, as He promised He would do, because He is not a man that He can lie, and He always keeps His covenants.

I provided the brief history lesson on the past few pages to bring you to the next few prophecies that confirm we are in the last generation.

Yet for all that, when they are in the land of their enemies, I will not cast them away, nor shall I abhor them, to utterly destroy them and break my covenant with them; for I *am* the LORD their God.
Leviticus 26:44 (NKJV).

As much as Satan has wanted to completely destroy Jews and Christians, Yahweh has not and will not allow it. Just as Yahshua, the voice of Father Yahweh, gave that prophecy to Moses that He would not cast away the Jewish people to be utterly destroyed, He also gave prophecies to other prophets regarding the re-gathering of the Jewish people one last time to become a nation again. It is written:

... that the LORD your God will bring you back from captivity, and have compassion on you, and gather you again from all the nations where the LORD your God has scattered you. ... Then the LORD your God will bring you to the land which your fathers possessed, and you shall possess it. He will prosper you and multiply you more than your fathers.
Deuteronomy 30:3, 5 (NJKV)

Behold, I will bring them from the north country *[Russia]*, and gather them from the ends of the earth ... They shall come with weeping, and with supplications I will lead them. ... "Hear the word of the LORD, O nations, and declare *it* to the isles afar off, and say, 'He who scattered

Israel will gather him, and keep him as a shepherd does his flock.' "
Jeremiah 31:8-10 (NKJV). *Bracketed words added for clarity.*

Therefore say, 'Thus says the Lord GOD: "Although I have cast them far off among the Gentiles, and although I have scattered them among the countries, yet shall I be a little sanctuary for them among the countries, yet I shall be a little sanctuary for them in the countries where they have gone." ' Therefore say, 'Thus says the Lord GOD: "I will gather you from the peoples, assemble you from the countries where you have been scattered, and I will give you the land of Israel." '
Ezekiel 11:16-17 (NKJV)

For I will take you from among the nations, gather you out of all countries, and bring you into your own land.
Ezekiel 36:24 (NKJV)

"Now learn this parable from the fig tree: When its branch has already become tender and puts forth leaves, you know that summer *is* near. So you also, when you see all these things, know that it *[the second coming of King Yahshua and the end of the last generation of this age]* is near—at the doors! Assuredly, I say to you, this generation will by no means pass away till all these things take place."
Matthew 24:32-34 (NKJV). *Bracketed words added for clarity.*

In saying all of these things, our Master Yahshua is including the Jews becoming a nation of people again on the land that God gave them through His covenant with Abraham nearly four thousand years ago. These amazing prophecies, along with the whole chapter of Ezekiel 37, are the most profound prophecies of our time. They are being fulfilled in this generation by many Jewish brothers and sisters, and also by many non-Jewish believers in Messiah who have come to realize that they are now grafted into the Olive tree and are Messianic Israelites being drawn by Elohim back to the Promised Land to restore the twelve tribes of Israel.

The following historical information is from the 1,878 years that the Jewish people were scattered throughout the world. The Jews were in a three-year war with Rome, called the Bar Kokhba Revolt, that ended in the year A.D. 135. After the Roman victory, the Caesar Hadrian <u>changed the name of the land from Judaea to Palestine</u>. The original land that God gave to Abraham and his descendants was to remain under the control of the Roman Empire until A.D. 611. The Persians overtook the land for a few years, and then the armies of Saladin took control in 637.

During the occupation of the Saladin, a self-proclaimed prophet named Mohammad created the religion of Islam. He wrote his book called the *Koran*. The religion of Islam grew very rapidly among the Arab people and today is one of the three major religions of the world. It is very sad and tragic that there are professing Muslims today, although they are a minority, who are committed to *Jihad*. *Jihad* means "holy war," and in the minds of the fanatics who are following the instruction from the *Koran*, it is their justification for destroying Israel, the Jewish people, and all who will not convert to Islam.

The Crusaders from Europe captured Jerusalem from the Muslims in 1099, and then lost it to them in 1187. The Ottoman Turks defeated the Muslims in 1291 and held the land in their possession until 1917. The British Army, under the command of General Allenby, captured Jerusalem from the Turks without firing a shot.

Persecution of the Jewish people in Russia during in the late 1800s led to the creation of a Jewish movement in Eastern Europe called *Zionism*. The Zionists worked hard to convince the leaders of the free nations of Western Europe to assist the Jewish people in reclaiming the land that belonged to their forefathers and that was promised to Yahweh's chosen people for all time. The first Jewish settlers began work in the barren marshlands and arid areas in 1880. The land was legally purchased from Arab owners who were not using the wasteland, except for some nomadic herding. By 1900, there were approximately 5,000 Jews back in the Promised Land. By 1917, during World War I, the population had increased to nearly 100,000 Jews. The Turks and Arabs were trying to establish control over this fast-growing area but were overwhelmed by the British.

The Balfour Declaration was the official document that was initiated in 1918 to proclaim that the small, insignificant, newly named area called *Palestine* had the approval of the British Empire to be a place where the Jewish people could move to and be protected. This led to a great influx of Jewish people into Palestine and increased tensions there since many Arabs were moving into the area also.

During the year 1939, England was being drawn into World War II and was weary of trying to keep a peaceful resolve between the Arabs and the Jews. Much of the conflict was due to the Arab control of the eastern part of Jerusalem, particularly the Temple Mount on the hill called Mount Moriah. This is where the followers of Mohammed built their al-Aqsa Mosque called the Dome of the Rock in approximately A.D. 660. The dome is the gold-covered, eight-sided structure seen on news reports or magazine pictures of the temple mount area that is above the Wailing Wall in the old section of Jerusalem. The mosque is a sacred place for Muslims to pray together. It is built on the site of a rock that is believed to be, according to legend, the rock on which Mohammed stood before he was taken up into heaven. This is the third holiest mosque for the people of the Islamic religion. Its location is beside the original foundations of the first and second temples of the Jewish people. This small, flat piece of ground is the most holy and sacred place on the face of the earth for the Jewish people.

It was during 1939 that England issued a document called the *White Paper of 1939* that was in favor of Arab independence and control over Palestine due to the greater influx of Arabs into the area.

The evil, horrible holocaust of World War II resulted in the murder of more than six million Jews and nearly that many Christians and others by the Nazis. This caused an even greater influx of Jews into Palestine, increasing the conflict in the already troubled area. The result was that, in 1947, England withdrew all support from the region and completely abandoned the Jews, leaving them to go it alone. This caused so many problems that the United Nations moved in to stabilize and divide the area. The Jews, as a result, elected leaders in their section and began to petition for statehood. After a lot of work and effort between the early Zionist leaders, the leaders of the United States, Russia, and the United Nations, Israel was accepted into the United Nations as a newly formed nation and officially became a nation on May 14, 1948. Israel was then a recognized nation with its own government and flag. This was, and is today, the single most significant fulfillment of prophecy in over 1,900 years.

It is truly a miracle of God that a nation and race of people could be utterly destroyed, with only a small number of surviving people scattered throughout the nations of the world, and then to have their descendents become re-established as a nation on the same land as their ancestors nearly 1,900 years later with their language and customs intact. This phenomenon could only have happened by the power and will of God (Elohim) Almighty. It is simply amazing and incredible!

I will now show with prophetic Scriptures, that Almighty Yah by His divine sovereignty, planned exactly in history the month and year that He desired for Israel to be reestablished as a nation. It is written:

> ... then say to them, Thus says the LORD God: I will take the people of
> Israel from the nations among which they have gone, and will gather
> them from every quarter, and bring them to their own land. I will make
> them one nation in the land, on the mountains of Israel; and one king
> shall be king over them all. Never again shall they be two nations, and
> never again shall they be divided into two kingdoms.
> Ezekiel 37:21-22 (NRSV)

Now here are the Scriptures that establish the timing of when
Almighty Yah in His Master Plan established that He would bring them
back into their own land. It is written:

> If you continue hostile to me, and will not obey me, I will continue to
> plague you sevenfold for your sins.
> Leviticus 26:21 (NRSV)

> Then lie on your left side, and place the punishment of the house of
> Israel upon it; you shall bear their punishment for the number of the
> days that you lie there. For I assign to you a number of days, three hun-
> dred ninety days, equal to the number of the years of their punishment;
> and so you shall bear the punishment of the house of Israel. When you
> have completed these, you shall lie down a second time, but on your
> right side, and bear the punishment of the house of Judah; forty days I
> assign you, one day for each year.
> Ezekiel 4:4-6 (NRSV)

You may be asking yourself, "What is this guy trying to explain with
these Scriptures that really don't make much sense?" Well, they don't
make sense until you look at them as pieces to a puzzle. Separated, they
are meaningless, but together, they reveal the picture.

The punishment that Almighty Yah was administering to the nation of
Israel was to be measured as each day that Ezekiel lay on his side, which
represented a year of time. He was to lie on his left side for 390 days, which
equals 390 years for the House of Israel (ten northern tribes that are currently, for the most part, still lost among the nations), and 40 days, which
equals 40 years for the House of Judah that, for the most part, is now

restored on the land. So 390 plus 40 equals 430 years times the seven times factor, as recorded in Leviticus 26, that Israel must pay for her sins, equals 2,520 years. The ancient Jewish calendar has 360 days a year, so 360 times 2,520 equals 907,200 days. Now we convert the days to our modern calendar by dividing 907,200 days by 365 and we have 2,485 years and 5 months.

Ezekiel was a prophet of Israel during some of the 70 years that the southern tribes of Judah were in captivity in Babylon. The key in knowing that what I am explaining here applies to the re-establishing of Israel as a nation for the last time that would come about to clearly establish the beginning of the last generation is: **"and never again shall they be divided into two kingdoms"** (Ezekiel 37:21-22 NRSV), and some verses I will include shortly.

The year from which we begin to count is 538 B.C. This is the year that King Cyrus, the Persian king who conquered the Babylonians—the empire that had conquered the Jews seventy years before—agreed to free the Jews so they could return to their native land Israel and rebuild their temple for worship. They did return and rebuilt the temple and the nation and remained intact until A.D. 70, when they were destroyed by the Romans and dispersed again into the nations of the world. That event was prophesied by Yahshua as recorded in Luke 19:41 through 44.

From A.D. 70 for another 1,878 years, the Jewish people were persecuted and dispersed throughout the earth from their native homeland nation. So we subtract 537 years from 538 B.C., which brings us to the end of the year 1 B.C. There is no zero year, so we count forward to the year 1948 and the fifth month of May. Amazingly, May 14, 1948, is the year the House of Judah part of Israel was returned to the covenant-promised land for the last time, exactly 2,485 years, 5 months forward from the year 538 B.C.

Since 1948, the Israelis have fought and, with God's help, won five wars against the surrounding countries. The most significant war, in relation to prophecy, was the Six-Day War in June 1967. During that campaign, the Israeli army expanded the area of the nation of Israel to include the land to the Jordan River that is called the West Bank, land in the northeast called the Golan Heights that had been claimed by Syria, and a narrow strip of land on the southwestern side by the Mediterranean Sea called Gaza. The new cease-fire border lines brought the nation of Israel a step closer to establishing the original dimensions of the land that God had given to His servant Abraham and Abraham's descendants.

For a few hours of the war, some of the Israeli soldiers were actually in control of the Temple Mount. This was the first time in over 1,900 years that any Jewish people had been able to stand on the most holy place on the earth. It has been recorded that the men wept like babies and were in awe. Their capture of the Temple Mount was short-lived. When the Syrian army learned of the occupation of that part of Jerusalem, the fighting became terribly intense, and the Israeli soldiers had to pull back. Since that time, the Jewish people have not been allowed to worship on the Temple Mount, the most sacred place on the earth to them. The closest point to the Temple Mount where they have freedom to go is the old western foundation wall, called the Wailing Wall.

A more recent war was in the summer of 2006 when Israel fought for their right to exist against the terrorist organization Hezbollah that is financed and equipped by the terrorist governments of Iran and Syria. The Israeli army defeated the Islamic terrorists and destroyed many of their missile launch sites and underground tunnels. Within six months, the Iranian- and Syrian-funded and supplied Hezbollah army was and is prepared to engage in the next war, which, as of the publishing of this book, has not yet started. I believe the next war that Israel must fight will escalate and be full blown and with several of the Islamic Arab nations. There is more on this in Chapter Ten.

The reason I have included these few pages of Israel's history is to help the reader understand the importance of the Temple Mount to the Jewish and Arab/Islamic people. This very small piece of real estate in Jerusalem is the most significantly important parcel of land in the world as it relates to end-time Bible prophecy. This bit of history has been included to also help you have some appreciation for how difficult the struggle has been and continues to be for the Jewish people to be able to survive on their small piece of the planet. They are completely surrounded by the Arab Muslim nations of people who hate them and are committed to wiping them off the face of the earth, as prophesied in Psalm 83.

In the New Testament, or new covenant, the Gospel writers Matthew, Mark, and Luke recorded many prophesies that were spoken by our Master Yahshua Messiah about the end of time. Thus saith the Lord:

"Therefore when you see the *abomination of desolation* [horrible, profane, sacrilegious being] standing in the holy place, then let those who are in Judea flee to the mountains.
Matthew 24:15-16 (NKJV). *Bracketed words added for clarity.*

The evil being that Christ referred to is the anti-Christ, or beast, who will be the human incarnation of Satan, just as our Yahshua was the human incarnation of Almighty God the Father Yahweh. In order for the third temple to be built on the Temple Mount in Jerusalem, Israel would have to be an established nation; this happened in 1948 to mark the beginning of the last generation. The "holy place" that Yahshua was referring to is the third and final temple that the Jewish people will build toward the end of this last generation on the famous Temple Mount where the Muslim Dome of the Rock is now located.

Much of the high-level negotiations that took place in the summer of 2006 were related to the Israeli government, the Hamas-led Palestine Liberation Organization (PLO), and delegates of the European Union, including the United States and the "Quartet," working out the details for President Bush's "Roadmap to Peace." These negotiations have been taking place for years in an attempt to bring about a settlement, so that the PLO will be granted enough land to have their own recognized nation and for the Jews to be granted the area of the Temple Mount where the first and second temples stood in order to build the third temple.

Earlier I made reference to the seventh week of Daniel's prophecy. This seventh week will be the final seven years of this age that will culminate with the coming of our Judge and King Yahshua in His glory. The significance of the beginning of the seventh week of Daniel is that it begins precisely when the Jewish leaders of Israel, along with key world leaders including the anti-Messiah, sign a peace treaty that is to, supposedly, bring a lasting peace between Israel and the surrounding Arab nations. This treaty will no doubt follow on the heels of an invasion from Russia and China that will lead to world war three. The next world war will bring the world as a whole together. They will be begging for peace and a world leader who can produce it. This amazing political leader will come on the scene with great deception, persuasion, financial backing, and charisma. He will be speaking great lies that will influence most of the world's population into accepting him. Most of the Jewish people will believe that he is the prophesied Messiah because he will be able to bring peace to their country and enable them to build the long-awaited temple on the holy Temple Mount. This will enable the Jews to begin having animal sacrifices in their temple, which has not happened in over nineteen hundred years.

I have referred to the treaty as the final one because the preliminary one was signed in September of 1993 at the White House in Washington,

D.C. Signers were Yasser Arafat from the PLO, and the former Prime Minister Yekshok Rabin, from the nation of Israel. This was an historical treaty, which laid the groundwork for the resolve of Israel, Jerusalem, and a new Palestinian State.

It was continued with Oslo I and II. Oslo II was to bring the final resolve during the summer of 1999. Some Bible prophecy students thought the treaty of 1993 was the one to start the countdown of the seventieth week of Daniel. It is clearly not. The final treaty that kicks off the final seven-year clock and countdown happens after Russia and its unified coalition of Arab nations join forces. This group is bent on taking Israel by force, which they will not be able to do. I believe at that time they will be able to take out the nation of America, which I believe is Babylon the great. There will be more on this later.

The final seven years begin when a new Palestinian state is established at the expense of many Jews who will be forced to leave their homes and businesses in the West Bank area of Judea and Samaria, as has already happened in Gaza during August 2005. When the final status of Israel and Jerusalem is recognized and the people of Israel are promised peace and security, then you can expect to witness the third temple being erected on the Temple Mount. These events precede the rule of the anti-Messiah beast that begins the Great Tribulation three and one-half years later.

There are other prophecies that we can see being fulfilled that reveal that we are in the last generation. One of our Master's closest disciples was the Apostle John, who wrote the *Gospel of John*, the *Epistles of John*, and the book of *Revelation*. These writings contain the following prophecies and were written about 1,905 years ago while John was in prison on the Isle of Patmos.

The sixth angel poured his bowl on the great river Euphrates, and its water was dried up in order to prepare the way for the kings from the east.
Revelation 16:12 (NRSV)

Prepared for what?

Then the sixth angel blew his trumpet, and I heard a voice from the four horns of the golden altar before God, saying to the sixth angel who had the trumpet, "Release the four angels who are bound at the great river

Euphrates." So the four angels were released, who had been held ready for the hour, the day, the month, and the year, to kill a third of humankind. The number of the troops of the cavalry was two hundred million; I heard their number.
Revelation 9:13-16 (NRSV)

The significance of these two prophecies is that, in the winter of 1990, the government of Turkey completed a major dam project on the Euphrates River for the purpose of creating a large reservoir for providing water to several cities.

The January 13, 1990, issue of the *Indianapolis Star*: "By damming up this great river, which is 1,700 miles long and quite wide, the Turkish government can basically allow the riverbed downstream to dry up if they choose or are forced to do so."

It is also possible that God may supernaturally cause the riverbed to dry up so the great army may cross. This happened before when God parted the waters at the Red Sea in order for the nearly two million Hebrew people and their livestock to cross and flee from the pursuing Egyptian army. This miraculous account is recorded in the 14th chapter of Exodus of the old covenant.

The powerful Chinese communist leader, Mao Tse-Tung, before he died in 1976, boasted in his diary that China could assemble an army of 200 million men. These two realistic scenarios could never have been possible until this generation. Why would the Chinese have an interest in taking control of the tiny land of Israel? I truly do not know, and I don't know if the huge army described is actually Chinese. Perhaps the prophecy is describing a huge army of Muslims from the many millions in the Arab nations who will attempt to fulfill their desires that they have conspired as recorded in Psalms 83:4.

Whatever the nationality of the army, is doesn't really matter. It states that out of their horses mouths (tanks and war machines) came fire, smoke, and brimstone (huge explosions as in nuclear) and that by the fire, smoke, and brimstone, a third of the population of mankind will be destroyed. I believe this ties in with the prophecies of Ezekiel 38 and 39 when Russia and China and a few other countries unite to take over Israel and America. I believe they will succeed in destroying the United States, but will be super-naturally defeated by Almighty Yah, as recorded in Ezekiel 39.

It is also interesting to know that in 1979, the government of China completed, with the assistance of other adjacent governments, what is called the Karakoram Highway. (*End Times Digest*, March 1980 issue, ppg. 7-8.) This super long highway runs from western China through northern Pakistan, through central Afghanistan, through northern Iran, into northern Iraq to the Euphrates River, just south of the border of Turkey. This highway was built as a military highway and not for commerce because it winds through desolate, rural areas of these countries away from cities. With the Karakoram highway in place, it is now possible to transport a 200 million-man army from China to the Middle East. This has not been possible in the history of the world until this generation.

In two other chapters of the book of Revelation, there are prophecies that refer to the gathering of the armies of the world to wage war against the coming of the Messiah.

And they [*spirits of demons*] **gathered them together to the place called in Hebrew, Armageddon.**
Revelation 16:16 (NKJV). *Bracketed words added for clarity.*

The word *Armageddon* means "the mountain of Megiddo." This mountain is located about 50 miles north of Jerusalem and is across the great plain of Jezreel from the Golan Heights on the southeastern Syrian border. This area of northern Israel is where the ultimate confrontation of the armies and leaders of this world, along with Satan and his host of fallen angels and demons, will attempt to destroy King Jesus (Yahshua) Messiah and His great army of mighty angels as they approach planet earth from heaven.

Then I saw heaven opened, and there was a white horse! Its rider is called Faithful and True, and in righteousness He judges and makes war. His eyes are like a flame of fire, and on His head are many diadems; and He has a name inscribed that no one knows but himself. He is clothed in a robe dipped in blood, and His name is called The Word of God. And the armies of heaven, wearing fine linen, white and pure, were following Him on white horses. ... Then I saw the beast and the kings of the earth with their armies gathered to make war against the rider on the horse and against His army.
Revelation 19:11-14, 19 (NRSV)

This incredible confrontation of good and evil is the second coming of King Yahshua to this earth. At that time He will completely destroy Satan's physical and spiritual kingdoms on this earth and will establish His Kingdom on earth as it is in heaven.

The material in the past few pages shows some of the events that have been happening in Israel over the last few years that clearly confirm we are in the last generation and, in fact, are nearing the end of the last generation leading up to the time of the great tribulation. Believers in Yahshua are called to be watchmen, bondservants, and overcomers until the very end. In the Book of Daniel, we learn an important prophecy.

"But you, Daniel, shut up the words, and seal the book until the time of the end; many shall run to and fro, and knowledge shall increase."
Daniel 12:4 (NKJV)

Yahweh was telling His prophet Daniel that understanding of the prophecies would not make sense until the time of the end when people would travel all over the place and knowledge would increase tremendously.

Before the industrial revolution of the early eighteen hundreds, the modes of transportation were as they had been for thousands of years. Now, at the beginning of the third millennium, people travel across the oceans in hours, humans have been to the moon several times, there is a working space station orbiting our planet, there are satellites in the heavens relaying information throughout the world in seconds, the every-day miracles of modern medicine are incredible, there are massive computers with the capacity to maintain an active file on every person on this earth, and on and on are the advances in technology. The computer experts estimate that the first time the total knowledge of the world doubled was around the year 1900. Since then, the total knowledge of the world has been doubling at a faster rate and in a shorter number of years. Presently, with the assistance of computers and the Internet, it is estimated that all the total knowledge in the world will double again in three years or less.

"… And I will give *power* to my two witnesses, and they will prophesy one thousand two hundred and sixty days, clothed in sackcloth." … When they finish their testimony, the beast that ascends out of the bottomless pit will make war against them, overcome them, and kill them. And their dead bodies *will lie* in the street of the great city

[Jerusalem)] **which spiritually is called Sodom and Egypt, where also our Lord was crucified. Then** *those* **from the peoples, tribes, tongues, and nations will see their dead bodies three-and-a-half days, and not allow their dead bodies to be put into graves.**

Revelation 11:3, 7-9 (NKJV). *Bracketed words added for clarity.*

The significance of these prophecies is that Almighty Yah is going to empower two men to be His main messengers during the last years of the tribulation (the 70th week of Daniel). I personally believe that the two men will be representatives imparted with the spiritual mantles of Moses and Elijah, representing the law and the prophets. Moses and Elijah were the two individuals who were with Yahshua during His transfiguration as recorded in Matthew 17 and the other Gospels. I also believe the two witnesses are Jewish and Gentile believers who make up the restored two houses of Israel, Ephraim and Judah. These two men, protected by God, will proclaim the coming kingdom of Messiah and continue to warn the people of the earth not to worship the beast (Satan in the flesh). At the end of their three and one half years of ministry, Almighty Yah will allow them to be killed by the antichrist. The prophecy tells us that the inhabitants of the earth will see their dead bodies. For centuries, people who have studied the end-time prophecies have tried to understand how people in different locations of the world would be able to see the dead bodies of the two witnesses. It was impossible until this generation of satellite television.

Another prophecy that clearly reveals we are in the last generation is that the numbers of individuals proclaiming to be Jesus Christ will increase, obviously on a much larger scale. It is written:

Now as He sat on the Mount of Olives, the disciples came to Him privately, saying, "Tell us, when will these things be? And what *will* **be the sign of Your coming, and of the end of the age?" And Jesus answered and said to them: "Take heed that no one deceives you. For many will come in My name, saying, 'I am the Christ,' and will deceive many.**

Matthew 24:3-5 (NKJV)

On August 25, 2006, as this book is being written, an individual named Dr. Jose Luis de Jesus Miranda proclaimed himself to be Jesus Christ on the NBC *Today* show. This man has a cult ministry called "Growing in Grace." His web site is www.growingingracespanish.com

where you can see and hear the interview. It is truly eye opening. This sad, deceived man is deceiving millions of people currently in thirty countries. His following and financial support are increasing very rapidly due to their large cable network and TV programs, through which he is programming people who don't believe the truth in the Holy Scriptures. There will be more imposters coming out right up to the last few years of this generation when the final, ultimate deceiver—the incarnation of Satan himself—asserts his power over most of the people of the earth and proclaims himself to be God Almighty, enforcing the worship of all people.

The following are other prophesies that relate to the capabilities of technology and computers in this last generation.

And he deceives those who dwell on the earth by those signs which he was granted to do in the sight of the beast, telling those who dwell on the earth to make an image to the beast who was wounded by the sword and lived. He was granted *power* to give breath to the image of the beast, that the image of the beast should both speak and cause as many as would not worship the image of the beast to be killed. He causes all, both small and great, rich and poor, free and slave, to receive a mark on their right hand or on their foreheads, and that no one may buy or sell except one who has the mark or the name of the beast, or the number of his name. Here is wisdom. Let him who has understanding calculate the number of the beast, for it is the number of a man: His number *is* 666.
Revelation 13:14-18 (NKJV)

The initiation of a single, worldwide economic system with the capability of tracking every person on this planet has never been possible until the last few years. I have seen copies of photographs of a small, clear plastic implant the size of a grain of rice that has been developed and is currently being tested on humans. The implant can be inserted under the skin quickly and with little discomfort. Contained inside the implant is a microcomputer chip and micro transmitter that can be scanned from outside of the body so that the person can be connected to their computer file in the huge, already-existing computer system. This system will enable the people of the world to have a cashless society. It is interesting to note that the only places the researchers have found that the implants work properly, is on the hand and the forehead. There will be more on this topic later.

We are living in a time that has been called the "new world order."

Former President George H. Bush, Sr., coined this phrase when he stated, "Iraq is the first test for the new world order." He was referring to the unification of the armies of many countries and the support of most of the world in the war against Iraq to liberate Kuwait. The agenda of the movers and shakers who are bringing in the new world order is to unite the governments, religions, and economies of the world so that there can be a more peaceful, manageable, co-existence of the human race. The efforts for unity are not all being pursued by any one group but by many individuals and organizations simultaneously. There will be more on the mark of the beast and the new world order in Chapter Seven.

Another proof that we are in the last generation is the obvious increase of violence, hate crimes, disrespect for the sanctity of human life, the love of self, the love of wealth, hedonism, and evil in general. It is written:

You must understand this, that in the last days distressing times will come. For people will be lovers of themselves, lovers of money, boasters, arrogant, abusive, disobedient to their parents, ungrateful, unholy, inhuman, implacable, slanderers, profligates, brutes, haters of good, treacherous, reckless, swollen with conceit, lovers of pleasure rather than lovers of God, holding to the outward form of godliness but denying its power. Avoid them!"
2 Timothy 3:1-5 (NRSV)

Never in the past 500 years have we seen such a downward spiral of the morals of people throughout the world as we see in our societies today. Some people are doing such evil things to other people that it is incomprehensible how they can do these things and live with themselves.

In the Gospel of Matthew, our Lord Jesus Messiah spoke a significant end time prophecy. Thus says the Lord:

And this gospel of the kingdom will be preached in all the world as a witness to all the nations, and then the end will come.
Matthew 24:14 (NKJV)

Christian organizations are pressing harder that ever to reach all peoples in all countries throughout the world. The Gideon's are distributing *King James Version* Bibles in over 177 countries at an amazing rate of one million Bibles every six days. Many large evangelistic crusades are taking place in countries where literally tens of thousands of people are accepting Jesus as their Savior and Lord. Even in communist countries such as China, there are great underground church movements to reach the lost and those who have never heard of the wonderful love of our Master Yahshua. Wherever there are catastrophes, such the tsunami in Indonesia in 2005 that killed an estimated 200,000 people, the death and destruction from Hurricane Katrina, and the long running famines, such as the one in Ethiopia, there are Christian organizations. Ministries such as Samaritan's Purse are usually the first workers on the scene, feeding and giving aid to the people. And as they meet their physical needs, they teach them the Gospel of the risen Savior and give them Holy Bibles in their own language to meet their spiritual needs. This tremendous out-reach of the preaching and teaching of our Messiah Yahshua's coming kingdom throughout the world is more proof that, as we have begun a new century and a new millennium, we are living in the last years of the last generation.

A very significant part of the end-time message of Father Yahweh's Kingdom coming to this earth is the universal restoration of all things before King Jesus comes visibly in the air. It is written:

Repent therefore, and turn to God so that your sins may be wiped out, so that times of refreshing may come from the presence of the Lord, and that He may send Messiah appointed for you, that is, Jesus, who must remain in heaven until the time of universal restoration that God announced long ago through His holy prophets.
Acts 3:19-21 (NRSV)

The Apostle Peter spoke these words, and, indeed, the restoration began as the first-century church followed in the footsteps of Messiah. By the second century, however, false doctrine began to enter the congregations, and the true Messianic Israelite teachings and observances were watered down and mingled with the teachings and observances of the pagan world that I have already covered in Chapter Four. In this, the last generation, Father Yahweh's end-time restoration has clearly begun in the rebuilding of the Tabernacle of David as recorded by the prophet Amos. It is written:

"For surely I will command *[draw them by the power of Holy Spirit]*, **and sift the house of Israel among the nations** *[cause all those Jews and non-Jews that are grafted into the Olive tree by accepting Yahshua]*, **as grain**

is sifted in a sieve; yet not the smallest grain shall fall to the ground. All the sinners of My people shall die by the sword, who say, 'The calamity [the great tribulation] **shall not overtake nor confront us** [because they believe they are going to be raptured out from the earth].' **On that day I will raise up the tabernacle of David, which has fallen down, and repair its damages; I will raise up its ruins, and rebuild it as in the days of old..."**
Amos 9:9-11 (NKJV). *Bracketed words added for clarity.*

These prophecies speak to us of modern-day Israelites coming to the revelation of who we are in Messiah. We realize how we have been deceived by many centuries of traditional teachings and customs from churches and synagogues that had their origin in the early Church of Rome. Remember that according to Romans 11 when the vast majority of the Jewish people of the first century did not accept Jesus as the Messiah, Father Yahweh made a provision for any person who would accept Yahshua (Jesus), and what He accomplished in His crucifixion, to be able to be grafted into the Olive tree, or family of Elohim (Yah Almighty), so that we can be effective witnesses of our heavenly Father's love, truth, mercy, and grace.

The Tabernacle of David has to do with the children of Israel following the instructions that King Yahshua gave to Moses that explains the Ten Commandments, the keeping of Father Yahweh's appointed feast gatherings, and dietary and hygiene instructions. If you remember from a few pages back, I covered the division of the nation Israel toward the end of King Solomon's reign. The ten northern tribes are known in Scripture by many titles, such as the "ten lost tribes of Israel," "House of Israel," but most importantly, "Ephraim."

Before the people of Ephraim were captured by the Assyrians in 722 B.C., they had begun to pull away from the instructions of Yahweh and the Tabernacle of David worship. The House of Israel had begun to accept some of the customs and traditions of the nearby pagan nations, which made a blend of the truth of Yahweh and the falsehood of the pagans. Their spiritual adultery was the cause of their downfall. Almighty Yah allowed them to be taken into slavery, assimilated into the other nations of the world, and to lose their identity in Yahweh. Our Creator is a very jealous Creator and requires that we be loyal and committed to Him only, as the First Commandment states, through relationship with Him by His Son Yahshua through the indwelling of *Ruach haKodesh* (His Holy Spirit).

You and I are living in the most awesome time in all of history because Father Yahweh is calling us and restoring us back into covenant relationship with Himself. By our desire to truly seek and love our Creator, Savior, and King Eternal with all of our being, our hearts are being spiritually circumcised and sanctified. It is written:

> **"Behold, the days are coming, says the Lord, when I will make a new covenant with the House of Israel and with the House of Judah—not according to the covenant that I made with their fathers in the day** *that* **I took them by the hand to lead them out of the land of Egypt** *[which represents sin and idolatry]***, My covenant which they broke, though I was a husband to them, says the LORD. But this** *is* **the covenant that I will make with the house of Israel after those days, says the LORD: I will put My Law** *[instructions from the* Torah*]* **in their minds, and write it on their hearts; and I will be their God, and they shall be My people ..."**
> Jeremiah 31:31-33 (NKJV). *Bracketed words added for clarity.*

How amazing is our Heavenly Father's love for us. Are you hungry for a deeper relationship with the Creator of the universe, the one true God of Abraham, Isaac, and Jacob? Then call upon the name of His Son Yahshua; hear and do His instructions; be free to talk to Him and worship Him anytime through the indwelling of His Spirit of Holiness. HalleluYah!!!

The following three chapters will address several of these prophecies and the current events that apply. By studying prophecies from both the old and new sections of the Scriptures and applying them to developments in the world, we can have a more clear picture of the great showdown battle that is being played out, and will continue to be played out here on planet earth through the people of this world in day to day events. King Yahshua, with the great power of His Holy Spirit Who gives truth, goodness, and light battles on one side. Satan is on the other with his powers of deception, evil, and darkness. There is a day coming, however, when King Yahshua will return with His great army of warrior angels to rescue His bride and pour out His wrath on those who have rejected Him. Those who have made the terrible decision to place their allegiance with the anti-Messiah have been deceived and are worshipping his master, Satan, instead. Please, dear reader, don't be deceived. Study and know the truth found in Almighty Yah's Holy Scriptures. When you know and live the truth, the truth will be make you free.

꙼

7

THE COMING OF MESSIAH, LION OF JUDAH

O n the first pages of this book—pages iii and iv—I referenced verses of prophecies from Revelation 19 and Matthew 24 that describe the coming of King Yahshua, the Messiah. In this chapter, I will present a summary interpretation of this great book of prophecy, along with some relevant prophecy verses from other books of God's Word as they apply to the coming of Messiah at the end of this, the last, generation.

I must reiterate what I have said in other parts of this book, that no one has the complete, correct interpretations of the entire end-of-time prophecies, nor do we have all of the answers to all of the questions regarding the end of this age. This book is based on many years of study, research, and most importantly, the inspiration of Holy Spirit. To the one true God Who is One God, Almighty Yah, Father, Son, and Holy Spirit be the glory!

The book of Revelation is complex and one that most preachers and Bible teachers avoid. Many hundreds of pages could be, and have been, written with interpretations of this one book. There are many books in print that make attempts to explain every detail. I have chosen to express my understanding of this great book, along with key verses of prophecy from other books of the Bible, in a brief summary as it applies to the great manifest coming in the air of our King, Savior, and Judge, Yahshua Messiah.

It may seem that I jump around in this chapter a lot, but stay with it. In order to see all art subjects of a large stained glass window clearly, we must back away a few feet from it in order to take it all in. That's much the way it is in making sense of the book of Revelation. In order to have a clear picture of what is to take place and what has taken place already, one must connect the prophecies that apply from all of the other books of the Bible.

My main goal in writing this book, as I have previously stated, is to help you understand the necessity of accepting Jesus (Yahshua) Messiah as your Creator, Savior, and Master, and to live in personal covenant relationship with Him. My secondary goal is to help you to have a better understanding from Yah's Word, by revelation from His Holy Spirit, of His purpose and plan for the final years of this age and how you can be used by the one true God to be a blessing to others. I believe it's not important that we understand every little detail of the many prophecies about the coming of King Yahshua, but that we have a good understanding of Father Yahweh's overall plan and how He would have us to live as we face the end of this world as we know it. I encourage you to open your Bible, read, and study each verse from it as you are reading along in this book. It will be a blessing to you and will help your understanding. Please pray and ask Holy Spirit to help you comprehend the truth in Yah's Holy Word.

The English word *revelation* is derived from the Latin word *revelatio* and the Greek word *apokalupsis*. Both words mean "disclosure of that which was previously hidden or unknown." As I stated on page two of the Introduction, the writers to whom Yahweh gave the prophecies did not understand most or any of what they were recording because it was meant for a time in the far distant future when humankind would be extremely technologically advanced. Only people living in this time, the last generation, can understand the prophecies that apply to the last generation. As it is written:

> **"But you, Daniel, shut up the words, and seal the book until the time of the end; many shall run to and fro, and knowledge shall increase." ...**
> **And he said, "Go *your way*, Daniel, for the words *are* closed up and sealed till the time of the end. Many shall be purified, made white, and refined, but the wicked shall do wickedly; and none of the wicked shall understand, but the wise shall understand. ..."**
> Daniel 12:4, 9-10 (NKJV)

Many of the prophecies that are recorded in the book of Daniel relate to the same events and individuals that the prophecies in Revelation refer to. Also, many prophecies have double meanings of similar events happening at two different times in history, hundreds of years apart.

I have read and studied the book of Revelation two hundred or more times, along with many expositions and commentaries of other writers on the subject. My conclusion is that, first, it is the prophetic revealing of our Master Yahshua Messiah's coming to this planet to establish His Kingdom, and the events leading up to His coming. Second, I do not believe that all of the verses of this book are written in an exact chronological order, as most writers expressing their interpretation of the book have insisted. I'm convinced that there are several verses in different chapters describing the same event or world condition that were described in other verses in a different way. Throughout the Holy Bible, in several sections of prophecy verses, events that are to happen first are in latter verses, and events that are to happen later are in the first verses that apply to the prophecy.

Yahshua chose His apostle John, the beloved, to give the amazing visions and journeys into heaven as a witness and to record all that he experienced for the benefit of all who read and study Yah's Word. John received the visions while he was held as a prisoner of the Roman empire. He was imprisoned on an island called Patmos off the coast of Western Turkey in the Aegean Sea. Historical records indicate that John wrote the book between the years A.D. 81 and A.D. 96 during the reign of Emperor Domitian. This Caesar had sentenced John to Patmos because he was a Christian. Being a Christian during the first, second, and early part of the third centuries was against the law of the Roman empire and was often punishable by death. All of the disciples of Yahshua Messiah were murdered as martyrs for their loyalty to Messiah, except John and Judas. Judas hung himself after he realized His Master Yahshua would be put to death because of his betrayal. (See Matthew 26:47-51.) It is believed that John died of natural causes in prison.

The atrocities of martyrdom are still happening today. A conservative estimate during the year 2006 is that approximately 200,000 people worldwide were murdered because they would not renounce their love and commitment to our Lord and Master, Jesus. Most of these murders and horrible atrocities took place in the country of Sudan by the hands of demon-possessed Muslims. It is with much sadness that I state that I believe the persecution of Christians, as well as believing and non-believing Jews, will continue to increase as we draw closer to the end of this age. Satan, the devil, wants to destroy the true believers who are spreading the truth about the true Messiah. The devil also comes to kill, steal, and destroy as many non-believers as possible to prevent them from hearing the true good news message that Almighty Yah loves them and has made a way for them to have forgiveness of their sins and relationship with Him through the shed blood of Yahshua. In the final years of this age, many individuals will be murdered because they will not worship the anti-Christ beast. You will have a better understanding of this statement after reading this chapter and the next.

John recorded all that he actually saw and heard as a witness for our benefit. Verse three of Revelation Chapter One reveals that there are blessings associated with reading and obeying what is written in the book.

Blessed is the one who reads aloud the words of the prophecy, and blessed are those who hear and who keep what is written in it; for the time is near.
Revelation 1:3 (NRSV)

The visions that John experienced were profound and graphic in nature. Our Master Yahshua, one of the twenty-four elders of high position, and some of Yah's angels were showing John, in his visions and trips to heaven, the many events that would take place and the conditions of the world during the final years of human experience leading up to the Day of Yahweh, or as John worded it in Chapter One, verse 10, "the Lord's Day." He was not referring to Sunday or to Saturday, the Sabbath, but to the time period of the coming of King Yahshua to establish His Kingdom that transitions into the 1,000-year Millennium. As I stated in Chapter Five, the weekly Sabbath on Saturday is a symbolic foreshadow of the seventh one thousand year period since creation that will be the one thousand year millennium when Yahshua will rule and reign on this planet without the influence of the adversary, Satan. So John was witnessing the day of the coming of Yahshua and the conclusion of this age of the world's history as we know it.

I believe John experienced fourteen different visions. In seven, he saw things happening in heaven, and in seven he saw things happening on the earth. I also believe that he experienced these visions at different times in order for him to be able to accurately record them. The visions are what he actually saw and heard after he had been transported up to heaven, near to the throne of our Heavenly Father Yahweh. Thus saith the Lord:

Write the things which you have seen, and things which are, and the things which will take place after this.
Revelation 1:19 (NKJV)

John wrote the entire account of what he saw in the form of a long letter. He was instructed by Yahshua to send the record of the visions and prophecies to seven particular congregations, or churches, of believers that were located on the eastern coastline of the Aegean Sea, which is today western Turkey. These first century churches had been established by the apostle Paul and other disciples of Yahshua. John introduces this most amazing letter with a salutation, the Gospel message, and then a description of the coming of the King of Glory in the clouds.

> **Grace to you and peace from him who is and who was and who is to come, and from the seven spirits who are before His throne, and from Jesus Christ** [*Yahshua Messiah*] **the faithful witness, the first-born of the dead, and the ruler of kings on the earth. To Him Who loves us and has freed us from our sins by His blood and made us a kingdom, priests to His God and Father, to Him be glory and dominion for ever and ever. Amen. Behold, He is coming with the clouds, and every eye will see Him, every one who pierced Him** [*not the actual people responsible for having Him put to death, but the Jewish race in general who are living at the time of His coming in the air; when they look upon Him, and mourn for Him and realize that He is the true Messiah according to Zechariah 12:10*]**; and all tribes of the earth will wail on account of him. Even so. Amen. "I am the Alpha and the Omega," says the Lord God, who is and who was and who is to come, the Almighty.**
>
> Revelation 1:4-8 (RSV). *Bracketed words added for clarity.*

My interpretation of this Scripture is that, when King Yahshua comes in the clouds, the whole world will be in complete, or nearly complete, literal, physical darkness. As He and His army of millions of great warrior angels approach earth from out in space, the great and bright brilliance of the host from heaven will be seen by all on the earth as the earth rotates eastward toward the sun and King Yahshua's coming.

The following is a passage from Matthew describing the same event.

> **"... For as the lightning comes from the east and flashes to the west, so also will the coming of the Son of Man be. ... Immediately after the tribulation** [*persecution of Christians and Jews*] **of those days the sun will be darkened, and the moon will not give its light; the stars will fall from heaven, and the powers from heaven will be shaken. Then the sign of**

the Son of Man will appear in heaven, and then all the tribes of the earth will mourn, and they will see the Son of Man coming on the clouds of heaven with power and great glory.
Matthew 24:27, 29-30 (NJKV). *Bracketed words added for clarity.*

The vision of the seven churches is recorded in Revelation Chapters Two and Three. I believe this vision has a three-fold interpretation. First, they were literal, first-century churches that our Master wanted to offer words of praise, to warn, to reprove, and give them His Kingdom promises through John's letters to them. They were under the constant threat of the described anti-Christ, who in their minds were the Caesars of the Roman Empire at that time. Persecution and martyrdom was widespread, and many believers probably were looking and praying for Messiah to return soon in their day.

Second, the letters are symbolic of the condition of the professing Christian churches, as a whole, throughout the history of the churches, from the first century to present day. And third, the warnings, reproofs, praises, and provisions contained in the letters will apply specifically to different people who make up the worldwide body of Messiah during the last three and one-half years of the great tribulation. This segment of time has been referred to as the latter half of Daniel's seventieth week, The Day of Yahweh, the time of great tribulation or persecution of Christians and Jews, and Jacob's trouble.

In Chapter Four of the book of Revelation, John records that he (and he alone; nothing here implies that this is the rapture bus) is taken up into heaven and is before the very throne of God the Father Almighty. He states clearly that he records all that he sees—the twenty-four elders, the four living creatures, etc.

In Revelation Chapter Five, John sees a very important scroll held in the right hand of Almighty Father God, Yahweh. John learns that there is no one worthy to open the scroll except the Lamb of God, Yahshua Messiah, Who is called the "Lion of the tribe of Judah, the Root of David," as it is written in verses 5-7.

In Chapter Six, the Lamb begins opening the seals, one by one. The interpretation I have of John's vision of the opening of seals one through five is that the seals symbolize an outline of the developments and events that have been going on for the past 1,900-plus years, and will carry over into the last three and one-half years of the great tribulation. These events that John sees taking place are natural catastrophes and terrible atrocities that evil people commit against singled-out groups of the human race and the environment. Our Master Yahshua told His disciples that the time referred to as the latter half of the final seven years (the great tribulation) would be the most terrible time in the history of the world since it was created. King Yahshua comes in time to put an end to the martyrdom of the saints and to destroy the anti-Messiah, his false prophet and their huge army that they have gathered in Jerusalem to attack King Yahshua and His army of angels as they approach planet earth. Thus says the Lord:

> **"... For in those days there will be suffering, such as has not been from the beginning of the creation that God created until now, no, and never will be. And if the Lord had not cut short those days, no one would be saved; but for the sake of the elect, whom He chose, He has cut short those days. ..."**
> Mark 13:19-20 (NRSV)

The great tribulation is finalized by the coming (advent) of Yahshua, as it is described in the opening of the sixth seal in Revelation 6:12-17. It is also described in Daniel 7:9-14, Joel 2:30-32, Matthew 24:29-31, and Revelation 11:15-19, 14:14-20, 16:14-21 and 19:11-21. The opening of the sixth seal encompasses the events that are described in the opening of the seventh seal, which carry through to the advent (coming) of our Master Yahshua in the clouds.

I believe that the apostle John's recording of the opening of the symbolic seventh seal begins his witnessing of the judgments of Yah that are to be sent to this world as described in detail in the record of the seven trumpets and seven bowl, or vial, judgments. I believe the timing of these terrible catastrophes places them near the end of the final three and one-half year period leading up to the blessed return of King Yahshua. These plagues are poured out on a large portion of the world's population, those who will have had many opportunities to accept the one true living God, but rejected Him and instead, accepted the deceptive world system of Satan's anti-Christ and his worship.

Our Master Yahshua spoke a list of prophecies to His disciples in private that are recorded in the gospels. These prophecies give clues to the timing of His return to this earth. They are found in Matthew 24, Mark 13, and Luke 21. The most detailed account is found in Matthew 24.

There is an obvious parallel between the verses of Matthew 24:3-13 and 29-31 and the descriptions in the breaking of the seals on the scroll found in Revelation Six. This is the outline of the conditions and catastrophes of the final years of this generation. The message in all of these prophecies is not that the conditions haven't always been happening, but that the closer humanity progresses to the end of this age, the more frequent and devastating these tragedies will be, and that they will be happening more simultaneously. I believe that the events described in the opening of the seven seals have been happening since the beginning of the first-century church, through present day events, and will continue on into the final seven years, only more intensely.

THE OPENING OF THE FIRST SEAL

The signs and seals prophecies are broken down as deceptions by false messiahs, wars, famines, pestilence, martyrdom, and the signs in the heavens of the coming of the true Messiah. The disciples of Yahshua had asked Him the following important questions.

> **Now as He sat on the Mount of Olives, the disciples came to Him privately, saying, "Tell us, when will these things be? And what *will be* the sign of Your coming, and of the end of the age?" And Jesus answered and said to them: "Take heed that no one deceives you. For many will come in My name, saying, 'I am the Christ** [Messiah]**,' and will deceive many.**
> Matthew 24:3-5 (NKJV). *Bracketed words added for clarity.*

And now, the parallel:

> **Now I saw when the Lamb opened one of the seals; and I heard one of the four living creatures saying with a voice like thunder, "Come and see." And I looked, and behold, a white horse. He who sat on it had a bow; and a crown was given to him, and he went out conquering and to conquer.**
> Revelation 6:1-2 (NJKV)

This character seems to fit the description of King Yahshua that is described in Revelation 19 but is clearly not. This is very important to remember: Satan is going to do everything in his power, up to and during the last years of this age, to deceive as many people as possible into believing that the coming of his anti-Christ beast is the coming of the real Messiah, King Jesus. Satan has been conquering by deception since he was successful in deceiving Adam and Eve into believing they could turn away from Yahweh's instructions (*Torah* Tree of Life) and survive by their own reasoning ability, the knowledge of good and evil.

Today in America, it is estimated that over 400 people claim to be Jesus in whatever comprehension of Jesus they have. The most notable one that surfaced in August 2006 is a delusional yoyo named Dr. Jose Louis De Jesus Miranda who was interviewed that month on the NBC *Today* show and has been interviewed on all of the major networks. To see these shocking and repulsive interviews go to the web site: www.CEGEnglish.com.

Followers of every major religion of this world are looking for and anticipating the coming of the great one in their religion. They believe that their great one will bring a lasting peace to the world and make all things right for all people. The sad reality is that all belief systems of the world were created and instituted by Satan working through people. The true Creator, the Elohim of Abraham, Isaac, and Jacob, through His Messiah Yahshua created and instituted the only true way, truth, and life.

The Shiite and Sunni Islamic Muslims are expecting the coming of the twelfth Imam, Mahdi, the successor of Mohammed. The Aztec Mayans are expecting their Messiah in the rebirth of Quetzalcoatl. The Hopi and Sioux Indians are looking for the true White Brother from the East. The Japanese Buddhists are waiting for their Messiah, Shintorsin. The Eskimos and Indonesians are looking for a great Messiah. The Hindu are anticipating the coming of the Krishna, the ninth and last Avatar incarnation. The Buddhists are looking for Maitreya, the world unifier who was prophesied by Buddha to be greater than himself, to be coming at the end of the age, bringing equality to all peoples. Members of the New Age cult are believing it is near the time for the great spiritual energy of the universe to come down and purge the earth of everything that is not in harmony, and to bring in the new age of spiritual energy and enlightenment. Jewish people are looking for a powerful, political, Messiah messenger of the Almighty God Yahweh, who will bring a final peace to the nation of Israel and restore the Jewish people to their status of the chosen people. This would provide a way for them to build the third temple on the Temple Mount in Jerusalem, so that animal sacrifices could be reinstated, and they would have assurance of redemption from their sins. The vast majority of Christians worldwide are looking for their Lord and Savior, Jesus Christ, to come at possibly any moment, to sweep them off the planet before the time of the horrible tribulation begins.

I believe you can see the picture clearly. There is tremendous deception all over the world today, even in the beliefs of Christians. The next chapter will provide much insight regarding the doctrine of the resurrection (rapture), when King Yahshua supernaturally resurrects His saved body of believers during His coming in the air from His throne in heaven to planet earth.

The Opening of the Second Seal

It is written:

And you will hear of wars and rumors of wars. See that you are not troubled; for all *these things* must come to pass, but the end is not yet. For nation will rise against nation, and kingdom against kingdom.
Matthew 24:6-7a (NKJV)

Now the parallel:

When he opened the second seal, I heard the second living creature saying, "Come and see." Another horse, fiery red, went out. And it was granted to the one who sat on it to take peace from the earth, and that *people* should kill one another; and there was given to him a great sword.
Revelation 6:3-4 (NKJV)

The recorded prophecy that King Yahshua spoke to his disciples and the recorded vision of symbolism that was shown to John are prophecies that apply to warfare in all generations. The prophecies apply especially to the last years of the last generation when more wars and threats of war, especially in Israel, are in the news. After world war three, when America (I believe America is Babylon the Great as recorded in Revelation 18 and 19) is destroyed to the point of no longer being a super power, the outcry from the two-thirds of the population that are left on the earth will be for peace at any cost.

Since the beginning of this century, the number of wars and the devastation in lives lost and damage has significantly increased from all prior centuries. So far in this century, the world has had approximately 250 wars, two of which were world wars. World War I, 1914-1918, claimed approximately 10 million casualties, and World War II claimed over 51 million. Most of the wars have been border conflicts, such as the United States and Vietnam War, Israelis and Arab Yom Kippur War, Iran and Iraq War, the Russian and Afghanistan War, the Falklands War, the Persian Gulf War, and the Serbs and Croatians War. There is more and more unrest in more and more places in the world. There are as many as 20 to 30 civil wars and military conflicts taking place on this planet every week of the year, most of which never make the headlines of secular, mainstream news.

Defense experts project that over 30 countries now have nuclear weapons capability. The major hot spots are North Korea, Pakistan, India, China and as always Russia. The latest threat from a country trying to manufacturer a nuclear bomb and missile delivery system is Iran, with the support of its ally, Syria. What increases the Iranian threat is that its leader is committed to the destruction of Israel. The reality is not a question of whether or not there will be wars among nations, and conflicts among the different races and social groups but, rather, when will be the next major outbreak of violence.

There are some very significant prophecies regarding the invasion of Israel and the outbreak of war in the Middle East found in the book of Ezekiel, Chapters 38 and 39. I am convinced that the invasion described in those chapters will cause the world to cry out for peace and a world leader who can deliver it. The leader will no doubt be the long prophesied anti-Christ who will produce a temporary peace for Israel. More detail of these events is covered later.

THE OPENING OF THE THIRD SEAL

Thus saith the Master:

And there will be famines, pestilence, and earthquakes in various places. All these *are* the beginning of sorrows.
Matthew 24:7b-8 (NKJV)

Now the parallel:

When He opened the third seal, I heard the third living creature say, "Come and see." So I looked, and behold, a black horse, and he who sat on it had a pair of scales in his hand [famine]. **And I heard a voice in the midst of the four living creatures saying, "A quart of wheat for a denarius, and three quarts of barley for a denarius; and do not harm the oil and the wine."**
Revelation 6:5-6 (NKJV). *Bracketed words added for clarity.*

Throughout history, there have been famines, pestilence, and earthquakes. Only in this last generation that we are living in have these terrible catastrophes increased in frequency and intensity and have occurred over larger areas.

During the past fifty years, climate changes and the control of food distribution by evil governments have caused the most devastating famines in the history of mankind. At this writing, there are famines in Ethiopia, Chad, Sudan, Northern India, Brazil, North Korean, Bangladesh, and parts of Russia and China. Today, there are approximately six billion people on planet earth. Over half of the people on the earth are underfed. Millions die each year as a result of famine. Millions are fed each day by many Christian and non-Christian agencies.

Pestilence is described as any fatal, epidemic disease. Destructive insects are also included in this cause of death and suffering. There are more strains of untreatable viruses and diseases now than ever before, the latest being avian flu from birds. Certainly, the most well known is the AIDS virus that has tragically taken the lives of millions worldwide. Most of the people dying from this horror live in poverty in third world countries. Research scientists are frustrated when they discover antibiotics and drugs that destroy the microorganisms of diseases, only to observe the diseases becoming immune to the treatments and rapidly growing again.

There are now over 300 different insects that scientists are calling "super-bugs" that have become resistant to the chemicals developed to control them. The spread of disease and the loss of crops from ticks, mosquitoes, locusts, mites, fire ants, and many types of beetles and rodents have accelerated in this generation. (*Parade Magazine* article, "Super-bugs: A new Biblical Plague?")

Over the last decade, there have been many devastating earthquakes, tsunamis, hurricanes, tornadoes, floods, and wildfires that have resulted in the deaths of tens of thousands of people and untold billions of dollars in the loss of property, homes, and businesses.

Earthquakes have been increasing in number and intensity each century. The 1976 *World Almanac* states that 38 of the 57 most powerful earthquakes in all of history have happened in this century. Since then, there have been dozens more, such as the one in Ecuador in March 1987 that killed many thousands and left over 100,000 people homeless, or the one in Iran in June of 1990 that killed over 45,000 people, or the quakes of the nineties that happened in California and Japan. There is an observatory in Strasbourg, France, that has recorded the number of reported major earthquakes for several of the past centuries. The number in the 17th century was 378; in the 18th century it was 640; in the 19th century it was 2,119. (*News From Israel*, September 1986 issue.)

Along with famines, pestilence, and earthquakes are floods, fires, hurricanes, and tornadoes that are increasing and reeking havoc throughout the world. In the fall of 2001, here in eastern North Carolina where my family and I live, we experienced a 500-year flood that caused over 35,000 people to apply for help from FEMA. This flood was the result of Hurricane Floyd that came on the heels of Hurricane Dennis a week before. We had approximately thirty inches of rain from these storms within a two-week period. This natural catastrophe has been the worst ever documented and possibly the most costly in the number of lives and property damage in our state's history. The statistics for Hurricane Katrina's damage and flooding are several times greater, as it was the worst natural disaster America has experienced up to the year 2005.

This information of natural catastrophes and devastation is not being presented to frighten you but to help you understand that the earth is being shaken. Our Savior, Yahshua, and other prophets of the Scriptures painted a picture of what the conditions of the world would be like a few years prior to and during the final seven years of the last generation.

The last part of Revelation 6:6 on the previous page, "and do not harm the oil and the wine," means that there will be protection and provision for a group of true Jewish and Gentile followers of Messiah. They will be spared from martyrdom during the last half of the tribulation so there will be a remnant waiting for Yahshua when He comes to receive them unto Himself, as is stated in the Scriptures (John 14:1-4). There is more on this subject in the final chapters.

The Opening of the Fourth Seal

When He opened the fourth seal, I heard the voice of the fourth living creature saying, "Come and see." So I looked, and behold, a pale horse. And the name of him who sat on it was Death, and Hades followed with him. And power was given to them over a fourth of the earth, to kill with sword, with hunger, with death, and by the beasts of the earth.
Revelation 6:5-8 (NKJV)

The symbolism in these verses is summarizing the end results of the devastation of the first three seals and also of what is described in the opening of the fifth seal. The "beasts of the earth" are the anti-Christ and the followers of his system who orchestrate the organized murder of millions of true Christians and Jews. The Scriptures reveal that death is going to come to at least one fourth (approximately 1.5 billion people) of the population of the earth during the tribulation period as the result of the wars, famines, pestilences, martyrdom, and asteroid catastrophes as described in the first four trumpet prophecies. People living on the earth at that time will be desperately desiring a change in the world's conditions, and crying out for a great leader to make life on planet earth better. All of the catastrophes that have been previously described are only part of the terrible events that are to come. The events described in seals one through five are revealing Satan's wrath poured out on the human race, especially on those who will not accept his new world order system and worship his child, the anti-Christ beast.

The following Scriptures show that beginning half way through the final seven years of this age, there will be undercover, hidden martyrdom on a large scale, during which many tens of millions will die. I believe the evil carnage will be carried out in a top-secret fashion, much like the holocaust of the Jews and Christians by the Nazis. The following Scriptures support this.

The beast *[anti-Christ and his system]* **was given a mouth uttering haughty and blasphemous words, and it was allowed to exercise authority for forty-two months** *[3-1/2 years]*. **... Also it was allowed to make war on the saints and to conquer them.**
Revelation 13:5, 7 (NRSV). *Bracketed words added for clarity.*

In the *New Revised Standard Version* the same verse says, "all this is but the beginning of the birth pangs." This means that it will happen just as a woman experiences birth pangs—labor contractions—before childbirth. In the beginning, her contractions will be mild and farther apart. As she progresses toward the birth, there is an increase in the intensity of pain and the closeness of her contractions. The described catastrophes will increase in the number of occurrences and the devastation in the years leading up to the return of King Yahshua, the true Messiah.

Trust Almighty Yah's Holy Word. The conditions of this world as a whole are not going to improve; they are only going to progressively worsen. As bad as the world's overall conditions are with the current wars, famines, pestilences, and natural disasters in this generation, as of this printing, spring of 2007, we have not yet entered into the final seven-year period. The final peace treaty between the Israeli Jews and the Palestinians has not been initiated by the anti-Christ as of the publishing of this book. The Scriptures indicate that the final peace treaty will be established soon after the Russian-Arab invasion of Israel, according to the prophecies in Ezekiel 38 and 39. The Scriptures for these events are covered in detail in Chapter Ten, "Signs and Events to Watch For."

THE OPENING OF THE FIFTH SEAL

Thus saith the Lord:

"**Then they will hand you over to be tortured and will put you to death, and you will be hated by all nations because of my name. Then many will fall away, and they will betray one another and hate one another. And many false prophets will arise and lead many astray. And because of the increase of lawlessness, the love of many will grow cold. But the one who endures to the end will be saved. ..."**
Matthew 24: 9-13 (NRSV)

Also in Luke,

"**But before all this occurs, they will arrest you and persecute you; they will hand you over to synagogues and prisons, and you will be brought** before kings and governors because of my name. This will give you an opportunity to testify. So make up your minds not to prepare your defense in advance; for I will give you words and a wisdom that none of your opponents will be able to withstand or contradict. You will be betrayed even by parents and brothers, by relatives and friends; and they will put some of you to death. You will be hated by all because of my name. But not a hair of your head will perish. By your endurance you will gain your souls."

Luke 21:12-19 (NRSV)

Now the parallel.

When He opened the fifth seal, I saw under the altar the souls of those who had been slaughtered for the word of God and for the testimony they had given; they cried out with a loud voice, "Sovereign Lord, holy and true, how long will it be before you judge and avenge our blood on the inhabitants of the earth?" They were each given a white robe and told to rest a little longer, until the number would be complete both of their fellow servants and of their brothers and sisters, who were soon to be killed as they themselves had been killed.

Revelation 6:9-11 (NRSV)

This is important to remember as you read through the remainder of this chapter, so that all the prophecies that relate to the events of the fifth seal and the martyrdom of the saints of the past and the future will make sense. The souls that John saw under the altar represent the many millions of believers who have been martyred through the centuries up to the time of the great tribulation of this last generation. The clue is the last part of verse eleven that states, "until the number would be complete ... who were soon to be killed..." This is the last huge martyrdom that will be carried out in secret much like the Nazi Holocaust.

During the first three centuries of the Christian church, many tens of thousands, possibly millions, were persecuted and martyred for their love of and commitment to Yahshua Messiah. Remember that He wasn't referred to as *Jesus* at that time. Since that time, millions have been martyred during such times and events as the Roman Catholic crusades and inquisitions, the tyrannical rule of the communist leaders of Russia and China, and Hitler's horrible holocaust. As I stated earlier, in the year

2005, approximately 200,000 people worldwide were put to death because of their belief in and commitment to Master Yahshua. Since Yahshua's first coming, the demonic realm has influenced the murder of peace-loving people in many countries of the world, especially Christians and Jews. This has been going on for over 1,970 years and will intensify up to the very end of this age.

The final seven-year countdown begins when the nation of Israel signs the much-desired peace treaty with anti-Christ, whom they will be deceived to believe is the true Messiah. The peace treaty will bring final resolve between the Jews, Muslims, the United Nations, and all other entities who are engaged so that the dividing of the land of Israel can take place in order to create a Palestinian State. Whenever this profound event happens, the clocks begins ticking down for the final seven years until Yahshua comes, and judgment for America is certain. We must understand the prophecies and signs of the times so we will be prepared to make a stand for Yahshua and not give in to the evil world system of the anti-Messiah when it is ushered in.

What will be the justification to the unbelieving, unsaved world for the systematic mass genocide of true Christians and Jews worldwide? If you reflect back to Chapter One of this book, I stated how Satan desires to have as many people as possible worship him. He ingeniously devises the conclusion of his master plan for world control and glorification of himself through the human anti-Christ and false prophet, whom he will totally possess and control. Satan will do everything within his power to try to copy what Almighty Yahweh does so that, through his perverted ways, he (Satan) is worshiped by the masses.

Let's study now, in this section, how Satan has used the most power-ful of the world's empires and evil dictators down through history to persecute Jews and Christians. As he has done in the past, so he will do in great mass in the future.

In establishing the world's final empire and dictatorship, Satan will draw worship to the anti-Christ and ultimately to himself. It is written:

Then I saw a beast coming up out of the sea. It had ten horns and seven heads; on each of its horns there was a crown, and on each of its heads there was a name that was insulting to God. The beast looked like a leopard, with feet like a bear's feet and a mouth like a lion's mouth. The dragon gave the beast his own power, his throne, and his vast authority.

One of the heads of the beast seemed to have been fatally wounded, but the wound had been healed. The whole earth was amazed and followed the beast. Everyone worshiped the dragon because he had given his authority to the beast. They worshiped the beast also, saying, "Who is like the beast? Who can fight against it?"
Revelation 13:1-4 (TEV)

These verses require a lot of clarification, so hang on. This part of John's vision is a scene of the beast made up of animal parts representing Euro, Mid-Eastern world empires of the past that had dominated and enslaved nations, especially the Hebrew/Jewish people. A clear parallel of this description of empires is found in the second and seventh chapters of Daniel. I encourage you to read along in your Bible.

In the seventh chapter, Daniel is given a vision from Yahweh and describes the four world empires of the civilized world. He begins with Babylon, his captor, whose national emblem was a lion with eagle's wings. The second was Medo-Persian, whose emblem was a bear. The third was Greece, whose emblem was the leopard. He did not give the national emblem of the fourth empire but described it as dreadful and terrible, exceedingly strong. It had huge iron teeth; it was devouring, breaking in pieces and trampling its victims under its feet. It was different from all the other beasts before it, and it had ten horns. This fourth symbolic empire was Rome.

An important point to remember is that, after the Roman Empire faded, the next kingdom to rule over the lands and cities of the Middle East, specifically Jerusalem, Israel, was the Muslim Ottoman Empire, also known as the Turkish Empire. It began in A.D. 1299 and ended in A.D. 1923. The capital was in Istanbul, Turkey, the former eastern capital of the Roman Empire named Constantinople. The Ottoman Turks were in control of Jerusalem during most of 724 years. After World War I, the empire was forced to give up its control of the lands in the Middle East, including Israel. Soon afterward, the empire fell apart.

A more detailed description of these empires is found in the vision that Daniel interpreted for King Nebuchadnezzar found in the second chapter of the book of Daniel. God had given the king a vision about the future empires of the world leading up to the King of kings coming to establish His kingdom on the earth. The king had seen a giant statue with a head of gold, representing Babylon, his kingdom of that time; the chest and arms of silver, representing the Medo-Persian empire; the belly and hips of bronze, representing the Greek Empire; and the legs of iron representing the Roman Empire; and its feet and ten toes of part iron and part clay, representing the final world-dominating empire that will manifest out from all of the previous ones. The two legs represent the two joining states of the ancient Roman Empire. The capital of the eastern state was Constantinople, with Rome as the capital of the western state.

The mighty Roman Empire lasted nearly six hundred years and ended in A.D. 475. It is likely that from out of both ends of that great empire will come forth the ruling authority of the final world empire. This last world-wide empire will be made up ten regional governments of the world, administered by ten presidents, or rulers, of the regions of the planet. There have been several interpretations of what the combination of toes representing ten powerful nations or world regional powers are about. Here is the Scripture.

And whereas thou sawest the feet and toes, part of potters' clay, and part of iron, the kingdom shall be divided; but there shall be in it of the strength of the iron, forasmuch as thou sawest the iron mixed with miry clay. And as the toes of the feet were part of iron, and part of clay, so the kingdom shall be partly strong and partly broken. And whereas thou sawest iron mixed with miry clay, they shall mingle themselves with the seed of men: but they shall not cleave one to another, even as iron is not mixed with clay.
Daniel 2:41-43 (KJV)

What is Holy Spirit trying to help us to understand in these verses? Verse 43 is very intriguing, as it tells us that *they will mingle with the seed of men; but they shall not cleave* (other translations use "adhere to one another"), *even as iron does not mix with clay*. The part of the verse stating, "they will mingle with the seed of men" sounds very similar to the Scripture of Genesis Chapter Six that was covered in Chapter One of this book. Genesis Six is explaining the existence of the fallen angels, called the "sons of God" and "Nephilim," who had bred with human women and had caused humanity to become so evil that God Almighty destroyed the world with the flood. Yahshua prophesized that His coming at the end of the end of the age would be as it was in the days of Noah. It is written:

But as the days of Noah *were*, so also will the coming of the Son of Man be. For as in the days before the flood, they were eating and drinking, marrying and giving in marriage, until the day that Noah entered the ark, and did not know until the flood came and took them all away, so also will the coming of the Son of Man be.

Matthew 24:37-39 (NKJV)

On the surface, these verses sound like everything is normal and everyone is living his or her life in a carefree manner. We must remember, however, why it was that Almighty Yah destroyed the human race, except for Noah and his family, with the great flood. It was because the fallen angels had perverted the thinking and actions of the human race to the point that, as the Scriptures state, everyone's thinking was continuously on evil things and sinning. The morals of society had broken down to the point that constant sinning had become the normal way of life. If Yahshua said that it will be that way just before He returns to bring in His kingdom, then it will be that way.

I believe that fallen angels have already bred with humans in this generation and will continue their sinister breeding to again totally possess humanity for Satan's greater influence. I believe these individuals are sold out Satanists who are, in many cases, some of the wealthiest, most powerful people in the world and make up a secret organization known as the Illuminati. By Satan's design and direct instructions, the deceived people of the Illuminati are working toward fulfilling his purpose of worship from most of humanity living on the earth during the final years of this age. I believe the shadow government of the U.S.A. has been involved with fallen angels that have been masquerading as aliens from outer space for many years, and are up to a lot of mischief as they plan and facilitate their New World Order police state. When our Lord Yahshua walked upon the earth as a human, He told His disciples that this will be when the deception of the human race will be at an all time high.

Now back to the interpretation of the beast. There is another section of Scripture that addresses this same beast with some more detail. In Revelation Chapter 17, it is written:

Then one of the seven angels who had the seven bowls came and said to me, "Come, I will show you the judgment of the great harlot who is seated upon many waters, with whom the kings of the earth have

committed fornication, and with the wine of whose fornication the dwellers on earth have become drunk." And he carried me away in the Spirit into the wilderness, and I saw a woman sitting on a scarlet beast which was full blasphemous names, and it had seven heads and ten horns. The woman was arrayed in purple and scarlet, and bedecked with gold and jewels and pearls, holding in her hand a golden cup full of abominations and the impurities of her fornication; and on her fore-head was written a name of mystery: "Babylon the great, mother of harlots and of earth's abominations." And I saw the woman, drunk with the blood of the saints and the blood of the martyrs of Jesus. When I saw her I marveled greatly. But the angel said to me. "Why marvel? I will tell you the mystery of the woman, and of the beast with the seven heads and ten horns that carries her. The beast that you saw was, and is not, and is to ascend from the bottomless pit and go to perdition; and the dwellers on earth whose names have not been written in the book of life from the foundation of the world, will marvel to behold the beast, because it was and is not and is to come. This calls for a mind with wisdom: the seven heads are seven mountains on which the woman is seated; they are also seven kings, five of whom have fallen, one is, the other has not yet come, and when he comes he must remain only a little while. As for the beast that was and is not, it is an eighth but it belongs to the seven, and it goes to perdition *[destruction]*. And the ten horns that you saw are ten kings who have not yet received royal power, but they are to receive authority as kings for one hour, together with the beast. These are of one mind and give over their power and authority to the beast; they will make war on the Lamb, and the Lamb will conquer them, for He is Lord of lords and King of kings, and those with Him are called chosen and faithful." And he said to me, "The waters that you saw, where the harlot is seated, are peoples and multitudes and nations and tongues. And the ten horns that you saw, they and the beast will hate the harlot; they will make her desolate and naked, and devour her flesh and burn her up with fire, for God has put it into their hearts to carry out His purpose by being of one mind and giving over their royal power to the beast, until the words of God shall be fulfilled. And the woman that you saw is the great city which has dominion over the kings of the earth."

Revelation 17:1-18 (TEV). *Bracketed words added for clarity.*

The following is my best paraphrase of this important chapter. As I stated in the Introduction, many hundreds of pages could be, and have been, written about the meaning of this book of the Bible called Revelation. I simply want to help you understand the most important Scriptures that are necessary for making the right decisions for your life in general, and to prepare you on how to react to major world events as they develop.

I will start by stating that the ten horns that are ten kings will be ten governmental leaders of the ten economic regions in the world that has already been divided by an Illuminati organization called the "Club of Rome." This think-tank organization was formed as recently as April 1968, with the clear blueprint to establish a world government by dividing the world into ten regions. Most of the directives for planning the world bank and government are coming from this group. The ten divisions of the world, which are referred to as "kingdoms," are more likely to be the fulfillment of Daniel 2:31-45 and 7:19-28; also Revelation 13 and 17:12-14. The ten kingdom regions appointed by the club are: North America; Europe; Japan; Australia; Russia; South America; North Africa and the Middle East, including Israel; Central and Southern Africa; India and Malaysia; and China. There was a little warning sign that passed relatively unnoticed recently that confirms the thought of the powers. It is the commemorative stamp issued at the second European elections. The scene is taken from a Greek myth called the "Rape of Europe" and shows a woman, Europa, riding a beast. If this was not a sign allowed by God, then it was a clear and brazen attempt by the Devil to rub our noses into the events unfolding right in front of us. You can read more regarding this article at the following website:

www.HigherPraise.com/nwo.htm#New%20World

To view many of the euro coins, stamps, and posters of the woman riding the beast, go to the following website:

www.OriginOfNations.org/prophecy/Euro_woman_beast.htm

The great harlot that is shown to John by the angel is a unified world religious system that brings all willing religions into conformity, and spiritual fornication, as people are deceived into believing the lies of the false prophet and reject the truth of God's Word. This universal religion should be in full swing at the beginning of the final seven years (remember the opening of the first seal), and it will have its foundation in the roots of the ancient pagan religion of the Babylonians founded by Nimrod. (I wrote about Nimrod and his self-proclaimed god family in Chapter Four of this book.) The initiation of the worship of humans, the sun, the moon, the constellations, etc., in order to attain a higher level of illumination has been the quest of the fallen human nature throughout the ages. It is defined in the Scriptures as "spiritual harlotry" and "whoredom." The progression in steps to attain higher consciousness and illumination is the core teaching within Freemasonry, Mormonism, and basically all false belief systems. If you are involved with any of these, please get out from them. Repent, renounce the sworn oaths, and plead the blood of Yahshua Jesus, for only pure, uncompromising relationship with Him will be acceptable to Him.

In the last few years before the time of the anti-Messiah and the great tribulation, Satan will be able to pull together all of the false belief systems—even Islam—that he has introduced into the human race, so that he can be worshipped through his son, the beast. At the time of this writing with the exception of fanatical Islam, we are witnessing at the time of this writing the blending of major religions with New Age humanism. There is a humanistic conforming, which is all about doing whatever you want to do as long as you do not hurt or offend anyone. The new mindset is that there are no absolutes, everything is relative, you have the power to become your own god. Sound familiar? Read Genesis 3:1-13 again.

Throughout the centuries, false religions have spread through all cultures and nations. The foundation for this united religion is being laid now as many millions of people worldwide are anticipating the coming of the great one in their own religion, as I stated in Chapter Three. Many millions are flocking to statues of the Virgin Mary, and places where apparitions and illuminations are appearing in order to worship and be dazzled by the supernatural. Some are being miraculously healed. Satan is starting to put on an impressive show through the work of his fallen angels and demons. His deceptive works will continue to increase magnitude and in the number of occurrences until the vast majority of the world's population has bought into his system of lies.

The anti-Christ beast will use his false prophet and the universal religion to help justify his cause for eliminating all who will not accept his one-world political and economic system. The harlot looks impressive, with wealth, religious prestige, and popularity. Anyone who is caught up in the ways of the world will think that being a part of this false system will be the proper thing to do. Just as millions were murdered by the unholy Roman Catholic Church during the crusades, many, many millions will be murdered by the justifications set forth from this future false religion, the great deception of the false prophet, and the brute power of the anti-Christ's world military police force.

The anti-Christ beast will become jealous of the worship received by the false religion and will destroy the very system that enabled him to rise to power. He will then require all the inhabitants of the world to worship him. This happens when he defiles the rebuilt temple in Jerusalem and sets up a large idol of himself, which is very similar to what Antiochus Epiphanes IV did in the second temple in 165 B.C. The coming anti-Messiah will use a one-world economic system and fascist government to force as many as possible into his deadly trap. As I stated earlier, the anti-Christ beast will be the incarnation of Satan (Satan in the flesh). From the time of Satan's rebellion long ago, he has desired worship from human beings, just as our Heavenly Father, Yahweh, and Master Yahshua desire our worship and obedience.

Now to the understanding of the beast, the seven heads of the beast, and the ten horns. The angel explains that the unsaved people of the world will marvel when they realize who the beast really is because the beast was, and then is not, and is to come. The seven heads that are seven mountains upon which the woman is seated are the seven empires that through history have had control over the Hebrew-Jewish people from their beginning as a society and nation of peoples. The angel goes on to explain that these empires each had a king, or ruler, and then the angel helps John to determine the first six that he would have been aware of, including the empire that he was imprisoned by at that time. John, being a Jew, would have been taught the history of his race's heritage as a nation, which began in Egypt.

In the first chapter of this book, I recorded the Scriptures that tell of the Hebrews being held as slaves by multiple pharaohs in Egypt for about 400 years. This was the first empire that made slaves of the Jewish people. The second was the Assyrians, led by King Shalmaneser, who conquered the ten northern tribes of Israel in 721 B.C. and carried many into slavery. The third, forth, and fifth empires were explained in the visions recorded in Daniel Chapters Two and Seven. The third was the Babylonian empire led by King Nebuchadnezzar. The fourth was the Medo-Persian Empire led by King Xerxes. The fifth was the Greek empire led by Alexander the Great. The sixth was the Roman Empire that was under the control of the evil dictators called Caesars. Caesars Nero and Domitian ruled during the Apostle John's life. It is believed that Nero was responsible for having the Apostles Peter and Paul put to death. So now we can begin to have understanding of the explanation the angel gave to John, using the time in which John was living as a point of reference.

Consider the following, with paraphrase:

"… also, they are seven kings, of whom five have fallen [the first five kingdoms before John's time], **one is living** [the terrible Caesar Domitian, who followed Nero] **and the other** [the seventh] **has not yet come; and when he comes, he must remain only a little while."**
Revelation 17:9b-10 (NRSV). *Bracketed words added for clarity.*

Now, let's examine this for clarity. Here is where we must look at history from the time of the empire that was dominating the Jewish people at the time the visions were given to John up to our modern time. In doing so, we should be able to determine when and what empire has enslaved the Jewish people that would qualify to be the seventh king or empire. I included in Chapter Four the fulfillment of the most significant prophecy relating to the second coming of King Yahshua. This fulfilled prophecy was the returning of the Jewish people from many parts of the world to become a nation, after being scattered without a nation for 1,878 years. The Jewish people experienced the Diaspora, or great dispersing, in A.D. 70. This was the year when the Roman army, led by General Titus under the order of Caesar Nero, murdered most of the Jews living at that time. The great temple and the city of Jerusalem were leveled. Those who survived fled Israel and migrated into many other countries.

From A.D. 70 until A.D. 1948, the Jewish people were abused and despised throughout the world, but only once during that span of time have they, as a race, been enslaved, persecuted, and murdered in great mass by an empire with a dictator who was in power for a short time. The dictator was Adolf Hitler who was in control of the German empire known as the "Third Reich." This understanding of who the seventh head of the prophecy is may come as a shock to you because it reveals the horrible reality of the Holocaust that happened not so long ago. Hitler called his evil regime the "Third Reich," recognizing as the First Reich, the great lineage of popes and kings of the un-Holy Roman Empire, and the Second Reich, which he proposed was the powerful German empire created by Kaiser Bismarck in 1871. There is a strong connection between the ancestry of the early German leaders and Roman Empire Caesars. The word *Kaiser* is derived from the Latin word *Caesar*.

Let's look now at the next verse of Scripture in Chapter 17, verse 11.

As for the beast that was and is not, it is an eighth but it belongs to the seven, and it goes to destruction.
Revelation 17:11 (NRSV)

Here is another verse that helps to clarify.

And I *saw* one of his heads as if it had been mortally wounded, and his deadly wound was healed. And all the world marveled and followed the beast. So they worshiped the dragon *[Satan]* who gave authority to the beast; and they worshiped the beast, saying, "Who *is* like the beast? Who is able to make war with him?"
Revelation 13:3-4 (NKJV). *Bracketed words added for clarity.*

As it is written:

"... The beast that you saw was, and is not, and is about to ascend from the bottomless pit and go to destruction. And the inhabitants of the earth, whose names have not been written in the book of life from the foundation of the world, will be amazed when they see the beast, because it was and is not and is to come. ..."
Revelation 17:8 (NRSV)

The wording in the Scripture is too specific to be interpreted as one of the former world empires, or belief systems, as is stated in the question, "Who is able to make war with him?" My guess is that the anti-Christ beast—the ruler and dictator of the end-time world economic, political and religious systems—will be an individual like Adolf Hitler who will be at the right place in history with the message that everyone wants to believe will improve the devastated conditions of society. So the conditions on this planet after World War III takes place will be fertile ground for a world dictator to take advantage of a world in chaos such as Hitler did after WW I. The really important information to glean from all of this is that this evil being who has raised from the pit of hell comes to power by great deception, camouflage, and stealth. The world in general will not have a clue that this person is anyone other that the greatest politician and mediator for peace (especially in Israel), the most appealing, charismatic, brilliant, polished, strong, super-hero leader that the world has ever witnessed. He will convince the world that he is the answer to all of the world's problems.

Remember the two legs of the statue in the prophet Daniel's vision? The legs represent the former Roman Empire with two regions—the west with Rome as its capital, and the east with Constantinople (now Istanbul, Turkey) as its capital. I am convinced that the anti-Messiah individual will emerge from one of the Middle Eastern nations that were long ago part of the eastern region of the Roman Empire. In order for the Jewish leaders of the nation of Israel to accept the anti-Christ as their disguised Messiah and put their trust in him, he will certainly have to have some Jewish ancestry in his family tree. He will also have to have favor with the Muslims and have them convinced that he is the 12th Inman, the Madi.

I have recently read an interesting book titled *Islam, Peace or Beast* by a great author, Rabbi Simon Altaf. He has also written a book titled *World War III, Unmasking the End Time Beast*. Rabbi Altaf is a former Sunni Muslim from Pakistan who is now a Holy Spirit-filled, born again Israelite who believes in and follows the *Torah* teachings of our Master Yahshua Messiah. He teaches in depth that the prophecies that refer to the end-time city called Babylon the Great are not referring to the city of Rome, Italy, or New York City, USA, but, rather, to Mecca, Saudi Arabia. This is a new angle to what most people who have studied end-time prophecy for years have believed about Rome being Babylon the Great. His teachings certainly have merit when you consider that many of the details he has presented that have happened, and will continue to happen up to the end, have taken place completely in the Middle East.

In Revelation 17, the great harlot is described as: "being seated on many waters and seven heads meaning seven mountains." The city of Mecca is certainly surrounded by seven mountains (Rome is surrounded by hills, not mountains), and the country of Saudi Arabia is surrounded by eight different bodies of water. Verse 17 continues: "with whom the kings of the earth have committed fornication, and with the wine of whose fornication the dwellers on earth have become drunk." Rabbi Altaf explains that this verse is referring to the kings, or country's leaders buying oil and being drunk with the power and wealth that goes with oil that everything in our modern world depends on. He states that the fornication is the deception that has been broadcast throughout the world that Islam is a peaceful religion. People of the world who are paying attention know from all of the evil that has been done in the name of the false god, Allah, that hearing or reading that Islam is a religion of peace is nothing more than lies. Yahshua made it clear that we would know a tree by the type of fruit it produced. What is hard to comprehend is that many of the world's leaders and people in general believe that Islam is a peaceful religion, and that we Christians and Jews worship the same god the Muslims worship and pray to five times a day. This is not true, and Satan is the father of all lies and false, deceptive belief systems.

Rabbi Altaf believes that what has happened in the past 25 years is the re-emergence of the Islamic empire of the Ottomans that was dealt the wound to the head and is now the end-time beast that is rising. It cannot be denied that the oil-rich Arab Muslim nations have made their presence known in the modern world more than any other race and belief of people on the earth.

I agree with much of Rabbi Altaf's teachings, and I certainly can see plainly the effects Islam is having with shaping end-time events. Rather than believing that Islam is the end-time beast system, however, I believe that radical Islam is being used by the Illuminati as a power player on their chess board to accomplish their evil objectives and that toward the beginning of the final seven years, radical Islam will have been reduced and subdued.

Rabbi Altaf's books are sold through Your Arms to Israel Ministry at: www.YourArmsToIsrael.org.

The great majority of the world masses will adore the anti-Messiah, whatever his modern name is at the time he is revealed. He will use his charm, his abilities from Satan, and his powerful influence to bring about a much-needed peace to Israel and solutions to the many plaguing problems of the world. However, after the first three and one-half years of the final seven years of the peace contract that he initiates with Israel and its enemies, he will turn against the religious system that enabled him to gain his world power, as well as the Jews of Israel that he made a covenant with, and all who will not bow down to him. At that time, when he makes known the truth of his real identity, the majority of the world will marvel after him, accepting his enforcement of genocide of all who will not accept his world system.

When King Yahshua came to earth the first time as the Lamb of Yahweh, He had a forerunner, the prophet John the Baptist, to prepare the way so the people would know the true Messiah had come. Satan will use a false prophet and a false messiah to deceive the world into believing that the true creator of the universe has come down to establish his kingdom and make all things right. Satan will accomplish this by working through the power and influence of world governments, the supernatural display of incredible events that he will produce in the sky, the performing of miracles, the fascination of computer technological advances, and most importantly, the unifying of all non-Christian religions, including Judaism.

When the time comes for Satan to make his move to establish universal worship of himself through his manipulation of his false prophet and anti-Christ, the unsaved people of the world will be willing to compromise their differences in order to have restored universal peace, prosperity, and health. People throughout the world will cry out for relief from the many catastrophes they have experienced, as previously described in the opening of seals one through four. As it is written;

The coming of the lawless one is apparent in the working of Satan, who uses all power, signs, lying wonders, and every kind of wicked deception for those who are perishing, because they refused to love the truth and so be saved. For this reason God sends them a powerful delusion, leading them to believe what is false, so that all who have not believed the truth but took pleasure in unrighteousness will be condemned.
2 Thessalonians 2:9-12 (NRSV)

I have listed in this section of the opening of the fifth seal, some of the most relevant verses of the book of Revelation. The verses are Revelation 12:7-14, 17-18. These verses help us to grasp the general picture of the final forty-two months, or three and one half years, of the seven-year tribulation period. This period will be the time when the fallen angels of Satan's kingdom will have their greatest impact on the inhabitants of earth just prior to the second coming of the King of the universe, Yahshua, the true Messiah, and the resurrection of the saved. As it is written:

Then war broke out in heaven. Michael *[God's top angel]* **and his angels fought against the dragon** *[Satan]*, **who fought back with his angels** *[demons and fallen angels]*; **but the dragon was defeated, and he and his angels were not allowed to stay in heaven** *[2nd heaven]* **any longer. The huge dragon was thrown out—that ancient serpent, named the Devil, or Satan, that deceived the whole world. He was thrown down to earth, and all his angels with him** *[sometime in the beginning of the final seven years]*. **Then I heard a loud voice in heaven saying, "Now God's salvation has come! Now God has shown His power as King! Now His Messiah** *[Yahshua]* **has shown His authority! For the one who stood before our God and accused our brothers day and night has been thrown out of heaven. Our brothers** *[followers of Yahshua]* **won the victory over him by the blood of the Lamb and by the truth which they proclaimed; and they were willing to give up their lives and die** *[testimony of the martyrdom of the saints]*. **And so be glad, you heavens, and all you that live there! But how terrible for the earth and the sea! For the Devil has come down to you, and he is filled with rage, because he knows that he has only a little time left." When the dragon realized that he had been thrown down to the earth, he began to pursue the woman** *[the Jewish race that Yahshua Messiah was born into]* **who had given birth to the boy** *[Yahshua]*. **She was given the two wings of a large eagle** *[possibly the remainder Christian organizations from what is left of America that are able, with God's help, to fly many Jews out from Israel and other nations to a protected place]* **in order to fly to her place in the desert, where she will be taken care of for three and a half years, safe from the dragon's attack. … The dragon was furious with the woman and went off to fight against the rest of her descendants, all those who obey God's commandments and are faithful to the truth revealed by Jesus.**

Revelation 12:7-14, 17-18 (TEV). *Bracketed words added for clarity.*

Now let's go back to Revelation Chapter 13 and glean some more information in order to understand this evil empire that is coming. The following Scripture introduces another beast who is a key player in assisting the anti-Christ in accomplishing their master Satan's plan.

Then I saw another beast coming up out of the earth, and he had two horns like a lamb and spoke like a dragon.

Revelation 13:11 (NKJV)

I believe this individual will rise to power just before the anti-Christ is positioned to begin his power sweep that will be made possible by this other beast, the false prophet, and will evolve from the one-world false religion of the final seven years and will be given much authority and power by Satan to enforce the worship of the anti-Christ.

> **And he exercises all the authority of the first beast in his presence, and causes the earth and those who dwell in it to worship the first beast, whose deadly wound was healed.**
> Revelation 13:12 (NKJV)

This person is referred to as the false prophet in Revelation 19:20, and his title will certainly be appropriate as he will be the master-mind of the mass deceptions created to manipulate the people of the earth into dictator worship.

> **He performs great signs, so that he even makes fire come down from heaven on the earth in the sight of men.**
> Revelation 13:13 (NKJV)

Satan will enable the false prophet to do amazing miracles, such as the display of fire coming down from heaven. No doubt these future events will be covered on the evening news for all to behold.

> **And he deceives those who dwell on the earth by those signs which he was granted to do in the sight of the beast, telling those who dwell on the earth to make an image of the beast who was wounded by the sword and lived. He was granted** *power* **to give breath to the image of the beast, that the image of the beast should both speak and cause as many as would not worship the image of the beast to be killed.**
> Revelation 13:14-15 (NKJV)

The false prophet, who will be like a right-hand man to the anti-Christ, will have tremendous powers of persuasion, so that he will be able to convince the majority of the world's population to make a graven image, or idol, of the likeness of the anti-Christ being, to have close at hand in order to worship. Here are some verses to support this.

But the rest of mankind, who were not killed by these plagues, did not repent of the works of their hands, that they should not worship demons, and idols of gold, silver, brass, stone, and wood, which can neither see nor hear nor walk. And they did not repent of their murders or their sorceries [from the Greek word pharmakeia meaning recreational drugs used for pleasure and occult practices] **or their sexual immorality or their thefts.**

Revelation 9:20-21 (NKJV). *Bracketed words added for clarity.*

A few pages back, I referenced Scripture from Revelation Chapter 12 that stated the Devil and his angels were thrown down to the earth. These verses indicate that the miracle-working false prophet will convince the masses who are caught up in the worship of the anti-Christ, who has temporarily smoothed out the problems of the world, to either make an image of the beast with their own hands or to purchase a mass produced one, and to keep it near them to worship. In doing so, the fallen angels, or demons, will occupy the idols and communicate to the lost human who is worshipping it, as well as communicating to Satan's world-control system if the person is not worshipping the anti-Christ image.

Rabbi Altaf teaches that the image the Scriptures are referring to is the image of Islam, the crescent moon and star that people will have tattooed either on their forehead or a mark on their body as a visible sign of their allegiance to the false moon god, Allah. It is all certainly worth pondering.

At this point in the book, you may be saying that this sounds a little nutty, but I ask you this: What other interpretation from these Scriptures is there? Verse 14 implies that everyone in the world makes an image—not one huge imagine that they all make collectively, which would be impossible, but an image for themselves individually. It very well could mean purchasing some new technology that would enable a person to assemble an idol themselves that would tie into the grid of the one-world, anti-Messiah, worship system.

Verse 15 implies that the false prophet will be granted power, or authority, to give breath or some type of life to the idol. I believe that Satan will delegate his fallen angels to possess the idols in order to control people by intimidation and fear. Fallen angels and demons are, and have been for centuries, speaking through individuals who have opened themselves up to channeling as a way of communicating with those who are supposed to be dead or with entities of higher intelligence. Almighty Yah's Word forbids people from pursuing these practices that are called divination, soothsaying, and having familiar spirits. (Ref: Leviticus 19:26; 20:6, 27; Acts16:16; and 1 Timothy 4:1)

> **He causes all, both small and great, rich and poor, free and slave to receive a mark on their right hand or on their foreheads, and that no one may buy or sell except one who has the mark or the name of the beast, or the number his name. Here is wisdom. Let him who has understanding calculate the number of the beast, for it is the number of a man: His number is 666.**
>
> Revelation 13:16-18 (NKJV)

Wow, this future false prophet is going to be one powerful, influential dude. He deceives the majority of the people of the world into believing they should worship the anti-Christ by having an idol of him and enforcing worship of it with the death penalty. So now, as implied in these verses, he initiates a world economic system that everyone must be a part of in order to have customary, normal, day-to-day buying and selling of goods. This future, world-controlling economic system requires that all human beings have either the mark, the name, or the number of the beast or anti-Christ on either their hand or their forehead. Again, these Scriptures may sound way out in left field, but remember this, Almighty Yah's Holy Word is truth.

The reality is that some of the current high-tech advancements are not so far off from what is being described in these verses. There are presently several companies, such as Applied Digital Solutions and Mondex, which are competing for the multi-billion dollar biometric chip implant market. This is a not some distant future market of supplying the necessary equipment to facilitate a total cashless society that everyone will be required to use. It is only a few years away.

Technology has advanced the microcomputer chip to the application of being so small that one can be inserted under the skin with a hypodermic needle. Individual identification chips have been used to track and keep record on livestock and pets for years. The research from the high-tech companies, such as Applied Technologies, has found that there are two places on the human anatomy where the microchips work best. You guessed correctly, the back of the hand and the forehead. These areas have the least amount of muscle and tissue between the skin and bone. This application provides the clearest signal transmission and reception for scanning and tracking.

Having a worldwide cashless society really makes good sense when we consider the benefits. In a few years from now, we will hear the spin from politicians and the banking industry explaining to us that, by taking the chip and going cashless, our world will be so much better. Their strong arguments will be: an end to identity theft, less drug trafficking, less personal theft and counterfeiting; greater ease of travel with your lifetime visa and driver's license embedded on your hand or noggin. Just imagine, banking and shopping with no cash, checks, or credit cards. All you do is walk up to the checkout counter with your items, have your hand or head scanned, and you are on your way out the door. Sounds like a great improvement, doesn't it? Well, it is supposed to sound that way because it's deception.

We cannot allow ourselves to be deceived into accepting this evil, pre-destined system that is coming soon if in any way it is tied to the worship of the anti-Christ. Here is what Yah's Holy Word says about it:

> **Then another angel, a third, followed them, crying with a loud voice, "Those who worship the beast and its image, and receive a mark on their foreheads or on their hands, they will also drink the wine of God's wrath, poured unmixed into the cup of His anger, and they will be tormented with fire and sulfur in the presence of the holy angels and in the presence of the Lamb. And the smoke of their torment goes up forever and ever. There is no rest day or night for those who worship the beast and its image and for anyone who receives the mark of its name." Here is a call for the endurance of the saints, those who keep the commandments of God and hold fast to the faith of Jesus. And I heard a voice from heaven saying, "Write this: Blessed are the dead who from now on die in the Lord." "Yes," says the Spirit, "they will rest from their labors, for their deeds follow them."**
> Revelation 14:9-13 (NRSV)

I pray that you are beginning to appreciate the importance of sharing these verses and Almighty Yah's plan of salvation with others. There will be more Scripture and paraphrasing regarding the events of the final seven years later in this book.

Now some hard reality as I attempt to paraphrase the Scriptures that reveal clues about the end-time beast system that has been around for many years. How will all that has been prophesied about the beast system actually materialize? The plans for the end-time, one-world economic, political, and religious systems have been in the planning and behind-the-scenes implementation stage for many centuries. The members of the Illuminati have been working their plan called the "New World Order" by manipulating governments to bring about their desired results. There are many people who are a part of several organizations that have been working in concert to create all sorts of chaos throughout the world. Out of the chaos they form, the end result they desire is shaping their New World Order.

The following article is extracted from an excellent analysis of the *New World Order (NWO)* by author Ken Adachi, which can be found at: www.educate-yourself.org.

The term *New World Order (NWO)* has been used by numerous politicians through the ages, and is a generic term used to refer to a worldwide conspiracy being orchestrated by an extremely powerful and influential group of genetically-related individuals (at least at the highest echelons) which include many of the world's wealthiest people, top political leaders, and corporate elite, as well as members of the so-called **Black Nobility** of Europe (dominated by the **British Crown**) whose goal is to create a **One World (fascist) Government**, stripped of nationalistic and regional boundaries, that is obedient to their agenda.

This is a statement from the Zionist banker, Paul Warburg: "We will have a world government whether you like it or not. The only question is whether that government will be achieved by conquest or consent." (February 17, 1950, as he testified before the US Senate).

The Illuminati's intention is to effect **complete and total control** over every human being on the planet and to dramatically reduce the world's population by two-thirds. This means that if you are alive at the time of anti-Messiah's beast system during the last three and one-half years of the great tribulation, you will either conform to their program, which means accepting the mark of the beast, or be exterminated, or be under divine protection from Almighty Yahweh.

While the name *New World Order* is the term most frequently used today to loosely refer to anyone involved in this conspiracy, the study of exactly who makes up this group is a complex and intricate one. I will give an overview, and you can research it more thoroughly if you desire to.

In 1992, **Dr, John Coleman** published *Conspirators Hierarchy: The Story of the Committee of 300*. With laudable scholarship and meticulous research, Dr Coleman identifies the players and carefully details the New World Order agenda of worldwide domination and control. On page 161 of the *Conspirators Hierarchy*, Dr Coleman accurately summarizes the intent and purpose of the Committee of 300 as follows:

"A One World Government and one-unit monetary system, under permanent non-elected hereditary oligarchies (government by a few) who self-select from among their numbers in the form of a feudal system as it was in the Middle Ages. In this One World entity, population will be limited by restrictions on the number of children per family, diseases, wars, famines, until 1 billion people who are useful to the ruling class, in areas which will be strictly and clearly defined, remain as the total world population.

"There will be no middle class, only rulers and the servants. All laws will be uniform under a legal system of world courts practicing the same unified code of laws, backed up by a One World Government police force and a One World unified military to enforce laws in all former countries where no national boundaries shall exist. The system will be on the basis of a welfare state; those who are obedient and subservient to the One World Government will be rewarded with the means to live; those who are rebellious will simply be starved to death or be declared outlaws, thus a target for anyone who wishes to kill them. Privately owned firearms or weapons of any kind will be prohibited."

Why is the conspiracy unknown by the general public? The sheer magnitude and complex web of deceit surrounding the individuals and organizations involved in this conspiracy is mind boggling, even for the most astute among us. Most people react with disbelief and skepticism towards the topic, unaware that they have been **conditioned** (brainwashed) to react with skepticism by institutional and media influences. Author and de-programmer Fritz Springmeier (*The Top 13 Illuminati Bloodlines*) says that most people have built in "slides" that short circuit the mind's critical examination process when it comes to certain sensitive topics. "Slides," Springmeier reports, is a CIA term for a conditioned type of response which dead ends a person's thinking and terminates debate or examination of the topic at hand. For example, the mention of the word "conspiracy" often solicits a slide response with many people.

What most people believe to be "Public Opinion" is in reality *carefully crafted and scripted propaganda* designed to elicit a *desired behavioral response* from the public. **Public opinion polls** are really taken with the intent of gauging the public's acceptance of the New World Order's planned programs. A strong showing in the polls tells them that the programming is "taking," while a poor showing tells the NWO manipulators that they have to recast or "tweak" the programming until the desired response is achieved.

The NWO Modus Operandi: The NWO global conspirators manifest their agenda through the skillful manipulation of human emotions, especially fear. In the past centuries, they have repeatedly utilized a contrivance that NWO researcher and author David Icke has characterized in his latest book, *The Biggest Secret*, as **Problem, Reaction,** and **Solution.**

The technique is as follows: NWO strategists create the **Problem**—by funding, assembling, and training an "opposition" group to stimulate turmoil in an established political power (sovereign country, region, continent, etc.) that they wish to impinge upon and thus create opposing factions in a conflict that the NWO themselves maneuvered into existence. In recent decades, so called opposition groups are usually identified in the media as 'freedom fighters' or 'liberators'.

At the same time, the leader of the established political power where the conflict is being orchestrated is demonized and, on cue, referred to as 'another Hitler' (take your pick: Saddam Hussein, Milosevic, Kadaffi, etc.). The 'freedom fighters' are not infrequently assembled from a local criminal element (i.e. KLA, drug traffickers). In the spirit of true Machiavellian deceit, the same NWO strategists are equally involved in covertly arming and advising the leader of the established power as well (the NWO always profits from any armed conflict by loaning money, arming, and supplying all parties involved in a war).

The conflict is drawn to the world stage by the controlled media outlets with a barrage of photos and videotape reports of horrific and bloody atrocities suffered by innocent civilians. The cry goes up "Something has to be done!" And that is the desired **Reaction.**

The NWO puppeteers then provide the **Solution** by sending in UN 'Peace Keepers' (Bosnia) or a UN 'Coalition Force' (Gulf War) or NATO Bombers and then ground troops (Kosovo), or the military to 'search for Weapons of Mass Destruction,' which of course are never found. Once installed, the 'peace keepers' never leave. The idea is to have NWO-controlled ground troops in all major countries or strategic areas where significant resistance to the New World Order takeover is likely to be encountered.

So who and what is the NWO? The corporate portion of the NWO is dominated by **international bankers, oil barons, and pharmaceutical** cartels, as well as other major multinational corporations. The **Royal Family of England,** namely **Queen Elizabeth II** and the House of Windsor, (who are, in fact, descendants of the German arm of European Royalty—the Saxe-Coburg-Gotha family—changed the name to Windsor in 1914), are high level players in the oligarchy which controls the upper strata of the NWO. The decision-making nerve centers of this effort are in **London** (especially the **City of London**), Basel, Switzerland, and **Brussels** (NATO headquarters).

The **United Nations,** along with all the agencies working under the UN umbrella, such as the **World Health Organization** (WHO), are full time players in this scheme. Similarly, **NATO** is a military tool of the NWO.

The **leaders of all major industrial countries** like the United States, England, Germany, Italy, Australia, New Zealand, etc. (members of the "G7/G8") are active and fully cooperative participants in this conspiracy. In this century, the degree of control exerted by the NWO has advanced to the point that only certain handpicked individuals, who are groomed and selected are even eligible to become the prime minister or president of countries like England,

Germany, or The United States. It didn't matter whether Bill Clinton or Bob Dole won the Presidency in 1996, or John Kerry or George W. Bush in 2000, the results would have been the same. All four of these men are playing on the same team for the same ball club. Anyone who isn't a team player is taken out: i.e., President Kennedy, Ali Bhutto (Pakistan) and Aldo Moro (Italy). More recently, Admiral Borda and William Colby were also killed because they were either unwilling to go along with the conspiracy to destroy America, weren't cooperating in some capacity, or were attempting to expose/thwart the takeover agenda.

The following is the Illuminati's role in shaping history. Most of the major wars, political upheavals, and economic depression/recessions of the past 100 years (and earlier) were carefully planned and instigated by the plotting of these elite, sick people. They include The Spanish-American War (1898), World War I and World War II; The Great Depression; the Bolshevik Revolution of 1917; the Rise of Nazi Germany; the Korean War; the Vietnam War; the 1989-91 "fall" of Soviet Communism; the 1991 Gulf War; the War in Kosovo; and the two Iraq wars. Even the French Revolution was orchestrated into existence by elements of the Illuminati.

The instigation of a trumped-up war as a cover for amassing fortunes can be dated back to at least the 12th Century when only a core group of nine members of the Knights Templar, kicked off The Crusades that lasted for over a century and a half.

The core group mentioned above has been reported as being the military arm of a secret society known as the Priory of Sion, but this has been proven to be a hoax.

In 1307, the king of France, Philippe the Fair, coveted the wealth and was jealous of the Templars' power. The French king set out to arrest all the Templars in France on October 13. While many Templars were seized and tortured, including their Grand Master, Jacques de Molay, many other Templars (who had been tipped off) escaped. They eventually resurfaced in Portugal, in Malta (as the Knights of Malta) and later in Scotland as The Scottish Rites of Freemasonry, with Albert Pike playing a key role in defining a plan for establishing a world government.

The following information is from a letter from Albert Pike to Mazzini as stated on the web site www.ThreeWorldWars.com/index.html.

It is a commonly believed fallacy that for a short time, the Pike letter to Mazzini was on display in the British Museum Library in London, and it was copied by William Guy Carr, former Intelligence Officer in the Royal Canadian Navy. The British Library has confirmed in writing to me that such a document has never been in their possession. Furthermore, in Carr's book, *Satan, Prince of this World*, Carr includes the following footnote: "The Keeper of Manuscripts recently informed the author that this letter is NOT catalogued in the British Museum Library.

It appears that Carr learned about this letter from Cardinal Caro Rodriguez of Santiago, Chile, who wrote *The Mystery of Freemasonry Unveiled*.

To date, no conclusive proof exists to show that this letter was ever written. It seems strange that a man of Cardinal Rodriguez's knowledge should have said that it WAS in British Museum Library in 1925." Nevertheless, the letter is widely quoted and the topic of much discussion.

Following are apparently extracts of the letter, showing how Three World Wars have been planned for many generations.

"**The First World War** must be brought about in order to permit the Illuminati to overthrow the power of the Czars in Russia and of making that country a fortress of atheistic Communism. The divergences caused by the 'agentur' (agents) of the Illuminati between the British and Germanic Empires will be used to foment this war. At the end of the war, Communism will be built and used in order to destroy the other governments and in order to weaken the religions." (Cmdr. William Guy Carr: Quoted in *Satan: Prince of This World*.)

Students of history will recognize that the political alliances of England on one side and Germany on the other, forged between 1871 and 1898 by Otto von Bismarck, co-conspirator of Albert Pike, were instrumental in bringing about the First World War.

"**The Second World War** must be fomented by taking advantage of the differences between the Fascists and the political Zionists. This war must be brought about so that Nazism is destroyed and that the political Zionism be strong enough to institute a sovereign state of Israel in Palestine. During the Second World War, International Communism must become strong enough in order to balance Christendom, which would be then restrained and held in check until the time when we would need it for the final social cataclysm." (Cmdr. William Guy Carr: Quoted in *Satan: Prince of This World*.)

After this Second World War, Communism was made strong enough to begin taking over weaker governments. In 1945, at the Potsdam Conference between Truman, Churchill, and Stalin, a large portion of Europe was simply handed over to Russia, and on the other side of the world, the aftermath of the war with Japan helped to sweep the tide of Communism into China.

(Readers who argue that the terms Nazism and Zionism were not known in 1871 should remember that the Illuminati *invented* both these movements. In addition, Communism as an ideology, and as a coined phrase, originates in France during the Revolution. In 1785, Restif coined the phrase four years before revolution broke out. Restif and Babeuf, in turn, were influenced by Rousseau—as was the most famous conspirator of them all, Adam Weishaupt.)

"The Third World War must be fomented by taking advantage of the differences caused by the "agentur" of the "Illuminati" between the political Zionists and the leaders of Islamic World. The war must be conducted in such a way that Islam (the Moslem Arabic World) and political Zionism (the State of Israel) mutually destroy each other. Meanwhile the other nations, once more divided on this issue will be constrained to fight to the point of complete physical, moral, spiritual and economical exhaustion...We shall unleash the Nihilists and the atheists, and we shall provoke a formidable social cataclysm which in all its horror will show clearly to the nations the effect of absolute atheism, origin of savagery and of the most bloody turmoil. Then everywhere, the citizens, obliged to defend themselves against the world minority of revolutionaries, will exterminate those destroyers of civilization, and the multitude, disillusioned with Christianity, whose deistic spirits will from that moment be without compass or direction, anxious for an ideal, but without knowing where to render its adoration, will receive the true light through the universal manifestation of the pure doctrine of Lucifer, brought finally out in the public view. This manifestation will result from the general reactionary movement which will follow the destruction of Christianity and atheism, both conquered and extermi-nated at the same time." (Cmdr. William Guy Carr: Quoted in his book, *Satan: Prince of This World*.)

Since the terrorist attacks of September 11, 2001, world events, and in par-ticular in the Middle East, show a growing unrest and instability between Modern Zionism *[Christianity as least by association]* and the Arabic World. This is completely in line with the call for a Third World War to be fought between the two, and their allies on both sides. This Third World War is still to come, and recent events show us that it is not far off.

The acquisition and consolidation of ever-greater wealth, natural resources, total political power, and control over others are the motivating forces which drive the decisions of the NWO leaders. The toll in human suffering and the loss of innocent lives are non-issues for these individuals.

There are literally thousands of pages of material on these subjects. I encourage you to do your own research, so you can better understand how the terrible prophecies that I covered a few pages back are being ful-filled before our eyes by the evil people that make up the NWO. Here are some excellent web sites that have a lot of information about the New World Order, which is the coming beast system.

www.threeworldwars.com/index.html
www.endtimez.com/
www.meguiar.addr.com/End_Times_Table_of_Contents.htm
www.meguiar.addr.com/Home_Page.htm#The%20Book%20of%20Revelation
www.conspiracyarchive.com/NWO/Freemasonry.htm
www.educate-yourself.org/nwo/nwonewsindex.shtml

On this last site, there is a really interesting article about a plan for huge deception with **Project Blue Beam** that you should read. There are many others, but these are the best I have found that will help you to be informed. Many of you that have read this section will be very skeptical of this material and the web sites I have referenced. I respect what you believe. Isn't it wonderful that we have the freedom to believe whatever we choose to believe is right and true. It's kind of like what you witnessed on that most tragic day in U.S. history to date, as you watched the huge twin tower buildings at the World Trade Center and the third building no. 7, rapidly crashing to the ground. And in the weeks and months afterward, you formed your opinion of what really happened based on what you learned from the news and reports. You either saw through the deception to the truth, or you didn't.

Just remember that, in the insanity that is playing out in these last years of this, the last, generation, Almighty Yah is in control. We all must be prepared to die whenever our time comes and someday stand before King and Judge Yahshua to give an account of our life.

The Opening of the Sixth Seal

"Immediately after the suffering of those days the sun will be darkened, and the moon will not give its light; the stars will fall from heaven, and the powers of heaven will be shaken. Then the sign of the Son of Man will appear in heaven, and then all the tribes of the earth will mourn, and they will see 'the Son of Man coming on the clouds of heaven' with power and great glory. And He will send out His angels with a loud trumpet call, and they will gather His elect from the four winds, [entire world] **from one end of heaven to the other."**
Matthew 24:29-31 (NRSV). *Bracketed words added for clarity.*

Note: The latter part of this verse as it is written in Mark 13:27 (NRSV) reads, **"from the ends of the earth to the ends of heaven."** Now the parallel.

When He opened the sixth seal, I looked, and there came a great earthquake; the sun became black as sackcloth, the full moon became like blood, the stars of the sky fell to the earth as the fig tree drops its winter fruit when shaken by a gale. The sky vanished like a scroll rolling itself up, and every mountain and island was removed from its place.

Then the kings of the earth and the magnates and the generals and the rich and the powerful, and everyone, slave and free, hid in the caves and among the rocks of the mountains, calling to the mountains and rocks, "Fall on us and hide us from the face of the one seated on the throne and from the wrath of the Lamb; for the great day of their wrath has come, and who is able to stand?"

Revelation 6:12-17. (NRSV)

These two sections of Scripture parallel and are describing several truly incredible events that are to happen in succession after the most horrible martyrdom of millions of born again believers and Jews in all of history. These events will take place during the final three and a half years of the world dictator's rule, as described in the previous section. These amazing events that Almighty Yah produces in the heavens and the earth are highlighted in this the opening of the sixth seal outline. I believe the future events that are described as taking place in the heavens will be the results of a large planet or dwarf star after it passes close enough to our planet to cause huge problems. This planet or star that has been named Planet X is scheduled to pass in front of our planet's orbital path. I believe that as planet earth passes through the debris of the tail of Planet X, earth will be bombarded with asteroids that will produce the destruction described in the Scriptures. There is more detail about Planet X explained in the first four trumpets Scriptures a few pages over.

The verses above are describing the coming of Yahshua Messiah with His huge army of warrior angels in great brilliance. King Yahshua and His army are fulfilling two very important parts of Almighty Yah's Master Plan as these prophecies are revealed. First is the destruction of the anti-Christ, his army, and all who make up and are loyal to his world system. Second is the literal, physical saving of the Jews and non-Jews who have accepted Yahshua (Jesus) prior to His coming and are taken up into the air and transformed with new resurrected bodies. King Yahshua and His army will come in the clouds in great brilliance against a pitch-black background either circling the earth or projecting Himself larger than life, so that, as the earth revolves, every person on the earth will see Him. This awesome event in the sky terrifies all those who do not know Him, those who have bowed down to and put their faith and trust in the anti-Messiah, thereby worshiping Satan. I believe the terrible plagues described in the next section will be poured out during the coming in the air of the true Messiah.

Some of the great host of angels will be zooming all over the earth, gathering the elect, the saved ones, in order for them to be transformed into their new resurrected bodies. All those who were saved when they died, beginning from the time when Yahshua was resurrected from the dead in approximately A.D. 30, will be given new resurrected bodies at that time, first before we who are alive at that incredible time.

All of the next chapter, "The Resurrection of the Elect," is a detailed explanation of the gathering of Yah's elect, or the rapture, as it is commonly known today. This event of the royal priesthood receiving new, resurrected, glorious bodies will truly be the most incredible event in Almighty Yah's Master Plan. This clearly happens at the end of the three and one-half year tribulation period when Yahshua comes.

There is an important question at the end of the description of the opening of the sixth seal.

> **"...For the great day of His wrath has come, and who is able to stand?"**
> Revelation 6:17 (NJKV)

The answer is then given and described in all of Chapter Seven. Almighty Yah is going to select precisely 12,000 descendants of each of the 12 tribes of Israel that currently mingled within the races throughout the earth. He will seal and protect these individuals just prior to the time of the great persecution by the anti-Christ and the timing of the meteorite events that are described in the first four trumpets of Revelation 8. These people that John sees on the earth will be born again Messianic Israelites from the House of Judah and the House of Ephraim. I believe that their sealing will be during the spring Feast of Passover in the year that is three and one-half years before the end, when Yahshua comes to establish His kingdom. Chapter 14 is where I believe a description of the sealing takes place. It is written:

> **Then I looked, and there was the Lamb, standing on Mount Zion! And with Him were one hundred forty-four thousand who had His name and the His Father's name written on their foreheads.**
> Revelation 14:1 (NRSV)

I understand the sealing by Master Yahshua to be with His true name and the true name of His Father Yahweh in their minds and hearts. I believe the sealing literally takes place on the Temple Mount of Mount Zion in Jerusalem. The way the Scriptures continue, it appears that this select, chosen group (many are called, but few are chosen), will proclaim throughout the earth the most important end-time messages that are described as being given to them by the three angels as recorded in Revelation 14. It is written:

> **They have been redeemed from humankind as first fruits** [Shavuot *makes sense to be the Feast time of their sealing because it is about first fruits and is when the Torah was given at Mt. Sinai and Holy spirit was given to 120 Messianic Jews during what is known in Christianity as Pentecost*] **for God and the Lamb, and in their mouth no lie was found; they are blameless. Then I saw another angel flying in midheaven, with an eternal gospel to proclaim to those who live on the earth—to every nation and tribe and language and people. He said in a loud voice, "Fear God and give him glory, for the hour of his judgment has come; and worship him who made heaven and earth, the sea and the springs of water." Then another angel, a second, followed, saying, "Fallen, fallen is Babylon the great! She has made all nations drink of the wine of the wrath of her fornication." Then another angel, a third, followed them, crying with a loud voice, "Those who worship the beast and its image, and receive a mark on their foreheads or on their hands, they will also drink the wine of God's wrath, poured unmixed into the cup of his anger, and they will be tormented with fire and sulphur in the presence of the holy angels and in the presence of the Lamb. And the smoke of their torment goes up forever and ever. There is no rest day or night for those who worship the beast and its image and for anyone who receives the mark of its name." Here is a call for the endurance of the saints, those who keep the commandments of God and hold fast to the faith of Jesus. And I heard a voice from heaven saying, "Write this: Blessed are the dead who from now on die in the Lord." "Yes," says the Spirit, "they will rest from their labors, for their deeds follow them."**
>
> Revelation 14:4b-12 (NRSV). *Bracketed words added for clarity.*

In order for these three very important messages to be delivered throughout the world, the 144,000 sealed Messianic Israelites will be given the messages from the three angels and then sent out like the 12 and 72 apostles were sent out by Master Yahshua, as recorded in

Matthew 10:1-23 and Luke 10:1-24. These sealed, and totally protected, Holy Spirit-filled individuals will be sent out, probably in groups of two, to all the nations proclaiming the three incredible messages stated above. They will be empowered to do the miraculous healings and deliverances like those that the 12 and 72 apostles performed when Yahshua sent them out before His death on the cross. The miracles will be testimonies as a witness that the 144,000 are proclaiming the truth and performing the miracles by the power of Holy Spirit in Yahshua's mighty name.

There has never been, nor will there ever be again, a time in human history when the power of Almighty Yah is manifested through so many people receiving so many healings and deliverances from demons as during the last three and one-half years of the great tribulation when the 144,000 are ministering. The timing of the ministry of the 144,000 will most likely coincide with the ministry of the two witnesses described in Revelation 11:3-12 as they are calling down the plagues that are described in the seven trumpets and seven vials. The 144,000 will be anointed and blessed by the leadership of the two witnesses who, I believe, will be EliYah and Moses as they prepare the people for the coming of Messiah Yahshua. HalleluYah! What a time that will be.

For a more detailed study of the ministry of the 144,000 during the three and one-half years of the great tribulation, I encourage you to order a copy of the book titled *The Mystery of Disunity* by Tim McHyde. His web site address is: www.EscapeAllTheseThings.com.

Don't these events sound a lot more exciting than sitting on a cloud playing a harp?

Another group is described in verses 9 through 17 of Revelation 7. These are the true followers of Yahshua Messiah who are overcomers through the tribulation but are not part of the chosen group of 144,000. When we accept Yahshua as our Savior, whether Gentile or Jew, and are born of His Holy Spirit, we then become a new creation in Him. We become part of His body, His family. We become what is described in Ephesians 2:11-16 "the one new man."

During the tribulation, many of the believing redeemed, both Jew and non-Jew, will be called upon by Yahshua to lay down their lives for Him because they will not deny Him as their Master and Savior. And some Yahweh will supernaturally protect and provide for during the evil reign of the dictator, anti-Christ beast. It is written:

And he said to me, These are they which came out of great tribulation, and have washed their robes, and made them white in the blood of the Lamb.
Revelation 7:14b (KJV)

Those who are overcomers, whether they lay down their lives for the cause of Messiah or are protected by Him until His coming, will have important roles in the new kingdom that King Yahshua will establish.

Then I saw thrones, and those who sat on them were given the power to judge. I also saw the souls of those who had been executed because they had proclaimed the truth that Jesus revealed and the word of God. They had not worshiped the beast or its image, nor had they received the mark of the beast on their foreheads or their hands. They came to life and ruled as kings with Christ for a thousands years. (The rest of the dead did not come to life until the thousand years were over.) This is the first raising of the dead. Happy and greatly blessed are those who are included in this first raising of the dead. The second death has no power over them; they shall be priests of God and of Christ, and they will rule with Him for a thousand years.
Revelation 20:4-6 (TEV)

We will each stand before our Creator, Savior, and King eternal, Yahshua, to give an account of our lives in either one of two judgments. The Judgment Seat of Christ, also called the Bema Seat Judgment of the saints, or elect, will be phase one of the judgment that He renders. The judgments are covered in greater detail in Chapter Nine, "Post Resurrection Events."

Recapping briefly, seals one through five describe events that have been happening throughout history, are happening now, and will intensify, especially during and after World War III, as described in Jeremiah 50 and 51, Ezekiel 38 and Revelation 17 and 18. World War III sets the stage for the New World Order beast system to take over.

The opening of the fifth seal gives us insight of clues about martyrdom of the true followers of Yahshua in all of the history of mankind for the past 1,900 plus years, of those that will be martyred during the great tribulation. The events described in the first five seals are to be understood as past and present tense. The events described in the sixth and seventh seals are specifically for the years just prior to and during the last three and one-half years of the Prophet Daniel's seventieth week.

The opening of the sixth seal gives us insight into the beginning of the Day of the Lord, as Almighty Yah responds to the evil and suffering that Satan produced during the past six thousand years. Included is the description of unparalleled cosmic and earthly catastrophes as Almighty Yah starts to shake things up in order to wake people up from their sleepy state of deception and complacency. The description of the events of the sixth seal is overlaid by the events described in the seven trumpets. Noteworthy is the events of the first four trumpets. I believe what is being described in the verses of Revelation 8:7-13 is the earth being bombarded by asteroids that come from a large sphere of some type that passes through in front of our earth's orbit path. It is written:

The first angel sounded: And hail and fire followed, mingled with blood, and they were thrown to the earth. And a third of the trees were burned up, and all green grass was burned up. Then the second angel sounded: And *something* like a great mountain burning with fire was thrown into the sea, and a third of the sea became blood. And a third of the living creatures in the sea died, and a third of the ships were destroyed. Then the third angel sounded: And a great star fell from heaven, burning like a torch, and it fell on a third of the rivers and on the springs of water. The name of the star is Wormwood. A third of the waters became Wormwood, and many men died from the water, because it was made bitter. Then the fourth angel sounded: And a third of the sun was struck, a third of the moon, and a third of the stars, so that a third of them were darkened. A third of the day did not shine, and likewise the night. And I looked, and I heard an angel flying through the midst of heaven, saying with a loud voice, "Woe, woe, woe to the inhabitants of the earth, because of the remaining blasts of the trumpet of the three angels who are about to sound!"
Revelation 8:7-13 (NKJV)

What scientific evidence is there that supports that events of the magnitude described above can happen, and since it is prophesied in the Scriptures, will happen? We start at the beginning of civilization after the great flood in which Noah, his family, and the animals survived.

Authorities of ancient history believe the oldest civilization to be that of Sumer, located in the vicinity of where the Garden of Eden was in modern-day Iraq. Sumer was founded by Nimrod. Remember him and his family from Chapter Four? Nimrod was responsible for building the Tower of Babel, which was a large, very tall ziggurat used for studying the stars, planets, and heavens.

Parts of the following article were taken from a report written by the late author Jim Rector. His excellent work can be found on his website Cornerstone Publications at: **www.CornerstonePublication.com.**

The ancient Sumerians were highly advanced astronomers in their understanding of our solar system. In 1976, a Russian-born, Palestinian-raised linguistic scholar named Zecharia Sitchin wrote the first of his best-selling "Earth Chronicles" series, titled "The Twelfth Planet." In his writings taken from his translation of the ancient Sumerian "Creation Tablets," is information about the nine planets of our solar system, our sun, and moon that the Sumerians counted as ten and eleven, and then a twelfth planet they called *Nibiru*, which means, "planet of passing."

According to the Sumerian texts, the planet *Nibiru* has a widely elliptical orbit of some 3,600 years in length. Two of the most critical aspects of the Sumerian creation epic are that the close proximity of *Nibiru* to the earth always produces an extended period of great cosmic and seismic upheaval and destruction, and according to the calculations, the planet *Nibiru* made its last flyby of the earth in or around the year 1587 B.C., and thus its 3,600-year orbit will effect its return in the year that appears in the title of this article, namely A.D. 2012. This, of course, begs the question, *Is there actually an additional planet in our solar system beyond the nine with which we are all familiar?* And the answer, believe it or not, may well be YES!

The famous astronomer Percival Lowell, builder of the world-class observatory in Flagstaff, Arizona, bearing his name, and perhaps most well known for promulgating the theory that there were canals on Mars of apparently intelligent design, was the leading scientist behind the quest for yet another constituent of the solar system during the first part of the 20th century. Interestingly, Lowell termed the object of his search as PLANET X, a designation that is still quite familiar and in use today,

Unbeknown to most people, modern astronomers have continued to search for Percival Lowell's *Planet X*. In fact, they have even retained the same name for this tenth member of the solar system. Continual perturbations in the orbits of Uranus and particularly Neptune large enough to dismiss the minuscule effect of Pluto kept scientists busy in the quest for a tenth planet. In 1982, it was finally discovered, acknowledged by NASA, and a year later was actually spotted by an Infrared Astronomical Satellite (IRAS). Cal-Tech's Jet Propulsion Laboratory (JPL), manager for NASA's Deep Space Program and the leading center in the U.S. for the robotic exploration of the solar system, also reported on the discovery of the so-called *Planet X*. In the early 1980s, articles attesting to the new finding appeared in major newspapers, including both the *New York Times* and the *Washington Post*. The *Post* story, in fact, began in the following manner:

"AT SOLAR SYSTEM'S EDGE GIANT OBJECT IS A MYSTERY - A heavenly body possibly as large as the giant planet Jupiter and possibly so close to Earth that it would be a part of this solar system has been found in the direction of the constellation Orion by an orbiting telescope called the IRAS. So mysterious is the object that astronomers do not know if it is a planet, a giant comet, a protostar that never got hot enough to become a star, a distant galaxy so young that it is still in the process of forming its first stars, or a galaxy so shrouded in dust that none of the light cast by its stars ever gets through."

Shortly after these public announcements, however, a shroud of silence has surrounded the project, and a seriously focused Federal government cover-up undertaken.

The scientific facts that have been determined thus far with regard to Planet X is that its orbit is highly elliptical, resembling that of a comet more than a typical planetary body. In addition, it's orbit is of far greater size than any of the current nine members of our solar system, carrying it far out into space over a revolutionary period of some 3,600 years. Planet X is also a very large celestial body, possessing a total mass in excess of 100 times that of the earth. Its magnetic core is exceedingly powerful and clashes with the electromagnetic fields of other planets. In spite of official silence concerning Planet X, research has continued apace since its 1982 discovery. It is now known that the Hubble Space Telescope has been repeatedly used to observe Planet X, with only a chosen few permitted to see the actual astrophotographs. The Hubble telescope is equipped with special technological equipment that prohibits any possible interception of its signals by any entity other than NASA. Over the last 10-12 years, the U.S. government has constructed a total of eight special observatories in various parts of the world for the express purpose of studying Planet X. Two of those institutions are located in the state of New Mexico.

Although there is much disinformation being promulgated with respect to Planet X, solid and dependable scientific evidence of its existence, discovery, and the research accomplished, both past and present, is readily available. Perhaps the most highly qualified member of the scientific community who has personal inside knowledge of this nature is Dr. James McCanney, a world-renowned astrophysicist, with a double doctorate in both mathematics and nuclear solid-state physics. He has served as professor of physics at Cornell University, and for several years was a consultant to NASA. He has had a number of scientific articles published, and has written at least three books and several technical manuals. Dr. McCanney knows about Planet X, and the U. S. government's ongoing efforts to learn more about it, and now that he is no longer working with NASA and is no longer bound to total silence, he has become something of a whistle-blower on this very sensitive subject.

According to Dr. McCanney, as well as a growing number of astronomers, astrophysicists, geologists, and cosmologists, Planet X has been having and continues to have an ever increasingly negative effect on our Sun, and consequently on our planet as well. Scientists have kept records of solar activity literally since the 1700s. Coronal Mass Ejections, or solar flares as we commonly refer to them, follow an 11-year cycle, five and one-half years increasing to a peak, then five and one-half years on the decline to a low. This cycle has been continuously repeated ever since astronomers have been keeping such records.

The last 11-year peak transpired in the year 2000, thus the scientific expectation would have been a consistent decrease in solar flare activity through most of 2005, but this has not at all been the case. Instead, coronal mass ejections have increased during this period, and that increase has been exceedingly substantial. In fact, the most extensive sun flares in all earth's known history with respect to both intensity and frequency have been recorded during the last five years, and the projections now are, interestingly and incredibly enough, for dramatic increase in solar storms between 2005 and, you guessed it, A.D. 2012 precisely!!

Astronomers and other scientists in related fields are acutely aware that something major is negatively affecting our Sun. Some of them are now beginning to seriously consider the likelihood that a fairly large celestial body is moving near to or actually may have already entered the solar system. That intruder is the mysterious Planet X, which is now no longer being relegated to the ranks of mere science fiction, as was once the case, but rather to the forefront of astronomical research. Experts, such as Dr. McCanney and others, are coming forth with admissions with regard to Planet X, its history, the intense research that has been on-going among the scientific community for at least the last 23 years, the classification of this project as above top secret, the massive government cover-up at the federal level, and the current thinking on this potentially destructive astral object threatening the earth and its population.

One of the questions that nags at critics of Planet X is why it has proven so difficult to physically observe and photograph (it most definitely has been seen and astrophotos certainly exist). Several fairly simple, but very profound facts contribute to this problem. First of all, the measurable perturbations in the orbits of Uranus and Neptune indicate a downward gravitational pull being exerted by Planet X on these two outer members of the solar system. This means that the object is approaching Earth from below the plane of the ecliptic, or the plane of the planetary solar orbits. This literally means that the best place on earth to view Planet X is at the South Pole, a region unlikely to permit professional astronomers the kind of access they would require to more fully and successfully investigate the approach. Additionally, due to its unusual orbital plane, the rogue planet can be viewed only during a very small window of time during the month of May. As far back as 1991, no less an authority than Dr. Robert S. Harrison, then director of the Naval Observatory, wrote an internal abstract covering nearly a decade of theoretical, mathematical, and observational astronomy by a team of NASA and other experts on the specific location and orbit of Planet X, reaching the above-stated conclusion.

Dr. McCanney has confirmed that Planet X is following the same path as the well-known Hale-Bopp comet, which means that indeed it is approaching from the southern hemisphere. His research has also led him to conclude that these two celestial objects are connected, and he revealed something else. Listed in the *New Illustrated Science & Invention Encyclopedia, 1987-89 Edition, Vol. 18,* he found heretofore-overlooked information regarding Planet X. Under the heading "Space Probes," there is a diagram that shows the 10th planet and a dark star (our Sun's dark twin). In addition, it is now known that both Pioneer 10 and 11 space probes were sent toward the southern hemisphere, and physically sighted both of these objects.

Secondly, Planet X, though a large celestial body compared to the size of the Earth, Mars, Venus, and Mercury, is nevertheless not a very bright space object. It may, in fact, be a kind of star known as a brown dwarf. Combining this information with the fact that atmospheric pollutants and haze make any kind of direct viewing very difficult, so much so that Dr. David Morrison, Director of Space & Astrobiology at NASA's Ames Research Center, admitted before the U.S. House of Representatives that, under such extreme conditions, a comet or possibly even a planetary body could literally blind-side the earth, escaping definitive detection until within only a few weeks from impact or close flyby.

In addition to the already measurably known interaction with the Sun, the approach of Planet X has begun to effect significant atmospheric and meteorological changes on the earth as well—changes with which most of us are acutely and painfully familiar. This trend has, in fact, been on-going since around 1960, and has shown appreciable increase since 1990 onward to the present time. There is little or no need to take up much time and space detailing the almost incomprehensible escalating weather, seismic, and volcanic catastrophes that have transpired upon the earth over the last several years. Anyone who attributes these incredible Earth changes in more recent times to some sort of familiar weather pattern that is simply repeating itself as it has done for thousands of years is, I am sad to say, grossly misinformed. Nothing could be farther from the truth!

The approach of Planet X almost certainly will not cause it to actually strike the Earth directly. The chances of that happening are extremely remote and would result in the utter obliteration of this planet, something that the Scriptures unquestionably rule out. The point, of course, is that with something the size of such a celestial body literally invading our solar system, it would not be necessary for it to strike our planet in order to precipitate unprecedented destruction—indeed chaos and upheaval of only Biblical prophetic proportions!

According to the ancient Sumerian Creation Tablets, Planet X or *Nibiru*, will return some 3,600 years from its last close passage to the Earth, which was about 1587 B.C.

Dr. Velikovsky, in his book "Worlds in Collision," painstakingly amassed evidence so strong as to be overwhelming that at the time of the Exodus and for the next 52 years, the Earth experienced one of the greatest cosmic encounters in its history. Unfortunately, he concluded that all the various upheavals and disruptions that transpired during the Exodus period were attributable to the planet Jupiter ejecting a large comet-like object that, after swinging by the Earth several times, eventually stabilized as the new planet

Venus. This now appears to be incorrect, but the remainder of research compiled by Dr. Velikovsky is unassailable in its veracity, and in its conclusion that the extraordinary catastrophes that struck the Earth during that ancient era were indeed caused by a planetary body moving into or close to the Earth's orbit. It is just that the correct answer is not Venus, but rather the *Planet X* or *Nibiru*!!

I have provided these pages of documentation for you because it is important for all of us to be as informed as we can be regarding the events that are fulfilling the end-time prophecies of the Scripture. The fulfillment of the prophecies of the first four trumpets is huge. The passing by of Planet X, or whatever it actually is, in front of our earth's orbit with earth passing through the debris trails of asteroids provides the believable scenario of the meaning of what Apostle John heard and saw in the vision of the four trumpets.

First trumpet: Fire thrown upon the earth burning up a third of the trees and all grass is the result of probably thousands of meteorites coming into the earth's atmosphere as the earth passes through the tail debris of Planet X.

Second trumpet: A great burning mountain, meaning very enormous, crashing into the sea would be a huge asteroid that would create tsunamis the size that have never been recorded before. The heat from it in the sea would boil the oxygen out of the water killing the sea life and creating a red algae tide.

Third trumpet: The gases emitted from a star that would appear to be falling from heaven and passing by earth, would be very poisonous and would spread throughout the earth's atmosphere. The poisonous gases would settle and fall on the rivers, springs, and lakes, thereby polluting much of the earth's drinking water. Wormwood means "very bitter" and in the case of verse 11 of Revelation Eight, very deadly, because it says that "many men died from the water."

Fourth trumpet: Here is a summary of the prophecies including the darkness of the fourth trumpet as stated in a June 1989 edition of the *National Geographic* magazine of what would happen if our planet were to be hit by a large asteroid or asteroids. Note how remarkably close the description given in the magazine is to the words of the Scriptures:

"Giant meteorite strikes Earth, setting the planet AFIRE. VOLCANOES erupt, TSUNAMIS crash into the continents. The SKY grows DARK for months, perhaps years. Unable to cope with the catastrophic changes in climate, countless species are wiped off the face of the planet" (p. 686).

Literally billions of people will be homeless by this time. There will be little or no electricity, little or no running water, extreme food shortages, massive chaos everywhere, with looting, rape, and murder abounding. Rioting will ensue in many locales. Travel will be virtually impossible. It will truly be the end of the world as we have known it.

During the summer of 2006, I read a very detailed book that I highly recommend regarding the subject of the rough star or planet the Sumerians named *Nibiru*. The book is titled "Planet X in Bible Prophecy" by an excellent author I have already referenced, Tim McHyde. You can learn more from his in depth research at his website: www.EscapeAllTheseThings.com.

THE OPENING OF THE SEVENTH SEAL

The opening of the seventh seal in verse one of Revelation Chapter Eight, begins with the description of many of the details of the terrible events that will take place on earth during the final short span of time at the end of the great tribulation. These details continue through the end of Chapter Twenty. These symbolic descriptions of Yah's wrath using His forces in nature, and allowing powerful fallen angels and demons to be unleashed on the earth, are found in Chapters Eight and Nine. More details of God's coming wrath are described symbolically in Revelation Fifteen and Sixteen. These symbolic descriptions are referred to as the seven last trumpet plagues and bowls, or vials of the wrath of Yahweh. The seven last plagues and wrath of God are part of what is described after the blowing of the seventh or last trumpet.

Then the seventh angel blew his trumpet, and there were loud voices in heaven, saying, "The power to rule over the world belongs now to our Lord and His Messiah, and He will rule forever and ever!" Then the twenty-four elders who sit on their thrones in front of God threw themselves face downward and worshipped God, saying: "Lord God

Almighty, the one who is and who was! We thank you that you have taken your great power and have begun to rule! The heathen were filled with rage, because the time for your anger has come, the time for the dead to be judged. The time has come to reward your servants, the prophets, and all your people, all who have reverence for you, great and small alike. The time has come to destroy those who destroy the earth!" God's temple in heaven was opened, and the Covenant Box *[Ark]* **was seen there. Then there were flashes of lightning, rumblings and peals of thunder, an earthquake, and heavy hail.**

Revelation 11:15-19 (TEV). *Bracketed words added for clarity.*

The latter events in verse nineteen correspond with the events of the seventh angel pouring out his bowl of plagues described in Chapter 16, verses 17-21.

At the end of this age, King Yahshua comes to destroy the fallen angels, demons, rulers, armies, and all the people of this world who have accepted and worshipped the anti-Christ beast, to cast the evil anti-Christ beast and his deceitful false prophet into the lake of fire and to bind Satan the devil. When the seventh angel blows the last trumpet, it's the event that signals the time for Yahshua to leave His throne in heaven and with His great army of warrior angels, to begin traveling across the vast universe to planet earth. While the great heavenly host is coming to earth, the seven bowl plagues are being poured out on the earth in quick and rapid succession. The anti-Christ, beast dictator will have gathered the armies of the then one-world economic, governmental, and political systems together, to attempt to destroy King Yahshua and His army as they approach earth in the sky. All the host of human armies and fallen angles are destroyed at the battle of Armageddon. As it is written,

Then I saw heaven opened, and there was a white horse! Its rider is called Faithful and True, and in righteousness He judges and makes war. His eyes are like a flame of fire, and on His head are many diadems; and He has a name inscribed that no one knows but Himself. He is clothed in a robe dipped in blood, and His name is called The Word of God. And the armies of heaven, wearing fine linen, white and pure, were following Him on white horses. From His mouth comes a sharp sword *[His powerful, righteous Word]* **with which to strike down the nations, and He will rule them with a rod of iron** *[after He establishes His kingdom* *on earth]*; He will tread the winepress of the fury of the wrath of God the Almighty. On His robe and on His thigh He has a name inscribed, "King of kings and Lord of lords." Then I saw an angel standing in the sun, and with a loud voice he called to all the birds that fly in mid-heaven, "Come, gather for the great supper of God, to eat the flesh of kings, the flesh of captains, the flesh of the mighty, the flesh of horses and their riders—flesh of all, both free and slave, both small and great." Then I saw the beast and the kings of the earth with their armies gathered to make war against the rider on the horse and against His army. And the beast was captured, and with it the false prophet who had performed in its presence the signs by which he deceived those who had received the mark of the beast and those who worshiped its image. These two were thrown alive into the lake of fire that burns with sulfur. And the rest were killed by the sword of the rider on the horse, the sword that came from His mouth; and all the birds were gorged with their flesh.

Revelation 19:11-21 (NRSV). *Bracketed words added for clarity.*

And then the lawless one will be revealed, and the Lord Jesus *[Yahshua]* will slay with him with the breath of His mouth and destroy him by His appearing and His coming.

2 Thessalonians 2:8 (RSV). *Bracketed words added for clarity.*

You watched while a stone was cut out without hands, which struck the image on its feet of iron and clay, and broke them in pieces. Then the iron, the clay, the bronze, the silver, and the gold *[all of the influences of the former world empires that make up the last world government]* were crushed together, and became like chaff from the summer threshing floors; the wind carried them away so that no trace of them was found. And the stone that struck the image became a great mountain and filled the whole earth.

Daniel 2:34-35 (NKJV). *Bracketed words added for clarity.*

And the Spirit of the Lord shall rest upon Him, the spirit of wisdom and understanding, the spirit of counsel and might, the spirit of knowledge and the fear of the Lord. And His delight shall be in the fear of the Lord. He shall not judge by what His eyes see, or by what His ears hear; but with righteousness He shall judge the poor, and decide with equity for

the meek of the earth; and He shall smite the earth with the rod of His mouth, and with the breath of His lips He shall slay the wicked.
Isaiah 11:2-4 (RSV)

From out of these ancient empires shall come a final world dominating empire that Satan will rule for a short time through his completely possessed man, the anti-Christ beast and his side kick, the false prophet. When Yahshua comes back to this earth, He will utterly destroy the ten kingdoms of this world that are in control at that time.

I am sure the thought of these prophecies actually coming true in the future, or possibly now as you are reading this, are somewhat scary. Please understand this, Almighty Yah allows these terrible catastrophes to happen in order for anyone in the human race that will, to have the opportunity to cry out to Him for help, for forgiveness, and for salvation, and to punish all people that worship the anti-Christ beast who will be the actual incarnation of Satan. As it is written in the second letter from the apostle Peter:

The Lord is not slow about His promise, as some think of slowness, but is patient with you, not wanting any to perish, but all to come to repentance. But the day of the Lord will come like a thief [*will come upon an unsuspecting world as a great surprise*]**, and then the heavens will pass away with a loud noise, and the elements will be dissolved with fire, and the earth and everything that is done on it will be disclosed.**
2 Peter 3:9-10 (NRSV). *Bracketed words added for clarity.*

If the symbolism of the coming of King Yahshua is that of being a thief, then from whom is He taking something, and what is it that He is taking? King Yahshua is coming visibly in the air to this earth at the end of this age to take from Satan, the devil, all the millions who have accepted Jesus (Yahshua) as their Lord and Savior, and been born of His Spirit. No one, including Satan, knows the exact year when King Yahshua is to come except our Heavenly Father Yahweh. That is the reason that Yahshua conveyed this message the way He did. It is to help us understand that the people of the world who do not have intimacy with Him will not have a clue as to what is happening, but His bride that is in love with Him will know the season of her Bridegroom's coming for her, because she has studied His prophecies and understands the symbolism of His holy Feasts. It is written:

Now concerning the times and the seasons, brothers and sisters, you do not need to have anything written to you. For you yourselves know very well that the day of the Lord will come like a thief in the night. When they say, "There is peace and security," then sudden destruction will come upon them, as labor pains come upon a pregnant woman, and there will be no escape! But you, beloved, are not in darkness, for that day to surprise you like a thief; for you are all children of light and children of the day; we are not of the night or of darkness.
1 Thessalonians 5:1-5 (NRSV)

"... Worship God! For the testimony of Jesus is the spirit of prophecy."
Revelation 19:10b (NRSV)

Satan, the devil, knows that our Master Yahshua Messiah will not leave His throne in heaven with Father Yahweh to come to this earth to destroy the kingdoms of this world and establish His kingdom until exactly the right time when our Holy Father gives the word to go. That precise time will be when the Jews and a portion of the true born again believers will be under heavy persecution by the evil anti-Christ empire. That time will be when the complete number of Gentiles have been born again and come into Yah's spiritual kingdom, and all the Jewish people living at that future time of evil have realized that the one they believed to be the Messiah proves himself to be the anti-Christ. The Jewish people will be crying out to Almighty Yah for help, and will be ready to accept the true Messiah. At that time, King Yahshua will come to save His people from complete annihilation by the anti-Christ. His terrible wrath of destruction will be poured out on the evil people of the world at that time. The following verses support the timing of that which was just stated.

So, when they had come together, they asked Him, "Lord, is this the time when you will restore the kingdom to Israel?" He replied, "It is not for you to know the times or periods that the Father has set by His own authority. But you will receive power when the Holy Spirit has come upon you; and you will be my witnesses in Jerusalem, in all Judea and Samaria, and to the end of the earth." When He had said this, as they were watching, He was lifted up, and a cloud took Him out of their sight. While He was going and they were gazing up toward heaven, suddenly two men in white robes stood by them. They said, "Men of Galilee, why do you stand looking up toward heaven? This Jesus, who has been taken up from you into heaven, will come in the same way as you saw Him go into heaven.

Acts 1:6-11 (NRSV)

Then the apostles went back to Jerusalem from the Mount of Olives, which is about half a mile from the city.

Acts 1:12 (TEV)

There is a secret truth, my brothers, which I want you to know, for it will keep you from thinking how wise you are. It is that the stubbornness of the people of Israel is not permanent, but will last only until the complete number of Gentiles come to God. And this is how all Israel will be saved. As the scripture says, "The Savior will come from Zion and remove all wickedness from the descendants of Jacob. I will make this covenant with them when I take away their sins."

Romans 11:25-27 (TEV)

Look! He is coming with the clouds; every eye will see Him, even those who pierced Him [Jewish race]; and on His account all the tribes of the earth will wail. So it is to be. Amen.

Revelation 1:7 (NRSV). *Bracketed words added for clarity.*

The LORD will bring all the nations together to make war on Jerusalem. ... At that time He will stand on the Mount of Olives ...

Zechariah 14:2, 4 (TEV)

On that day the Lord will put a shield about the inhabitants of Jerusalem so that the feeblest among them on that day shall be like David, and the house of David ... "And I will pour out on the house of David and the inhabitants of Jerusalem a spirit of compassion and supplication, so that, when they look on Him whom they have pierced, they shall mourn for him, as one morns for an only child, and weep bitterly over Him as one weeps over a first-born.

Zechariah 12:8, 10 (RSV)

On that day there shall be a fountain opened for the house of David and the inhabitants of Jerusalem to cleanse them from their sin and uncleanness.

> **"And now, friends, I know that you acted in ignorance, as did also your rulers. In this way God fulfilled what He had foretold through all the prophets, that His Messiah would suffer. Repent therefore, and turn to God so that your sins may be wiped out, so that times of refreshing may come from the presence of the Lord, and that He may send the Messiah appointed for you, that is, Jesus, who must remain in heaven until the time of universal restoration that God announced long ago through His holy prophets.**
>
> Acts 3:17-21 (NRSV)

The restoration the apostle Peter was speaking of is that of a representation of the whole House of Israel being reestablished a final time in the land of present-day Israel. This restoration includes members of all twelve tribes that make up both houses—the descendants of the former Southern Kingdom of ancient Israel known as Judah, and the descendants of the Northern Kingdom of ancient Israel known as the ten lost tribes of Israel. Some today are learning of their Hebraic roots and connection to the ancient tribes by the revealing of this from the Holy Spirit. All non-Jews who accept Yahshua as their Savior and follow His teachings are grafted into the olive tree of Almighty Yah and become part of the tribe of Ephraim. All Jews who accept Yahshua as their Savior and follow His teachings are grafted into the olive tree of Almighty Yah and become part of the tribe of Judah (Romans 11.) This is the fulfilling of the prophecy in Ezekiel 37 when we become the "one new man" in Father Yahweh's hand. More on this subject in Chapter Eleven, "How Do We Prepare for the Coming of Messiah?"

King Yahshua Messiah will not leave His throne in heaven until our Holy Heavenly Father Yahweh gives the instruction at the seventh trumpet. That will be when the majority of unbelieving Jewish people are ready to receive Yahshua, the Lamb of God, as their Messiah and King eternal, and the body of Messiah, His bride, is prepared to be gloried in Him at His coming.

8

THE RESURRECTION
OF THE SAVED

In this chapter, we will study some of the great promises of the blessings of Almighty Yah's coming Kingdom, as found in His Holy Word.
The most important event in all of human history was the first coming of our Creator, Savior, and King in fulfillment of the prophecies. He
laid down His life as the spotless Lamb of Yahweh and was resurrected
with a new immortal body as the first of many fruits.

In Yahshua's first coming to earth, He fulfilled all the prophecies and
symbolism associated with the spring feasts that were covered in Chapter
Five. He laid down His life and accepted the penalty of death for our sins.
Of His own free will, He offered up His body to be tortured for our healing. He offered up His blood to be shed for the atonement of our sins. He
paid off a debt that He did not owe for lost humanity that owed a sin debt
that could not be paid. It was impossible for us to pay off our sin debt ourselves. He lived and died in order that we would have the opportunity of
accepting Him and what He did for us. He made the way for us to be able
to come into covenant relationship with Him, and to have a life of happiness and joy unspeakable, forever.

If you die of a heart attack after you go to sleep tonight, are you sure
you are ready to meet the Creator of the universe and the Judge of your
life when you pass over to the other side? Have you asked Messiah
Yahshua into your heart and repented of your sins? If you haven't, please
don't put off another minute the most important decision and act of
responsibility there is in all of life. What a loving Creator, Savior, King,
and Friend He is. He is worthy of all praise, honor, and glory!

The most wonderful and exciting event in all of human history will
be when King Jesus Messiah fulfills the prophecies of His second coming

to planet earth, accompanied by millions of His angels, to resurrect all of the saved individuals. This event will include all of those who have accepted Him as the full manifestation of Father Yahweh—the one true, living God of Abraham, Isaac, and Jacob—before He walked the earth as the man Yahshua, the redeemed, born again believers of Yahshua, or Jesus, who have died in Jesus since His resurrection in approximately A.D. 30, and those who are alive and saved at the time of His coming in the clouds from heaven to planet earth.

The definition of the word *resurrection* is "the act of raising from the dead, or returning to life." In the context of God's Holy Word, it is that, but actually means, "the raising of not the former body, but a new, immortal body." The word *rapture* is the English translation of the Greek word *rapozia*, which means, "to snatch away quickly." *Rapture* is another word that is used in our time for the resurrection of the saints.

King Yahshua defeated and overcame death, and so will all people who have been born of His Holy Spirit. The following verses describe this most wonderful event, but do not produce evidence of the timing of it, except that it occurs at the sounding of the last trumpet. It is written:

> But if we have died with Christ [Messiah], we believe that we will also live with Him. We know that Christ [Messiah], being raised from the dead, will never die again; death no longer has dominion over Him. The death He died, He died to sin, once for all; but the life He lives, He lives to God. So you also must consider yourselves dead to sin and alive to God in Christ Jesus [Messiah Yahshua].
>
> Romans 6:8-11 (NRSV). *Bracketed words added for clarity.*

> But the truth is that Christ has been raised from death, as the guarantee that those [born of God's Spirit] who sleep [rest] in death will also be raised. For just as death came by means of a man [Adam], in the same way the rising from death comes by means of a man [Yahshua].
>
> 1 Corinthians 15:20-21 (TEV). *Bracketed words added for clarity.*

> What I mean, brothers [and sisters], is that what is made of flesh and blood cannot share in God's Kingdom, and what is mortal cannot possess immortality. Listen to this secret truth: we shall not all die, but when the last trumpet sounds, we shall all be changed in an instant, as quickly as the blinking of an eye. For when the trumpet sounds, the dead

[in Yahshua] **will be raised, never to die again, and we shall all be changed. For what is mortal must be changed into what is immortal; what will die must be changed into what cannot die. So when this takes place, and the mortal has been changed into immortal, then the scripture will come true: "Death is destroyed; victory is complete!" "Where, Death, is your victory? Where, Death, is your power to hurt?"**

1 Corinthians 15:50-55 (TEV). *Bracketed words added for clarity.*

For since we believe that Jesus died and rose again, even so, through Jesus *[Yahshua],* **God will bring with Him** *[from heaven]* **those who have died** *[in Yahshua].* **For this we declare to you by the word of the Lord, that we who are alive, who are left until the coming of the Lord, will by no means precede** *[be raised before]* **those who have died. For the Lord Himself, with a cry of command, with the archangel's call and with the sound of God's trumpet, will descend from heaven, and the dead in Christ will rise first. Then we who are alive, who are left, will be caught up in the clouds together with them to meet the Lord in the air; and so we will be with the Lord forever. Therefore encourage one another with these words.**

1 Thessalonians 4:14-18 (NRSV). *Bracketed words added for clarity.*

What kind of body did our Master Yahshua have when He was with His disciples, and what kind does He have now after being raised from the dead? As it is written:

Now it came to pass, as He sat at the table with them, that He took bread, blessed and broke *it,* **and gave it to them. Then their eyes were opened and they knew Him; and He vanished from their sight. ... So they rose up that very hour and returned to Jerusalem, and found the eleven and those** *who were* **with them gathered together, saying, "The Lord is risen indeed, and has appeared to Simon** *[not one of the original 12]***!" And they told about the things** *that had happened* **on the road, and how He was known to them in the breaking of bread. Now as they said these things, Jesus Himself stood in the midst of them, and said to them, "Peace to you." But they were terrified and frightened, and supposed they had seen a spirit** *[ghost].* **And He said to them, "Why are you troubled? And why do doubts arise in yours hearts? Behold My hands and My feet, that it is I Myself. Handle Me and see, for a spirit does not**

have flesh and bones as you see I have." When He had said this, He showed them His hands and His feet. But while they still did not believe for joy, and marveled, He said to them, "Have you any food here?" So they gave Him a piece of a broiled fish and some honeycomb. And He took *it* and ate in their presence.

Luke 24:30-31, 33-43 (NKJV). *Bracketed words added for clarity.*

Wow! What a truly amazing resurrected body Yahshua has and we will have on our resurrection day. When we see Him, we will be like Him. It will be awesome to have a body that can transcend time and space and pass through walls, and by the supernatural creative power of God (Elohim), also be capable of solidifying to enjoy food. It will truly be wonderful to have a new body that will never become sick, experience pain, or die.

The Holy Scriptures teaches us that we will be like Him.

Beloved, we are God's children now; what we will be has not yet been revealed. What we do know is this: when He *[King Yahshua]* is revealed, we will be like Him, for we will see Him as He is. And all who have this hope in Him purify themselves, just as He is pure.

1 John 3:2-3 (NRSV). *Bracketed words added for clarity.*

Our Heavenly Father, Who works through our Master Yahshua and His Holy Spirit, is full of goodness and worthy of all praise.

When King Yahshua Messiah returns to the earth that He created long ago, He will destroy all of those who have the mark of the beast and have been worshiping the anti-Messiah. He will be glorified in His saints. As it is written,

... since *it is* a righteous thing with God to repay with tribulation those who trouble you, and to *give* you who are troubled rest with us when the Lord Jesus is revealed from heaven with His mighty angels, in flaming fire taking vengeance on those who do not know God, and on those who do not obey the gospel of our Lord Jesus Christ. These shall be punished with everlasting destruction from the presence of the Lord and from the glory of His power, when He comes, in that Day to be glorified in His saints and to be admired among all those who believe, because our testimony among you was believed.

2 Thessalonians 1:6-10 (NKJV)

Then I heard what seemed to be the voice of a great multitude, like the sound of many waters and like the sound of mighty thunderpeals, crying out, "Hallelujah! For the Lord our God the Almighty reigns. Let us rejoice and exult and give Him the glory, for the marriage of the Lamb has come, and His bride has made herself ready; to her it has been granted to be clothed with fine linen, bright and pure"—for the fine linen is the righteous deeds of the saints.
Revelation 19:6-8 (NRSV)

This is the marriage of the Bridegroom (King Yahshua, the head of His body) and His bride, all who have accepted Him, been born of His Spirit and have been chosen. Many are called into His Kingdom but few are chosen to be part of His bride. I will cover the called and the chosen in more detail in the eleventh chapter in the section, "Identifying the Bride of Messiah." The marriage supper event is the fulfillment of the symbolism of the last of the fall feasts, the Feast of *Sukkot,* also called the Feast of the Ingathering. HalleluYah! There are no words to convey what an awesome experience that will be.

You may be wondering when this incredible event happens in relation to all of the end-time prophecy events that were covered in Chapter Five. As we learned in Chapter One, we need Almighty Yah's Holy Spirit working in us to help us understand His Word in all doctrines (principles or basic truths). It is important to understand that all doctrines of the Messianic believer's faith must be supported by Scriptures. Notice that "Scriptures" is plural, meaning "more that one verse." Sound doctrine must be established by taking into account all of the Scriptures of the Bible that apply and in their proper context. Taking a single verse, or a few verses, out of context and twisting their meaning to fit the doctrine has resulted in the establishment of many false doctrines, cults, and denominations within Christianity and Judaism.

Today, there are many different interpretations of when the resurrection, or rapture, will happen. Some believe and teach that it will happen before the great tribulation begins. Others believe it begins during the middle of the final seven years of the seventh week that Daniel prophesied. Some teach that it will happen near the end, before the symbolic seven bowls, or vials, of God's wrath are poured out. Some have adopted the "pan position" and are content to wait and see how it's all going to pan out. The most popular belief is that the rapture, or resurrection, will happen before the tribulation period begins. There are many books, videos, and movies that teach this doctrine. I will explain in detail the origin and the truth of this false doctrine later in this chapter. It is extremely important that we understand the truth from God's Word concerning the most awesome event in all of human history.

THE TIMING OF THE RAPTURE FROM YAH'S WORD

The Bible clearly reveals that the coming of the Lord for the gathering of His saved saints (the rapture, or resurrection) takes place as King Yahshua is bringing His judgment and wrath of destruction upon this sinful world, as symbolized in the Feast of *Yom Kippur*. The following verses of Scriptures from several different books of the Bible support the doctrine that there is only one second coming of the Lord and that it happens at the end of the great tribulation, or Daniel's seventh week, as described in the previous chapter. My paraphrase is added in brackets.

> **The LORD** *[Father Yahweh]* **said to my Lord** *[Master Jesus Messiah]*, **"Sit at My right hand, till I make Your enemies Your footstool."**
> Psalm 110:1 (NKJV). *Bracketed words added for clarity.*

> **And He** *[King Yahshua]* **will destroy on this mountain the surface of the covering** *[the domination of Satan through the reign of the beast]* **cast over all people, and the veil** *[deception]* **that is spread over all nations. He will swallow up death forever, and the Lord GOD will wipe away tears from all faces** *[of the saved]*; **the rebuke** *[oppression]* **of His people He will take away from all the earth; for the LORD has spoken. And it will be said in that day: "Behold, this *is* our God; we have waited for Him, and He will save us. This *is* the LORD; we have waited for Him; we will be glad and rejoice in His salvation."**
> Isaiah 25:7-9 (NKJV). *Bracketed words added for clarity.*

> **Your dead shall live; together with my dead body they shall arise. Awake and sing, you who dwell in dust; for your dew *is like* the dew of herbs, and the earth shall cast out** *[resurrection]* **the dead. Come, my people, enter your chambers, and shut your doors behind you; hide yourself, as it were, for a little moment, until the indignation is past. For behold, the**

LORD comes out of His place to punish the inhabitants of the earth for their iniquity; the earth will also disclose her blood, and will no more cover her slain.

Isaiah 26:19-21 (NKJV). *Bracketed words added for clarity.*

"At that time Michael *[archangel]* **shall stand up, the great prince who stands** *watch* **over the sons of your people** *[all who are saved, "... for in Christ Jesus (Messiah Yahshua) you are all children of God (Yahweh) through faith. ... There is no longer Jew or Greek ... for all of you are one in Christ Jesus (Messiah Yahshua)." Galatians 3:26, 28 (NRSV)],* **and there shall be a time of trouble, such as never was since there was a nation,** *even* **to that time. And at that time your people shall be delivered, every one who is found written in the book** *[those who have already died in Jesus (Yahshua) and those alive at the time of His coming].* **And many of those who sleep in the dust of the earth shall awake, some to everlasting life** *[first resurrection],* **some to shame** *and* **everlasting contempt** *[second resurrection of the dead for judgment at the end of the 1,000-year millennium].*

Daniel 12:1-2 (NKJV). *Bracketed words added for clarity.*

Thus saith the Lord:

"... I will return again to My place, till they *[Jewish race]* **acknowledge their offense** *[the rejection of Yahshua, as the Messiah].* **Then they will seek My face** *[truth and relationship with Messiah];* **in their affliction (persecution of the tribulation) they will earnestly seek Me"** *[after they realize the true identity of the anti-Christ whom they had been deceived into accepting as the Messiah].* **Come, and let us return to the LORD; for He has torn, but He will heal us; He has stricken** *[allowed persecution to open their eyes],* **but He will bind us up. After two days** *[two thousand years from the time of the rejection of King Jesus Messiah; remember, a day with the Lord is as a thousand years]* **He will revive us; on the third day** *[early part of the third millennium]* **He will raise** *[resurrect]* **us up, that we may live in His sight** *[Yah's Kingdom on earth].*

Hosea 5:15; 6:1-2 (NKJV). *Bracketed words added for clarity.*

As I encouraged you at the beginning of this book, I encourage you again to think for yourself. Ask Father Yahweh, through the Holy Spirit in the name of Yahshua, to reveal the truth to you so you will know the truth, for the truth will set you free.

> **Another parable He put forth to them, saying: "The kingdom of heaven is like a man** *[Yahshua]* **Who sowed good seed** *[those that are born of the Holy Spirit]* **in His field** *[the world]***; but while men slept, his enemy** *[Satan]* **came and sowed tares** *[a tare is a plant of the Middle East that looks exactly like wheat until it sprouts its grain head, which is black instead of golden brown; the tares represent all who profess Jesus (Yahshua), but do not follow Him]* **among the wheat and went his way. But when the grain** *[redeemed, born again believers]* **had sprouted and produced a crop** *[good fruit or works for the Lord]***, then the tares also appeared. So the servants of the owner came and said to Him, 'Sir, did you not sow good seed in your field? How then does it have tares?' He said to them, 'An enemy has done this.' The servants said to Him, 'Do you want us then to go and gather them** *[tares]* **up?' But He said, 'No, lest while you gather up the tares you also uproot the wheat with them. Let both grow together until the harvest** *[the end of the age and the coming of the Master]***, and at the time of harvest I will say to the reapers** *[angels]***, "First gather together the tares and bind them** *[all who have the mark of the beast]* **in bundles to burn them, but gather** *[rapture]* **the wheat** *[all who are overcomers]* **into My barn** *[the kingdom of King Yahshua]***. " "**
>
> Matthew 13:24-30, 37-43 (NKJV). *Bracketed words added for clarity.*

Thus saith the Lord:

> **"Immediately after the tribulation** *[persecution]* **of those days** *[the last half of the seventh week of Daniel]* **the sun will be darkened, and the moon will not give its light, and the stars will fall from heaven, and the powers of the heavens will be shaken; then will appear the sign of the Son of man in heaven, and then all of the tribes** *[those with the mark of the beast]* **of the earth will mourn** *[be afraid]***, and they will see the Son of man coming on the clouds of heaven with power and great glory; and he** *[King Yahshua]* **will send out his angels with a loud trumpet call, and they will gather** *[rapture, or first resurrection]* **his elect** *[all the overcomers, dead and alive]* **from the four winds** *[the whole world over]***, from one end of heaven to the other** *[the soul/spirits of the elect who*

will have been saved by putting their trust in Jesus, who have deceased and are in heaven at that time will be brought with the angels to receive their new resurrected bodies, along with those alive on the earth at that time who are resurrected afterward].

Matthew 24:29-31 (RSV). *Bracketed words added for clarity.*

"But about that day and hour no one knows *[literally, no one will know the exact day of the Feast of Trumpets because of the sighting of the new moon, or time of day of the Master's coming, but all true believers of that time will know the approximate time of His coming because of the fulfilled prophecies that they will have witnessed due to their watchfulness and discernment],* **neither the angels of heaven, nor the Son** *[Yahshua],* **but only the Father** *[Yahweh].* **For as the days of Noah were, so will be the coming of the Son of Man. For as in those days before the flood they were eating and drinking, marrying and giving in marriage** *[people of the world and beast system will be living normal worldly lifestyles while true followers of Yahshua and Jewish people will be persecuted under cover, without exposure from the anti-Christ controlled media, with many simply disappearing from society],* **until the day Noah entered the ark, and they knew nothing until the flood came and swept them all away, so too will be the coming of the Son of Man.** *[Noah had warned the people of his day, but they were oblivious to their judgment until they saw the flood waters quickly rising. The people who will bare the mark of the beast will be warned, but will also be oblivious to their judgment until they see King Yahshua coming in the clouds with His great host of mighty angels, and they will realize that their destruction will be swift. Almighty Yah saved Noah and all that were aboard the ark from destruction of the flood. King Yahshua will perform the greatest miracle ever when He saves, by the rapture, all His true followers at His coming, from His great consuming fire.]* **Then two will be in the field; one will be taken and one will be left. Two women will be grinding meal together; one will be taken and one will be left. Keep awake therefore, for you do not know on what day your Lord is coming. But understand this: if the owner of the house had known in what part of the night the thief was coming, he would have stayed awake and would not have let his house be broken into. Therefore you also must be ready, for the Son of Man is coming at an unexpected hour.** *[The word* imminent *means "about to occur," or "impending." We know by the proof of the Scriptures that this word can-*

not apply to the coming of Yahshua now, as in any moment. It can only apply to the last few weeks or days of the end of the great tribulation during the fall feast of a future year not yet known. The important message from this verse is that anyone alive at the time of Messiah's coming must be ready to go up to meet the Master and not have received the mark of the beast.]

Matthew 24:36-44 (NRSV). *Bracketed words added for clarity.*

"Then the kingdom of heaven shall be likened to ten virgins *[all who profess to be true believers of Yahshua]* **who took their lamps** *[lives]* **and went out to meet the bridegroom. Now five of them were wise, and five** *were* **foolish. Those who** *were* **foolish took their lamps and took no oil with them** *[Oil in Yah's Word is symbolic of the presence and power of Holy Spirit. I believe that in this context oil also refers to obedience to Yah's instructions from His Holy Word.]*, **but the wise took oil in their vessels with their lamps. But while the bridegroom was delayed, they all slumbered and slept. And at midnight** *[the great tribulation, the darkest time in human history]* **a cry was** *heard*: **'Behold, the bridegroom is coming;** *[the great end-time warning message given by the two witnesses, the 144,000 selected ones from the blood descendants of the twelve tribes of Israel and many other overcomers spreading the truth about the evil anti-Christ system, the true Gospel message and the second coming of King Yahshua]* **go out to meet Him!' Then all those virgins arose and trimmed their lamps. And the foolish said to the wise, 'give us** *some* **of your oil, for our lamps are going out'** *[when the persecution comes, a person must be born of Father Yahweh's Holy Spirit and be prepared to die for Yahshua's sake; if not, they will cave in to the pressure that will come from the beast if confronted with it]*. **But the wise answered, saying, 'No, lest there should not be enough for us and you; but go rather to those who sell, and buy for yourselves.'** *[When the terrible persecution begins, panic will set in, and it will be very difficult for a person to have time to accept Yahshua and have enough faith in Him to not take the mark of the beast. The wise virgins represent believers who have matured in their daily relationship with Yahshua by learning and following His Torah instructions and have developed intimate relationship with Him in keeping His weekly Sabbath and annual Feasts that are set-apart times for His meeting with His Bride.]* **And while they went to buy, the bridegroom came, and those who were ready went in with Him to the**

wedding *[rapture]*; **and the door was shut. Afterward the other virgins came also, saying, 'Lord, Lord, open to us!' But He answered and said, 'Assuredly, I say to you, I do not know you.'** *[This parable is teaching us that we must be born of His Spirit and have a deep relationship with Him through obedience, so that He will know us and we Him. We must be able to stand for Him in the time of testing.]* **Watch therefore, for you know neither the day nor the hour** *[the exact timing]* **in which the Son of man is coming** *[His return to earth to establish His kingdom].*

Matthew 25:1-13 (NKJV). *Bracketed words added for clarity.*

"... Likewise, just as it was in the days of Lot: they were eating and drinking, buying and selling, planting and building, but on the day that Lot left Sodom, it rained fire and sulfur from heaven and destroyed all of them—it will be like that on the day that the Son of Man is revealed. *[The meaning of this verse is the same as the analogy about the days of Noah a few verses back. The difference is that the method of destruction is the same as it will be when the Lord returns. Notice that Lot was saved from the destruction the same day that the destruction came to Sodom.]* **On that day,** *[the coming of Yahshua]* **anyone on the housetop who has belongings in the house must not come down to take them away; and likewise anyone in the field must not turn back.** *[I believe this to be a literal, direct order from our Creator.]* **Remember Lot's wife.** *[She was turned into a pillar of salt after she was warned not to look back at the life of sin they were escaping from.]* **Those who try to make their life secure will lose it, but those who lose their life will keep it.** *[We must have complete faith and trust in our Lord Jesus Messiah, whether we are alive at the time of His coming, or if we die before we finish reading this book.]* **I tell you, on that night** *[when the Lord comes in the air]* **there will be two in one bed; one will be taken and the other left. There will be two women grinding meal together; one will be taken and the other left." Then they** *[the Master's disciples]* **asked Him, "Where** *[will the ones left be]*, **Lord?" He said to them, "Where the corpse is, there the vultures will gather."** *[After our Lord's angels gather the elect from the earth at the Lord's coming, the huge armies of the nations of the world that will have gathered in Israel will be destroyed, and there will be many corpses.]*

Luke 17:28-37 (NRSV). *Bracketed words added for clarity.*

"... This is indeed the will of My Father, that all who see the Son and believe in Him may have eternal life; and I will raise them up on the last day *[the last day of this age before the millennium begins]*.**"**

John 6:40 (NRSV). *Bracketed words added for clarity.*

It is written,

Jesus said to her, "Your brother will rise again." Martha said to Him, "I know that he *[Lazarus]* **will rise again in the resurrection on the last day." Jesus** *[Yahshua]* **said to Her, "I am the resurrection and the life. Those who believe in me, even though they die, will live, and everyone who lives and believes in me will never die. Do you believe this?" She said to Him, "Yes, Lord, I believe that You are the Messiah, the Son of God, the one coming into the world."**

John 11:23-27 (NRSV). *Bracketed words added for clarity.*

"... Repent therefore, and turn to God so that your sins may be wiped out, so that times of refreshing *[indwelling of the Holy Spirit]* **may come from the presence of the Lord, and that He may send the Messiah appointed for you, that is, Jesus, who must remain in heaven until the time of universal restoration that God announced long ago through His holy prophets. ..."**

Acts 3:19-21 (NRSV). *Bracketed words added for clarity.*

But in fact Christ has been raised from the dead, the first fruits of those who have died *[saved ones]*. **For since death** *[of the body and separation from God due to sin and rebellion]* **came through a human being, the resurrection of the dead** *[saved ones]* **has also come through a human being, for as all die in Adam, so all will be made alive in Christ. But each in his own order: Christ** *[Yahshua]* **the first fruits, then at His coming** *[only one coming]* **those who belong to Christ. Then comes the end, when He hands over the kingdom to God the Father, after He has destroyed every ruler and every authority and power.**

1 Corinthians 15:20-24 (NRSV). *Bracketed words added for clarity.*

Behold, I tell you a mystery: We shall not all sleep *[die in Yahshua]*, **but we shall all** *[those already in heaven and those alive at the coming of Messiah]* **be changed—in a moment, in the twinkling of an eye, at the**

last trumpet. *[As I detailed in the previous chapter, the last trumpet is the seventh trumpet.]* **For the trumpet will sound, and the dead will be raised incorruptible, and we shall be changed.**

1 Corinthians 15:51-52 (NKJV). *Bracketed words added for clarity.*

Now concerning the times and the seasons *[of the coming of the Master]*, **brothers and sisters, you do not need to have anything written to you. For you yourselves know very well that the day of the Lord will come like a thief in the night** *[unexpectedly]*. **When they say, "There is peace and security"** *[the anti-Christ and his leaders tell the world not to fear the great light that is coming in the heavens because they have assembled the massive armies and weapons of destruction, and will destroy that which is coming to earth from outer space]*, **then sudden destruction will come upon them, as labor pains come upon a pregnant woman, and there will be no escape! But you, beloved, are not in darkness** *[of deception and unaware of what is really happening]*, **for that day to surprise you like a thief; for you are all children of light and children of the day** *[saved and in the know]*; **we are not of the night or of the darkness. So then let us not fall asleep** *[being complacent and focused on the pleasures of this world; unconcerned and oblivious to the truth of Yahshua's coming]* **as others do, but let us keep awake and be sober** *[humble, repentant, and watching for the signs]*; **... For God has destined us not for wrath** *[destruction of the ungodly at the coming of King Jesus Messiah]* **but for obtaining salvation through our Lord Jesus Christ, who died for us, so that whether we are awake or asleep we may live with Him.**

1 Thessalonians 5:1-6, 9-10 (NRSV). *Bracketed words added for clarity.*

As to the coming of our Lord Jesus Christ and our being gathered *[raptured]* **together to Him, we beg you, brothers and sisters, not to be quickly shaken in mind or alarmed, either by spirit or by word or by letter, as though from us, to the effect that the day of the Lord is already here. Let no one deceive you in any way; for that day** *[the coming of Messiah]* **will not come unless the rebellion** *[apostasy of many who professed to be followers of Yahshua, but turned away from the truth and damned themselves by accepting the mark of the beast in order to not suffer persecution]* **comes first and the lawless one** *[the anti-Christ beast, who will be Satan in the flesh; demanding to be worshipped]* **is revealed,**

the one destined for destruction. **He opposes and exalts himself above
every so-called god or object of worship, so that he takes his seat in the
temple of God,** [*the temple that the Jews will be allowed to build on the
Temple Mount and reinstate animal sacrifices*] **declaring himself to be
God. Do you not remember that I told you these things when I was still
with you** [*the apostle Paul when he was with the church in
Thessalonica*]**? And you know what is now restraining him, so that he
may be revealed when his time comes. For the mystery of lawlessness**
[*Satan's plan*] **is already at work, but only until the one who now
restrains it is removed.** [*The one doing the restraining of Satan is the
archangel Michael, as it is written in Revelation 12:7-9. When Almighty
Yah gives the command to Michael to not hold back Satan any longer
and to cast him and his millions of fallen angels to earth, Satan will come
to planet earth to totally possess the body and soul of a human man, the
anti-Christ.*] **And then the lawless one will be revealed, whom the Lord
Jesus will destroy with the breath of His mouth, annihilating him by the
manifestation of His** [*King Yahshua's*] **coming.** [*The body of the anti-
Christ will be destroyed, but Satan will continue to live and will be cast
into the bottomless pit for a thousand years, as it is written in Revelation
20:1-3.*] **The coming of the lawless one is apparent in the working of
Satan, who uses all power, signs, lying wonders, and every kind of
wicked deception for those who are perishing, because they refused to
love the truth and so be saved.** [*Satan's deceptions are going to be
extremely difficult for anyone to withstand who is not grounded solidly
in a personal relation with Yahshua.*] **For this reason God sends them a
powerful delusion,** [*the great delusion has for years been planned and is
being orchestrated by the New World Order led by the Illuminati who
are under Satan's control*] **leading them to believe what is false, so that
all who have not believed the truth but took pleasure in unrighteousness will be condemned.**

2 Thessalonians 2:1-12 (NRSV). *Bracketed words added for clarity.*

Almighty Yah is going to allow Satan to use amazing miracles and
fallen angel (alien) influence to usher in the anti-Christ and his evil
system upon the world through the NWO. Don't trust what I say. Trust
what Almighty Yah's Word says and apply it to what is happening in the
world today. Ask yourself, "Could this really come true?"

Following are a few more references of Scripture to show that there is only one second coming of King Yahshua, and the timing of it is at the end of the great tribulation period.

> **For Christ did not enter a sanctuary made by human hands, a mere copy of the true one, but entered into heaven itself, now to appear in the presence of God on our behalf** [*interceding*]**. Nor was it to offer Himself again and again, as the high priest enters the Holy Place year after year with the blood that is not his own; for then He** [*Yahshua*] **would have had to suffer again and again since the foundation of the world. But as it is, He has appeared** [*was born into this world*]**, once for all at the end of the age** [*Master Yahshua brought an end to the Mosaic animal sacrifice covenant age, and after His resurrection and the outpouring of the Holy Spirit, the church age began, which will continue until He returns to end this church age and begin the Day of the Master's age that includes His millennial reign on earth*]) **to remove sin by the sacrifice of Himself. And just as it is appointed for mortals** [*all people*] **to die once** [*physical death as a result of the disobedient sin of Adam and Eve*]**, and after that the judgment** [*the first judgment is for the saved after the return of King Yahshua and is not really a judgment, but a very special ceremony in which our Master Yahshua gives recognition to His body of saints and delegation to all He chooses for different positions in His Kingdom that has come to earth. In the Scriptures this event is called the Judgment Seat of Christ (Messiah); the second judgment, called the Great White Throne Judgment, takes place a thousand years later when the unsaved are resurrected and judged for the life they lived with their sins not being covered by the Blood of the Lamb from our Savior Yahshua. I believe that all those who never had an opportunity to respond to the Gospel because they never heard it will be judged fairly by our Master Yahshua based on the way they treated others and the intentions of their hearts.*]**, so Christ, having been offered once to bear the sins of many** [*all who will accept Him and His way*]**, will appear a second time** [*only one second time*]**, not to deal with sin, but to save those who are eagerly waiting for Him.** [*Those who live through the terrible persecution and the calamity of the seven trumpet and seal events that are coming on this earth, as described in the previous chapter, will definitely be eagerly waiting for our Master to hurry up and come to save us.*]
>
> Hebrews 9:24-28 (NRSV). *Bracketed words added for clarity.*

For this they willfully forget: that by the Word of God *[the Logos, King Jesus]* **the heavens were of old, and the earth standing out of water and in the water, by which the world that then existed perished** *[the days of Noah]*, **being flooded with water. But the heavens and the earth which are now preserved by the same Word, are reserved for fire until the day of judgment and perdition** *[destruction]* **of ungodly men.** *[This fire and final judgment is referred to as the great white throne judgment in Revelation 20:11-15, comes at the end of the thousand year millennial reign.]*

2 Peter 3:5-7 (NKJV). *Bracketed words added for clarity.*

The coming of Yahshua will bring to conclusion the age of grace, and it will begin the Millennial age of rest and restoration.

Our Heavenly Father loves us and desires that all people come out of the deception and falsehood that is throughout the world. He desires that we, too, come to the truth that is written in His Word that will save us if we accept it and turn to Him. It is written:

The Lord is not slack concerning *His* promise *[to come and resurrect us]*, **as some would count slackness, but is longsuffering toward us, not willing** *[desiring]* **that any should perish but that all should come to repentance.** *[Our Heavenly Father Yahweh loves us so much that He sent His only Son, our Master Yahshua, to come to this earth and show us the way to salvation and eternal life by accepting His precious blood that He allowed to be shed willingly of His own choice, because He loves us and does not want any of us to die the second death, which is eternal separation from Him and the Father. Salvation is a process in which we believe, accept His gift, are born of His Spirit, and we repent, or turn away from our sins. I ask you once more, dear reader; if you die of a heart attack while asleep this day or night, are you positive that you are saved from God's judgment and a saint of the first resurrection? If you are not sure, please re-read Chapter Three again and pray, asking the Holy Spirit to help you in Yahshua's name.]* **Therefore, beloved, looking forward to these things, be diligent to be found by Him in peace, without spot and blameless ...**

2 Peter 3:9, 14 (NKJV). *Bracketed words added for clarity.*

The Revelation *[the events leading up to and the second coming]* **of Jesus**

Christ, which God *[Yahweh]* **gave Him to show to His servants—things which must shortly take place.** *[The apostle John must have thought that the Caesar Nero was the end-of-time anti-Christ because of his brutal persecution of Christians and Jews.]* **And He sent and signified** *it* *[the visions of the Revelation of King Jesus]* **by His angel to His servant John, who bore witness to the word of God, and to the testimony of Jesus Christ, to all things that he saw. Blessed** *is* **he who reads and those who hear** *[understand]* **the words of this prophecy, and keep those things which are written in it; for the time** *is* **near. John, to the seven churches** *[actual Messianic Congregations of John's time and are examples for us now]* **which are in Asia: Grace to you and peace from Him who is and who was and who is to come,** *[our Heavenly Father, God Almighty, Yahweh]* **and from the seven Spirits who are before His throne, and from Jesus Christ,** *[Messiah, the Lamb of Yahweh]* **the faithful witness, the firstborn from the dead,** *[first to be raised from the dead and have a new resurrected body]* **and the ruler over the kings of the earth. To Him who loved us and washed us from our sins in His own blood, and has made us kings and priests** *[in His millennium kingdom after He comes to earth]* **to His God and Father, to Him** *be* **glory and dominion forever and ever, Amen** *[truly approvable, so let it be]*. **Behold, He is coming with clouds,** *[literal clouds and clouds of angels]* **and every eye will see Him, even they who pierced Him** *[the descendants of the Jews and all who were responsible for His crucifixion]*. **And all the tribes** *[all the unsaved Jewish people and unsaved people of all races that are alive at that time]* **of the earth will mourn** *[grieve]* **because of Him. Even so, Amen.**

Revelation 1:1-7 (NKJV). *Bracketed words added for clarity.*

The moment that the unsaved Jewish people and others throughout the world see King Yahshua Messiah coming with great brilliance, their eyes will be opened to the truth. They will know that they have been deceived by the evil anti-Christ beast and by all of the lies they have believed that encouraged them not to believe that Yahshua is the true Messiah of the Holy Scriptures. This will be the fulfillment of the prophecy as it is written in Isaiah:

Listen! That loud noise in the city, that sound in the Temple, is the sound of the LORD punishing His enemies! "My holy city is like a woman who suddenly gives birth to a child without ever going into labor. Has any-

one ever seen or heard of such a thing? Has a nation ever been born in a day? Zion will not have to suffer long, before the nation is born. Do not think that I will bring my people to the point of birth and not let them be born." The Lord has spoken.

Isaiah 66:6-9 TEV)

Then I looked, and behold, a white cloud, and on the cloud sat *One* like the Son of Man, having on His head a golden crown, and in His hand a sharp sickle. And another angel came out of the temple, crying with a loud voice to Him who sat on the cloud, "Thrust in Your sickle and reap, for the time has come for You to reap, for the harvest of the earth is ripe." So He who sat on the cloud thrust in His sickle on the earth, and the earth was reaped. *[This is symbolic of the resurrection or rapture.]* And another angel came out from the altar, who had power over fire, and he cried with a loud cry to him *[angel]* who had the sharp sickle, saying, "Thrust in your sharp sickle and gather the clusters of the vine of the earth, for her grapes are fully ripe." So the angel thrust his sickle into the earth and gathered the vine of the earth *[all who receive the mark of the beast will be connected like grapes on a vine]*, and threw it into the great winepress of the wrath of God. And the winepress was trampled outside the city *[the battle of Armageddon with the armies of the anti-Christ, will be gathered a few miles away from Jerusalem, to wage war against King Yahshua and his huge army of angels coming in the sky]*, and blood came out of the winepress, up to the horses' bridles, for one thousand six hundred furlongs. *[This detail is too specific to ignore. A furlong is about 220 yards, times 1,600, equates to about 189 miles, which is nearly the length of the plain of Jezreel that runs from the northern to the southern border of the country of Israel. I believe the blood really will look to be about 4 feet deep in this vast area, because there will be several hundred million men who will die there.]*

Revelation 14:14-20 (NKJV). *Bracketed words added for clarity.*

Then I saw thrones, and those seated on them were given authority to judge. I also saw the souls of those who had been beheaded *[literally, and martyred by other means]* for their testimony to Jesus and for the word of God. They had not worshiped the beast or its image and had not received its mark on their foreheads or their hands. They came to life and reigned with Christ a thousand years *[the millennium in which all the saved live on earth with King Jesus].* **(The rest of the dead** *[unsaved]* **did not come to life until the thousand years were ended.)** **This is the first resurrection** *[the second coming of King Jesus which includes the rapture, or snatching up of the saved].* **Blessed and holy are those who share in the first resurrection** *[there is only one first resurrection].* **Over these** *[all who are saved]* **the second death has no power, but they will be priests of God and of Christ** *[Messiah]*, **and they will reign with Him a thousand years.**

Revelation 20:4-6 (NRSV). *Bracketed words added for clarity.*

The timing of the second and only coming of King Yahshua will be in some future year during the first of the fall feasts, the Feast of Trumpets (*Yom Terurah,* as covered in Chapter Five). In relation to biblical prophecy Scriptures, the Lord's coming is most accurately described as follows, after the seventh and last symbolic trumpet is blown.

Then the seventh angel blew his trumpet, and there were loud voices in heaven saying, "The kingdom of the world *[Satan's kingdom]* **has become the kingdom of our Lord** *[Yahweh]* **and His Messiah** *[Yahshua]*, **and He will reign forever and ever." Then the twenty-four elders** *[actual priests of high authority; not the raptured church]* **who sit on their thrones before God fell on their faces and worshiped God, singing, "We give you thanks, Lord God Almighty** *[Elohim]*, **who are and who were, for you have taken Your great power and begun to reign. The nations raged, but your wrath has come, and the time for judging the dead, for rewarding your servants, the prophets and saints and all who fear your name, both small and great, and for destroying those who destroy the earth." Then God's temple in heaven was opened, and the ark of His covenant was seen within His temple; and there were flashes of lightning, rumblings, peals of thunder, an earthquake, and heavy hail** *[This is a reference of the very heavy hail that is described in Revelation 16:21 weighing a talent, which is 75 pounds per hail stone].*

Revelation 11:15-19 (NRSV). *Bracketed words added for clarity.*

Verse 19 is describing the same events that are recorded in Revelation 16:17, which is the seventh angel pouring out the final wrath of God (Elohim) as King Yahshua is seen by all coming to earth.

As our Master and Savior, King Yahshua, returns to earth, He will supernaturally first give new immortal bodies to all saved believers who have died in Him and are not living on the earth at the time of His coming (1 Thessalonians 4:16-17). Secondly, He will give new immortal bodies to all the overcomers who are alive on the earth at the time of His coming. Those who are of the redeemed and alive at the end of the great tribulation will be in great need of being saving from the horrors of the beast system that will be taking place, along with the earthquakes, catastrophic weather and asteroid conditions that will be happening on the earth.

As King Yahshua approaches earth, millions of Jewish people will be saved on that day, HalleluYah! Their hearts will be miraculously transformed as they see Him coming in the sky, and they will accept Him as their Messiah, weeping and repenting of their sins. The physical bodies of millions of people who chose to reject Yahshua as their Savior and Master and accepted the mark of the beast will be destroyed by the brilliance of His coming. The terribly tragic reality for them is that, as it is written:

> **Then another angel, a third, followed them, crying with a loud voice, "Those who worship the beast and its image, and receive a mark on their foreheads or on their hands, they will also drink the wine of God's wrath, poured unmixed** [undiluted] **into the cup of His anger, and they will be tormented with fire and sulfur in the presence of the holy angels and in the presence of the Lamb. And the smoke of their torment goes up forever and ever. There is no rest day or night for those who worship the beast and its image and for anyone who receives the mark of its name." Here is a call for endurance of the saints, those who keep the commandments of God and hold fast to the faith of Jesus** [Yahshua].

Revelation 14:9-12 (NRSV). *Bracketed words added for clarity.*

THE IMPORTANCE OF THE WORD *PAROUSIA*

There is very important significance in understanding the use of the word *coming* as used in the New Testament. The English word *coming*, was translated from the Greek word *parousia*. By understanding the meaning and use of *parousia*, further support for the truth of the Lord's coming at the end of the tribulation is realized.

The definition of the word *parousia* as found in the *American Heritage Dictionary* is: "The Second Coming (referring to Jesus), arrival;

to be present."

The great Hebrew and Greek scholar, E.E. Bullinger, in his exhaustive work of the *Companion Bible*, reveals the following footnote on page 1364 as reference to the word *coming* found in Matthew 24:3.

> *Parousia*. This is the first of twenty-four occurrences of this important word (Matt. 24:3, 27, 37, 39. 1 Cor. 15:23; 16:17. 2 Cor. 7:6,7; 10:10. Phil. 1:26; 2:12. 1Thess. 2:19; 3:13; 4:15; 5:23. 2 Thess. 2:1, 8, 9. James 5:7, 8. 2 Peter 1:16; 3:4, 12. 1 John 2:28). The Papyri show that "from the Ptolemaic period down to the second century A.D. the word is traced in the East (Persian, or modern day Iran) as a technical expression for the arrival, or the visit of the king or the emperor", also of other persons in authority, or of troops. The Greeks had borrowed this word from the Persians, because of the many words the Greeks had to convey *coming*, the word *parousia* worked better in everyday conversation.

The Greek language is the most detailed and specific of all languages. God (Elohim) had pre-ordained the first-coming mission of King Jesus Messiah at exactly the right time in history—during the Roman empire when the New Testament books containing the Gospel message would be recorded in the Greek language. The Greek language was the most widely used language in the final centuries of the Roman empire, and the good roads and mail service enabled the rapid spread of Christianity.

The significance of *parousia* is that this word is used by the writers of the New Testament to convey the Lord's coming from heaven and the coming of others from one place to another. The following are some examples.

When He was sitting on the Mount of Olives, the disciples came to Him privately, saying, "Tell us, when will this be *[the destruction of the temple]*, **and what will be the sign of your coming and of the end of the age?"**

Matthew 24:3 (NRSV). *Bracketed words added for clarity.*

I rejoice at the coming of Stephanas and Fortunatus and Achaicus, because they have made up for your absence ...

1 Corinthians 16:17 (NRSV)

For since we believe that Jesus died and rose again, even so, through
Jesus, God will bring with Him those who have died [the saved whose
souls have gone to be with Lord Jesus in paradise and whose souls He is
bringing back to provide with new resurrected bodies]. For this we
declare to you by the word of the Lord, that we who are alive, who are
left until the coming of the Lord, will by no means precede those who
have died [in Jesus].

1 Thessalonians 4:14-15 (NRSV). *Bracketed words added for clarity.*

Nevertheless God, who comforts the downcast, comforted us by the
coming of Titus, and not only by his coming, but also by the consolation
with which he was comforted in you, when he told us of your earnest
desire, your mourning, your zeal for me, so that I rejoiced even more.

2 Corinthians 7:6-7 (NKJV)

As to the coming of our Lord Jesus Christ and our being gathered together
to Him, we beg you, brothers and sisters, not to be quickly shaken in
mind or alarmed, either by spirit or by word or by letter, as though from
us to the effect that the day of the Lord is already here.

2 Thessalonians 2:1-2 (NRSV)

And being confident of this, I know that I shall remain and continue
with you all for your progress and joy of faith, that your rejoicing for
me may be more abundant in Jesus Christ by my coming to you again.

Philippians 1:25-26 (NKJV)

And now, little children, abide in Him, that when He appears, we may
have confidence and not be ashamed before Him at His coming.

1 John 2:28 (NKJV)

The coming of the lawless one [anti-Christ, beast] is apparent in the
working of Satan, who uses all power, signs, lying wonders, and every
kind of wicked deception for those who are perishing, because they
refuse to love the truth and so be saved.

2 Thessalonians 2:9-10 (NRSV)

The definition of the word *parousia*, or *coming*, and the use of the
word in many verses of Scripture make it clear to us that the coming of

King Yahshua Messiah will be visible to all who are alive at the time. There is not anything secret or quiet in the description of His coming, but just the opposite, as clarified in the following verses.

"**And He** [*Yahshua*] **will send out His angels with a loud trumpet call** [*the NKJV states* great sound of a trumpet*], **and they will gather His elect** [*those alive at that time*] **from the four winds** [*all over the earth*], **from one end of heaven to the other.**" [*Those who are at rest in heaven come with Him to receive their new resurrected bodies first.*]
Matthew 24:31 (NRSV). *Bracketed words added for clarity.*

Listen to this secret truth: we shall not all die, but when the last trumpet [*seventh*] **sounds, we** [*all who are saved, dead and alive at that time*] **shall all be changed in an instant, as quickly as the blinking of an eye. For when the trumpet sounds, the dead will be raised** [*souls coming from heaven and resurrected with new, angel-like bodies*], **never to die again, and we** [*those alive during the Master's coming*] **shall all be changed** [*given the new bodies also*].
1 Corinthians 15:51-52 (TEV). *Bracketed words added for clarity.*

For the Lord Himself will descend from heaven with a shout, with the voice of an archangel, and with the trumpet of God. And the dead in Christ will rise first.
1 Thessalonians 4:16 (NKJV)

Then the seventh [*last*] **angel blew his trumpet, and there were loud voices in heaven, saying, "The kingdom of the world has become the kingdom of our Lord and of His Messiah, and He will reign forever and ever."**
Revelation 11:15 (NRSV). *Bracketed words added for clarity.*

These first two sections of this chapter should have provided you with the necessary Scripture and proper definition and context of the word *parousia*, to support the description and timing of the coming of our Savior, King Jesus. Since it is apparent that the *parousia* of King Yahshua is at the end of the seven-year tribulation period, then where did the false doctrine originate of the Lord coming in secret to rapture the church (all that are saved) out of the world before the tribulation begins?

PRE-TRIBULATION RAPTURE ORIGIN AND TRUTH

Throughout the world today, most Christians are interested in books, tapes, movies, and conversation about the timing of the second coming of our Lord Jesus Messiah. There are many opinions that have formed many doctrines. Some believe that the Apostle John, in his writing of the book of Revelation, was describing events that were happening in his day, and that the anti-Christ was Nero. This doctrine is called the *Preterist*. Its originator, James Stuart Russell, teaches in his book, *The Parousia*, published in 1878, that the second coming of King Yahshua happened soon after His resurrection, during the establishing of the first century church before the destruction of Jerusalem in A.D. 70. This belief to me is totally unscriptural and bizarre. Many of Yahshua's prophecies warning of the destruction of Jerusalem were for the believers living in the area of Jerusalem at that time and were given so they would know what was coming and to prepare them for escape. The writings of Josephus, the great Roman historian, reveal that the followers of Yahshua escaped before the Roman General Titus and his army invaded the city. The same prophecies, however, have significant meaning for future events at the end of the tribulation. To teach that all of the prophecies regarding the second coming of Messiah have already happened and took place in the first century before A.D. 70 is totally ludicrous to me.

Another doctrine called *a-millennialism* believes that Messiah is now reigning through the church and that there will not be a 1,000-year millennial age. Still others are in the *post millennium* camp and believe that there will be a gradual victory over the evil in the world by the spreading of the Gospel, and therefore, the great commission will be fulfilled.

Do you remember what I stated earlier about establishing a biblical doctrine with one or a few verses of Scripture, rather than using all of what the Bible says on the subject?

Most Christians who believe in the second coming of King Yahshua fall into the category of *futurist*. In this category are several camps that differ basically on their interpretation of the timing of the Master's coming. There are some who believe that Yahshua will come during the middle of the seven-year tribulation. Others believe in what is known as the pre-wrath rapture, when He returns to rapture the saints from the on-going carnage of the anti-Christ at the end of the tribulation period, just before the plagues of Almighty Yah's wrath are being poured out on the world as described in John's account of the seven trumpets and seven vials.

Possibly the smallest percentage of believers are in the group that embraces and supports the post-tribulation rapture doctrine. This is the doctrine that I believe and have explained to you in detail with the support of Scripture in this and the previous chapter.

By far, the most popular doctrine of the timing of the second coming of King Yahshua Messiah in relation to the tribulation period is the pre-tribulation rapture doctrine. This false doctrine is currently being taught *en mass*, and has been taught for decades in many theological seminaries. I believe that most evangelists and pastors of our time preach this doctrine. They believe it and teach it because it is what they were taught. It is sad to me that many ministers of Yah's Word have not taken the time to study the Holy Scriptures in order to challenge and either prove or disprove this doctrine and others. People worldwide desperately need to understand the truth of Almighty Yah's plan of salvation, but nearly as important is understanding the truth about the second coming of our Master and King, Yahshua. Those alive at the time of the terrible persecution from the anti-Christ need to know the truth from Yah's Holy Word in order to know what to do and what not to do.

The pre-tribulation rapture doctrine has its origin from a book that was first printed in Latin in around 1791. The four-volume set was translated into Spanish in 1799. In 1816, the book titled, *The Coming of Messiah in Glory and Majesty,* by Juan Josafat Ben-Ezra, who was supposed to be a converted Jew, was translated into English.

The following account is some of the background information on the author named Juan Josafat Ben-Ezra. This Spaniard from Chile, South America, was a Roman Catholic Jesuit priest whose real name was Emanual Lacunza (1731-1801). He had used a Jewish name as author, so that the masses of Protestants throughout the world would be more receptive to his book. Emanual spent the last thirty years of his life studying Yah's Word, especially the prophecies of the second coming of King Jesus Messiah. The last twenty of those thirty years were consumed with the writing of his great work. He died fifteen years before his book was translated into English and officially published in London. The book was widely distributed throughout Europe and probably contributed more to the awakening of the study of the second coming of Messiah than any other book of that time. (*Prophetic Faith of Our Fathers,* vol. 3; LeRoy Edwin Froom, 1946.)

I agree with Lacunza's belief in a literal interpretation of the end-time prophecies that apply to the Lord's second coming, unless the Scriptures contain obvious symbolism. I am in agreement with him regarding the literal establishment of an evil anti-Christ system of Satan with a single individual as its leader, and the literal coming from heaven of King Yahshua Messiah to resurrect His saints and destroy the beast system at the end of the tribulation period. Much of the balance of his book that I have read deals with doctrine of Roman Catholicism that I cannot support with Scripture.

From the beginning of the Protestant faith in the early 1500s until Lacunza's time, many people were able to read the Holy Bible in their own language and form beliefs about the end-time prophecies. Knowing that the unholy Roman Catholic Church was responsible for the murder of millions of people who would not convert to the Church of Rome during the dark ages of the inquisitions, Protestants began believing the position of the pope was that of the anti-Christ. It would seem that Lacunza was a devoted Roman Catholic priest. It is plausible that he desired to use his book to divert the attention of the rapidly growing Protestant church.

He chose to describe himself as a converted Jewish Rabbi with a Jewish name in order to deceive the Protestants, who would be eager to read his massive volumes with the intriguing title. It is also plausible that he knew his book would be banned and condemned by the church he served, which made the book even more sought after.

Sometime during 1813, three years before the book was published in English, a manuscript in Spanish was introduced to the Roman Catholic Church. Lacunza hinted that he did not believe a pope, or a man, would be the anti-Christ, but that the beast would be a religious system. The book review board for the Church of Rome obliviously decided that there were too many connections in Lucanza's writings between the pope and the anti-Christ. The manuscript was soon banned after its first reading and placed on Rome's Index of Prohibited Books.

In 1826, a Reverend Edward Irving (1792-1834) of London read the 1812 edition of Lacunza's book and became obsessed with it. In 1828, he translated Lacunza's Spanish manuscript into English and had it published by L.B. Seeley and Son, London England, under the title *The Translator's Preliminary Discourse In The Coming of Messiah in Glory and Majesty*. After it was published in English, the banned book became a hot commodity across Europe.

I have given the historical background of this important book to introduce to you the following paragraph that is very significant. On page

99 of *The Coming of Messiah in Glory and Majesty,* Lacunza records the famous Scriptures of 1 Thessalonians 4:13-18, and then he made the following statement:

> "When the Lord returns from heaven to earth, upon His coming forth from heaven, **and much before His arrival at the earth,** He will give His orders, and send forth His commandments as King and God omnipotent."

I agree with Lacunza in his interpretation of King Jesus giving the commands to the angels to gather the elect (saved) from the earth before His literal arrival to earth. I believe that, near the very end of the tribulation period, the earth will be cast into darkness, as it is written in Revelation 16:10. During this time, King Yahshua will leave His place at the right hand of His Father's throne and begin His journey to planet earth. The great white brilliance of His coming with His host of millions of warrior angels will no doubt be seen by telescopes long before His arrival and His command for the rapture to take place. I estimate that the rapture will take place a few weeks, possibly days, before King Yahshua unleashes His justified wrath on the millions who will be gathered outside of Jerusalem to wage war against Him and His army as they approach from outer space.

Reverend Edward Irving, who translated Lacunza's book into English, believed and taught a different interpretation of the timing of the rapture. Irving became one of the most influential preachers of the British Great Advent Awakening conferences that began in the 1820s. In 1826, after his translated book was published and began to sweep across the British Isles, he began to preach to large crowds. At one point in a large church in Regent Square, London, more than a thousand people were packing the church Sunday after Sunday. In 1828, he began to tour Scotland where he preached outdoors to crowds of up to 20,000 people. He preached with great zeal about the near second advent of Christ. (*Prophetic Faith of Our Fathers,* vol. 3, pp. 516; LeRoy Edwin Froom, 1946.)

Irving had a great passion for Yah's Word and yearned for lost souls. He desired for the church to grow in the power of the Holy Spirit and to become like the first-century church as described in the book of Acts. He wanted to see people healed from diseases and prophecy to go forth to warn people because he truly believed that the coming of the Master was to be in his lifetime. At the beginning of the dedication of his translation of Lacunza's book, he stated, "My soul is greatly afflicted because of the present un-awakened and even dead condition of all the churches, with respect to the coming of our Lord Jesus Christ, which draweth nigh, and which, as I believe, is close at hand." (*The Translator's Preliminary Discourse In The Coming of Messiah in Glory and Majesty*, Vol. 1, pp. 16-20; Edward Irving, 1826.) He believed the events of the French Revolution would usher in the fulfillment of the prophecies of the book of Revelation.

Irving's fame grew, and he was invited to speak at many of the prophecy conferences that were being organized during the early years of the British Advent Awakening. He was one of the key speakers at the Albury Park Conferences that went on from 1826 through 1830. From these opportunities to express beliefs and opinions, three volumes called *Dialogues on Prophecy* were recorded. The recorded expressions were the beginnings of a new belief system of pre-tribulationism, a secret rapture, the "gap" theory and dispensationalism. This new belief system began to be accepted as doctrine during the conferences held at Powerscourt Castle in Ireland in 1830. The doctrine was based on the "rapture" of the church, as described in 1 Thessalonians 4:17, happening before the beginning of the great tribulation. The rest of the human race would be left to go through the horrible three and one-half years of persecution from the anti-Christ beast system. (*The Prophetic Faith of Our Fathers, The Historical Development of Prophetic Interpretation*, Vol. IV, pps. 421-422; LeRoy Edwin Froom, 1946.)

In October of 1831, while at his London home congregation of over a thousand members called the Catholic Apostolic Church, the first utterances of unknown tongues broke out. This was very encouraging to Irving. He believed that this was a great manifestation of the gifts of the Holy Spirit, and surely the Lord would be coming soon. His best friend and associate pastor, Robert Baxter, was one of the first to speak in the utterances and continued to do so in many worship services for the following two years.

One of the greatest Greek scholars and editor of the *Greek New Testament*, Dr. S. P. Tregelles, LL.D., from London, England, lived during the British Advent Awakening. He attended some of the prophecy conferences. The following is from a section titled "Origin of the Secret Rapture Theory" from the book, *The Prophetic Outlook Today*, pp. 19, E.P. Cachemaille, MA, 1918. Dr. S. P. Tregelles, who was originally connected with the remarkable awakening at Plymouth, England, in 1830-31, says:

"I am not aware that there was any definite teaching that there would be a Secret Rapture of the Church at a Secret Coming (of the Master), until this was given forth as an utterance in Mr. Irving's church from what was there received as being the Voice of the Spirit. But whether anyone ever asserted such a thing or not, it was from that supposed revelation that the modern doctrine and the modern phraseology arose. It came not from Holy Scripture, but from that which falsely pretended to be the Spirit of God."

Cachemaille continues his record of the great apostasy with the following account:

"To the testimony of Dr. Tregelles is added that of Mr. Robert Baxter, the principal actor in the Irving scandals. He was their most notable prophet, and for a time one of the most deluded men known in Church History. There is an astounding list of the statements uttered by him, and accepted as truths by the deluded congregations. Prior to the fanatical outbreak in Mr. Irving's church and before the Plymouth revival, Mr. Irving had publicly taught on the subject that was adopted by Mr. Robert Baxter. In the extravagance of the excitement Mr. Baxter's prediction's were greedily accepted by professed believers, and more and more widely afterwards."

Mr. Baxter subsequently repented deeply for his part in the impiety. Humbly confessing his sin, he separated himself wholly from the partisans of the "fables" and published an account of his part in giving the utterances titled, *Narrative of Facts*. He constantly maintained that the manifestations with which he had been connected were supernatural, but that Satan, not the Holy Spirit, was their author.

The following statements are from Mr. Baxter's own words. I will reference each page number from his book.

"The facts of the manifestations must speak for themselves, how far the delusion has been weak or strong, ordinary or extraordinary. But the men who have been involved in it, and have drank it in a full cup, will not hesitate to say it was indeed strong delusion." (*Narrative of Facts*, Second Edition, Preface, page 16, Robert Baxter, 1833.)

"Holding in mind the fact of the sincerity of the persons involved; the course of the manifestations certainly develops throughout either a most wonderful exercise of a spiritual power with all the appearance of an angel of light, giving forth power, signs, and lying wonders, in the power of utterance and conviction, in the fulfillment of many signs, and in the wonderful reading of the thoughts and mind of others; or if this not be admitted, the necessary inference must be, that the minds of all concerned were so darkened, that they mistook the natural workings of their own minds for a supernatural power working on them—mistook also a natural utterance for a supernatural one—mistook coincidences or accidents for signs—the exercise of natural discernment for supernatural discernment, and that the hundreds who daily attended upon these utterances, and experienced the spiritual influence of the work to their own perfect conviction, were altogether infatuated into a belief of it as supernatural. The delusion must be as strong in the one case as the other." (Preface, page 17.)

"An opinion had been advanced in some of Mr. Irving's writings, that before the second coming of Christ, and before the setting in upon the world of the day of vengeance, emphatically so called in the Scriptures, the saints would be caught up to heaven like Enoch and Elijah; and would be thus saved from the destruction of this world, as Noah was saved in the ark, and as Lot was saved from Sodom. This was an opinion I never could entertain; conceiving, as I did, that our refuge in and through the days of vengeance, would be some earthly sanctuary, until the Lord should come, the dead be raised, and those remaining alive should be caught up. (1 Thess. IV. 17.) In the interval I have alluded to I did, however, experience a sudden change of opinion; the passages in Mat. 24:40 & 41, Two shall be in the field, one shall be taken, and the other left; two women shall be grinding at the mill, the one shall be taken, and the other left, were brought to me in the power, and accompanied with the sudden conviction I have before described—"This is the translation of the saints, while the rest of the world are left in their usual occupations." My wife, though agreeing with me in general, on doctrine and in faith, was never able to believe in the utterance and power as of God; but considered it to be a deceit of Satan, and was most violently opposed to it, and all views connected with it." (Pages 17 & 18.)

My comment here regarding Mr. Baxter's testimony is that he was correct in believing and teaching that verses 40 and 41 of Matthew 24 are referring to the resurrection of the saints at the coming of Lord Jesus. The deception was—then and today—in the belief that the resurrection is before the great tribulation. The Scriptures of the Holy Bible clearly teach that the resurrection of the saints is at the end of the great tribulation just before Almighty Yah's wrath is poured out as a consuming fire.

Now back to Mr. Baxter's statements from his book.

"We all felt as though the Lord was indeed resolving our doubts, and graciously condescending by His Spirit to teach us by open voice. Mr. Irving seemed most fully confirmed in the belief, and I was myself exceedingly composed and strengthened. Looking back upon it now, I can only say, all this seeming demonstration of truth and holiness would not have been permitted to deceive us, if we had not forgotten the scripture that Satan himself is transformed into an angel of light." (Page 23.)

"Nevertheless, as upholding Mr. Irving on all occasions, I am ready to confess myself justly involved in the delusion, and my own personal offences in prophetic speculations and lofty imaginations, would, even apart from these heresies, sufficiently explain my punishment. One circumstance of these manifestations cannot but force itself upon observation; that is, the continual use which was made of the doctrine of the second advent of the Lord. This was the leading theme of the utterances. The nearness of it, its suddenness, and the fearful judgments which would accompany it, were the continual arguments which were used to excite our minds, and stimulate our decision; as well as to support us under difficulties, and to induce us to lay all other things aside to further the work. The same thing has, as far as we are informed, attended every putting forth of assumed prophetic power from the earliest times. With regard to those manifestations, which have been nearer our own times, we know certainly that it has been so. With the French prophets, who arose about the beginning of the last century, and with the followers of Joanna Southcote, in our own days, the nearness of the second coming has been the leading doctrine. The inevitable effect of this fanatical use of the doctrine is to create prejudice, and to induce a persuasion that it is a dangerous doctrine. We must, however, be on our guard against any such hastiness of decision. Previously to the first advent of our Lord, many false Christs arose, and drew away many; and the nearer the advent, the more frequent and powerful were the delusions. Doubtless they excited in the minds of the Jews a strong prejudice, which led them practically to deny our Lord when He came, though they yet professed to wait for Him. We are also expressly warned with reference to the second advent, that there shall arise false Christs and false prophets, and shall show great signs and wonders, insomuch that if it were possible, they shall deceive the very elect. And our Lord's caution upon it is, Behold I have told you before, wherefore if they shall say unto you, Behold he is in the desert, go not forth: behold he is in the secret chamber, believe it not. For as the lightning cometh out of the east, and shineth even unto the west, so shall also the coming of the Son of Man be. We must not, therefore, suffer ourselves to be brought into an unbelief of His coming, so as to join the company of the scoffers, and say, Where is the promise of His coming? But we must remember our Lord's injunction, Take ye heed, watch and pray ... for ye know not when the master of the house cometh ... lest coming suddenly he find you sleeping. And what I say unto you I say unto all, watch! The device of satan, doubtless, is to cast odium *(hatred)* upon the doctrine, lull men into a state of forgetfulness, that the coming of the Lord draweth nigh. Without, however, dwelling further upon this subject, I would say; whilst, it appears to me, these circumstances ought in no wise to prevent our watchfulness, or patient waiting for the coming of the Lord; they certainly call upon us to humble ourselves, under the remembrance that there must have been much error, in our view of the manner and circumstances of the coming of the Lord, or we could not have been so deceived. May God grant us grace to confess our faults, and proving all things, hold fast that which is good. (*Narrative of Facts*, Second Edition, pps. 23, 142 & 143, Robert Baxter, 1833.)

There are only nine known copies of this very rare book. I was very fortunate that Duke University, School of Divinity Library had a copy and was willing to let me have access to it with white cotton gloves under close watch.

Baxter published his *Narrative of Facts* about two years after Reverend Edward Irving's teachings and the phenomenon of the utterances became controversial. The following is a recorded account.

Controversy developed over the origin of the phenomenon—whether of divine or demonic possession. The attempted prosecution for heresy in December 1830 had led to Irving's withdrawal from the jurisdiction of the London Presbytery. But he was soon thereafter removed from his pulpit by the church trustees, in 1832. The Presbytery of Annan, on the charge of heresy, deprived Irving from his status as a clergyman in the Church of Scotland after an ecclesiastical trial in 1833. After traveling in Scotland, preaching to crowds in the open air, he returned to London to find himself suspended, virtually deposed by his own congregation, and occupying a minor position. His health declined rapidly, and he died in Glasgow in 1834. All the ministers of Glasgow attended his funeral service, as that of a minister of Christ. (*Prophetic Faith of Our Fathers*, Vol. 3, pg. 516 & 517, LeRoy Edwin Froom, 1946.)

The accounts of Reverend Irving reveal that he was a devout man of God who sincerely sought the truth from God's Word. The records show that he, his close friend, Robert Baxter, and many other devout men of the early prophecy conferences were truly seeking insight from the utterances and interpretations. These men believed that they were receiving new revelation from God about the events of the second coming of our Messiah. Two of these men, John Nelson Darby and B. W. Newton, were from the Plymouth Brethren. The following is an account from an historical writer that defends the doctrine of the Plymouth Brethren.

It was in these meetings that the precious truth of the rapture of the Church was brought to light; that is, the coming of the Lord in the air to take away His church before the great tribulation should begin on earth. The views brought out at Powerscourt Castle not only formed the views of the Brethren elsewhere, but as years went on obtained wide publication in denominational circles, chiefly through the writings of such men as Darby, Bellett, Newton, and others.

Belief No. (9): Secret rapture of the saints—caught up to be with Christ:

Yes, if this be heresy, "Brethren" are heretics; for they indeed teach that the coming of the Lord, to be in the air and all His saints will be caught up to meet Him, and the world left to pass through the great tribulation. But he is a bold man who would dub this "blessed hope" heresy in the face of 1 Cor. 15:51-56, 1 Thes. 4:13-18, and kindred passages. And again, be it remarked, "Brethren" are in good company, for Dr. Strong need not go outside his own denomination to find a host of honored servants of Christ who believe as thoroughly as "Brethren" do in the "secret rapture of the saints." (*A Historical Sketch of the Brethren Movement*, ppg. 23, 212 & 213; Dr. Henry Allen Ironside, 1942.)

Dr. Ironside uses these two sections of Scripture to support the false pre-tribulation rapture doctrine that was originated by Irving, Darby, and some of the early Plymouth Brethren. These two sections of Scripture do indeed describe the blessed event of the resurrection (rapture) of all saints when we receive new immortal bodies. The timing of this amazing event is not before the evil tribulation, but at the end of it, at the last trumpet, which is the seventh according to Yah's Word.

The following is a section of the English translation of a Greek manuscript discovered by Bryennious in 1873. The manuscript titled *Teaching of the Twelve Apostles*, or *Didache* as it is also known, has been a confirmed authentic document by the historical writings of Clement of Alexandria who lived around A.D. 200, and other historical writers of the second and third centuries.

The *Didache* is believed to have been written approximately in the year A.D. 60 by some of the original, later surviving apostles of King Yahshua Messiah. From the *Didache* it is stated, "For in the last days the false prophets and corrupters will abound, and the sheep will be turned into wolves, and love will be turned into hate. As lawlessness increases they will hate and persecute and betray one another. And then the deceiver of the world will appear as a son of God and "will perform signs and wonders, and the earth will be delivered into his hands, and he will commit abominations the likes of which have never happened before." Then all humankind will come to the fiery test, and "many will fall away" and perish; but "those who endure" in their faith "will be saved" by the accursed one himself (King Yahshua Messiah). And "then there will appear the signs" of the truth: first the

sign of an opening in heaven, then the sign of the sound of a trum-
pet, and third, the resurrection of the dead—but not of all; rather, as
it has been said, "The Lord will come, and all of his saints with him."
Then the world "will see the Lord coming upon the clouds of heaven."
(*The Apostolic Fathers*, Second Edition, page 158; J.B. Lightfoot &
J.R. Harmer, 1989, First Edition, 1891.)

I will conclude this section of the origin of the false doctrine of the
secret coming of King Yahshua any moment, rapture of the saints, with
these documented, historical statements:

"It was not until the first decade of the twentieth century that
dispensationalism, the pre-tribulation rapture theory, and the separation of the seventieth week from the previous sixty-nine weeks
of Daniel 9, became accepted doctrine in the then, newly formed
Fundamentalist wing of Protestantism. This was largely brought
about by the acceptance of Dr. C. I. Scofield's bold and revolutionary
thesis, and the aggressive support given this postulate by the Moody
Bible Institute of Chicago. This, be it remembered, was around the
turn of the century." (*The Prophetic Faith of our Fathers*, Vol. IV, pps.
1203-1204; LeRoy Edwin Froom, 1946.)

"Set in impiety, the doctrine of the Lord's secret Coming, before the
manifestation of the man of sin and before the great tribulation, was
then first openly promulgated in England. It was adopted by the late
J. N. Darby, and was taught far and near, and hailed as enchanted
teaching. There has since been much scheming to give the doctrine
a reputable origin, scheming by those who did not know the original
facts, not being contemporaries of Dr. Tregelles. Also, great efforts
have been made to prove it from scripture, in the face of the plain
statements that have already been referred to. No such direct proof
can be found; indirect inferences, but insufficient, are made to do
service instead. It is disastrous fiction that the Rapture will be before
the Tribulation, and that the Lord will take away His people before the
man of sin is revealed. The saints themselves are those that endure
the Tribulation (Rev. 7:14), so they must be on earth while it is taking
place." (*The Prophetic Outlook To-Day*, pps. 20-21; E.P. Cachemaille,
M.A., 1918.)

The supernatural resurrection of the elect by the power of our Master and King Yahshua as He approaches earth will absolutely be the most awesome, brilliant, and longed-for time of rejoicing and reunion of the redeemed that has ever been or ever will be. Imagine, if you are alive on the earth at the time of Yahshua's coming, uniting with our precious Bridegroom, and reuniting with family members and friends who have formerly died and gone on to be with Almighty Yah. And to make the event even more astounding, instantly being blessed with a new resurrected, supernatural body, as was described from Scripture previously in this chapter. The uniting with King Yahshua will be the marriage of Himself, the Bridegroom, and His bride. All of us who make up His body, also called His true *ekklesia*, or *called out ones* who are set apart from the world, will partake in this most blessed of all events in human history. How long we are with Yahshua in the air above the earth before He and His army begin to destroy Satan's kingdom is not clear in the Scriptures. Anyone's opinion on this is nothing more that speculation. I believe the marriage supper, which will be a celebration of the union of King Yahshua and His body of saved believers, will happen later in the sequence of events, after the destruction of the gathered armies of the world around Jerusalem. There is more detail on the post-resurrection events in the condensed next chapter.

9

POST RESURRECTION
EVENTS

From the very first word in this book, I have sought to be completely open in sharing the information that I have collected from my research on the end-of-days and the return of Messiah. No one on this earth knows the exact timing or the order of all of the end-of-this-age and post-resurrection events. I am convinced by the evidence of the understanding of the Scriptures that the post-resurrection events take place on this earth and not in heaven, and that all of the events associated with King Yahshua's second coming will be fulfilled during the fall feasts at the end of the last year of the tribulation period of a yet unknown year. There are many details of the many events that happen after King Yahshua returns to this planet. Rather that list every detail of every event in all of the Scriptures that relate to His establishing His Kingdom, I have chosen to list what I believe are the most important events. Some of the prophecy Scriptures have been stated previously and are being referenced again with a different application. We learn new insights from Yah's Holy Word by reading and studying it more than once.

The event of the coming of Yahshua Messiah will be the most wonderful and welcomed time possible for His body of redeemed believers. It will also be the most terrifying, horrible, and fear-consuming time of despair there has ever been or ever will be for those who have accepted the mark of the beast and worshiped Satan through his deceptive system.

The huge army of the world's united confederation will be gathered outside of Jerusalem and will have taken control of the city. As they see the brilliance of the heavenly host coming in the sky, their focus will change from abusing the people of the city to preparing to do battle with King Yahshua and His mighty angels in an attempt to prevent Him from coming to establish His Kingdom in Jerusalem.

I believe that King Yahshua will physically touch down on the Mount of Olives following the resurrection but prior to His giving the command to His army of angels to unleash His wrath of fire upon the gathered armies of the world, the anti-Christ, the false prophet, and all who have accepted the mark of the beast. At that time, I believe that He will be joined by the 144,000 chosen Israelites who will have fulfilled their important ministry during the tribulation years. He then will cause an earthquake that will split the mountain in half and provide a place of protection for the many Jewish people who will have been persecuted in and around Jerusalem. The surviving Jews will be those who will have overcome testing through the fires of persecution from the anti-Christ because they did not accept the mark of the beast, but they will have not at that time accepted King Yahshua as their true Messiah. Jews, as all people, must accept that Jesus Yahshua is the Messiah, put their faith in His blood for atonement and be born of His Spirit in order to be accepted into Father Yahweh's Kingdom, according to His Holy Word. They will be yearning for Him and seeking Him with all of their hearts when they see Him coming in the sky with His magnificent host.

As I stated earlier in this book, prophecy Scripture has often been recorded by the original writers in reverse chronological order, which is why prophecy is often difficult to understand. The following verses are an example of this as they apply in context to King Yahshua coming to earth and standing on the Mount of Olives. As it is written:

Behold, the day of the LORD cometh, and thy spoil shall be divided in the midst of thee. For I will gather all nations against Jerusalem to battle; and the city shall be taken, and the houses rifled, and the women ravished; and half of the city shall go forth into captivity, and the residue [*remaining remnant*] **of the people shall not be cut off from the city. Then shall the LORD go forth, and fight against those nations, as when He fought in the day of battle** [*close conflicts of previous battles and wars involving the Jews and the nation of Israel*]**. And His feet shall stand in that day upon the mount of Olives, which is before Jerusalem on the east, and the mount of Olives shall cleave** [*split*] **in the midst thereof toward the east and toward the west, and there shall be a very great valley; and half of the mountain shall remove toward the north, and half of it toward the south. And ye** [*Jewish remnant*] **shall flee to the valley**

of the mountains; for the valley of the mountains shall reach unto Azal *[a new place yet to be identified on a map]*; **yea, ye shall flee, like as ye fled from before the earthquake in the days of Uzziah king of Judah: and the LORD my God** *[Elohim]* **shall come, and all the saints with thee** *[meaning warrior angels bringing with them the souls of all those who have died in Yahshua just prior to the resurrection of all who are a part of the first resurrection of the body of Messiah as recorded in Matthew 24:29-31 and 1 Thessalonians 4:16-17]*.

Zechariah 14:1-5 (KJV). *Bracketed words added for clarity.*

The following verses, from a different prophet of the old covenant, refer to the same events that are to occur during the end of the great tribulation.

LORD, in trouble *[tribulation]* **they have visited You, they poured out a prayer** *when* **Your chastening** *was* **upon them. As a women with child is in pain and cries out in her pangs,** *when* **she draws near the time of her delivery, so have we been in Your sight, O LORD. We have been with child, we have been in pain; we have, as it were, brought forth wind** *[grieving in their spirit]*; **we have not accomplished any deliverance in the earth, nor have the inhabitants of the world** *[beast system]* **fallen. Your dead** *[all who belong to Yahweh, those before Yahshua lived as a man, and since His resurrection]* **shall live;** *together with* **my dead body** *[the prophet Isaiah's]* **they shall arise. Awake and sing, you who dwell in the dust; for your dew** *is like* **the dew of herbs, and the earth shall cast out the dead. Come, my people** *[the Jewish remnant that have not accepted Yahshua as their Messiah that will be in Jerusalem at that time]*, **enter your chambers, and shut your doors behind you** *[figuratively; flee into the Lord's protection in the new valley at the Mount of Olives]*; **hide yourself, as it were, for a little moment, until the indignation is past. For behold, the LORD** *[King Yahshua]* **comes out of His place** *[at the right hand of Father Yahweh in heaven]* **to punish the inhabitants of the earth for their iniquity; the earth will also disclose her blood, and will no more cover her slain.**

Isaiah 26:16-21 (NJKV). *Bracketed words added for clarity.*

Also from the prophet Zechariah:

The word of the Lord concerning Israel: Thus says the Lord, who stretched out the heavens and founded the earth and formed the spirit

of man within him: "Lo, I am about to make Jerusalem a cup of reeling to all the peoples round about; it will be against Judah *[those Jews that have been deceived by and accepted the anti-Christ]* also in the siege against Jerusalem. On that day I will make Jerusalem a heavy stone for all the peoples; all who lift it shall grievously hurt themselves. And all the nations of the earth will come together against it. On that day, says the Lord, I will strike every horse with panic *[disable the military equipment from functioning properly]*, and its rider with madness *[confuse the soldiers of all the armies]*. But upon the house of Judah I will open my eyes *[regard with favor the Jewish people there]*, when I strike every horse of the peoples with blindness. Then the clans of Judah shall say to themselves, 'The inhabitants of Jerusalem have strength through the Lord of hosts, their God.' On that day I will make the clans of Judah like a blazing pot in the midst of wood, like a flaming torch among sheaves; and they shall devour to the right and to the left all the peoples round about, while Jerusalem shall still be inhabited in its place, in Jerusalem *[the army of Israel will once again prevail against its enemies with the Master's intervention]*. And the Lord will give victory to the tents of Judah first, that the glory of the house of David and the glory of the inhabitants of Jerusalem may not be exalted over that of Judah. On that day the Lord will put a shield about the inhabitants of Jerusalem so that the feeblest among them on that day shall be like David, and the house of David shall be like God *[have great strength from Almighty Yah]*, like the angel of the Lord, at their head. And on that day I will seek to destroy all the nations that come against Jerusalem. And I will pour out on the house of David and the inhabitants of Jerusalem a spirit of compassion and supplication, so that, when they look on Him *[King Yahshua]* whom they have pierced, they shall mourn for Him, as one mourns for an only child, and weep bitterly over him, as one weeps over a first-born *[the blindness of the Jewish people in Jerusalem at that time, those descendants of the Jewish leaders who were responsible for seeking the death of Jesus Messiah, will be removed and they will believe and mourn]*.

Zechariah 12:1-10 (RSV). *Bracketed words added for clarity.*

During the future siege of the city of Jerusalem, the great armies of the world will gather at Megiddo, or Armageddon. Their attention will be diverted by the brilliance of the incoming King Yahshua and His huge army of warrior angels. All of the soldiers of the world's army, and those who have accepted the mark of the beast who are alive at that time, will be destroyed physically by Almighty Yah's consuming fire, as the full measure of His wrath is poured out on the manifestation of Satan's evil empire.

As it is written:

For it is indeed just of God *[Yahweh]* **to repay with affliction those who afflict you, and to give relief to the afflicted as well as to us, when the Lord Jesus is revealed from heaven with his mighty angels in flaming fire, inflicting vengeance on those who do not know God and on those who do not obey the gospel of our Lord Jesus. These will suffer the punishment of eternal destruction, separated from the presence of the Lord and from the glory of His might, when he comes to be glorified by his saints and to be marveled at on that day among all who have believed, because our testimony to you was believed.** *[As stated previously, the saints, dead and alive at that time, will be given newly resurrected bodies, as He and His bright host are visibly seen approaching earth from a great distance. The amount of time between the rapture and the outpouring of the fire of His wrath cannot be accurately determined by the Scriptures.]*

2 Thessalonians 1:6-10 (NRSV). *Bracketed words added for clarity.*

For our God *is* **a consuming fire.**
Hebrews 12:29 (NJKV)

And the rest were killed by the sword of the rider *[King Yahshua]* **on the horse, the sword that came from His mouth ...**
Revelation 19:21 (NRSV). *Bracketed words added for clarity.*

I believe the correct interpretation of this last verse is that God's Word is all powerful in the execution of His master plan from beginning to end, for creation, instruction for living, redemption, prophecy, and judgment. It is written:

Indeed, the word of God is living and active, sharper than any two-edged sword, piercing until it divides soul from spirit, joints from marrow; it is able to judge the thoughts and intentions of the heart. And

before Him no creature is hidden, but all are naked and laid bare to the eyes of the one to whom we must render an account.
Hebrews 4:12-13 (NRSV)

He had in His right hand seven stars, out of His mouth went a sharp two-edged sword, and His countenance was like the sun shining in its strength.
Revelation 1:16 (NKJV)

I believe when King Yahshua gives His powerful command out of His mouth, the mighty angels will begin the process of first gathering all the resurrected saints, as it is written in Matthew 24:29-31, Mark 13:24-27 and Luke 21:25-28. Then the angels will slay with fire the gathered armies and those with the mark of the beast after the anti-Christ and the false prophet are captured and cast into their eternal place of torment, the lake of fire, as it is written in Revelation 19:20.

The following verse describes how the armies that have gathered to destroy Jerusalem will be slain. It is written:

And this shall be the plague with which the LORD will strike all the people who fought against Jerusalem: Their flesh shall dissolve while they stand on their feet, their eyes shall dissolve in their sockets, and their tongues shall dissolve in their mouths.
Zechariah 14:12 (NKJV)

This described event reminds me of the scene in the movie, "Raiders of the Lost Ark," when the Nazi commanders removed the lid from the top of the ark of the covenant and the release of the energy from within consumed the men, causing them to dissolve into nothing. The entire chain of events leading up to, during, and after the second coming of Yahshua Messiah reads like scenes in a science fiction movie. But we know that by the evidence of the fulfillment of the all of the prophecies relating to the first coming of our Master and Judge, that all of the prophecies relating to His second coming will likewise come true. It is written:

For the LORD *is* good; His *mercy is* everlasting, and his truth *endures* to all generations.
Psalms 100:5 (NKJV)

Sanctify them by Your truth. Your word is truth.
John 17:17 (NKJV)

This last verse is part of the prayer Yahshua prayed to His Heavenly Father, Yahweh, testifying to His truth.

God's Holy Word reveals to us that there will be immensely wonderful events that take place after King Yahshua returns to destroy Satan's kingdom and to begin the process of establishing His kingdom on earth. Satan will be bound for a thousand years.

Then I saw an angel coming down from heaven, having the key to the bottomless pit and a great chain in his hand. He laid hold of the dragon, that serpent of old, who is *the* Devil and Satan, and bound him for a thousand years; and he cast him into the bottomless pit, and shut him up, and set a seal on him, so that he should deceive the nations no more till the thousand years were finished. But after these things he must be released for a little while.
Revelation 20:1-3 (NJKV)

It is implied that, along with Satan, all of the fallen angels and demons are bound also because, during the millennium reign of King Jesus, there will be peace, order, and righteousness throughout the world.

The LORD [*Father God Yahweh*] **said to my lord** [*Jesus*]**, the king, "Sit here at my right side until I put your enemies under your feet." From Zion the LORD will extend your royal power. "Rule over your enemies," he says. On the day you fight your enemies, your people will volunteer. Like the dew of early morning your young men will come to you on the sacred hills.**
Psalms 110:1-3 (TEV). *Bracketed words added for clarity.*

For out of Zion shall go forth the law, and the word of the Lord [*King Yahshua*] **from Jerusalem. He shall judge between many peoples, and shall decide for strong nations afar off; and they shall beat their swords into plowshares, and their spears into pruning hooks; nation shall not lift up sword against nation, neither shall they learn war any more ...**
Micah 4:2b-3 (RSV). *Bracketed words added for clarity.*

Yahshua will usher in a true and lasting peace with order, not just in a few places, but throughout the entire world.

I believe that as soon as Satan and his kingdom has been defeated and removed from influencing human beings that a time of wonderful restoration begins. I believe that after King Yahshua brings law and order to Israel and the world in general, that He transforms the landscape all around Jerusalem and Israel supernaturally by His power, also changing the climate and nighttime darkness to daylight. I believe that the city of Jerusalem and the third temple on the Temple Mount will either be cleansed or a new temple will be built and made ready for His coronation. Remember that there will have to be a third temple built on the foundation of the first and second temples, in order for the Jewish people to be able to reinstate animal sacrifices that the anti-Christ stops mid-way through his time of authority. Being that the Mount of Olives is located on the east side of Jerusalem, I envision a huge procession moving from the Mount of Olives toward the Eastern Gate of the city, and as many as possible proceeding in to the Temple Mount area. King Yahshua will take His rightful place on His throne, the throne of His ancestor, King David. As it is written:

> **The whole region, from Geba in the north to Rimmon in the south, will be made level. Jerusalem will tower above the land around it; the city will reach from the Benjamin Gate to the Corner Gate, where there had been an earlier gate, and from the Tower of Hananel to the royal wine presses. The people will live there in safety, no longer threatened by destruction.**
>
> **When that time comes, there will no longer be cold or frost, nor any darkness. There will always be daylight, even at nighttime. When this will happen is known only to the LORD. When that day comes,** *[the second coming of King Yahshua]* **fresh water will flow from Jerusalem, half of it to the Dead Sea and the other half to the Mediterranean. It will flow all year long, in the dry seasons as well as the wet. Then the LORD will be king over all of the earth; everyone will worship Him as God and know Him by the same name.**

Zechariah 14:10-11 & 6-9 (TEV). *Bracketed words added for clarity.*

And behold, you will conceive in your womb and bring forth a Son, and shall call His name JESUS. *[This was fulfilled in His first coming. Remember, His name* Yahshua, *means* salvation from Yah.*]* **He will be**

great, and will be called the Son of the Highest; and the Lord God *[Elohim Adonai]* **will give Him the throne of His father David. And He will reign over the house of Jacob** *[all people that have accepted Him are one people group called Israel, or House of Jacob made up of Jew and non-Jew born again believers]* **forever, and of His kingdom there will be no end.**

Luke 1:31-33 (NKJV). *Bracketed words added for clarity.*

I believe next in order, according to the Scriptures, will be a long series of judgments. It is written:

A shoot shall come out from the stump of Jesse *[one of the prophecies of the first coming of Messiah was that He would be a direct descendant of Jesse the father of King David, the second king of ancient Israel]*, **and a branch shall grow out of his roots. The Spirit of the LORD shall rest on Him,** *[Yahshua]* **the spirit of wisdom and understanding, the spirit of counsel and might, the spirit of knowledge and the fear of the Lord** *[Almighty Yah]*. **His delight shall be in the fear of the LORD. He** *[King Yahshua]* **shall not judge by what His eyes see, or decide by what His ears hear; but with righteousness He shall judge the poor** *[impoverished of the truth]*, **and decide with equity for the meek** *[patient oppressed ones]* **of the earth; and He shall strike the earth with the rod of His mouth, and with His breath of His lips He shall kill the wicked. Righteousness shall be the belt around His waist, and faithfulness the belt around His loins.**

Isaiah 11:1-5 (NRSV). *Bracketed words added for clarity.*

... for we shall all stand before the judgment seat of Christ *[Messiah Yahshua]*. **For it is written, As I live, says the Lord, every knee shall bow to me, and every tongue shall confess to God** *[Elohim]*. **So then every one of us shall give account of himself to God.**

Romans 14:10b-12 (KJV). *Bracketed words added for clarity.*

There are many different judgments recorded in the Holy Scriptures. I have included below the four I believe to be the most significant. They are:

1. the *Bema* Seat, or Judgment Seat, of Christ;
2. the judgment of people of the nations of the world in regards to their treatment toward blood-line Jewish people and the true

followers of Messiah during the tribulation time;

3. the judgment of the fallen angels, and

4. the Great White Throne Judgment, which covers all other non-believing people of all times who either had the opportunity to accept Jesus as their Lord and Savior and didn't, or who never had the opportunity to receive the truth that the Messiah, the Creator of the universe, was Almighty Yahweh Who was born into the human race as Yahshua.

I have given some detail of the understanding to number one below and number four in the latter part of this chapter. Some details for number two are in Chapter Eleven, as this applies to how we treat each other during the most difficult time in all of history. The Scripture references for number three, the judgment of fallen angels are: 1 Corinthians 6:3, 2 Peter 2:4, and Jude 6.

Bema is the Greek word used in the original manuscripts that means *judgment seat of Christ.* He will establish His place of rule and judgment. It will be a great, white (pure and righteous) throne that is raised up because He alone is to be exalted. The judgment is the most high court of King Yahshua Messiah, that is phase one of judgment, and begins after He has brought restoration to the world at the beginning of the Millennial reign. The *Bema* judgment is similar to the second resurrection judgment, in that each person is judged according to his or her works done in this life. The paramount difference is that those in the first resurrection have accepted Jesus, Yahshua, as their Savior and have been born of His Holy Spirit. Therefore, they have no fear of being sentenced to eternal separation from the one true God, Almighty Yah.

The following Scriptures confirm the happening of the event and give some description, but they give no clue to the length of the process. As I stated previously, I believe the order of the events in this and other prophecies give indication that the judgments happen after King Yahshua comes from heaven and unleashes His wrath on Satan's physical army and leaders. It is written that after the seventh angel blows his trumpet:

"The nations raged, but your wrath has come, and the time for judging the dead, for rewarding Your servants, the prophets and saints and all who fear Your name, both small and great, and for destroying those who destroy the earth."

Revelation 11:18 (NRSV)

Every human being will be required to stand before our eternal Creator, Savior, King and Judge. Those of us that are part of the first resurrection will have a review of our lives after receiving the blood of Yahshua that covers our sins and being born of His Spirit, to be judged by our Master as to how we lived the remainder of our lives.

For all of us [redeemed, set apart ones] **must appear before the judgment seat of Christ, so that each may receive recompense** [payment given for doing Yahweh's will and the knowledge of awards that would have been given had the person been obedient in doing His will] **for what has been done in the body, whether good or evil.**
2 Corinthians 5:10 (NRSV). *Bracketed words added for clarity.*

The time has come for judgment to begin, and God's [Yah's] **own people are the first to be judged. If it starts with us, how will it end with those who do not believe the Good News from God?**
1 Peter 4:17 (TEV). *Bracketed words added for clarity.*

For no one can lay any foundation [of truth from the one true, living God] **other than the one that has been laid; that foundation is Jesus Christ** [the true Word from Yahweh Almighty, all that He accomplished in His first coming and requires of us, His people.] **Now if anyone builds on the foundation with gold, silver, precious stones** [good works with the right motive in the person's heart; to love Almighty Yah and our fellowman, and to bring glory to our Heavenly Father and His Son, King Yahshua]**, wood, hay, straw** [good works with the wrong motive in the person's heart; to bring glory to themselves, to seek the praise and recognition of people, to have a hidden agenda that give the person some unworthy gain]**—the work of each builder will become visible, for the Day** [the Day of Yahweh, which begins with the second coming of Messiah Yahshua, and continues through to the end of the thousand year millennium reign, ending with the creation of a new earth and heaven which will usher in eternity] **will disclose it, because it will be revealed with fire, and the fire will test what sort of work each has done. If what has been built on the foundation survives, the builder will receive a reward. If the work is burned up, the builder will suffer loss; the builder will be saved, but only as through fire** [receiving the Holy Spirit; see Matthew 3:11-12].
1 Corinthians 3:11-15 (NRSV). *Bracketed words added for clarity.*

All people who are not part of the first resurrection will be judged after the second resurrection at the end of the millennium according to how they lived with what light they received in their lives. The main truth to understand is that everyone will one day stand in front of Almighty Yahshua. We can face up to Him boldly if we have done that which He has required us to do and have been obedient to the leading of His Holy Spirit.

I encourage you to love our Creator and Redeemer with all of your heart, mind, and being, and to love all people in your life as you love yourself. Allow the person of the Holy Spirit *(Ruch HaKodesh)* to lead you to do what is our Heavenly Father's will, in loving Him and His Son, Yahshua, and in helping to meet the needs of others. Do all that you do with the right intent in your heart, which is to bring glory to Yah Almighty. HalleluYah! It is written:

My conscience is clear, but that does not prove that I am really innocent. The Lord is the one who passes judgment on me. So you should not pass judgment *[in regards to salvation and eternity]* **on anyone before the right time comes. Final judgment must wait until the Lord comes; he will bring to light the dark secrets and expose the hidden purposes of people's minds. And then everyone** *[all who are in Messiah Yahshua]* **will receive from God the praise he deserves.**
   1 Corinthians 4:4-5 (TEV). *Bracketed words added for clarity.*

My brethren, let not many of you become teachers, knowing that we shall receive a stricter judgment. For we all stumble in many things.
   James 3:1-2a (NKJV)

Our friend and advocate, Holy Spirit, begins the process of preparing us to be able to stand boldly before our Creator, Savior, King, and Judge the moment we accept Yahshua into our hearts. The process of chastening, cleansing, and developing the holy character of Yahshua in us begins and is ongoing throughout our entire life on earth.

During the Judgment Seat of Messiah, King Yahshua establishes His administrative government that will have been given to Him by our Holy Father. He then delegates authority to those of the first resurrection, some as priests, some as kings, as well as the many other tasks that will be delegated. As it is written:

Unto to Him that loved us, and washed us from our sins in his own blood, and hath made us kings and priests unto God and His Father; to him be glory and dominion for ever and ever. Amen.

Revelation 1:5b-6 (KJV)

The **LORD** [*Father Yahweh*] **said unto my Lord** [*King David is here refer-ring to Master Yahshua, our Savior*]**, Sit thou at my right hand, until I make thine enemies thy footstool.**

Psalms 110:1 (KJV). *Bracketed words added for clarity.*

Then to Him was given dominion and glory and a kingdom, that all peo-ples, nations, and languages should serve Him. His dominion is an ever-lasting dominion, which shall not pass away, and His kingdom is the one which shall not be destroyed.

Daniel 7:14 (NKJV)

He will reign over the house of Jacob [*all of redeemed, born again Israel*] **forever, and of His kingdom there will be no end.**

Luke 1:33 (NRSV). *Bracketed words added for clarity.*

Then the kingdom and dominion, and the greatness of the kingdoms under the whole heaven, shall be given to the people, the saints of the Most High [*King Yahshua*]**. His kingdom is an everlasting kingdom and all dominions shall serve and obey Him.**

Daniel 7:27 (NKJV). *Bracketed words added for clarity.*

But the meek [*humble, patient, obedient, set apart ones*] **shall inherit the earth; and shall delight themselves in the abundance of peace.**

Psalms 37:11 (KJV). *Bracketed words added for clarity.*

"Blessed are the meek, for they shall inherit the earth."

Matthew 5:5 (RSV)

They sang a new song: "You [*King Yahshua*] **are worthy to take the scroll and to break open its seals. For You were killed, and by your sacrificial death you bought** [*purchased*] **for God** [*Father Yahweh*] **people from every tribe, language, nation, and race. You have made them a kingdom of priests to serve our God, and they shall rule on earth."**

Revelation 5:9-10 (TEV). *Bracketed words added for clarity.*

From now on there is reserved for me *[the Apostle Paul]* **the crown of right-eousness, which the Lord, the righteous judge, will give me on that day, and not only to me but also to all who have longed for His appearing.**
2 Timothy 4:8 (NRSV). *Bracketed words added for clarity.*

Then I saw thrones, and those *[King Yahshua and other heavenly appointed beings]* **seated on them were given authority to judge** *[judging and rewarding]*. **I also saw the souls of those who had been behead-ed** *[literally, but implied all martyrs who died for the cause of Jesus, Yahshua, down through the ages and during the great tribulation]* **for their testimony of Jesus and for the word of God. They had not wor-shiped the beast or its image and had not received its mark on their fore-heads or their hands. They came to life and reigned with Christ a thou-sand years. (The rest of the dead did not come to life until the thousand years were ended.) This is the first resurrection. Blessed and holy are those who share in the first resurrection** *[all who have accepted Yahshua]*. **Over these the second death has no power, but they will be priests of God** *[Father Yahweh]* **and of Christ** *[His Anointed One]*, **and they will reign with Him a thousand years.**
Revelation 20:4-6 (NRSV). *Bracketed words added for clarity.*

The Millennial reign is the first thousand years of Messiah's never-ending, eternal reign. During the one thousand years of the Millennial Kingdom, the many millions of inhabitants of the earth who had not taken the mark of the beast and had survived the catastrophes of the tribulation period will experience a great time of healing and of experi-encing the goodness of Yahshua, our Creator. All people of the world will be taught the ways of the Lord and will be required to come to Jerusalem and worship our Creator, Savior, and King Eternal, Yahshua, to His glory and the glory of Father Yahweh. It is written:

And it shall come to pass in the last days, that the mountain of the LORD's house shall be established in the top of the mountains, and shall be exalted above the hills; and all nations shall flow unto it. And many people shall go and say, Come ye, and let us go up to the mountain of the LORD, to the house of the God of Jacob; and he will teach us of His ways, and we will walk in His paths: for out of Zion shall go forth the law, and the word of the LORD from Jerusalem. And He shall judge

among the nations, and shall rebuke many people: and they shall beat their swords into plowshares, and their spears into pruninghooks: *[the focus of leaders and people in general will not be on military weapons and security, etc., but will be on providing food and the basic needs of all people]* **nation shall not lift up sword against nation, neither shall they learn war any more.**

Isaiah 2:2-4 (KJV). *Bracketed words added for clarity.*

And it shall come to pass *that* **everyone who is left of all the nations which came against Jerusalem** *[all the surviving inhabitants of the earth after Yahshua comes and establishes His kingdom]* **shall go up from year to year to worship the King** *[Yahshua]*, **the LORD of hosts, and to keep the Feast of Tabernacles. And it shall be** *that* **whichever of the families of the earth do not come up to Jerusalem to worship the King, the LORD of Hosts, on them there will be no rain.**

Zechariah 14:16-17 (NJKV). *Bracketed words added for clarity.*

Apparently, there will be people in the early years of the millennium who, even after the influence of Satan and his host are removed from the human experience, will continue to be rebellious and not love Master Yahshua with all of their hearts. Even during the millennium, people will still have free will to choose to love and serve their Creator. All of us who are resurrected at Messiah's coming will be delegated the responsibility of helping the people of the millennium to learn the ways of Almighty Yah as taught in His *Torah*, and to love Him above all else.

At the end of the millennial reign, the old adversary of the human race will be allowed to come out of his confinement in order to test and deceive as many people on earth as possible one last, short season of time. Again, the human beings who were not part of the first resurrection who live during the millennium will have to choose whom they will follow and serve, whether it is the Master, Yahshua, or Satan, the devil. All who choose the devil will be destroyed and separated from the love and presence of our Creator for all eternity.

Now when the thousand years have expired, Satan will be released from his prison *[bottomless pit]* **and will go out to deceive the nations which are in the four corners of the earth, Gog and Magog** *[as implied, not the same as Ezekiel 39]*, **to gather them together to battle, whose number** *is*

as the sand of the sea. **They went up on the breadth of the earth and surrounded the camp of the saints and the beloved city** *[Jerusalem]*. **And fire came down from God** *[Yahweh]* **out of heaven and devoured them. The devil, who deceived them, was cast into the lake of fire and brimstone where the beast and the false prophet** *are*. **And they will be tormented day and night forever and ever.**
  Revelation 20:7-10 (NKJV). *Bracketed words added for clarity.*

These Scriptures reveal that the truly justified place for Satan's final, eternal torment for the pain and evil caused throughout all of human history until eternity begins is the same place of eternal torment that the beast and the false prophet had been suffering during the millennium. Sometime during the time that King Yahshua is dealing with Satan is when He will judge the fallen angels. As it is written:

And the angels that did not keep their own position but left their proper dwelling have been kept by Him in eternal chains in the nether gloom until the judgment of the great day ...
  Jude 1:6 (RSV)

The apostle John continues with the vision he is given that describes the final judgment of all people who have ever lived that were not part of the first resurrection.

And I saw a great white throne *[indicating holiness and righteousness and is phase two of the judgment of King Yahshua]* **and him who sat on it; from whose face the earth and the heaven fled away; and there was found no place for them** *[this indicates that the final judgment takes place somewhere in space away from heaven and earth during eternity]*. **And I saw the dead, small and great, standing before God; and the books** *[detailed records of each person's life like a video]* **were opened: and another book was opened, which is the book of life:** *[the book that contains the names of all the people who are saved, and who will spend eternity with Adonai Elohim, the one true God made up of Father, Son, and Holy Spirit]* **and the dead were judged out of those things which were written in the books, according to their works. And the sea gave up the dead which were in it; and death and hell** *[the graves]* **delivered up the dead which were in them: and they were judged every man according to their works. And death and hell were cast**

into the lake of fire. This is the second death. And whosoever was not found written in the book of life was cast into the lake of fire.
Revelation 20:11-15 (KJV). *Bracketed words added for clarity.*

I have prayed much about these five verses of Scripture. I have asked the Holy Spirit to help me to have clarity about the truth regarding the great white throne judgment, just as I have regarding all that is written in this book. Almighty Yah's Word does not provide a lot of detail regarding this judgment. The consensus of most believers in Jesus Christ regarding the Great White Throne Judgment is that all human beings who did not make it on the first resurrection will be condemned to the eternal lake of fire after the judgment. I do not believe that to be the work of a loving, merciful Creator Who was born in this world as a human, lived a life without sin, and freely gave His life as a blood atonement offering to cover every sin of every person who has ever lived. Our Master Yahshua gave too much to save only a small percentage of humanity.

At the end of this section are Scriptures that I believe support the understanding that every person who has ever been conceived and was born and lived, or was conceived and not born, was and is recorded in Yah's book of life. The challenge for every human being is not whether their name has been written in the Lamb's (Yahshua's) book of life, but whether their name will be blotted out and removed from the book. We know from previously stated Scripture that those who are part of the first resurrection are sealed and in the book of life, with no possibility of being removed because they did what was required by a loving Creator/Savior— they responded correctly to the truth about Messiah and accepted Him, by inviting His Holy Spirit into their hearts. But what about all of the millions, possibly billions, of people who have been born on this planet through the many centuries of time who never had an opportunity to hear and understand the wonderful truth of our Savior Yahshua, how He has redeemed us from our sins by dying in our place as described in Chapters Two and Three. Yah's Holy Word establishes that it is our Heavenly Father's desire or will that all people be saved. It is written:

The Lord is not slack concerning His promise, as some men count slackness; but is longsuffering to usward, not willing that any should perish, but that all should come to repentance.
2 Peter 3:9 (KJV)

The Scriptures also establish that there is not any way for a person, including an unborn baby, to be saved and permitted to enter into God's Kingdom except by accepting Jesus as their Savior God and receiving His Holy Spirit. It is written,

> **There is salvation in no one else, for there is no other name** [except that of Jesus, or Yahshua] **under heaven given among mortals by which we must be saved.**
> Acts 4:12 (NRSV). *Bracketed words added for clarity.*

> **Jesus answered, "I am telling you the truth: no one can see the Kingdom of God unless he is born again** [birthed or engendered by the Holy Spirit from above, which happens when we put our faith and trust in Yahshua and ask Him into our hearts to help us repent of our sins so we can live for Him]**."**
> John 3:3 (NEV). *Bracketed words added for clarity.*

So now I pose the question, "How is it possible for human beings, who have been created by Almighty Yah in His great process, to receive the understanding of His plan of salvation—becoming complete in Messiah and being born of His Holy Spirit in order to have eternal life with Him—if they were born with a mind that could not comprehend or were never exposed to the truth about King Jesus?"

There has to be a span of time during the Great White Throne Judgment, before the creation of the new heaven and new earth, when our great holy Creator and righteous Judge, King Yahshua, will provide the opportunity for all people who did not have the opportunity during their one life on earth to understand the necessity of accepting His perfect blood to cover their sins and the importance of loving our Creator God with all of their hearts. I believe that the millions of aborted babies will be resurrected in a developed state of God's design to have the capability of understanding the need for the redeeming blood of Yahshua and the freedom to choose to accept Him or not to accept Him as their Savior and King eternal. Also I believe, as the Scriptures indicate, that there will be millions of people who will be born, live, and die during the millennium who will choose to accept Yahshua and live for Him. I believe their names will remain written in the Lamb's book of life and will not be blotted out.

The following Scriptures address the names in the Lamb's (Yahshua's) book of life and the fact that many names will be blotted out of His book. It is written,

> **Then Moses returned to the LORD and said, "Oh, these people have committed a great sin, and have made for themselves a god of gold! Yet now, if You will forgive their sin—but if not, I pray, blot me out of Your Book which you have written." And the Lord said to Moses, "Whoever has sinned against Me, I will blot him out of My book."**
> Exodus 32:31-33 (NKJV)

> **Add to them punishment upon punishment; may they have no acquittal from thee. Let them be blotted out of the book of the living; let them not be enrolled among the righteous.**
> Psalm 69:27-28 (RSV)

> **"No one can come to Me unless the Father who sent Me draws him, and I will raise him up at the last day.** *[The last day is the period that covers the second coming of Yahshua, the first resurrection, His establishing His Kingdom, the millennial reign, the final revolt after Satan's release from the bottomless pit, the second resurrection, and the process of the Great White Throne Judgment before eternity begins the new creation.]* **It is written in the Prophets: 'They will all** *[no exceptions]* **be taught by God.' Everyone who listens to the Father and learns from him comes to Me." ... "I am the living bread that came down from heaven. If anyone eats of this bread, he will live forever. This bread is My flesh,** *[His body and blood sacrificed for our sins and atonement]* **which I will give for the life of the world."** *[He spoke this before He gave His life of His own free will to be crucified to pay the price for all people's sins from the first person to the last.]*
> John 6:44-45 & 51 (NKJV). *Bracketed words added for clarity.*

> **"He who overcomes shall be clothed in white garments, and <u>I will not blot out his name from the Book of Life</u>; but I will confess his name before My Father and before His angels. He who has an ear** *[anyone who is interested in listening and wants to understand]*, **let him hear what the Spirit says to the churches."** *(Emphasis added.)*
> Revelation 3:5-6 (NKJV). *Bracketed words added for clarity.*

All people will be judged fairly with righteousness by the one true righteous Judge Himself, King Yahshua Messiah. Everyone will be judged according to the light he or she received in his or her life. As it is written:

Therefore you have no excuse, whoever you are, when you judge others; for in passing judgment on another you condemn yourself, because you, the judge, are doing the very same things. You say, "We know God's judgment on those who do such things is in accordance with truth." Do you imagine, whoever you are, that when you judge those who do such things and yet you do them yourself, you will escape the judgment of God? Or do you despise the riches of His kindness and forbearance and patience? Do you not realize that God's kindness is meant to lead you to repentance? But by your hard and impenitent heart you are storing up wrath for yourself on the day of wrath, when God's righteous judgment will be revealed. For He will repay according to each one's deeds; to those who by patiently doing good seek for glory and honor and immortality, he will give eternal life; while for those who are self-seeking and who obey not the truth but wickedness, there will be wrath and fury. There will be anguish and distress for everyone who does evil, the Jew first and also the Greek [Gentiles, all other races], **but glory and honor and peace for everyone who does good, the Jew first and also the Greek. For God shows no partiality. All who have sinned apart from the law will also perish apart from the law, and all who have sinned under the law will be judged by the law. For it is not the hearers of the law who are righteous in God's sight, but the doers of the law who will be justified. When Gentiles, who do not possess the law, do instinctively what the law requires, these, though not having the law, are a law to themselves. They show that what the law requires is written on their hearts, to which their own conscience also bears witness; and their conflicting thoughts will accuse or perhaps excuse them on the day when, according to my gospel, God** [Father Yahweh], **through Jesus Christ** [Yahshua], **will judge the secret thoughts of all.**

Romans 2:1-16 (NRSV). *Bracketed words added for clarity.*

Say among the heathen that the LORD reigneth: ... he shall judge the people righteously. ... for he cometh, for he cometh to judge the earth: he shall judge the world with righteousness, and the people with his truth.

Psalms 96:10 & 13 (KJV)

The one who rejects me and does not receive my word has a judge; on the last day *[span of time of the events of the coming of King Yahshua, the establishing of His Kingdom on earth, judgments, etc.]* **the Word that I have spoken will serve as judge, for I have not spoken on my own, but the Father who sent me has himself given me a commandment about what to say and what to speak. And I know that his commandment is eternal life. What I speak, therefore, I speak just as the Father has told me.**

John 12:48-50 (NRSV). *Bracketed words added for clarity.*

For the Son of Man *[Yahshua Messiah]* **shall come in the glory of his Father with His angels; and then He shall reward every man according to His works.**

Matthew 16:27 (KJV). *Bracketed words added for clarity.*

It is not revealed in the Scriptures if the many hundreds of millions of humans who have lived and not heard and understood the true message of Yah's salvation plan through the life, death, and resurrection of Yahshua will have that opportunity before or during the Great White Throne Judgment. Only Almighty Yah knows. Since there is no evidence either way, we cannot rule out the possibility. One thing is for sure, according to the Scripture, all who do evil and live wicked lives refusing the good influence of their conscience, the protection of their angels, the prompting of the Holy Spirit, and refuse to accept Jesus will be condemned.

And the sea gave up the dead in it, Death and Hades *[the grave]* **gave up the dead in them, and all were judged by what they had done. Then Death and Hades were thrown into the lake of fire. This is the second death, the lake of fire; and if anyone's name was not found written in the book of life, he was thrown into the lake of fire.**

Revelation 20:13-15 (RSV). *Bracketed words added for clarity.*

How about you? Have you accepted Jesus, or by His Hebrew name Yahshua, as the true Messiah, the Savior, and invited Him to live in you? Are you sure that when you stand before the Great Judge of your life that your name has not been rubbed out of His book of life?

You have created a great burden upon yourself by reading and comprehending the contents of this book. If you have not believed that He is Who He says He is in His Holy Word and invited Him into your heart so you can have forgiveness from your sins and fellowship with Him, then you have no excuse when you stand before Him on your judgment day. If you have not made the most important decision in all of life, do it now and don't put it off. Cry out to Master Yahshua with all of your heart. It is written:

> We then, *as* workers together *with Him,* also plead with *you* not to receive the grace of God in vain. For He says: *"In an acceptable time I have heard you, and in the day of salvation I have helped you."* Behold, now *is* the accepted time; behold, now *is* day of [your] salvation.
> 2 Corinthians 6:1-2 (NKJV). *Bracketed words added for clarity.*

One of the most wonderful events that will happen after King Yahshua establishes His kingdom here on earth is the great marriage supper. The timing of this is not clear, whether it is before or after the *Bema* Seat Judgment. Most Christians believe this great event takes place in heaven, but I believe it will be a part of the millennial events here on earth. I have encouraged you throughout this book to read Yah's Holy Word and think for yourself.

This joyous, happy event will be the largest marriage supper celebration in all of history, and it will be prepared by our Creator, Savior, and King eternal, our Bridegroom, Yahshua. As it is written,

> On this mountain the Lord of hosts *[Lord over all in heaven and earth]* will make for all peoples *[all in the first resurrection]* a feast of fat things *[really good foods]*, a feast of wine on the lees *[aged, preserved]*, of fat things full of marrow *[life]*, of wine on the lees well refined. And He will destroy on this mountain the covering *[sin and deception]* that is cast over all peoples, the veil *[spirit of unbelief]* that is spread over all nations. He will swallow up death forever *[after the Millennium]*, and the Lord *[Master]* God *[Yahshua]* will wipe away tears from all faces, and the reproach of His people He will take away from all of the earth; for the Lord has spoken. It will be said on that day, "Lo, this is our God *[Almighty Yah]*; we have waited for him; let us be glad and rejoice in His salvation."
> Isaiah 25:6-9 (RSV). *Bracketed words added for clarity.*

Thus saith the Lord:

Then He took the cup and gave thanks, and gave *it* **to them, saying, "Drink from it, all of you. For this is My blood of the new covenant, which is shed for many for the remission of sins. But I say to you, I will not drink of this fruit of the vine from now on until that day** *(the marriage feast of the Lamb after Messiah's second coming)* **when I drink it new with you** *[resurrected redeemed saints that make up His bride and bridesmaids]* **in My Father's kingdom** *[that will have come to earth with Him].*
   Matthew 26:27-29 (NJKV). *Bracketed words added for clarity.*

Then the Scriptures tell of the apostle John being shown the new heavens and new earth being created with the new city of Jerusalem coming down out of heaven. This will be the eternal dwelling place of all of Yah's children whose names were found written in the Lamb's Book of Life. It is written:

Now I saw a new heaven and a new earth, for the first heaven and the first earth had passed away. Also there was no more sea. Then I, John, saw the holy city, New Jerusalem, coming down out of heaven from God, prepared as a bride adorned for her husband. And I heard a loud voice from heaven saying, "Behold, the tabernacle of God *is* **with men, and He will dwell with them, and they shall be His people. God Himself will be with them** *and be* **their God.** *[Our Heavenly Father Yahweh and Messiah Yahshua are Almighty. Yah will have kept His promise at that appointed time as recorded in Isaiah 7:14 and Matthew 1:23. He will be IMMANUEL, Elohim with us.]* **And God will wipe away every tear from their eyes; there shall be no more death, nor sorrow, nor crying. There shall be no more pain, for the former things have passed away."**
   Revelation 21:1-4 (NKJV). *Bracketed words added for clarity.*

IDENTIFYING THE BRIDE AND BRIDESMAIDS
WITHIN THE BODY OF MESSIAH

I am finishing this chapter with a very important short teaching that is needed for identifying who the bride and bridesmaids of Messiah are and are not. Most of this teaching I received from a dear brother in Yahshua, Eddie Chumney, who gave me permission to include this material in this book. Some of this material is revelation from Holy Spirit.

I will begin by laying a foundation of the understanding the grouping of threes that we find in the Scriptures that provides great revelation of Who our Creator is, who we are in Him, and His marvelous Master Plan that He taught though His design of the tabernacle in the wilderness.

Almighty Yah is the one true, eternal God of Abraham, Isaac, and Jacob Who has manifested Himself in three different entities as Creator Holy Father, Redeemer Holy Son, and Comforter and Teacher Holy Spirit. Almighty Yah's full measure and expression of Himself to humanity was through His Son Yahshua, Who came in His Father Yahweh's name.

Almighty Yah gave His servant Moses the design for the tabernacle in the wilderness for His chosen race of people, the Israelites, that by His strong arm, they would have a place to worship Him and learn of His steps of progression that He instituted for His followers to draw closer and closer to Him in obedience and intimacy.

The entrance to the outer court was through one door that had curtains of four colors hanging down for the person to part and go through, as described in Exodus 25 through 27. The curtain veils separating the outer court from the holy place, and the veil separating the holy place and the most holy place were made using the same four colors. Also, the inside lining of the ceiling of the tabernacle and the garments of the high priest where made of the same four colors.

The first was **sky blue**, representing the eternalness of Almighty Yahweh, our Creator, whose name means *I have always been, I Am now,* and *I will always be all knowing, all powerful, all sovereign, and omnipresent.*

The next curtain color was **purple**, representing the royal majesty and kingship of Yahshua as the rightful King of the universe. As you know, it takes the mixing of the two primary colors of blue and red to make the color purple.

The next was **scarlet red**, representing Yahweh coming forth as His Son Yahshua Who would shed His precious blood for the forgiveness of our sins and to be given to purchase us back from our fallen state in Satan's kingdom.

The fourth curtain color is **pure white**, made from fine twisted linen. White represents purity, righteousness, and holiness.

Upon entering the outer court of the tabernacle, a person was to go to the **bronze altar** to burn their offering of an animal or grain unto Almighty Yah for any of the five applications as recorded in the first seven chapters of the book of Leviticus.

The next process was to proceed to the **bronze laver** that was filled with water for the common person and priest to wash their hands. The basin of the laver was lined with mirrors so the person taking water up into their hands would be able to see their reflection. This is symbolic of looking at ourselves when we receive water baptism, so we can reflect on our past sinful nature and turn from it and turn to our Master as he leads us down paths of righteousness.

The teaching and symbolism of all that was going on in the outer court was that we enter into relationship with Almighty Yah through His Son Yahshua, Who is the only <u>Way</u> to the Father. When we know that we have sin in our lives and that we are in need of a Savior from the death penalty of sin, then we ask our Father Yahweh for forgiveness and accept Yahshua as our Redeemer, making Him Master of our life. We are then blessed with the indwelling of His Holy Spirit, our Comforter and Teacher. We must repent and turn away from our previous sin and begin our walk with our High Priest and King, Yahshua. This is the Passover, Unleavened Bread, and First Fruits experience of our faith journey. Though we were born naturally from a corruptible seed, we now have His incorruptible Seed living and growing in us by being born of His Holy Spirit. Yahshua was the first of the firstfruits, and now we are part of His firstfruits for the first resurrection when He returns to earth to give us our new resurrected bodies that will be like His. HalleluYah!!!

When we first have our outer court experience and embrace our blessed Redeemer and Master, the Way, we are like young infants that can only drink milk. This is the good way of doing Almighty Yah's will. It is written:

> **Jesus said to him, "I am the way, and the truth, and the life. No one comes to the Father except through me."**
> John 14:6 (NRSV)

> **I am writing to you, little children, because your sins are forgiven on account of his name.**
> 1 John 2:12 (NRSV)

It is truly the best when a person has the life changing, salvation experience, but we should not stay in the Passover, outer court, infant-in-Messiah state. We should press on to grow in Him and Him in us. Sadly, after being saved a very high percentage of born-again believers spend their whole life at this level within the body of Messiah. This saddens our Father Yah's heart because His desire is for us to mature in Him by His Spirit, so we can become His bride that He has chosen for His Son, Yahshua. This is very hard for me to state, but I believe that nearly all of the born-again believers who are alive just before and during the last three and one-half years of the terrible tribulation will be in positions of having to lay down their lives in order to not take the mark of the beast. Revelation 20 verse 4 indicates that those who will be killed because of their witness to Jesus and the Word of God will be those who had not accepted the mark of the beast nor worshiped him. They are part of the first resurrection and will live and reign with Messiah during the millennium. It will be very difficult for anyone having to face that reality. The good news is that those martyrs will be part of the bride of Messiah as recorded in this Scripture, even if they had not progressed from the outer court, Passover experience.

Many saved and redeemed believers are in the position of being carnal Christians because they won't turn loose of their sin and worldliness that keeps them from progressing in the maturity walk that Yah desires for each born again believer. Carnal Christians make up the vast majority of Christians who are content with the Passover, outer-court, feeding-on-the-milk-of-the-Word experience. The parables in the Scriptures below teach us that not all redeemed believers of the body of Messiah make up the bride of Messiah. They are actually a small percentage (few). It is written:

> **And He went through the cities and villages, teaching, and journeying toward Jerusalem. Then one said to Him, "Lord, are there few who are saved?" And He said to them, "Strive to enter through the narrow gate, for many, I say to you, will seek to enter and will not be able. When once the Master of the house has risen up and shut the door, and you begin to stand outside and knock at the door, saying, 'Lord, Lord, open for us,' and He will answer and say to you, 'I do not know you, where you are from,' then you will begin to say, 'We ate and drank in Your presence, and You taught in our streets.' But He will say, 'I tell you I do not know you, where you are from. Depart from Me, all you workers of iniquity.' There will be weeping and gnashing of teeth, when you see Abraham and Isaac and Jacob and all the prophets in the kingdom of God, and yourselves thrust out."**
> Luke 13:22-28 (NKJV)

"I tell you, many will come from east and west and will eat with Abraham and Isaac and Jacob in the kingdom of heaven, while the heirs of the kingdom will be thrown into the outer darkness, where there will be weeping and gnashing of teeth."
Matthew 8:11-12 (NRSV)

"But when the king came in to see the guests, he noticed a man there who was not wearing a wedding robe, and he said to him, 'Friend, how did you get in here without a wedding robe?' And he was speechless. Then the king said to the attendants, 'Bind him hand and foot, and throw him into the outer darkness, where there will be weeping and gnashing of teeth.' For many are called, but few are chosen."
Matthew 22:11-14 (NRSV)

Now for deeper understanding of what these verses mean. The words "workers of iniquity" are very important to understand because the correct interpretation of these words has been overlooked in Christianity due to 1,650 years of not having Hebraic roots, Messianic Judaism understanding. However, I believe that Almighty Yah planned it that way. Remember the prophecy from the book of Daniel about sealing up important revelation understanding until the end times? We are in the end times, and the revelation understanding that we so desperately need is now being revealed in this book that you are holding in your hands and many other works that Almighty Yah is bringing forth through His servants to gather His bride and body before the end.

What are the workers of iniquity doing? The word *iniquity* is a translation from the Greek word *anomos*, which is Strong's word number 459. It is made up of the two words *a* and *nomos*. *A* comes from the negative participle in Greek which means *without*. The second part of the word, *nomos*, is the Strong's word number 3551, which means *law*, or a better rendering is *Torah*. So the real meaning of *the workers of iniquity* is that these are people who are without *Torah* in their lives and are actually teaching and practicing the breaking of the *Torah* instructions. It is written:

"Enter by the narrow gate; for wide *is* the gate and broad *is* the way that leads to destruction, and there are many who go in by it. Because narrow *is* the gate and difficult *is* the way which leads to life, and there are few who find it. ... Not everyone who says to Me, 'Lord, Lord,' shall

enter the kingdom of heaven, but he who does the will of My Father in heaven. Many will say to Me in that day, 'Lord, Lord, have we not prophesied in Your name, cast out demons in Your name, and done many wonders in Your name?' And then I will declare to them, 'I never knew you; depart from Me, you who practice lawlessness!'"

Matthew 7:13-14; 21-23 (NKJV)

"Do not think that I have come to abolish the law or the prophets; I have come not to abolish but to fulfill. For truly I tell you, until heaven and earth pass away, not one letter, not one stroke of a letter, will pass from the law until all is accomplished. Therefore, whoever breaks one of the least of these commandments, and teaches others to do the same, will be called least in the kingdom of heaven; but whoever does them and teaches them will be called great in the kingdom of heaven. For I tell you, unless your righteousness exceeds that of the scribes and Pharisees, you will never enter the kingdom of heaven.

Matthew 5:17-20 (NRSV)

In the first verses, Master Yahshua is making it clear that many will not make it into His Kingdom. He then teaches about being least and great in the kingdom. The symbolism here is like the Kingdom having a large outer court where the vast majority of the redeemed of the body will be. Then there will be a smaller area of the kingdom like the holy place where a small percentage of the redeemed of His body will be. Then there will be an even smaller area of His kingdom like the Holy of Holies in the tabernacle where His bride will be with Him when the marriage is fully consummated after the first resurrection takes place at His coming in the air.

The clarification of *the place of outer darkness* is that there are two different interpretations to this Hebrew idiom that have hidden meanings. One meaning is the place of hell that is complete separation from Almighty Yah and His Kingdom, a place of literal darkness that is devoid of everything that is beautiful with light, color, music, love, etc. The other meaning, and the one that applies to these Scriptures, is a place of shade or shadow that requires man's light. It is not the place of the glorious light from Yah as when He manifested Himself above the mercy seat in the Holy of Holies and the burning bush on the mountainside where He met with Moses several times. When Master Yahshau was talking about casting this group of people who had done works in His name into a place of outer darkness, He was speaking of places on the outer edge of His Father's kingdom.

Understanding the symbolism of the outer court brings understanding to Master Yahshua's words. The people in that category are redeemed and will make it into His Kingdom, but they will be looking from a distance at the wedding feast and the marriage of Yahshua to His bride. They will be grieving with weeping and regretfulness because they did not study His Holy Word, seek His Holy Spirit for understanding and knowledge of the *Torah* instructions, and then apply those instructions in their life each day. It is written:

> **"Then the kingdom of heaven will be like this. Ten bridesmaids took their lamps and went to meet the bridegroom. Five of them were foolish, and five were wise. When the foolish took their lamps, they took no oil with them; but the wise took flasks of oil with their lamps. As the bridegroom was delayed, all of them became drowsy and slept. But at midnight there was a shout, 'Look! Here is the bridegroom! Come out to meet him.' Then all those bridesmaids got up and trimmed their lamps. The foolish said to the wise, 'Give us some of your oil, for our lamps are going out.' But the wise replied, 'No! there will not be enough for you and for us; you had better go to the dealers and buy some for yourselves.' And while they went to buy it, the bridegroom came, and those who were ready went with him into the wedding banquet; and the door was shut. Later the other bridesmaids came also, saying, 'Lord, lord, open to us.' But he replied, 'Truly I tell you, I do not know you.' Keep awake therefore, for you know neither the day nor the hour."**
>
> Matthew 25:1-13 (NRSV)

All of the bridesmaids were born again, saved believers, but the foolish ones were not following the Bridegroom's instructions. If they had been following His *Torah* instructions, they would have been wise and not foolish.

Oil is symbolic of the anointing presence of Holy Spirit. If we do not have consistent communication and intimate relationship with Almighty Yah through His Holy Spirit Who comes in the name of Yahshua, then we grieve Him. Truly knowing our Bridegroom Yahshua requires communication with Him, just like we do with our closest family members and loved ones. Yah uses the terminology of *bride* and *groom* to teach us about how much He desires intimacy with us. When we are filled with His Holy Spirit each day, maintaining constant communication with Him, operating in the positions in which He predestined for us, exercising the manifestations of Holy Spirit with which He blesses us, and are teaching and living His *Torah* instructions, then we are assured of being not just a part of His body, or the bridesmaids, but we will be His bride.

The second level of maturity in our faith journey is becoming priests while learning in the holy place of the tabernacle. The holy place of the tabernacle is symbolic of our Pentecost experience of receiving the spiritual gifts and offices from Holy Spirit. The holy place contained the seven-branch menorah, the table of the twelve loaves of showbread, and the altar of incense that was placed in front of the curtain that separated the holy place from the most holy place where the Ark of the Covenant was set.

The holy place experience is where we learn the great revelations of wisdom and truth from Yah's Holy Word and where we embrace "The Truth, Yahshua." Remember, He is the Way, the Truth, and the Life. The menorah was to be refilled with fresh oil and wicks as needed each day. This was the work of the priest. As priests, we are to seek Almighty Yah each new day and ask to be refilled with His anointing and Holy Spirit so that His light shines bright in us and out to those in the world we come in contact with. At the end of each week, twelve new, fresh loaves of bread were brought in and placed on the table. The twelve loaves represent the twelve tribes of the nation and people of Israel. The priests were to eat the loaves that were replaced with the fresh ones during the new week after the Sabbath. This is symbolic of eating and consuming the Holy Word of Yahweh each day for spiritual nourishment to mature from drinking milk as children to eating the meat of the Word as young men.

It is written:

I am writing to you, young people, because you have conquered the evil one.
1 John 2:13b (NRSV)

For though by this time you ought to be teachers, you need *someone* to teach you again the first principles of the oracles of God; and you have come to need milk and not solid food. For everyone who partakes *only* of milk *is* unskilled in the word of righteousness, for he is a babe. But

solid food belongs to those who are of full age, *that is,* those who by reason of use have their senses exercised to discern both good and evil.
Hebrews 5:12-14 (NKJV)

The priests were to study the Word and seek revelation from Holy Spirit so they could teach the people of the twelve tribes of Israel. That has not changed. We are to do the same today.

The third item in the holy place was the altar of incense. Each day the priests were to place incense made from five different fragrant plants on top of coals that they would bring in from the altar of sacrifice. The incense would smolder and give off a wonderful smoke fragrance. The priests were to pray for all of the people of the twelve tribes of the nation of Israel as they came to confess their sins and bring their offerings of gratitude to be present before Almighty Yah.

The symbolism of the sweet-smelling smoke rising up is that we are to pray and intercede for people on a regular basis. Pray for the lost who are not redeemed, those with diseases and infirmaries, those possessed and oppressed with demon spirits, those who are in prisons, those who serve as soldiers, our loved ones, and our enemies. The list of people and situations that we can pray for goes on and on. The Apostle Paul said that we are to pray without ceasing.

All of these functions of the priest in the holy place required work that took effort. Worshipping and seeking Almighty Yah each day, studying His Holy Word so we can share it with others, living by the *Torah* instructions, leading by example of His ways, and praying without ceasing all requires putting forth effort and work. This is why Yahshua said that there are few who commit themselves to walk the narrow path of being Spirit filled and living a called-out, *Torah*-obedient life to become His kings and priests.

The third part of the tabernacle was the most holy place. In that small room was one piece of furniture, and it was the Ark of the Covenant containing the two stone tablets that the ten instructions to mankind were written on, Aaron's budded rod, and a golden pot of the manna that Yah fed the Israelites for forty years. This progression of our faith journey to the Holy of Holies is symbolic of the Feast of *Sukkot,* or Tabernacles, or the ingathering of Yahshua's bride at the end of the tribulation. This level of maturity in Messiah comes from being obedient in all that He has instructed us to do and being led by Holy Spirit to worship Yah in spirit and in truth. The truth is about living the *Torah* instructions, not just studying about them. That is like having a head full of information about Who Jesus, Yahshua, was and is, but not having a close, personal, intimate relationship with Him. When we meet Him in the most holy place, we are in His presence, and He is pleased and delighted that we want to be in fellowship with Him and that we know Him in our obedience. The third part of the verse in John 14:6 says that He is the life. This is what John was referring to as fathers. It is written:

I am writing to you, fathers, because you know him who is from the beginning.
    1 John 2:13a (NRSV)

There you have it, dear reader, the teaching of the threes. The outer court, Passover, blood, the Son Yahshua, the Way; the children drinking milk who are forgiven because of His name's sake, the holy place, Pentecost, fire, Holy Spirit that comes in the name of Yahshua, the Truth, young men who are strong because the Word of Yah that abides in them and they have overcome the wicked one, the most holy place, *Sukkot*, smoke, the divine presence of Almighty Yah, the Life, the fathers who are completely sold out, obedient, know Him because they know they are in covenant relationship with Him.

How does this revelation information apply to the redeemed of these three different groups during the last three and one-half years of the great tribulation time of persecution. I believe that those who are a part of the body of Messiah who are here in America when the attack comes from Russia and China will die then as I have described in other places in this book. Those who are instructed by Holy Spirit to escape Babylon and move to Israel or other places will either be martyred by the beast system as described in Revelation 12:11, or they will be directed by Holy Spirit to a place of refuge, as the Woman that flees in the wilderness described in Revelation 12:6, 14-17. It indicated in verse 14 that those taken to a place(s) of refuge will be protected and provided for. I believe this group is made up of the people who are the bridesmaids referred to in Matthew 25 in the parable of the ten virgins. In the parable that Yahshua taught, the five foolish ones did not have what was necessary to make it in to the marriage supper with King Yahshua when He comes. It looks to me like they fall into apostasy and backslide during the tribulation time and move themselves back with the outer court members of Messiah's body of redeemed people. Then in verse 17 of Revelation 17, the anti-Messiah beast system turns to make war on the rest of the body of Messiah who keep the commandments of Almighty Yah and have the testimony of Yahshua Messiah. I believe this group is the true Bride of Yahshua, the chosen 144,000 who will be supernaturally protected throughout the tribulation time. They will be instructed to go forth throughout the earth proclaiming the messages of the three angels as recorded in Revelation 14:1-13, and they will witness the destruction by King Yahshua of the wicked who take the mark of the beast and worship him and Satan. There is more teaching on the 144,000 in Chapter 11.

I finish this chapter with these words of Scripture for you to study and pray over. It is written:

For, behold, the day cometh, that shall burn as an oven; and all the proud, yea, and all that do wickedly, shall be stubble: and the day that cometh shall burn them up, saith the LORD of hosts, that it shall leave them neither root nor branch. But unto you that fear my name shall the Sun of righteousness arise with healing in his wings; and ye shall go forth, and grow up as calves of the stall. And ye shall tread down the wicked; for they shall be ashes under the soles of your feet in the day that I shall do this, saith the LORD of hosts. Remember ye the law of Moses my servant, which I commanded unto him in Horeb for all Israel, with the statutes and judgments. Behold, I will send you Elijah the prophet before the coming of the great and dreadful day of the LORD: And he shall turn the heart of the fathers to the children, and the heart of the children to their fathers, lest I come and smite the earth with a curse.

Malachi 4 (KJV)

10

EVENTS AND SIGNS
TO WATCH FOR

O ur Master Yahshua instructed His followers no less than sixteen times to watch what is going on in the world, as is recorded in Matthew 24, 25, and 26; Mark 13 and 14; and Luke 12 and 21. The instructions applied to the apostles at the time Yahshua gave them for their coming persecution, and the warnings also apply to us in this the last generation.

Webster's New World Dictionary gives the following definition:

watch

noun

1. *The act or fact of keeping awake, especially in order to protect or guard.*
2. *Close observation for a time, as to find out something.*

verb

1. *To be looking or waiting attentively.*
2. *To keep informed about.*
3. *To keep watch over; tend; watching; on the lookout—watch out, to be alert and on one's guard.*

It is written:

"Now learn this parable from the fig tree: When its branch has already become tender, and puts forth leaves, you know that summer is near. So you also, when you see these things happening, know that it is near—at the doors! Assuredly, I say to you, this generation will by no means pass away, till al these things take place. Heaven and earth will pass

away, but My words will by no means pass away. But of that day and
hour no one knows, not even the angels in heaven, nor the Son, but only
the Father. Take heed, watch and pray; for you do not know when the
time is. *It is* like a man going to a far country, who left his house and
gave authority to his servants, and to each his work, and commanded
the doorkeeper to watch. Watch therefore, for you do not know when
the master of the house is coming—in the evening, at midnight, at the
crowing of the rooster, or in the morning—lest, coming suddenly, he
find you sleeping. And what I say to you, I say to all: Watch!"
   Mark 13:28-37 (NKJV)

   Our Master Yahshua has made it very clear that there is no way for us
to know the exact day or the exact hour of His coming. He has instructed us to watch what is going on around us in the world so that when we
see things happening that apply to the end of this age, we will know that
His coming is near.
   I explained in Chapter Five that the holy feast days of the spring were
prophetic shadows of the first coming of Messiah, and that the holy feasts
of the fall are a prophetic foreshadow of His second coming. Remember,
no one knows when the Feast of Trumpets begins until there is a confirmed sighting of the new moon in the seventh month of *Tishri*. We know
from what we have already learned that King Yahshua's second coming to
establish His Kingdom on the earth will be during the fall feast times of
some future year.
   I am truly amazed as I watch events taking place that are relevant to
the fulfillment of end-time Bible prophesies. Applying the interpretation
of the Scriptures to the events is like watching some huge production of
a world-changing movie coming together. It is as if all of the different
facets of the production are being brought to fruition simultaneously.
That's the way it is with the drama being played out through the human
race that will culminate in the final battle of this age between the forces
of good and the forces of evil. I will break down the different events and
signs that are important to watch for by the categories of spiritual/
religious, political, and economic.
   Due to its importance, some of this material is a more detailed version of things that were covered in Chapter Seven. When you travel from
one geographical location to another, you see large billboard signs adver-
tising events or places of interest. As you approach the place that was

advertised on the sign, you see confirming signs that you are near that place. In the same way, let the signs that I am teaching you about in this book be points of reference, like road signs warning of increasing danger up ahead. You can reflect back on them for help in discerning the state of the world in regards to the events of the last generation. I do not know of any greater gift that we receive from Holy Spirit than the gift of being able to discern truth from falsehood and to have discernment about the events happening in our world as they apply to end-time prophecy. I encourage you to pray for Holy Spirit to give you discernment about what is being taught in the world today.

Our Savior Yahshua gives us an outline of the events and signs to watch for when He spoke to His disciples on the Mount of Olives, as recorded In Matthew 24, Mark 13, and Luke 21. In the arena of religious signs to watch for, His first instruction is:

"Beware that no one leads you astray. For many will come in My name, saying, 'I am the Messiah!' and they will lead many astray."
Matthew 24:4-5 (NRSV)

Pressing into King Yahshua, the one Whom we know is the true Messiah, is most important and will become more of a challenge for people as spiritual and religious deception increases. Even now, many people throughout the world are being taught about a man claiming to be the World Teacher. A professor in England named Benjamin Crème is currently promoting him, and his popularity is increasing. The World Teacher's name is Lord Maitreya, which means "Lord of Love."

In Chapter Seven of this book, in the section "Opening the First Seal," I stated that within all major religions is the teaching of a great one who is to come to bring world peace and make right all the ills of the world. Lord Maitreya claims to be the great one that is expected to come and bring unity of the world's major religions and harmony to the races. He claims to be the Messiah the Jewish people are waiting for, the Buddha the Buddhists are waiting for, and Imam Mahdi the Muslims are looking for.

In his effort to prove that he is the Christian Messiah, he even claims to have fulfilled the prophecy of Jesus coming in the clouds, as recorded in 1 Thessalonians 4:16-17, when he descended in the clouds from the Himalayas in an airplane. He claims that Jesus was simply a master of wisdom, just as were Krishna, Mohammed and Buddha. Maitreya claims that he was the energy source that gave power to Jesus and that he over-shadowed Him, using His body to fulfill the tasks for that life. Maitreya also claims that he was the one who resurrected the body of Yahshua from the grave, and that the man Jesus, through the process of evolution, became a Son of God as will every other human being eventually. All of this is foolish deception to me, but to people who don't know any better, it may be exactly what they want to hear and where they want to place their faith.

Lord Maitreya made his first appearance before six thousand people in Nairobi, Africa, in June 1988. He simply appeared at an outdoor prayer and healing meeting where he was instantly recognized and believed by the people there to be the true Messiah, Jesus. Maitreya's following is increasing as the manifestations of deception increase with his appearances. From 1991 to the present, Maitreya has been appearing miraculously before gatherings of different orthodox religious groups throughout the world. When he appears, he addresses the people in their own language. During the meetings, the people recognize him as the long-awaited teacher or great master of their belief system. Benjamin Crème claims that Maitreya creates healing springs of water near the areas where his appearances are to be. Supposedly, Maitreya has created healing waters in Mexico, Germany, and India, where millions of people have visited, with some miraculous healings reported. Benjamin Crème promotes Maitreya as the true Messiah and World Teacher who will unite and represent all the faiths of the world. This is getting pretty weird, isn't it? Hang on to your hats, the balance of this report is even more bizarre.

According to Crème, Lord Maitreya claims that the Master Jesus became manifest as a man several hundred years ago and is currently living in Rome. He claims this Jesus will eventually take over the throne of St. Peter. I interpret that to mean the office of the Pope of the Roman Catholic Church. He further states that when that happens, the Christians of the world, along with all people of all other religions, will then be able to receive the divine revelation of the unification of all the world's faiths. Maitreya refers to this future revelation event as "The Day of Declaration." Maitreya claims that when The Day of Declaration comes, he will telepathically communicate to each person on earth in his or her own language and project an image before their eyes of what they believe their Messiah looks like, so they will know that he is their great one.

How will this entity that may actually be Satan masquerading as the

Teacher of the World and the Lord of Love be able to pull this off? My only explanation is that Satan may be using his huge host of fallen angels and demons to deceive individuals who are not grounded in the truth found in the Word of Almighty Yah. He may even work through high tech satellites with lasers that can project 3-D holograms in the sky to really dazzle unsuspecting people. If you are interested, do a web search for *Project Blue Beam*. I have just described to you a very important sign to watch for. The following is a very important warning. It is written:

The coming of the lawless one is apparent in the working of Satan, who uses all power, signs, lying wonders, and every kind of wicked deception for those who are perishing, because they refused to love the truth and so be saved. For this reason God sends them a powerful delusion, leading them to believe what is false, so that all who have not believed the truth but took pleasure in unrighteousness will be condemned.
2 Thessalonians 2:9-12 (NRSV)

For false messiahs and false prophets will appear and produce great signs and omens, to lead astray, if possible, even the elect [those who received and applied the truth from God's Holy Word].
Matthew 24:24 (NRSV). *Bracketed words added for clarity.*

I know this information seems bizarre, but this is the very type of major deception that Satan will use to achieve his brainwashing by the false prophet that prepares the way for the anti-Messiah. So be watchful!

If you are interested in learning more about Lord Maitreya, you can visit Benjamin Crème's web site at: www.shareinternational.com. At the time the anti-Messiah is revealed, if he is this Lord Maitreya, he may be presenting himself under the name of Apostikane. Be watchful, and don't allow yourself to be deceived by the miracles and delusions that Satan will produce through his pawns.

Another religious sign to watch is the position of the last Pope of the Roman Catholic Church. During the time of Nostradamus in the early 12th century, there lived another much less known seer prophet named Malachay. Malachay had visions of all of the Popes, from Celestine II of his day, in the year A.D. 1143, all the way down through our present day and to the end of the age. Malachay wrote down in Latin phrases title descriptions of each Pope he saw in his visions. Each title description has been accurate of each Pope. I will state Malachay's title description and historical commentary of Pope John Paul II, the three Popes preceding him, and Malachay's title description with commentary of the last two Popes.

Malachay called Pope John XXIII, 1958-1963, "Pastor and Mariner." John was a pastor to the world of the Roman Catholic Church and was much beloved. This Pope was the Patriarch of Venice, Italy. Malachay's connection to "mariner" from his prophecy nearly 800 years prior to John's life is amazing.

The next Pope, whom Malachay called the "Flower of Flowers," was Pope Paul VI, who served from 1963-1978. Paul's coat-of-arms has three flowers on it.

Following Paul was Pope John Paul I, 1978-1978, who Malachay described as "Of the Half Moon." John Paul I was elected Pope on August 26, 1978, which was the night of a half moon. He died 33 days later. Some believe he was murdered.

Pope John Paul II replaced John Paul I in 1978. Malachay described this Pope as "The Labor of the Sun." John Paul did more traveling than any other Pope in history. He addressed huge crowds everywhere he went. He was once shot in an attempted assassination, but continued to travel, even through he was in his early eighties and was in poor health. Like the sun which never ceases to labor and provides light each day, this Pope was incessant. John Paul II was born on May 18, 1920. During the morning on that date, there was a near total eclipse of the sun over Europe and his native country of Poland. Pope John Paul II died at the age of 84 on April 2, 2005.

Malachay's title description for the next Pope to come after John Paul II is "The Glory of the Olive." On May 9, 2005, Cardinal Joseph Ratzinger from Germany, who chose the name Pope Benedict XVI, was voted in as the new Pope. The symbols of the Order of Saint Benedictine include olive branches. Though Cardinal Ratzinger was not from that order, by choosing the name Benedict, the Pope became linked with St. Benedict, who is distantly connected to the Olivetans, a small sub-order of Benedictines. I believe there is validity in the predictions of Malachay. The man had too much accurate insight in writing down the phrases that revealed some small identity connection with all of the Popes over a span of almost 900 years to simply be discounted as unreliable. We will see.

Malachay's title for the final Pope is **Peter the Roman**. His closing words for the last Pope are as follows. "In the final persecution of the Holy Roman Church there will reign Peter the Roman who will feed his flock among many tribulations; after which the seven-hilled city *(Rome, the seat of the Vatican)* will be destroyed and the dreadful Judge will come to judge the people."

I believe the final Pope will be the main influential leader behind the deceptive religious system that is described in Revelation 13:11 as "another beast coming up out of the earth." This position of authority is also known as the "false prophet." The last Pope, with the support of the modern-day universal (Catholic) Roman Church and the support of the many deceived ecumenical Protestant denominations, will be successful in bringing about the worship of the anti-Christ. This unified false belief system will draw all other mainstream false belief systems into it, primarily Christianity, Judaism, and Islam. Someone like Lord Maitreya coming on the scene at the right time could be instrumental in helping to pull Satan's great plan of deception together.

In conjunction with the coming one-world economic system, Satan will have a short time of control over the vast majority of the peoples of the world to receive what he has always desired: to be worshipped as the creator and savior of mankind. Remember from Chapter Seven that the false prophet is responsible for deceiving the world into making an image of the anti-Messiah beast so they can worship it.

The title for the Pope in Latin is "Vicarius Filii Dei," which means in English, "The Vicar of the Son of God." The total of the Roman numerical value of the Latin words equals the number 666. Great authority will be given to this individual and his institution. It is written:

> He was granted *power* to give breath to the image of the beast, that the image of the beast should both speak and cause as many as would not worship the image of the beast to be killed. He causes all, both small and great, rich and poor, free and slave, to receive a mark on their right hand or on their foreheads, and that no one may buy or sell except one who has the mark or the name of the beast, or the number of his name. Here is wisdom. Let him who has understanding calculate the number of the beast, for it is the number of a man: His number *is* 666.
>
> Revelation 13:15-18 (NKJV)

Malachay's word says that Peter the Roman will feed his flock among many tribulations. I believe this refers to his feeding lies of deception to the majority of the world's population that is caught up in the one-world, ecumenical church system religion. The Roman Emperor Constantine, in the year A.D. 325 during the Council of Nicæa, was responsible for changing the biblical, Israelite day of rest and worship from Saturday—the Sabbath—to Sunday, the first day of the week. It was an easy way to keep the sun-worshipping pagans in the empire happy, to assert the Papal authority he was putting into place, and to attempt to destroy Judaism. During the Inquisition and the Crusades, many millions of people were murdered and tortured to death. Those brave martyrs would not bow down to the Papal authority by renouncing their Savior Jesus and conform to forced worship on Sunday. Father Yahweh long ago blessed and ordained the Sabbath as His fourth instruction of the ten He gave to Moses for all generations. It is written,

> **"So I led them out of the land of Egypt and brought them into the wilderness. I gave them my statutes and showed them my ordinances** *[instructions in the Ten Commandments and Torah in Leviticus]*, **by whose observance man shall live. Moreover I gave them my sabbaths,** *[weekly Sabbath and the seven annual Feasts of the Lord]* **as a sign between me and them, that they might know that I the Lord sanctify** *[set apart as special]* **them. But the House of Israel rebelled against Me in the wilderness; they did not walk in my statues but rejected my ordinances, by whose observance man shall live; and my sabbaths they greatly profaned. ... And I said to their children in the wilderness, Do not walk in the statues of your fathers, nor observe their ordinances, nor defile yourselves with their idols. I the lord am your God; walk in My statutes, and be careful to observe my ordinances, and hallow my sabbaths that they may be a sign between me and you, that you may know that I the LORD am your God. But the children rebelled against Me; they did not walk in my statues, and were not careful to observe my ordinances, by whose observance man shall live; they profaned my sabbaths."**
>
> Ezekiel 20:10-13; 18-21 (RSV). *Bracketed words added for clarity.*

I believe it is possible that when the end-time world political, economic, religious system is established, mandatory Sunday observance may be enforced. If you hear of this happening in conjunction with news of technology advancements being implemented to have electronic economic control over your life, know that it is the mark of the beast. Remember this end-time sign, for it may be the most important one of all. Since Almighty Yah has told us in His Word that the Sabbath is a sign between Him and the Israelites, then it must have significance in relation to the end times and the second great exodus. If the sign of Almighty Yah is His seventh-day Sabbath and His holy name Yahweh and that of His Son Yahshua in the foreheads of His set apart people, then the sign of the anti-Messiah could be forced Sunday observance as history has been known to repeat itself. This is another road sign to remember. I encourage you to seek the truth in Yah's Word in all of these things, for only in knowing Yahshua and living His truth will a person be prepared for the tribulation.

In the political realm of end-time prophesy signs and events to watch for, be expecting a very powerful leader to emerge from the unified Europe (EU) as the area of the former Roman empire resurfaces. This great leader, whomever he is, will have a false prophet (possibly the Pope or someone like Lord Maitreya) producing incredible miracles and pumping out propaganda in order to prepare the way for the anti-Messiah by deceiving the world and drawing them into a one-world belief system. Remember the anti-Messiah will be a political figure who is able to establish a temporary peace agreement between the nation of Israel and the Islamic nations that try to destroy Israel. A key component of the agreement will be a provision allowing the Orthodox Jews access and permission to erect the third temple on the Temple Mount in order to re-instate animal sacrifices. I believe that the timing for the peace agreement takes place sometime after the end of the Gog-Magog war that I will cover in the next few pages.

I am certain that as this book is being written, the anti-Christ is alive. There is a man in the world today that I am keeping my eye on and who, I believe, bears watching as he and his family work behind the political scenes in Europe to gain more and more power. The family I am referring to has controlling interest in over 200 of the most powerful corporations in the world. Their family crest and coat of arms have the symbolism of the anti-Messiah. The lead male of this very wealthy family in Europe was responsible for initiating, behind the scenes, the peace accord between former Prime Minister Rabin of Israel and Yasser Arafat, former leader of the PLO, in September 1993. It is believed that this individual is the top person in the very secretive organization called the Order of the Garter, which is the top echelon of the Masonic Order of Freemasonry. This is huge in the realm of power and influence worldwide. There are photographs showing this individual wearing a knitted skullcap that is popular with men that are Muslims, and it is rumored that he converted to Islam in the late 1980s. This man's father is known to have ties with the Illuminati and has made statements alluding to the reduction of the world's population to one billion.

The powerful man I'm referring to had two significant accomplishments in 2002. In April, he launched a multi-faith campaign called RESPECT. His vision in this endeavor is to bring the religions of the world together to better understand each other and overcome prejudices. At the program's launch were leaders from the Roman Catholic Church, the Protestant Church, Islam, Hindu, Buddhist, the Bahá'í Faith, and others as stated in the April 18, 2002, edition of the *The Times* of India. Later that year, this lead figure was recognized in **news.Telegraph.co.uk** as the model environmentalist for his efforts in preserving the rainforests of the Amazon in South America. The article has a picture of a two-foot tall sculpture model that was used in the making of the full size sculpture that is approximately 16-feet tall and made from bronze. The statue is that of a man with very large wings, like those of an angel, standing on a globe depicting the many peoples of humanity, with outstretched arms and wearing a loincloth. In a ceremony, the governor of the State of Tocantins, in the heart of the Amazon rain forest, honored this individual with the dedication of the statue and called the individual "the savior of the world." It makes you wonder if the statue of this person will end up in a future temple that will be built on the Temple Mount in Jerusalem and fulfill the prophecy of Daniel in 12:11 that refers to "the abomination that maketh desolate set up" will be the actual image that the anti-Messiah sets up for the world to worship.

A more recent event involving this individual was reported on *BBC News* on March 25, 2006. The report states that this man was the first Westerner to deliver a speech to many scholars of several Arab nations at the Imam Muhammad bin Saud University in Riyadh, Saudi Arabia.

Okay, enough mystery. This individual is Prince Charles of Wales. He has certainly made many humane and worthy accomplishments throughout the world and has great influence behind the scenes.

On the coat of arms and crest of his last name is a picture of a beast, as described in Revelation 13:2, with the body of a leopard, with the feet of a bear, and the head of a lion. The crest also has a picture of a red dragon. I am not stating that this man is absolutely the anti-Messiah, only that there is a lot of evidence that he could be. If you are interested in learning more about this subject, I recommend the book, *The AntiChrist and a Cup of Tea,* by Tim Cohen. Remembering this information and keeping a watchful eye on this individual and his family is certainly good advice as the end-time events unfold. You can find more information about Tim's book and other end-time topics at his web site: http://www.prophecyhouse.com/

The technology for electronically tracking every human on this planet is available now and can be mass produced for government implementation. In 2002, the first family to receive implantation of a device that has Global Positioning Satellite (GPS) capability, was the Jacobs family from Boca Raton, Florida. The company, Applied Digital Solutions, received the patent for its technology product December 10, 1999. The trademark registration for the implant product was given the strangely ironic name, "Digital Angel." The biometric computer chip implant is being marketed under the name of VeriChip, as in verification.

The company's initial sales pitch is to meet the medical application of patients implanted with the device being readily identified if rushed to a hospital emergency center. The implant is about the size of a grain of rice and can be implanted with a large syringe and needle. The microscopic chip inside has enough memory to store the patient's name and vital medical statistics.

At the time of the patent of Digital Angel, there was no other product like it. With a micro antenna, the VeriChip is capable of real time transmission of the implanted person's body temperature, pulse rate, and other vitals when satellite linked for internet access. There are many positive medical applications that are being pursued from this technology, such as blood sugar tracking for diabetics, irregular heartbeats, and controlled administration of nearly every kind of drug. There are also many banking, IRS, and crime prevention applications using this type of technology. Having a cashless society eliminates the counterfeiting of dollar bills and theft of money. It makes possible more accurate tracking of earnings by the IRS and removes the means of exchange for most crimes, such as drug dealing and illegal gambling. It also provides a way for the governments of the world to verify a person's identity by scanning an implanted identification chip, thereby eliminating the problem of identity theft.

In the fifth seal section of Chapter Seven, I stated that the biometric chip implant companies have found that the chips work best in the back of the hand and the forehead of the human anatomy. According to the *Strong's Concordance*, the word *mark* in Revelation 13:16-18 is translated from the Greek words *charagma* meaning "a scratch, etching or stamp"; *charakter* meaning "an exact copy or representation"; and *charax* meaning "to sharpen to a point." The Apostle John could have used several different words to describe what he saw during the vision that our Lord Yahshua gave him of the end time events. In using what has been translated into English as the word *mark*, he is describing something with a sharp point scratching or penetrating into the hand or forehead that would be an exact representation of something that would be required in order for a person to legally buy or sell. I am certain, not insinuating, that Applied Digital Solutions has patented and is marketing a product that will be used as the mark of the beast. The advancements in this potentially helpful technology is another sign to watch for in the end times, especially if you learn from news sources that it is being mandated for the general population.

As you know, the greatest atrocities ever to happen to citizens of the United States took place on September 11, 2001. The evil attacks of the terrorists who crashed jetliners into the World Trade Center towers, the Pentagon, and the thwarted attack that crashed in the Pennsylvania countryside resulted in the premeditated murder of over 3,000 innocent lives. Those suicide/murders shocked many Americans into understanding the brutal realities of terrorism that the Jewish people and citizens of Israel have been experiencing for decades. Other victims of terrorism include places such as Darfur, Sudan, where they have been experiencing these atrocities for several years. The events of that September day will certainly be remembered as the day many things in our world changed. Life as we have known it here in the safe shores of the most blessed country of the world will never quite be the same again.

As you remember, soon after the terrorist attacks of September 11, our President declared war on terrorism. Our military engaged in a worldwide operation of wiping out the followers of Osama bin Laden and terrorists beginning with destroying his headquarters in Afghanistan. This led to the buildup of war with and the defeat of the nation of Iraq and its dictator, Saddam Hussein. The war in Iraq has mushroomed into igniting terrorist-type warfare in many parts of the world by fundamentalist Muslims whose crusade is to destroy America and Israel and eventually all peoples that will not convert to Islam. The reality that I see that has evolved since September 11, 2001, is the bringing to fruition of the plan for World War III that Albert Pike, the Illuminati architect, laid, as stated back in Chapter Seven. Fasten your seatbelts, folks. The New World Order that is ushering in the end-time tribulation and beast system is in full swing.

I'm sure that much of what you have read in this chapter and in Chapter Seven is shocking. It was and is for me as well. I am committed to teaching the truth, no matter how difficult it is for people to receive and no matter what the cost. We must be informed so that we can at least have the opportunity to prepare for the worst, if we choose to do so, the best we can. The truth is that the three and one-half years of the great tribulation that is detailed in several places in the Scriptures and in this book is not a time period that is far off in the distant future—many decades or centuries away. Based on the accuracy of the end-time prophecies and the overwhelming evidence we see in current events, it is clear that we are within a few years of the beginning of the rule of the anti-Messiah. We must prepare for all that we see coming ahead. I offer some excellent advice about how to prepare for the coming tribulation in the next chapter.

In several places within this book, I have stated, with Scripture, that when King Yahshua returns to this earth, He will come with great power and authority to destroy the physical and spiritual kingdom of Satan and all those who have aligned themselves with our adversary through the beast system. The core and root of deception in the world that has been working throughout history and that is accelerating today is the anti-Messiah, anti-Yahweh spirit.

Nowhere is the spirit of hate and rebellion more prevalent and obvious than in the country of Israel. This small nation is where the great and final battle—the Battle of Armageddon—between the forces of holiness and evil will be played out. I believe before that horrific day comes there will be two major wars fought that will involve the nations of Israel and America. Understanding the timing of these wars, along with observing the many other signs of the tribulation period, should enable us to determine the sequence of events and the next significant event to happen on an international scale.

The constant attacks by the H-bombs, meaning the *human* bombs, of the terrorists are Satan's attempts to press the Israeli government into a decision to allow a Palestinian state that would divide the land. This should not be allowed to happen, but the current (2007) "Roadmap to Peace" that was originated by think tanks in the United States and Saudi Arabia, go figure, has forced the government of Israel to give up the Gaza Strip in phase one. Most of the West Bank, which is a much larger area and more heavily populated than in Gaza, is to be given up in phase two. The bloodshed in Israel is much more that physical encounters with brainwashed Islamic radicals who have been deceived and lied to, with their family members being paid up to $20,000.00 US to encourage them to commit suicide. The *Jihad* martyr believes that after he or she dies from strapping a high powered plastics bomb to his or her torso and walking into a crowded public place in an Israeli city and murdering as many innocent men, women, and children as possible, he or she will receive great rewards in the false god Allah's heaven. Fanatical Islamic *Jihad* is Satan's present-day futile attempt to destroy Father Yahweh's progress in restoring the nation of Israel that began in 1948. Now that Israel is established, Satan knows that we are clearly in the last generation and that his time is running out. Bible prophecy reveals that there will be other attempts to destroy Israel in the years to come. You can be assured that our old adversary, Satan, the devil, has many more tricks up his sleeve. Continuously, until the end of this age, he will use every deceptive and evil way he can to foil Almighty Yah's plans, and to take as many souls with him to the lake of fire as possible. Please pray for the Jewish people in Israel and throughout the world to remember their Creator Yahweh and the covenant that He made with their ancient ancestor, Abraham. Pray that they will stand firm in the midst of a deceived and weak government and that Holy Spirit will draw them to the truth of Messiah Yahshua and accept Him as their Redeemer and Messiah.

How about you? Have you accepted Yahshua (Jesus) as your Creator God and Redeemer (Lord and Savior)? Have you put your complete trust in the one, true, living Elohim of Abraham, Isaac, and Jacob? If you have not made this most important of all decisions and commitments in life, please do it now, and don't put it off any longer. Holy Spirit is constantly searching the hearts of individuals for those who are sincerely crying out to be redeemed and set free from sin.

There are four major wars to come before the return of King Yahshua Messiah. The first two future wars are certainly important signs to watch for. The third war is the war between the army of the anti-Messiah and the countries that make up the king of the north and those that make up the king of the south, as described in Daniel 11. I am not going to expound on this war, as it happens well into the final three and a half years of the tribulation. If you and I are alive then, we will be wherever we are to be, and I don't believe there will be opportunity to change anything at that point.

The final war deserves clarification because it is the great climax and showdown of the war between good and evil. The setup is when the anti-Messiah gathers a huge worldwide army to the valley of Megiddo for the purpose of destroying Jerusalem and the remaining Jews. When the Jews witness the abomination that brings desolation (the placing of a large idol of the anti-Messiah in the third temple), they are instructed in Matthew 24:15-20 to flee to the mountains. This is when, I believe, they escape as a group 200 miles south to Bozrah, which is known as Petra, the ancient fortress in southern Jordan.

This mass exodus of the Jews, very similarly to the exodus of the ancient Israelites from Egypt and Pharaoh, will incite the anti-Messiah to send his army in pursuit. When the army of several hundred million men is stretched out for 200 miles south of Jerusalem, King Yahshua will come in the clouds with His warrior angels and slay the great army, and the prophecy in Revlation 14:19 through 20 will be fulfilled. It is written:

So the angel swung his sickle over the earth and gathered the vintage of the earth, and he threw it into the great wine press of the wrath of God. And the wine press was trodden outside the city, and blood flowed from the wine press, as high as a horse's bridle, for a distance of about two hundred miles.
Revelation 14:19-20 (NRSV)

This will truly be the most awesome event in history because the Jewish people who survive the terrible tribulation will become born-again believers *en masse* when they see King Yahshua coming to rescue them as He did similarly with His mighty acts of parting the Red Sea in the Great Exodus. It is written:

And I will pour out a spirit of compassion and supplication on the house of David and the inhabitants of Jerusalem, so that, when they look on

the one whom they have pierced, they shall mourn for him, as one mourns for an only child, and weep bitterly over him, as one weeps over a firstborn.
   Zechariah 12:10 (NRSV)

The saved Jews of the House of Judah and the born-again believers that make up the House of Ephraim, or Israel, described in Revelation 12:6 and 14 as "the woman that is taken to the wilderness and provided for," will be united with the 144,000, all with new resurrected bodies, and will proceed with King Yahshua back to the Mount of Olives for His coronation. This will fulfill the prophecy of the restored Houses of Judah and Ephraim as Israel becoming a nation in a day. It is written:

Who has heard of such a thing? Who has seen such things? Shall a land be born in one day? Shall a nation be delivered in one moment? Yet as soon as Zion was in labor she delivered her children. Shall I open the womb and not deliver? says the LORD: shall I, the one who delivers, shut the womb? says your God. Rejoice with Jerusalem, and be glad for her, all you who love her; rejoice with her in joy, all you who mourn over her—that you may nurse and be satisfied from her consoling breast; that you may drink deeply with delight from her glorious bosom.
   Isaiah 66:8-11 (NRSV)

See, the day is coming, burning like an oven, when all the arrogant and all evildoers will be stubble; the day that comes shall burn them up, says the LORD of hosts, so that it will leave them neither root nor branch. But for you who revere my name the sun of righteousness shall rise, with healing in its wings. You shall go out leaping like calves from the stall. And you shall tread down the wicked, for they will be ashes under the soles of your feet, on the day when I act, says the LORD of hosts.
   Malachi 4:1-3 (NRSV)

When Yahshua comes, the two houses that have been separated for over 2,700 years will be restored by Him back to His one nation of Israel that will be His nation of kings and priests throughout the Millennium kingdom, as prophesied in Jeremiah 30 and 31.
   As I am observing the situations in the Middle East, the early stages of the first of the two remaining wars that I believe Israel will be involved

in happened in the summer of 2006 in the war with the Hezbollah. It ended up being a battle victory for Israel that the United Nations and the United States forced Israel to end too soon. Now, in early 2007, a much larger war is in the making that I believe will escalate and, at some point, will involve the United States.

In the spring of 2006, after many years of work, the America government finished construction of the largest military base there is in Israel. Something is definitely up in the land of Jacob's trouble. Actually, by the time you read this book, the war could already have happened. The buildup to the war is that a high percentage of the terrorists entering Israeli cities are being trained and equipped in Syria, Lebanon, and Iran. The two main organizations responsible are Hezbollah and Amal.

Probably the most influential sect stirring the pot of terrorism and hatred of Jews and Christians in the world is the Wahhabi Muslims of Saudi Arabia. This group of extreme Jihad Muslim clerics is responsible for inciting and supporting Osama bin Laden and many of the fighters in al Qaeda that have come from a country Americans believed to be an ally. The Jihad that the Muslim extremist pursues is called the third level, or physical Jihad. It is not about producing a peaceful resolve to the Israeli/Palestinian conflict by creating a new Palestinian country; it is about destroying Israel and, ultimately, destroying America, also. This radical, unholy war mindset is about destroying all Jews and Christians in Israel and America. It is truly a spiritual and religious issue; the God of Islam versus the God of Israel.

As you know, Yasser Arafat is dead and was replaced by Abass, a man that is basically an Arafat clone. The forced removal of approximately 9,000 Jews from their homes in the southwestern area of Israel call Gaza began the week of August 21, 2005. Before the week was over, Hurricane Katrina was developing and on August 30 slammed into the Gulf coast states of Louisiana and Mississippi, leaving behind the most destruction of any kind of event in the history of the USA, and probably the world. I don't believe it was coincidence that the storm came on the heels of the forced removal of the Jewish people from their homes in Gaza. This was one of many natural catastrophes that have happened in this country when our leaders have been involved with a plan for forcing the dividing of the land of Israel. Almighty Yah is not pleased with the nations that do these things. It is written:

For then, in those days and at that time, when I restore the fortunes of Judah and Jerusalem, I will gather all the nations and bring them down to the valley of Jehoshaphat, and I will enter into judgment with them there, on account of my people and my heritage Israel, because they have scattered them among the nations. They have divided my land, and cast lots for my people, and traded boys for prostitutes, and sold girls for wine, and drunk it down.

    Joel 3:1-3 (NRSV)

The U.S. government and the others that are pushing the "Roadmap to Peace" are committed to the next forced removal of other Jews from their homes along the much larger West Bank areas of Samaria and Judea. We are now well on the way to a major regional war in the Middle East.

The first of the two wars that set the stage for the final years of the anti-Messiah system will be a regional war involving Israel against the countries of Syria, the Palestinians, Jordan, and Lebanon. In Isaiah Chapter Eleven, we see the layout of the regional war. As I have stated previously in this book, prophecy chapters of the Bible will often include a section of prophecy in the beginning of the chapter that is about events that happen after the events described in the latter section of the chapter. That is the case in Isaiah Eleven. The forced evacuation of the Jewish people who lived in Gaza will definitely set the stage for the regional war. As the buildup of terrorists and weapons escalates and the potential of Iran to wipe Israel off the face of the earth is recognized when that country has completed their quest of having long range missiles with nuclear warheads, Israel will have no other option but to make a first strike.

The first eleven verses of Isaiah Eleven are about the peaceful Millennium reign of King Jesus after He returns to earth to establish His Kingdom. Verse twelve begins the Scriptures that describe the significant regional war that Israel engages in that has not happened as of the date of the publishing of this book. In verse thirteen, Ephraim represents, the ten northern tribes that were taken into slavery by the Assyrians over one hundred years before Isaiah recorded these prophecies. So the prophecies have to be about the current day restored nation of Israel consisting of descendants of the tribes of Judah and the ten northern tribes that have returned to the land. As it is written:

In that day the Lord will extend His hand yet a second time to recover the remnant which is left of His people, from Assyria [Syria], from Egypt, from Pathros *[northern Egypt]*, **from Ethiopia, from Elam** *[NE Iraq]*, **from Shinar** *[same area]*, **from Hamath** *[southern Syria]*, **and from the coastlands of the sea** *[east Mediterranean]*. **He will raise an ensign for the nations, and will assemble the outcasts of Israel, and gather the dispersed of Judah from the four corners of the earth** *[the reestablishment of the nation of Israel in modern times]*. **The jealousy of Ephraim shall depart, and those who harass Judah shall be cut off; Ephraim shall not be jealous of Judah, and Judah shall not harass Ephraim** *[unity of Messianic believers that are Jews and non-Jews, and that is part of the restoration of both Houses of Israel that Father Yahweh is bringing about now in this last generation before Messiah returns]*. **But they** *[Israel, with backing from the USA]* **shall swoop down upon the shoulder of the Philistines** *[Palestinians]* **in the west** *[Gaza]*, **and together they shall plunder the people of the east** *[Arab Islamic nations]*. **They shall put forth their hand against Edom** *[Saudi Arabia]* **and Moab** *[Jordan]*, **and the Ammonites shall obey them.**

Isaiah 11:11-14 (RSV). *Bracketed words added for clarity.*

According to the prophecy, it seems that Israel will have control of some of the oil-rich areas of the Arab nations. I also believe there will be discoveries of huge oil reserves and expensive minerals in the Dead Sea and huge oil reserves in the West Bank area that will make Israel a very wealthy nation. It makes sense because the war between Israel and the Arab nations will have to happen in order to set the stage for the next war, possibly a major world war that involves the superpowers.

The following is another prophecy that I believe is about the same event.

"Behold, Damascus will cease from *being* a city, and it will be a ruinous heap."

Isaiah 17:1 (NKJV)

Damascus, the capital of Syria, is considered to be one of the world's oldest cities. Even though Damascus was captured in 632 B.C. by the Assyrian king, Tiglathpileser, the city was not destroyed and has stood through modern times. As of the time of the publishing of this book, the prophecy above is still future.

When this regional war is concluded, I believe Israel will occupy some of the land east of the Jordan River that now belongs to the country of Jordan. The area I am referring to is part of the original land area that Almighty Yahweh gave to His servant Abraham and on which the tribes of Gad, Reuben, and half of Manasseh settled when the twelve tribes came out of the desert wilderness under Joshua's leadership. This war will likely bring an end to the attacks on Israeli citizens by the Muslim fanatics who have violated them for years with their suicide missions.

The few years of temporary peace following this regional war will not be a result of the anti-Messiah establishing a peace treaty with the leaders of Israel and the other nations. I see this described time of peace being a result of the Vatican making its move to gain control of the old historical section of Jerusalem. In doing so, the Roman Catholic Church (RCC) will be able to divide the old city into three sections: one for the Jewish people, one for the Muslim people, and one for the Christian people. This plan has been in the making for many years and will empower the Pope to have administrative control over the three sections and to create a second Vatican in Jerusalem. It is believed that the last Pope of the RCC, previously referred to as Peter the Roman, while occupying his new headquarters in Jerusalem, will be part of the fulfillment of end-time prophecies leading up to Armageddon, the final conquest between King Yahshua and Satan, the devil. The last Pope will, most likely, fulfill the role of the false prophet who deceives most of humanity and prepares the way of the dreaded anti-Messiah.

When Israel defeats some of the key terrorist Arab nations in the regional war and the complete destruction of Damascus takes place, the stage will be set for the coming of World War Three. As stated earlier, Israel will become a very wealthy nation and will have peace with its neighbors for a few years. I believe Israel's wealth and prosperity at that time will cause Russia and a confederacy of Islamic nations that were not humbled during the regional war to make a plan to invade Israel in order to destroy its people and take control of its wealth. The prophet Ezekiel gives us the prophecies. It is written:

> **Now the word of the LORD came to me, saying, "Son of man, set your face against Gog** [nations to the north and east of Israel] **of the land of Magog,** [ma means people of; Magog is the name of one of the sons

Japheth, one of the sons of Noah Gen. 10:2] **the prince of Rosh** *[chief nation, Russia]*, **Meshech** *[Turkey]*, **and Tubal** *[southern Russia in the Caucasus area]*, **and prophesy against him, and say, 'Thus says the Lord GOD: "Behold, I** *am* **against you, O Gog, the prince of Rosh, Meshech, and Tubal. I will turn you around, put hooks into your jaws, and lead you out, with all your army, horses, and horseman, all splendidly clothed, a great company** *with* **bucklers and shields, all of them handling swords** *[a well equipped, modern army]*. **Persia** *[Iran]*, **Ethiopia** *[Sudan]*, **and Libya** *[west of Egypt]* **are with them** *[note that all of the countries listed are Muslim]*, **all of them** *with* **shield and helmet; Gomer** *[another section of Turkey]* **and all its troops; the house of Togarmah** *[Armenia]* **from the far north and all its troops—many people** *are* **with you. Prepare yourself and be ready, you and all your companies that are gathered about you; and be a guard for them. After many days you will be visited** *[many centuries from the time Ezekiel received the prophecy]*. **In the latter years** *[last years of the last generation that we are in]* **you will come into the land of those brought back from the sword** *[This refers to the believing and non-believing Jews who are called to make Aliyah return to their homeland of Israel and occupy the land fulfilling the prophecy of Ezekiel 37 of the two tribes of Judah and Ephraim coming together again as the one new man in Messiah.]* **and gathered from many people on the mountains of Israel, which had long been desolate; they were brought out of the nations, and now all of them dwell safely. You will ascend, coming like a storm, covering the land like a cloud, you and all your troops and many peoples with you." 'Thus says the Lord GOD: "On that day it shall come to pass** *that* **thoughts will arise in your mind, and you will make an evil plan: You will say, 'I will go up against a land of unwalled villages** *[I believe at this future time the walls around Jerusalem will have been removed]*; **I will go to a peaceful people, who dwell safely, all of them dwelling without walls, and having neither bars nor gates'—to take plunder and to take booty** *[gain control of the great oil reserves that Israel will have acquired in the regional war]*, **to stretch out your hand against the waste places** *that are again* **inhabited, and against a people gathered from the nations, who acquired livestock and goods, who dwell in the midst of the land. Sheba, Dedan, the merchants of Tarshish, and all their young lions will say you, 'Have you come to take plunder? Have you gathered your army to take booty** *[take control of Israel's wealth]*, **to carry away silver and gold, to take away livestock** and goods, to take great plunder?'"' "Therefore, son of man, prophesy and say unto Gog *[Russia, Iran, and others]*, 'Thus says the Lord GOD: "On that day when My people Israel dwell safely, will you not know *it*? Then you will come from your place out of the far north, you and many peoples with you, all of them riding on horses, a great company and a mighty army. You will come up against My people Israel like a cloud, to cover the land. It will be in the latter days *[last years of the last generations of this age]* that I will bring you against My land, so that the nations may know Me, when I am hallowed in you, O Gog, before their eyes." Thus saith the Lord GOD: "Are *you* he of whom I have spoken in former days by My servants the prophets of Israel, who prophesied for years in those days that I would bring you against them? And it will come to pass at the same time when Gog comes against the land of Israel," says the Lord GOD, "*that* My fury will show in My face. For in My jealousy *and* in the fire of My wrath I have spoken: 'Surely in that day there shall be a great earthquake in the land of Israel, so that the fishes of the sea, the birds of the heaven, the beasts of the field, all creeping things that creep upon the earth, and all men who *are* on the face of the earth shall shake at My presence. The mountains shall be thrown down, the steep places shall fall, and every wall shall fall to the ground.' I will call for a sword against Gog throughout all My mountains," says the Lord GOD. "Every man's sword will be against his brother. And I will bring him to judgment with pestilence and with bloodshed; I will rain down on him, on his troops, and on the many peoples who are with him, flooding rain, great hailstones, fire, and brimstone. Thus I will magnify Myself and sanctify Myself, and I will be known in the eyes of many nations. Then they shall know that I *am* the LORD.'"

"And you, son of man, prophesy against Gog, and say, 'Thus says the Lord GOD: "Behold, I *am* against you, O Gog, the prince of Rosh, Meshech, and Tubal; and I will turn you around and lead you on, *[in the King James version it says: and leave but the sixth part of thee]* bringing you up from the far north, and bring you against the mountains of Israel. Then I will knock the bow out of your left hand, and cause the arrows to fall out of your right hand. You shall fall upon the mountains of Israel, you and all your troops and the peoples who *are* with you; I will give you to birds of prey of every sort and *to* the beasts of the field to be

**devoured. You shall fall on the open field; for I have spoken," says the
Lord GOD. "And I will send fire on Magog, and on those who live in
security in the coastlands. Then they shall know that I *am* the LORD. So
I will make My holy name known in the midst of My people Israel, and
I will not *let them* profane My holy name any more. Then the nations
shall know that *I am* the LORD, the Holy One in Israel."**

Ezekiel 38; 39:1-7 (NKJV). *Bracketed words added for clarity.*

I type this with much sadness. I believe that when the events
described in Ezekiel 38 happen, the part referencing those who live in
security in the coastlands is speaking about the United States of America.
It's apparent to me that, in all of history, America has been the greatest
nation of all nations. I believe there is strong evidence to support that
America is the end times Babylon described in the Scriptures, and if not
the Babylon, certainly a part of it. Below is a list of clues with Scripture
notations that you can study for yourself. This list was compiled by Larry
Meguiar. He has produced a truly incredible amount of information with
excellent teaching on his web site for those who want to know more of
what is going on in this world. His website address is:

www.meguiar.addr.com

As we watch, read, and study the prophecies of the Scriptures and current events, you can see the New World Order and beast system of the end
times materializing before our eyes.

If you have not done so, do a study in the Scripture prophecies concerning Babylon in the last days. You will find that:

1. It continually says, "in those days" and "in that time" and in the "day of
   trouble." This is a reference to the time of Jacob's trouble or the birth
   pangs of the Messiah (Isaiah 13:8, 13. 21:3; Jeremiah 50:4, 20, 51:2, 43).
2. Babylon is a rich and economically prosperous country (Jeremiah 50:37,
   51:13; Revelation 18:3, 19).
3. Babylon is a land of "mixed/mingled people" (Jeremiah 50:37).
4. Babylon is a world military power (Jeremiah 51:53).
5. Babylon is a land that sits among many waters (Jeremiah 51:13).
6. Babylon is a country that has a heritage in the Elohim of Israel but has
   sinned and has turned from Almighty Yah (Jeremiah 50:11, 14, 24, 29,
   38, 51:7).
7. The Elohim of Israel would have healed the land of Babylon if she would
   have repented, but she will not repent (2 Chronicles 7:14; Jeremiah

51:8-9).

8. The good news of Messiah is going forth from the land of Babylon but it will be "cut off" in "the time of harvest," which is the end of the age (Jeremiah 50:16).

9. Babylon is a country that does not believe it will experience the wrath and judgment of Yahweh (be a widow) (Isaiah 47:5, 7-10; Revelation 18:7-8).

10. The attacking power against Babylon is from "THE NORTH COUNTRY" (Jeremiah 50:3, 9, 26, 41, 51:48).

11. Babylon is destroyed by extremely accurate arrows (missiles) and the attack is devastating (Jeremiah 50:9, 14, 29, 42, 51:3, 11).

12. A fire is kindled in the cities of Babylon from the accurate arrows (missiles) (Jeremiah 50:32; Revelation 18:8).

13. Babylon will be destroyed similar to the way that Sodom and Gomorrah were destroyed (Isaiah 13:19; Jeremiah 50:40).

14. When Babylon is destroyed, it will never be inhabited again (Isaiah 13:19-20; Jeremiah 50:3, 13, 26, 39-40, 51:2-3, 26, 29, 37, 43, 63-64).

15. The nations of the world tremble and shake in fear at the defeat of Babylon (Jeremiah 50:46; Revelation 18:9-10).

16. The house of Judah (Judaism) and the house of Israel (Christianity) who live in Babylon are called to flee from Babylon and go to Zion (Isaiah 13:14; Jeremiah 50:4-5, 16-19, 28, 33, 51:9, 45; Revelation 18:4).

17. When Babylon is destroyed, the sins of the house of Judah (Judaism) and the house of Israel (Christianity) will be pardoned (the exile will be over and the house of Judah and the house of Israel will be restored) (Jeremiah 50:20).

18. When the house of Judah (Judaism) and the house of Israel (Christianity) flees the land of Babylon to go to "Zion," they will enter into an ETERNAL covenant that will not be forgotten (Jeremiah 50:4-5; Ezekiel 37:26-27).

When you ponder about how it would be possible for a one-world economy to happen, and it is actually going to happen, America will have to be neutralized, subdued, and stripped of its Constitution and freedoms. Look around, it is happening now and has been for several years. It will be a sad set of circumstances when that happens. I believe the destruction of America will come about from an all-out, in-concert attack from Russia and China using their huge fleets of nuclear submarines and long-range, inter-continental ballistic missiles, as well as internally from Muslim terrorist cells using suitcase nuclear bombs. I believe this attack will come very quickly, without warning, and will take place at the same time that Russia makes its move to capture Israel. I believe also that this horrible set of events will happen on the heels of tremendous devastation to America from the effects of a meteorite storm that takes place with the passing of Planet X in front of the earth's path that will fulfill the prophecies of the first through the fourth trumpets in Revelation Eight that I covered earlier.

When this final world war takes place, as planned by the Illuminati, the survivors of the world will be in a similar state of mind as were the people of Germany after World War II. They were desperate and were willing to listen to and comply with any leader who could tell them what they wanted to hear and deliver peace and prosperity. History has repeated itself many times and in many different ways.

During the final three and one-half years of the great tribulation, the masterminds of the New World Order will have finally been successful in creating great chaos and, out of the chaos, they will have created the kind of order they have desired all along: total control of the world, which will be the beast system.

The end-times battle between the Creator of the universe, Who is worthy of the worship of every human being on the earth, and the god of this world that is doing everything in his power to steal the worship that is due Almighty Yah will come to its grand finale.

The question I have for you, dear reader, is this. Are you prepared for the end and the coming first of Satan's son, whatever his name will be, and then the coming of Almighty Yahweh's Son, Whose name is Yahshua? I pray for your sake throughout all eternity that you are prepared. Amen.

11

HOW DO WE PREPARE FOR THE COMING OF MESSIAH?

M y brother-in-law emailed me the afternoon of September 11, 2001, to ask what I thought was happening. I assured him it was not the end of the world and told him to pray for the families of those who had been killed, those who were injured, our President, our national leaders, our nation as a whole, and for Israel. I explained to him that as horrible as this evil event was, Father Yahweh would turn that which Satan, the devil, did for evil, destruction, and pain into something positive and good.

I believe now as I did on that shocking day that as a result of so many of our people dying so quickly and so close to home, many have sought out the one true and living God, Who by His Holy Spirit is constantly searching into the hearts of people, looking for anyone who is crying out to Him to be saved. We are beginning to witness the good fruit of revival that has come forth as a result of the blood of over 3,000 innocent victims being poured out. People are searching for answers, truth, and understanding as never before. The events of September 11 were and are a true sign and wake up call for all of us from our Creator. We should all be seeking to press into our Heavenly Father Yahweh and Savior, King Yahshua, with all of our hearts, seeking His wisdom and discernment as the days are becoming more difficult.

I was very blessed to be able to attend an intercessor's prayer gathering in Washington, D.C., two weeks after the horror of September 11. As I awoke and lay in bed for a few minutes the morning I was to leave to go to the gathering, Holy Spirit gave me the following Scripture:

For God has not given us a spirit of fear, but of power and of love and of a sound mind.
2 Timothy 1:7 (NKJV)

The gathering had been planned in early June, three months before the terrorist attack, for the purpose of praying for revival in America. Many, if not all, in attendance were touched by Holy Spirit in special ways with visions, prophetic words, and such unity in a body of believers that I haven't witnessed before. Almighty Yah is doing new things in His Body of believers to prepare them for the different ministries of the end times. It was confirmed during the gathering that Almighty Yah was going to release new anointings and gifts of the Spirit to accomplish His end-time work throughout the earth. It was also revealed that the mighty Sword of the Spirit, which is the true Word of the one true, living God would go forth in a greater way than ever before, with restoration of believers to foundational truths that Yahshua taught and lived.

In the last years of this last generation before King Yahshua returns the most significant signs of the working of the Holy Spirit will be greater deliverance and healing ministries than the world has ever known. Also, new teaching ministries will come forth, such as the one you are learning from right now, that will restore the true Hebrew names of our heavenly Father, Yahweh, and Himself as His manifested Son, whose name is Yahshua, our Messiah. Also in this great end-time work of Holy Spirit is the restoration of believers to our Hebraic Roots of embracing the instructions of Yah's *Torah* and desiring to be *Torah*-observant because it pleases our Creator.

In thinking about how we are to prepare for all that is coming upon the earth and in our rapidly changing societies, it is imperative that we as believers of the one true, living God of Abraham, Isaac, and Jacob be absolutely grounded in His Holy Word and filled with His Holy Spirit. Master Yahshua is coming back to this earth to marry His bride that has been tried by His fire and has been empowered to overcome all the deceptions, temptations, and persecutions that Satan can throw at her.

We prepare for the coming of Messiah by learning to hear Holy Spirit talking to us with His unique voice. It is written:

Pilate therefore said to Him, "Are You a king then?" Jesus answered, "You say *rightly* that I am a king. For this cause I was born, and for this

**cause I have come into the world, that I should bear witness to the
truth. Everyone who is of the truth hears My voice."**
    John 18:37 (NKJV)

**"Very truly, I tell you, anyone who does not enter the sheepfold by the
gate but climbs in by another way is a thief and a bandit. The one who
enters by the gate is the shepherd of the sheep. The gatekeeper opens
the gate for him, and the sheep hear his voice. He calls his own sheep
by name and leads them out. When he has brought out all his own, he
goes ahead of them, and the sheep follow him because they know his
voice. They will not follow a stranger, but they will run from him
because they do not know the voice of strangers.**
    John 10:1-5 (NRSV)

**Now we have received, not the spirit of the world, but the Spirit who is
from God, that we might know the things that have been freely given to
us by God. These things we also speak, not in words which man's wisdom teaches but which the Holy Spirit teaches, comparing spiritual
things with spiritual.**
    1 Corinthians 2:12-13 (NKJV)

Hearing the still small voice of Holy Spirit is necessary for our growth
as mature believers and empowers us in our daily walk with Yahshua. By
learning to hear His voice, we receive instruction, council, and discernment from the One Who created us. He knows what is best for us and
desires His best for us. It is up to us to be plugged into Him in a complete, sold-out relationship so we can hear Him speak to us. Hearing Him
speak to us directly in our heart of hearts and from His Holy Word is so
important as we begin to prepare for the tribulation times and His coming to defeat evil in the earth and establish His awesome kingdom.

Each time I have sat down at the keyboard to begin typing on this
book, I have prayed and asked Holy Spirit to speak to me and guide my
thoughts so I would teach in this work the words that He wants on these
pages for you, the reader, to benefit from. I'm convinced that second in
importance to you receiving Master Yahshua as your Savior and allowing Him to live within you is your preparing yourself for His return and
coming kingdom. We must be in covenant relationship with Him,
following His instructions from His whole word. He is the Word, the

"Living *Torah*."

We prepare for Messiah's coming by learning to personally hear from Him in our day-to-day decisions and also from the instructions in His Word. When we are born again of His Holy Spirit, His spiritual kingdom dwells within us; therefore His kingdom is being established within us. In these last years before Yahshua returns, He is calling people all over the earth to repent from their sins and to be redeemed, to return and be obedient to His instructions that He gave to His servant Moses, and to restore the true and pure worship He desires from His people. These prophecies are for our times. As it is written:

> **Repent therefore, and turn to God so that your sins may be wiped out, so that times of refreshing may come from the presence of the Lord, and that He may send the Messiah appointed for you, that is, Jesus, who must remain in heaven until the time of universal restoration that God announced long ago through his holy prophets. Moses said, "The Lord your God will raise up for you from your own people a prophet like me** [*Moses*]. **You must listen to whatever He tells you. And it will be that everyone who does not listen to that prophet will be utterly rooted out of the people."**
>
> Acts 3:19-23 (NRSV). *Bracketed words added for clarity.*

> **"For surely I will command, and will sift the house of Israel** [*Jew and non-Jew believers*] **among all nations, as *grain* is sifted in a sieve; yet not the smallest grain shall fall to the ground. All the sinners of My people shall die by the sword, who say, 'The calamity** [*tribulation*] **shall not overtake us nor confront us.' On that day I will raise up the tabernacle of David, which has fallen down, and repair its damages; I will raise up its ruins, and rebuild it as in the days of old ..."**
>
> Amos 9:9-11 (NKJV). *Bracketed words added for clarity.*

Almighty Yah is preparing His kingdom people for His return. Yahshua must remain in heaven and not come to earth until all things are restored according to His plan. He restored the land of Israel by making the way for it to become a nation again in May 1948. He has kept the Hebrew language intact for all the many centuries the Jews were dispersed throughout the world and is now restoring the language to many non-Jewish believers in Yahshua as a second language. He is restoring a passion in many believers to understand how to live His instructions that He gave to Moses, not only all ten of the familiar Ten Commandments, but the other instructions regarding dietary, issues of blood, and the importance of keeping His Holy Feasts and new moon celebrations. He is restoring pure worship from His people who are free in Yahshua to return to His holy days and appointed times, and are not bound up by religion and the false doctrines of man. It is written:

> **"But the hour is coming, and now is, when the true worshipers will worship the Father in spirit and truth; for the Father is seeking such to worship Him. God *is* Spirit, and those who worship Him must worship in spirit and truth."**
> John 4:23-24 (NKJV)

All of these restorations are part of the rebuilding of the tabernacle of David and the bringing together of the two houses of Israel—the house of Judah and the house of Ephraim, believing, redeemed Jews and non-Jews who form the One New Man in Messiah. It is written:

> **Behold, the days are coming, says the Lord, when I will make a new covenant with the house of Israel** *[Gentile believers]* **and the house of Judah** *[Jewish believers]*—**not according to the covenant that I made with their fathers in the day *that* I took them by the hand to lead them out of the land of Egypt, My covenant which they broke, though I was a husband to them, says the Lord. But this *is* the covenant that I will make with the house of Israel** *[both houses united in Yahshua as the one new man]* **after those days** *[all the generations up to the last generation when all of the restorations began]*, **says the Lord: I will put My law** *[ten commandments and other instructions]* **in their minds, and write it on their hearts; and I will be their God, and they shall be My people."**
> Jeremiah 31:31-33 (NKJV). *Bracketed words added for clarity.*

This is the same new covenant that the writer of Hebrews was referring to in Chapter Eight. As it is written:

> **Now the main point in what we are saying is this: we have such a high priest** *[Yahshua]*, **one who is seated at the right hand of the throne of the Majesty in the heavens, a minister in the sanctuary and the true tent**

that the Lord, and not any mortal, has set up. For every high priest is appointed to offer gifts and sacrifices; hence it is necessary for this priest also to have something to offer. Now if he were on earth, he would not be a priest at all, since there are priests who offer gifts *(animal, grain, wine, and oil)* according to the law. They offer worship in a sanctuary that is a sketch and shadow of the heavenly one; for Moses, when he was about to erect the tent, was warned, "See that you make everything according to the pattern *[all of the items that were used in the Tabernacle in the wilderness, the tent of meeting with Almighty Yah]* that was shown you on the mountain." But Jesus has now obtained a more excellent ministry, and to that degree he is the mediator of a better covenant, which has been enacted through better promises. For if that first covenant had been faultless, there would have been no need to look for a second one. God finds fault with them when he says: "The days are surely coming, says the Lord, when I will establish a new covenant with the house of Israel and with the house of Judah; not like the covenant that I made with their ancestors, on the day when I took them by the hand to lead them out of the land of Egypt; for they did not continue in my covenant, and so I had no concern for them, says the Lord. This is the covenant that I will make with the house of Israel after those days, says the Lord: I will put my laws *[Torah instructions]* in their minds, and write them on their hearts *[this is the promise and work of Yah through His Holy Spirit]*, and I will be their God, and they shall be my people. And they shall not teach one another or say to each other, 'Know the Lord,' for they shall all know me, from the least of them to the greatest. For I will be merciful toward their iniquities, and I will remember their sins no more." In speaking of "a new covenant," he has made the first one *[animal, grain, wine, and oil sacrifices]* obsolete. And what is obsolete and growing old will soon disappear.

Hebrews 8:1-13 (NRSV). *Bracketed words added for clarity.*

This is relating to the promises of the coming of Holy Spirit that transpired during the awesome time of the Feast of *Shavuot* (Pentecost) as recorded in Acts Chapter Two. Holy Spirit does many things to help us, but one of the most important is to lead us into all truth so that Father Yahweh's instructions are written on our hearts and imbedded in our minds that we can come out of falsehood. The people of the twelve tribes of Israel that Moses lead out of Egypt did not have the benefit of being born of Holy Spirit of Father Yahweh that comes to us in the name of our Master Yahshua, or Jesus. This is all part of the way Father Yahweh desired for His Master Plan to unfold. Isn't this awesome to behold and to realize that we are being drawn by Him to be a part of this end-time ministry of sharing the truth with others so they too can receive eternal life and be prepared for the coming of Messiah. It is written:

> **"... say to them, 'Thus says the Lord GOD: "Surely I will take the stick of Joseph, which *is* in the hand of Ephraim** [Gentile believers]**, and the tribes of Israel, his companions; and I will join them with it, with the stick of Judah** [Jewish believers]**, and make them one stick, and they will be one in My hand."'**
>
> **"They shall not defile themselves anymore with their idols, nor with their detestable things, nor with any of their transgressions; but I will deliver them from all their dwelling places in which they have sinned, and will cleanse them. Then they shall be My people, and I will be their God. David My servant** [a reference to Yahshua, Messiah, son of David] ***shall be* king over them, and they shall all have one shepherd; they shall also walk in My judgments and observe My statutes, and do them.**
>
> Ezekiel 37:19, 23-24 (NKJV). *Bracketed words added for clarity.*

We are to be new covenant people with our Master Yahshua's blood covering us and Father Yahweh's *Torah* instructions written on our hearts as we live each day according to His instructions.

We prepare for the coming of Messiah by repenting from what we have learned and practiced from the ignorance we have been taught according to the teachings of man that don't line up with God's Word. We also prepare by holding on to the covenant promises that Master Yahshua has given to us. I believe the Scriptures that most profoundly address the areas of false teachings, discernment, and His awesome promises for particularly the people of this last generation are in the letters to the seven churches recorded in the book of Revelation, Chapters Two and Three. We are called by our Creator and Master to be overcomers to the end.

This is the first letter, and my paraphrases are in parentheses.

> **"To the angel of the church of Ephesus write, 'These things says He who holds the seven stars in His right hand, who walks in the midst of the seven golden lampstands** [menorahs]: **"I know your works, your labor,**

your patience, and that you cannot bear those who are evil. And you have tested those who say they are apostles and are not, and have found them liars; and you have persevered and have patience, and have labored for My name's sake and have not become weary. **Nevertheless I have *this* against you, that you have left your first love** [the passionate love for our Creator/Savior and our love for one another]. **Remember therefore from where you have fallen; repent and do the first works, or else I will come to you quickly and remove your lampstand from its place—unless you repent. But this you have, that you hate the deeds of the Nicolaitans** [a personal name meaning "conqueror of the people"] **which I also hate. He who has an ear, let him hear what the Spirit says to the churches. To him who overcomes I will give to eat from the tree of life, which is in the midst of the Paradise of God."'**

Revelation 2:1-7 (NKJV). *Bracketed words added for clarity.*

The first reproof (*reproof* means *to bring a misdeed to someone's attention for correction*) in this passage of Scripture is to return to the first love and do the first works. I believe Yahshua was telling His body of believers down through the centuries that it is very important to have discernment about how people act and our position regarding social issues so as to be able to correctly make a stand for the things that are right according to Yahweh's Holy Word.

In all of our understanding and making a stand for what is right, and in all of our persevering, having patience, laboring for His name's sake, and not becoming weary, if we aren't loving people the way our Master has taught in His Word and by His example, then we are falling short and not fulfilling His purpose in us. This grieves His heart. We must learn to love unconditionally the way He has taught us. It is written:

Beloved, let us love one another, for love is of God; and everyone who loves is born of God and knows God. He who does not love does not know God, for God is love. In this the love of God was manifested toward us, that God has sent His only begotten Son into the world, that we might live through Him. In this is love, not that we loved God, but that He loved us and sent His Son *to be* the propitiation for our sins. Beloved, if God so loved us, we also ought to love one another. No one has seen God at any time. If we love one another, God abides in us, and His love has been perfected in us. By this we know that we abide in

Him, and He in us, because He has given us of His Spirit. And we have seen and testify that the Father has sent the Son *as* Savior of the world. Whoever confesses that Jesus is the Son of God, God abides in him, and he in God. And we have known and believed the love that God has for us. God is love, and he who abides in love abides in God, and God in him. Love has been perfected among us in this: that we may have boldness in the day of judgment; because as He is, so are we in this world. There is no fear in love; but perfect love casts out fear, because fear involves torment. But he who fears has not been made perfect in love. We love Him because He first loved us. If someone says, "I love God," and hates his brother, he is a liar; for he who does not love his brother whom he has seen, how can he love God whom he has not seen? And this commandment we have from Him: that he who loves God *must* love his brother also.

1 John 4:7-21 (NKJV)

The second reproof is not to be like the Nicolaitans who strive for status and control in the church and teach false doctrines about the acceptance of immorality and idolatry. During the Apostle John's life, there were a group of first-century believers who followed the teachings of a man named Nicolaitan who twisted the true meaning of the *Torah* Scriptures and the teaching of the apostles and prophets to create his own denomination. He was thereby leading believers astray by teaching falsehood and manipulating the people to be under his control without questioning what he taught.

Do we have people in the Catholic and Protestant churches and Jewish synagogues today who strive for status, teach that people within a congregation are to be under the pastor's or rabbi's authority, teach idolatry, and that immoral practices are acceptable? I encourage you to question everything that you have ever been taught by your rabbi, pastor, and teacher of the Scriptures and line it up beside the Holy Word of Almighty Yahweh to determine if what you have been taught is accurate.

Our Lord hates striving. We are to follow in His footsteps in all things and be servants to all, especially those who are less fortune that we. Our Master and King hates sin and lies. It is written:

He who overcomes shall inherit all things, and I will be his God and he shall be My son. "But the cowardly, unbelieving, abominable,

murderers, sexually immoral, sorcerers, idolaters, and all liars shall have their part in the lake which burns with fire and brimstone, which is the second death.

Revelation 21:7-8 (NKJV)

Our Messiah Yahshua's first promise to those who overcome is that He will bless them to be able to eat from the Tree of Life. We will be allowed to eat from the same tree that Adam and Eve had access to in the Garden of Eden. They chose not the Tree of Life but the tree of the knowledge of good and evil that leads, then and now, to death. Yahshua is the "Living *Torah*" and the "Tree of Life." If we choose wisely, we eat from Him now, as all who are overcomers will be doing throughout the coming tribulation and His coming millennial kingdom here on earth.

The second letter:

"And to the angel of the church in Smyrna write, 'These things says the First and the Last, who was dead, and came to life *[Yahshua, the Messiah]***: "I know your works, tribulation, and poverty, (but you are rich** *[in spirit]***); and** *I know* **the blasphemy of those who say they are Jews and are not, but are a synagogue of Satan. Do not fear any of those things which you are about to suffer. Indeed, the devil is about to throw** *some* **of you into prison, that you may be tested, and you will have tribulation ten days. Be faithful until death, and I will give you the crown of life. He who has an ear, let him hear what the Spirit says to the churches. He who overcomes shall not be hurt by the second death."'**

Revelation 2:8-11 (NKJV). *Bracketed words added for clarity.*

There is no reproof here, only instruction and promise. The instructions are very strong and are for those who will be called to lay down their lives as believers and followers of Yahshua, the Messiah, and not of this world. We must be willing to lay down our lives for our Master and King because He laid His life down for us, not only because He loves us, but also because He desired to redeem us back to Himself so we can have eternal life together. Remember, we were born into Satan's kingdom, with all of its trappings, curses, sickness, death penalty, and destiny of eternal separation from our Heavenly Father Yahweh. When we accept Yahshua as our Savior and invite Him into our hearts, we are re-born spiritually (born again) into Yahshua's kingdom and are in position to receive all of the covenant blessings, along with eternal life. During the three and a half year tribulation period, we who are alive at that time will be tested greater than any people in any generation of the history of mankind. We must be prepared to be able to stand firm. It is written:

> **"Then they will hand you over to be tortured and will put you to death, and you will be hated by all nations because of my name. Then many will fall away** [*cave in under the pressure to accept the mark of the beast to survive, which will be connected with worshiping Satan through his son the anti-Messiah*]**, and they will betray one another and hate one another. And many false prophets will arise and lead many astray. And because of the increase of lawlessness, the love of many will grow cold. But the one who endures to the end will be saved."**
> Matthew 24:9-13 (NRSV). *Bracketed words added for clarity.*

Remember that a person cannot accept the mark of the beast and be received into Yahweh's kingdom. Receiving the mark of the beast is the ultimate curse and judgment sentence. It is written:

> **Then a third angel followed them, saying with a loud voice, "If anyone worships the beast and his image, and receives *his* mark on his forehead or on his hand, he himself shall also drink of the wine of the wrath of God, which is poured out full strength into the cup of His indignation. He shall be tormented with fire and brimstone in the presence of the holy angels and in the presence of the Lamb. And the smoke of their torment ascends forever and ever; and they have no rest day or night, who worship the beast and his image, and whoever receives the mark of his name." Here is the patience of the saints; here *are* those who keep the commandments of God and the faith of Jesus. Then I heard a voice from heaven saying to me, "Write: 'Blessed *are* the dead who die in the Lord from now on.'" "Yes," says the Spirit, "that they may rest from their labors, and their works follow them."**
> Revelation 14:9-13 (NKJV)

Study the Holy Scriptures and the information in this book so that you will be prepared not to fall into the deception of Satan's horrible trap.

Our first promise in this second letter is that if we are faithful until death, we will be given the crown of life. From the Apostle James we hear:

> **Blessed is anyone who endures temptation. Such a one has stood the test and will receive the crown of life that the Lord has promised to those who love Him.**
> James 1:12 (NRSV)

And from the Apostle Paul,

> **As for me, I am already being poured out as a libation, and the time of my departure has come. I have fought the good fight, I have finished the race, I have kept the faith. From now on there is reserved for me the crown of righteousness, which the Lord, the righteous judge, will give me on that day, and not only to me but also to all who have longed for His appearing** [the one coming of Messiah Yahshua to establish His kingdom, destroy the kingdoms of this earth, and reward His servants].
> 2 Timothy 4: 6-8 (NRSV). *Bracketed words added for clarity.*

These are some of the last words the Apostle Paul wrote before he was beheaded by the Romans because he would not acknowledge Caesar as Lord. He refused to deny and renounce that Yahshua was his Master. I don't believe that a person can loose their salvation; I believe that is a false teaching. Human beings, when in full faculty of mind, are capable of making independent decisions right up until the last breath. We must know Almighty Yahweh's truth and be fully persuaded and confirmed in what we believe, or we will be washed away by the river currents of deception. When a person is born of Almighty Yah's Holy Spirit by inviting Yahshua (Jesus) into their hearts, that person is completely saved and sealed, and no matter what kind of torture and persecution comes their way, that person will not deny their Savior. Will you be able to stand in the day when the greatest of all tests for humanity comes upon the earth?

Our second promise in this letter is that we will not be hurt by the second death.

> **Then I saw thrones, and those seated on them were given authority to judge. I also saw the souls of those who had been beheaded for their testimony to Jesus and for the word of God. They had not worshiped the beast or its image and had not received its mark on their foreheads or their hands. They came to life and reigned with Christ a thousand years. (The rest of the dead did not come to life until the thousand years were**

ended.) **This is the first resurrection. Blessed and holy are those who share in the first resurrection. Over these the second death has no power, but they will be priests of God and of Christ, and they will reign with Him a thousand years.**
Revelation 20:4-6 (NRSV)

"I tell you, my friends, do not fear those who kill the body, and after that can do nothing more. But I will warn you whom to fear: fear him who, after he has killed, has authority to cast into hell. Yes, I tell you, fear him! Are not five sparrows sold for two pennies? Yet not one of them is forgotten in God's sight. But even the hairs of your head are all counted. Do not be afraid; you are of more value than many sparrows.
Luke 12:4-7 (NRSV)

Our Bridegroom has promised us in His instruction that He will be with us all the way to the end. It is written:

"… teaching them to observe all things that I have commanded you; and lo, I am with you always, even to the end of the age." Amen.
Matthew 28:20 (NKJV)

Yahshua is faithful, and He requires that we be faithful to the end.
The third letter:

"And to the angel of the church in Pergamos write, 'These things says He who has the sharp two-edged sword [*Yahshua's word of truth that has the power to judge all people and nations*]**: I know your works, and where you dwell, where Satan's throne** *is.* **And you hold fast to My name, and did not deny My faith even in the days in which Antipas** *was* **My faithful martyr, who was killed among you, where Satan dwells. But I have a few things against you, because you have there those who hold the doctrine of Balaam, who taught Balak to put a stumbling block before the children of Israel, to eat things sacrificed to idols, and to commit sexual immorality. Thus you also have those who hold the doctrine of the Nicolaitans, which thing I hate. Repent, or else I will come to you quickly and will fight against them with the sword of My mouth. He who has an ear, let him hear what the Spirit says to the churches. To him who overcomes I will give some of the hidden manna to eat. And I**

will give him a white stone, and on the stone a new name written which no one knows except him who receives it."'
Revelation 2:12-17 (NKJV). *Bracketed words added for clarity.*

The believers were holding fast to Yahshua's name and were not denying their faith in Him, which is of primary importance for salvation. The reproof is that there were some among them who had accepted false teaching that had crept into the congregations by false teachers who were influenced by the traditions of men of the cultures in surrounding nations, such as Greece and Rome. Something interesting to note is that Pergamos was in ancient Turkey, which Yahshua identifies as being where Satan has an earthly throne. I believe that the anti-Messiah beast will come out from the country of Turkey, not necessary a native citizen from there, but someone with close association.

The strong reproof here is regarding the teaching of Balaam and again the teaching of the Nicolaitans. We have already learned that the teaching of the Nicolaitans is that of those who strived for status in the church and taught false doctrines about the acceptance of immorality and idolatry. The account of Balaam is found in the book of Numbers from Chapters 22 through 31. Balaam was a prophet for profit. He was hired by the evil king Balak of Moab to curse the invading Israelites. Each time Balaam when to the Israelites to pronounce a curse upon them, he was unable, and instead, by the power of Yahweh, he would pronounce a blessing. This infuriated Balak so that he insisted that Balaam come up with a plan to destroy the Israelites. After much thought, Balaam recommended that young women of Moab be sent to seduce the men of Israel into marriage and accepting their false Baal gods. The plan worked. After a few years, Moses had to deal with many from the twelve tribes who had fallen into idolatry.

So the teaching of Balaam is referring to teaching against the truth from the *Torah* that was given to Moses as instructions for all people, not just the Israelites of that time, but for all people then and now, excluding animal sacrifices. We become the people of Yahweh's Israel when we accept Yahshua as our Redeemer and ask to be born of His Holy set-apart Spirit. We are then grafted into the olive tree of Israel, the Kingdom of Yahweh (Romans 11).

The examples of eating things sacrificed to idols and committing acts of immorality are referring to not following the instructions from the

Holy Scriptures about how to live right. The mindset and teaching of Balaam for the Israelites then and born-again Israelites today says that we don't need to pay attention to the teaching of Moses because, after Yahshua the Messiah came and gave His life to pay our death sentence so we could be reconciled back to Father Yahweh, the teachings of Moses were then finished and done away with. Nothing could be farther from the truth. We cannot live like people of the world who do not know Yahshua. We are called to be set apart and different. We who are putting our complete trust in Yahshua and following the instruction that He gave to Moses in the *Torah* are, and will continue to be, labeled as mean-spirited, judgmental, Bible fanatics, and insane heretics. Yahshua followed His and our Heavenly Father's instructions being lead by His *Ruach HaKodesh*, and we are to follow in Yahshua's footsteps.

The promises here are that we will be given a white stone and on it written a new name that no one will know except the one who receives it. I believe this speaks to us of a new name our Creator and King will give to us when He establishes His kingdom on this earth at the end of the tribulation. In His new kingdom, we will have new names and positions that He will place us in according to the abilities He has given us for the purpose of assisting Him in the management of the earth during the Millennium.

The second promise in the preceding Scriptures indicates that there will be some overcomers during the tribulation time for whom He will provide food as He did for the more than one million Israelites during the forty years in the wilderness prior to their entering the promised land. Our promised land is the millennium kingdom and later the New Jerusalem. I believe there will be a group of people from all over the world that Father Yahweh has chosen to be divinely protected and provided for during the horrible time of the coming holocaust. It is written.

> So when the dragon *[Satan]* saw that he had been thrown down to earth, he pursed the woman *[Israel, those who accept Yahshua as Messiah]* who had given birth to the male child *[Yahshua]*. But the woman was given the two wings of the great eagle, so that she could fly from the serpent into the wilderness, to her place where she is nourished for a time, and times, and half a time *[three and one-half years]*.
> Revelation 12:13-14 (NRSV). *Bracketed words added for clarity.*

There is no doubt in my mind that the people chosen to be in that group will be completely surrendered to the will of Yahweh, in loving relationship with Him, and will be following His instructions (*Torah*). What are the modern-day prophets and preachers of today telling us about the end times? What about the many ministries that are teaching people the ridiculous doctrine of the pre-tribulation rapture, giving trusting believers false hope that they will not have to face the many challenges of the last three and one-half years of this age because they are going to be snatched away, leaving the Jews and unbelievers behind to deal with it all?These false teachings are absolute apostasy. They cause people to be deceived into assuming they have all of the answers they need from our Creator because they have not taken the time to study the truth as revealed in our only source of truth—all 66 books of the Holy Bible. Wake up, folks! It's way past time to come out of falsehood and into the truth. The truth will set you free.

The fourth letter:

"And to the angel of the church in Thyatira write, 'These things says the Son of God, who has eyes like a flame of fire [*eyes that can penetrate into the very spirit and soul of a person to determine not only thoughts, but even motives*], **and His feet like fine brass** [*in the Scriptures, brass represents judgment*]: "I know your works, love, service, faith, and your patience; and as for your works, the last are more than the first. Nevertheless I have a few things against you, because you allow that woman Jezebel, who calls herself a prophetess, to teach and seduce My servants to commit sexual immorality and eat things sacrificed to idols. And I gave her time to repent of her sexual immorality, and she did not repent. Indeed I will cast her into a sickbed, and those who commit adultery with her into great tribulation, unless they repent of their deeds. I will kill her children with death, and all the churches shall know that I am He who searches the minds and hearts. And I will give to each one of you according to your works. Now to you I say, and to the rest in Thyatira, as many as do not have this doctrine, who have not known the depths of Satan, as they say, I will put on you no other burden. But hold fast what you have till I come. And he who overcomes, and keeps My works until the end, to him I will give power over the nations—'He shall rule them with a rod of iron; they shall be dashed to pieces like the potter's vessels'—as I also have received from My Father; and I will give**

him the morning star. He who has an ear, let him hear what the Spirit says to the churches."'
Revelation 2:18-29 (NKJV). *Bracketed words added for clarity.*

The reproof here is all about following the ways of Jezebel, whose name means "where is the prince?" Jezebel was the daughter of the king of the Sidonians, which is now in the area of Lebanon. She married the king of Israel named Ahab, one of the worst rulers of ancient Israel during the time when the leaders and people were plunging head first into idolatry. The spirit of Jezebel is that of seduction. In Jezebel's case, she seduced Ahab to turn away from serving Almighty Yahweh and accepting the pagan gods of her people.

So Ahab worshiped Baal (which means *husband*) and built altars for worshiping Baal. He led the people into terrible idolatry and immoral practices. The spirit of Jezebel comes from Satan and wants to seduce all believers into accepting the wrong husband—not Yahshua, but Satan—and to fall for the deception and lies that Satan has infiltrated into the minds of people since creation. We are betrothed to our Bridegroom, Messiah Yahshua, and none other. Satan is setting the stage to deceive the whole world with his false prophet and his false bridegroom, the anti-Messiah.

We must have wisdom that comes from studying the Holy Scriptures and the revelation of the deep meanings that are revealed to us from the awesome power of Yahweh's Holy Spirit. Yahshua is saying that believers should not tolerate the lying spirit of Jezebel that has been prominent in the churches for 1,650 years. This spirit leads the servants of Yahweh astray, enticing them to commit acts of immorality and spiritual adultery by accepting and practicing false, man-initiated customs and traditions and not following the instructions that Father Yahweh gave in His *Torah*. If believers don't repent (turn away) from compromising with the humanistic belief systems of the world and committing spiritual adultery, as I described in detail in Chapter Five, *Satan's Plan of Deception After Messiah's First Coming,* we will be judged by our righteous judge Yahshua. For it is written:

"As I live, says the LORD, every knee shall bow to Me, and every tongue shall confess to God." So then each of us shall give account of himself to God.
Romans 14:11-12 (NKJV)

And I saw the dead, small and great, standing before God, and books were opened. And another book was opened, which is the Book of Life. And the dead were judged according to their works, by the things which were written in the books. And anyone not found written in the Book of Life was cast into the lake of fire.
Revelation 20:12, 15 (NKJV)

Dear reader, please hear me. You cannot afford to compromise the truth that is before you in Yahweh's Holy Word. All redeemed, born-again believers will be judged first. It is written:

For the time *has come* for judgment to begin at the house of God; and if *it begins* with us first, what will *be* the end of those who do not obey the gospel of God? Now *"If the righteous one is scarcely saved, where will the ungodly and the sinner appear?"*
1 Peter 4:17-18 (NKJV)

These examples—Nicolaitan, Balaam, and Jezebel—are showing us the lying deception of Satan, the father of lies. He has been and will continue to do everything within his ability to draw people away from the truth and from having a relationship with Yahweh/Yahshua.

In His promises from this letter, Master Yahshua encourages us to hold fast until He comes, and those who overcome will be given authority over the nations. This means that those who overcome will be given positions by Him to assist in governing the peoples of the world with Him when He establishes His kingdom here on earth during the thousand-year reign. He also promises to give us the morning star. This speaks to us of Holy Spirit pouring into us the light of understanding and revelation knowledge from the Word that equips us and empowers us to be overcomers. Yahshua gives us the light of His love so that, through us, His knowledge, love, and power shine forth into the darkness in this world. The morning star speaks to us of His power that He makes available to us to be His bondservants, to be obedient to His instructions, and to be effective ministers to others. As we draw nearer to Him in love, obedience, and respect, He draws nearer to us and blesses us with more of His power to do His work. The next chapter addresses these areas.

The fifth letter:

"And to the angel of the church in Sardis write, 'These things says He who has the seven Spirits of God [as described in Isaiah 11:2] **and the seven stars** [symbolic of many angels assigned to congregations world-wide]**: "I know your works, that you have a name that you are alive, but you are dead** [dead spiritually; asleep to knowing and living the truth]**. Be watchful, and strengthen the things which remain, that are ready to die, for I have not found your works perfect before God. Remember therefore how you have received and heard; hold fast and repent. Therefore if you will not watch, I will come upon you as a thief, and you will not know what hour I will come upon you. You have a few names even in Sardis who have not defiled their garments; and they shall walk with Me in white, for they are worthy. He who overcomes shall be clothed in white garments, and I will not blot out his name from the Book of Life; but I will confess his name before My Father and before His angels. He who has an ear, let him hear what the Spirit says to the churches."'**

Revelation 3:1-6 (NKJV). *Bracketed words added for clarity.*

The reproof here was for believers of the Sardis congregation then and for us today. Many, then and now, have the appearance of being right with Yahweh, but they are not. Many believe in Yahshua and believe that He is who He claimed to be, the Son of Yahweh. They think believing that and having their name on a church membership somewhere is all that is required of them to be a child of Yahweh. Yahshua has made it clear in His Word that in order to enter into His Kingdom, we must be born of His Spirit. The Spirit will then lead us to walk in His ways, for our faith must manifest into works of righteousness (right standing before Him). If we have no works of righteousness (fruit), our faith is a dead faith.

The Apostle Paul established all of the seven congregations in Asia Minor and taught the truth from the Holy Scriptures, or the *Tanak* (old testament), as it was called in his day. The letters Paul wrote to some of these congregations and to fellow bondservants who were spreading the good news about Yahshua, the Messiah, revealed that Paul's teaching and instruction were from the teaching of Moses as recorded in the *Torah*. It is written:

Do we then make void the law through faith? Certainly not! On the contrary, we establish the law [instructions].

Romans 3:31 (NKJV). *Bracketed words added for clarity.*

The writer is referring to the law, or instructions, that were given to Moses for the Israelites then and for us today. Yahweh does not change. The Apostle James, the half brother of Messiah, gave it to us this way:

> **What good is it, my brothers and sisters, if you say you have faith but do not have works? Can faith save you? If a brother or sister is naked and lacks daily food, and one of you says to them, "Go in peace; keep warm and eat your fill," and yet you do not supply their bodily needs, what is the good of that? So faith by itself, if it has no works, is dead. But someone will say, "You have faith and I have works." Show me your faith apart from your works, and I by my works will show you my faith. You believe that God is one; you do well. Even the demons believe— and shudder. Do you want to be shown, you senseless person, that faith apart from works is barren? Was not our ancestor Abraham justified by works when he offered his son Isaac on the altar? You see that faith was active along with his works, and faith was brought to completion by the works. You see that a person is justified by works and not by faith alone.**
> James 2:14-22, 24 (NRSV). *Bracketed words added for clarity.*

Our complete faith and trust in Yahshua does save us, but our testimony to the world that we are saved and in covenant relationship with the Creator of the universe is the kind of fruit we bear, as reflected by the good works we do to help our fellow man.

The congregation in Sardis had been taught well. They had received the truth and had been walking it out. They had, however, obviously fallen into apostasy and turned away from living according to the instructions that had been taught from the Word. Does that sound like many in churches today? There is much that should be taught from the instructions found in the *Torah* that would be beneficial to the growth of believers. Instead, we are taught that all of the *Torah* instruction (Law) has been done away with and that we don't need it. Many are taught that we should follow partial truth and pagan-influenced customs that have come down to us from 1,650 years of traditions that our Creator did not initiate. Yahshua, Who is the Living *Torah,* told the people of Sardis, through John's letter, to repent of falsehood and sin and to hold fast to the truth. This first reproof in this letter has the same message for us today.

In two places in this letter, Master Yahshua addresses being watchful and not watching. These verses are definitely prophetic and apply to this last generation. The two chapters of Matthew 24 and 25 are detailed instructions for us now in these end times to learn from the clues and to watch and discern the current events, so we can apply them in the proper context of the prophecies. King Yahshua said for us to watch for the signs of His coming to establish His Kingdom, to be about doing His will, and to know that prophecy is for us to help us. It is written:

"For the testimony of Jesus is the spirit of prophecy."
Revelation 19:10b (NKJV)

The second reproof is that if we do not watch, we will not be prepared when Messiah comes, and His coming will be like a thief. Once He begins heading from outer space, His coming will be quick, and there will not be time for people to prepare to meet Him when He arrives. The last three verses of the parable of the ten virgins sums this up very well. It is written:

"Afterward the other virgins came also, saying, 'Lord, Lord, open to us!' But he answered and said, 'Assuredly, I say to you, I do not know you.' Watch therefore, for you know neither the day nor the hour in which the Son of Man is coming [*this statement is to be taken literally and not in general, as in having no clue as to the timing because we do according to other Scriptures throughout the Word, such as 2 Thess. 2:1-4 and 1 Thess. 1:3-11*].
Matthew 25:11-13 (NKJV). *Bracketed words added for clarity.*

The five foolish virgins were out trying to buy oil for their lamps that they carelessly had let run out, and while they were gone, the Bridegroom came. What is this oil that the five foolish virgins had to go out to try to obtain? It is the deep, intimate relationship with Him that can only come from constant communication with Him and loving Him with all of your heart, soul, and strength, and by following His commandment instructions. It is written:

"Hear, O Israel: The LORD our God, the LORD *is* one! You shall love the LORD your God with all your heart, with all your soul, and with all your strength. And these words which I command you today shall be in your heart. You shall teach them diligently to your children, and shall

**talk of them when you sit in your house, when you walk by the way,
when you lie down, and when you rise up. You shall bind them as a sign
on your hand, and they shall be as frontlets between your eyes. You shall
write them on the doorposts of your house and on your gates."**
Deuteronomy 6:4-9 (NKJV)

Obeying His commandments means keeping the weekly Sabbath, His
seven annual set-apart feast times, eating only the foods that He has
instructed to eat according to His Word, and dealing properly with the
issues of blood. It's all in His Holy Scriptures. They are to be on our minds
each day all during the day as *Ruach HaKodesh* leads us in following
them. The choice is ours as to whether we want to choose life and receive
His blessings, or death and curses. I will choose life and blessings anytime
I have a choice because I love Yahshua, and I want to please Him, even if
that decision causes people I love not to be pleased with me. It is okay
because I know Who my Creator, Savior, Master, King, Judge, and best
Friend is. I encourage you to prepare for Yahshua's coming by having the
oil you need in your lamp, so that when He arrives you won't hear, "Truly,
I tell you, I don't know you."

The acknowledgment and promise in this letter to the church at Sardis
is that there were a few in Sardis who had not defiled their garments and
that they would walk with Messiah, for they were worthy. Again, He is
telling us that those who overcome shall be clothed in white garments and
that He will not blot out their names (nor ours) from the Book of Life. He
will confess our name before Father Yahweh and His holy angels.

Among the great masses of people living on the earth in this last
generation, only a small percentage will be willing to receive this
profound message of true love, restoration, warning, and promised hope.
The reason is because it requires making changes in a person's relationship with our Creator and in the way a person lives. I believe that every
human being's name has been written in Master Yahshua's Book of Life
since before the foundation of the universe. It's tragically sad that many
will not choose life and keep their names in the Master's Book for all
eternity. We have the free will to choose Yahshua (Jesus) as our Savior
and not leave this life unredeemed right up until we draw our last breath.
If we are truly born of Almighty Yah's Holy Spirit, we will be secure and
will not give in to a false belief system because we cannot lose our salvation once we are sealed. The Apostle Paul instructs us to be thoroughly

persuaded in our belief and walk. It is up to us individually to stay true to our calling and know that our names will not be blotted out from His Book of Life as we prepare to stand before His judgment that every person will experience.

I am committed to keeping my name in His Book of Life, and I so look forward to the day when my great Intercessor and High Priest confesses my name before Father Yahweh and His angels. Are you prepared to meet face to face with the Creator of the universe and the Judge of all of the human beings that will have ever lived on this planet? This is more important than there are words to properly convey. If you are not prepared, now is an excellent time to start while you still can. None of us has a guarantee that we will wake up tomorrow morning in this world.

The references of white garments speak to us of saints taking responsibility for their walk with Almighty Yahweh and purifying ourselves by being submissive to the leading of Holy Spirit and the washing of minds with the supernatural Holy Word of God. White garments or robes are symbolic of our righteous actions and right standing in our relationship with our Creator Yahweh/Yahshua. It is written:

> And he said, "Go *your way* Daniel, for the words *are* closed up and sealed till the time of the end. Many shall be purified, made white, and refined, but the wicked shall do wickedly; and none of the wicked shall understand, but the wise *[virgins dressed in white garments with the right oil]* shall understand.
> Daniel 12:9-10 (NKJV). *Bracketed words added for clarity.*

> Then one of the elders addressed me, saying, "Who are these, robed in white, and where have they come from?" I said to him, "Sir, you are the one that knows." Then he said to me, "These are they who have come out of the great ordeal *[the tribulation that believers who are alive at that time will overcome]*; they have washed their robes and made them white in the blood of the Lamb.
> Revelation 7:13-14 (NRSV). *Bracketed words added for clarity.*

This is more important than you taking your American Express Card with you as you leave for a trip. Do you have the right oil for your lamp, and do you have garments that you have washed in the blood of the Lamb and by the water of His Holy Word? Don't leave this life without them.

The sixth letter:

> **"And to the angel of the church in Philadelphia write, 'These things says He who is holy, He who is true, _"He who has the key of David, He who opens and no one shuts, and shuts and no one opens"_: I know your works. See, I have set before you an open door, and no one can shut it; for you have a little strength** _[small in number]_**, have kept My word** _[those who keep Yahweh's commandments and His ordinances]_**, and have not denied My name** _[I believe this is referring to the sanctified, restored name of Father Yahweh and His name, Yahshua, that He was given when He was born into the human race to become the salvation from Yah]_**. Indeed I will make** _those_ **of the synagogue of Satan, who say they are Jews and are not, but lie—indeed I will make them come and worship before your feet, and to know that I have loved you. Because you have kept My command to persevere** _[overcome]_**, I also will keep you from the hour of trial which shall come upon the whole world, to test those who dwell on the earth. Behold, I am coming quickly! Hold fast what you have, that no one may take your crown. He who overcomes, I will make him a pillar in the temple of My God, and he shall go out no more. And I will write on him the name of My God and the name of the city of My God, the New Jerusalem, which comes down out of heaven from My God. And** _I will write on him_ **My new name. He who has an ear, let him hear what the Spirit says to the churches."**
>
> Revelation 3:7-13 (NKJV). _Bracketed words added for clarity._

There is no reproof in this letter, only positive commendations, hidden instructions, and great promises. Master Yahshua is the only One Who is holy and true. The key that David had was the knowledge of understanding the ways of Father Yahweh and the wisdom of living in His ways. It is written:

> **Oh, how I love Your law** _[Torah instructions]_**! It** _is_ **my meditation all the day.**
>
> Psalm 119:97 (NKJV). _Bracketed words added for clarity._

King Yahshua certainly has the key of David because He is the only One who has ever lived perfectly the will of Father Yahweh by being completely obedient to all of the instructions that were given to Moses and following all of Father Yahweh's instructions as He heard by Holy Spirit. He is the only One Who could qualify as the Perfect Lamb of God. Master Yahshua has all power and authority in opening and closing doors, which is referring to the doors of His kingdom. I am committed to be a part of this small group of believers because King Yahshua has promised them an open door into His kingdom that no person, demon, or Satan himself has the ability to prevent from happening. Also, this small group is promised protection and provision during the three and a half years of the great tribulation period.

Our King and Judge, Yahshua, knows our works, how we have followed His instructions found in His Holy Scriptures, and if we have not denied His holy name. For the second time, He addresses those of the synagogue of Satan and says that He will make those who say they are Jews and are not, but lie, to come and worship at the feet of this small remnant, and that He will make known His love for them.

To break this down, let's define who a Jew is as explained in the Scriptures. This is not referring to the people group who are the bloodline descendants of Judah or Levi, but rather those who have been birthed by Father Yahweh's Holy Spirit and have been given new hearts, even if they are not of Jewish descent. I refer you to John Chapter Three with the understanding that in verse 36, *believe* means *to obey*. It is written:

Whoever believes in the Son has eternal life; whoever disobeys the Son will not see life, but must endure God's wrath.
John 3:36 (NRSV)

For he is not a Jew who *is one* outwardly, nor *is* circumcision that which *is* outward in the flesh; but *he is* a Jew who *is one* inwardly, and circumcision *is that* of the heart, in the Spirit, not in the letter; whose praise *is* not from men but from God.
Romans 2:28-29 (NKJV)

What I believe is being taught here is that there are people who truly believe they are living right. They are going to places of worship to worship, pray, and give of themselves, but they are not in the right relationship with Almighty Yah. Throughout history, the greatest persecutions have come from religious people who believed they were in right relationship with the one true God but were not. Yahshua was sought out, lied about, condemned, and put to death because of the actions of religious people who thought they were in right relationship with our Creator. I state this as an example because we know that we all were responsible for His death because we all have committed sin and are all in desperate need of a savior. No one took His life from Him; He laid it down of His own free will as a gift to pay our death penalty. The Jews whom Yahshua refers to in verse nine of Chapter Three and verse nine of Chapter Two are those in this last generation who have an outward appearance of being pious and right with Yahweh but are not. I believe that some from this group will be the very ones who will bring much persecution to those who are of the small group that keep the commandments of Yahweh, do not deny His name, and will not accept the mark or the name of the beast.

Yahshua continues on to say to the church in Philadelphia that:

> **"Because you have kept My command to persevere** [*a better translation is, "have guarded My Word of endurance"*]**, I will also keep** [*guard*] **you from the hour of trial which shall come upon the whole world, to test those who dwell on the earth."**
> Revelation 3:10 (NKJV). *Bracketed words added for clarity.*

Let's look closer at the word "from" in verse ten. In the *Companion Bible,* edited by E.W. Bullinger from the *1611 Authorized Version of the King James Bible*, is an exhaustive Appendix. The late Mr. Bullinger was a leading Hebrew and Greek scholar of his era who devoted much of his life's work in producing the *Companion Bible,* which is an excellent resource for breaking down words used in the original manuscripts for better understanding. The word "from" as used in Revelation 3:10 is from the Greek word *ek*, which means *out from* with an immediate origin, as regarding something or someone that is within. The Greek word that means *away from* as in *not present at all*, is the word *apo* and was not the word the Apostle John used in this verse. The best analogy I can think of to use to convey the proper understanding of this as it applies to this important promise in this letter to the elect is the account of the three Hebrew men who would not bow down and worship the false god image that King Nebuchadnezzar had set up and commanded everyone to worship. The penalty for anyone not following the king's orders was that they would be thrown into a furnace of fire to be burned. As it is written:

Wherefore at that time certain Chaldeans came near, and accused the Jews. They spake and said to the king Nebuchadnezzar, O king, live for ever. Thou, O king, hast made a decree, that every man that shall hear the sound of the cornet, flute, harp, sackbut, psaltery, and dulcimer, and all kinds of musick, shall fall down and worship the golden image: And whoso falleth not down and worshippeth, that he should be cast into the midst of a burning fiery furnace. There are certain Jews whom thou hast set over the affairs of the province of Babylon, Shadrach, Meshach, and Abednego; these men, O king, have not regarded thee: they serve not thy gods, nor worship the golden image which thou hast set up. Then Nebuchadnezzar in his rage and fury commanded to bring Shadrach, Meshach, and Abednego. Then they brought these men before the king. Nebuchadnezzar spake and said unto them, Is it true, O Shadrach, Meshach, and Abednego, do not ye serve my gods, nor worship the golden image which I have set up? Now if ye be ready that at what time ye hear the sound of the cornet, flute, harp, sackbut, psaltery, and dulcimer, and all kinds of musick, ye fall down and worship the image which I have made; well: but if ye worship not, ye shall be cast the same hour into the midst of a burning fiery furnace; and who is that God that shall deliver you out of my hands? Shadrach, Meshach, and Abednego, answered and said to the king, O Nebuchadnezzar, we are not careful to answer thee in this matter. If it be so, our God whom we serve is able to deliver us from the burning fiery furnace, and he will deliver us out of thine hand, O king. But if not, be it known unto thee, O king, that we will not serve thy gods, nor worship the golden image which thou hast set up. Then was Nebuchadnezzar full of fury, and the form of his visage was changed against Shadrach, Meshach, and Abednego: therefore he spake, and commanded that they should heat the furnace one seven times more than it was wont to be heated. And he commanded the most mighty men that were in his army to bind Shadrach, Meshach, and Abednego, and to cast them into the burning fiery furnace. Then these men were bound in their coats, their hosen, and their hats, and their other garments, and were cast into the midst of the burning fiery furnace. Therefore because the king's commandment was urgent, and the furnace exceeding hot, the flame of the fire slew those men that took up Shadrach, Meshach, and Abednego. And these three men, Shadrach, Meshach, and Abednego, fell down bound into the midst of the burning fiery furnace. Then Nebuchadnezzar the king was astonished, and rose up in haste, and spake, and said unto his counsellors, Did not we cast three men bound into the midst of the fire? They answered and said unto the king, True, O king. He answered and said, Lo, I see four men loose, walking in the midst of the fire, and they have no hurt; and the form of the fourth is like the Son of God. Then Nebuchadnezzar came near to the mouth of the burning fiery furnace, and spake, and said, Shadrach, Meshach, and Abednego, ye servants of the most high God, come forth, and come hither. Then Shadrach, Meshach, and Abednego, came forth of the midst of the fire. And the princes, governors, and captains, and the king's counsellors, being gathered together, saw these men, upon whose bodies the fire had no power, nor was an hair of their head singed, neither were their coats changed, nor the smell of fire had passed on them. Then Nebuchadnezzar spake, and said, Blessed be the God of Shadrach, Meshach, and Abednego, who hath sent his angel, and delivered his servants that trusted in him, and have changed the king's word, and yielded their bodies, that they might not serve nor worship any god, except their own God. Therefore I make a decree, That every people, nation, and language, which speak any thing amiss against the God of Shadrach, Meshach, and Abednego, shall be cut in pieces, and their houses shall be made a dunghill: because there is no other God that can deliver after this sort. Then the king promoted Shadrach, Meshach, and Abednego, in the province of Babylon.

Daniel 3:8-30 (KJV)

From this Scripture analogy and a better understanding of the words found in the original manuscripts, we glean a better understanding of the text, which in my paraphrase reads as follows. *Because you have kept the word of my patience, which ties back to verse 8 regarding keeping His instructions and not denying His name, I (Yahshua) will guard (protect) you within or through the hour of temptation, that is the three and one-half years of great tribulation, which shall come upon all the world, to try them that dwell upon the earth.*

Another Scriptural analogy that would apply is the account of the great flood and the protection through the great destruction of the human race by flood of Noah, his family, and the pairs of all the animals that were on the ark.

What an awesome promise for the group of believers who will not accept the mark, name, and system of the beast, anti-Messiah, during the last years of this age, and who will be protected and given provision from our Master because He knows their works.

King Yahshua goes on in His letter to the church in Philadelphia to give the instruction to hold fast, to hold on tightly to His promises and continue following Him as they have, so that no one will be able to cause them to fall into apostasy and loose their crown, as many of the professing believers who are not saved will do when that most difficult time of testing comes. Here is further confirmation as it is written:

> "And now I am no longer in the world, but they are in the world, and I am coming to you. Holy Father, protect them in your name that you have given me, so that they may be one, as we are one. While I was with them, I protected them in your name that you have given me. I guarded them, and not one of them was lost except the one destined to be lost, so that the scripture might be fulfilled. But now I am coming to you, and I speak these things in the world so that they may have my joy made complete in themselves. I have given them your word, and the world has hated them because they do not belong to the world, just as I do not belong to the world. I am not asking you to take them out of the world, but I ask you to protect them from the evil one. They do not belong to the world, just as I do not belong to the world. Sanctify them in the truth; your word is truth. As you have sent me into the world, so I have sent them into the world. And for their sakes I sanctify myself, so that they also may be sanctified in truth. I ask not only on behalf of these, but also on behalf of those who will believe in me through their word, that they may all be one. As you, Father, are in me and I am in you, may they also be in us, so that the world may believe that you have sent me. The glory that you have given me I have given them, so that they may be one, as we are one, I in them and you in me, that they may become completely one, so that the world may know that you have sent me and have loved them even as you have loved me. Father, I desire that those also, whom you have given me, may be with me where I am, to see my glory, which you have given me because you loved me before the foundation of the world. Righteous Father, the world does not know you, but I know you; and these know that you have sent me. I made your name *[What name? The name Yahweh, not God]* known to them, and I will make it known, so that the love with which you have loved me may be in them, and I in them."

John 17:11-25 (NRSV). *Bracketed words added for clarity.*

As we read this, we comprehend two important prayer requests that our Master Yahshua is making on our behalf. First, He is asking our Heavenly Father to protect us in the name that Father Yahweh gave Him. What name is that? *Yahshua* (also *Yahushua* or *Yeshua*) that is now being restored to the people of this last generation after being poorly translated and hidden for the past 1,670 years by Constantine Christianity.

Second, Master Yahshua is asking that we be sanctified, meaning *to be set apart in the truth*. What truth? The truth that is revealed from the Scriptures, from all of the Scriptures, not just the New Testament. This ties us back to Revelation 3:8b, *"... for you have little strength, have kept My word, and have not denied My name."* What word? The instructions of the *Torah*, the first five books that Moses wrote. What name? The name of the One Who has been granted all power and authority in heaven and on earth, the name of Yahshua, the Messiah.

I encourage you to read Chapter Four again so you can refresh your understanding of how great deception was established within humanity by Nimrod, first Emperor of the first world empire. Nimrod, his wife, and their son established the false belief system of sun god worship and elevated themselves as gods that were worshiped by the people in their kingdom.

This process continued down through the centuries and had huge significance when the emperor, Constantine, initiated the formation of the Church of Rome. The Church of Rome created a new belief system that was and is different from that of the first-century Apostles and early believers in Yahshua. Satan was successful in creating this new belief system, which was a mix of paganism from the Roman Empire blended with the Way of the Nazarenes, the true followers of Messiah. The end result was that people were being forced into accepting and following the dictates of this new empire-administrated belief system, or they would suffer persecution and often death. Everything associated with Messianic Judaism was abolished, including the keeping of the Sabbath, dietary instructions, and Father Yahweh's seven annual feasts. The people were brainwashed into believing that they were following the proper instructions from the Holy Scriptures when, in actuality, they were following the false teachings of egotistical men (spirits of Nicolaitans, Balaam, and Jezebel) who were empowering themselves in order to have control over the masses.

Today, most believers are swimming in a sea of ignorance of not knowing what the true instructions from Father Yahweh are in order to be able to be obedient. Most believers, when presented with these biblical truths, respond with comments like, "It doesn't matter because all of that Old Testament stuff was nailed to the cross, and it doesn't apply to us now," or, "That's legalistic; you're trying to be saved by works." What was nailed to the cross was humanity's death sentence, the consequence of not following the instructions of *Torah*, that no one could keep perfectly except Yahshua, and the instructions for animal sacrifices because there was and is no longer a need for them. Being *Torah* observant does not save anyone. We do it because Almighty Yah has instructed us to do so, and we love Him and want to be obedient. He prefers our obedience to His instructions more than our sacrifices that we make to Him. It is written:

> **And Samuel said, "Has the LORD as great delight in burnt-offerings and sacrifices, as in obeying the voice of the LORD? Surely, to obey is better than sacrifice, and to heed than the fat of rams. For rebellion is no less a sin than divination [witchcraft], and stubbornness is like iniquity and idolatry. Because you have rejected the word of the LORD, he has also rejected you from being king."**
> 1 Samuel 15:22-23a (NRSV). *Bracketed words added for clarity.*

We have all been deceived and have blindly followed the traditions of man that are not scriptural because that is what everybody else is doing, and that is the way we have always done it all the way back 1,670 years ago. Until the year 2001, I had not understood anything about the importance of keeping the true Sabbath, the Feasts, and the other instructions found in Yah's *Torah*. I had never been taught the truth about these significant subjects from the pulpits in churches or from anywhere else.

Heavenly Father, in the name of your Son, Yahshua, please help us to wake up and come out of our stupor and repent of our sins and shortcomings. Help us to be led by your Holy Spirit to follow Your instructions that we have missed all these years and be prepared to receive your protection during the great tribulation time. Amen.

The truth has been presented to you. The choice is yours. What you are learning from this book that has been compiled from much study and research is vital for you and your loved ones.

According to the revelation within the Scriptures, Father Yahweh has planned another great exodus for His people, except the next one will be even greater and more amazing than the first that is recorded in the Book of Exodus. Just prior to the last three and one-half years of the great tribulation and prior to King Yahshua's return, there will be what has become known as the second great exodus, or greater exodus. Just as with the first exodus led by Moses approximately 3,400 years ago, Father Yahweh will provide divine protection and provision for the end-time, born-again Messianic Israelites. I have included a section toward the end of this chapter about the second (greater) exodus that ties in with this letter from Master Yahshua to the Church in Philadelphia.

Dear reader, I am committed to being under Father Yahweh's protection. Don't you want to make sure that you and your family and friends are protected when the end time events of the Day of the Lord as described in Scriptures begin to happen?

Our Master Yahshua promises protection and provision through the great tribulation to those who are overcomers, and our reward is that He will make each one a pillar in the temple of His Elohim; he shall go out no more. And he will write on him the name of His Elohim and the name of the city of His Elohim, the New Jerusalem, which comes down out of heaven. This is our promised land that we are marching toward. He will write on His remnant His new name. These are marriage covenant words conveying Messiah's bride receiving His name and Father Yahweh's name and receiving a new permanent home. Our new home is not in heaven because King Yahshua is coming to this earth to establish His kingdom. I believe much about our new home has to do with our new resurrected bodies that we will live in, not some mansion on a hill. It is written:

> **"Let not your heart be troubled; you believe in God, believe also in Me. In My Father's house are many mansions** [spiritual dwelling places]**; if it were not so, I would have told you. I go to prepare a place for you. And if I go and prepare a place for you, I will come again and receive you to Myself; that where I am, there you may be also. ... I will not leave you orphans; I will come to you. A little while longer and the world will see Me no more, but you will see Me. Because I live, you will live also. At that day you will know that I am in My Father, and you in Me, and I in you. He who has My commandments and keeps them, it is he who loves Me. And he who loves Me will be loved by My Father, and I will love him and manifest Myself to him."**
>
> John 14:1-3; 18-21 (NKJV). *Bracketed words added for clarity.*

Being born of Father Yahweh's Holy Spirit, putting our complete faith and trust in Master Yahshua, keeping His Sabbaths, His Feasts, His *Torah* instructions, and carrying His name sets us apart from the rest of the world. All that we do and believe must be done in pure love for Him and all people, especially our brethren. With the one true God of Abraham, Isaac, and Jacob, all things are possible. HalleluYah!

The seventh letter:

"And to the angel of the church of the Laodiceans write, 'These things says the Amen, the Faithful and True Witness, the Beginning of the creation of God: "I know your works, that you are neither cold nor hot. I could wish you were cold or hot. So then, because you are lukewarm, and neither cold nor hot, I will vomit you out of My mouth. Because you say, 'I am rich, have become wealthy, and have need of nothing'— and do not know that you are wretched, miserable, poor, blind, and naked—I counsel you to buy from Me gold refined in the fire, that you may be rich; and white garments, that you may be clothed, *that* **the shame of your nakedness may not be revealed; and anoint your eyes with eye salve, that you may see. As many as I love, I rebuke and chasten. Therefore be zealous and repent. Behold, I stand at the door and knock. If anyone hears My voice and opens the door, I will come in to him and dine with him, and he with Me. To him who overcomes I will grant to sit with Me on My throne, as I also overcame and sat down with My Father on His throne. He who has an ear, let him hear what the Spirit says to the churches."'"**
Revelation 3:14-22 (NKJV)

There are no words of commendation in this last letter from Master Yahshua, as is found in the other six letters—commendations, warnings, and promises that have been for believers who have lived throughout the generations gone by, as well as those of us living now and until He returns. If you are a believer, this letter describes a sad state to be in. I know because I have been in a backslidden condition of professing to be a follower of Jesus (as I called Him at that time), but yet looked and acted like people in the world who are lost with no knowledge of Father Yahweh's master plan of redeeming mankind through the holy blood of Messiah Yahshua. I wanted to party and chase the buzz, but I wanted also to be looked upon in the community and in the eyes of the pious church folks as living right, at least by the standards that I perceived were in the church during that part of my faith journey. I was trying to straddle the fence, attempting to have one foot in Yah's Kingdom and one foot in the world, which leads to death and eternal separation from Almighty Yah's Kingdom. What a hypocrite I was. I had deceived myself into believing that my lifestyle and relationship with my Savior was okay. I believed in Jesus and was saved because I know I had been born again, but I had not made Him Master of my life.

In 1993, after years of living a double standard, Holy Spirit rocked my world down to the core of my foundation. He was not going to give up on me; it was time for me to get on His program. I wept as I realized how much I must have hurt the heart of Almighty Yah and grieved Holy Spirit by being rebellious and pursuing my self-centered way. I realized that part of the reason I was living the double-standard lifestyle was that I had not received the right teaching at the church I attended. I had not thought for myself, nor had I really studied Yah's Word to reap the wisdom from it.

Dear reader, you may be in a similar lukewarm state of relationship with our Creator, Savior, Master, and Judge of our souls. Oh, what a horrible state to be in. It is a matter of life and death. We must repent and separate ourselves from sin and the ways of the world, even from the appearance of sin. Satan will do everything he can to keep you from the truth that includes following all of Father Yahweh's instructions as given by His Son, The Word, Yahshua, the Living *Torah*. Please, dear reader, if you have a lukewarm relationship with Jesus (Yahshua) and have not made Him Master of your life to the point that you are willing to do whatever it takes to know that you are in His perfect will, then stop and humble yourself before Him. Ask Him to help you get your relationship with Him right so that you can live in His complete peace, His *shalom*.

Oh, how easy it is to be deceived by the adversary into justifying the sins and lifestyles that pull us away from truth and our dear and precious Bridegroom. Satan has been very successful at manipulating humans into creating thousands of false belief systems. They are like deadly, enticing lures for the mind to pursue in the quest for greater understanding of what life is all about, what happens after death, and what the purpose is for us being here. All false belief systems are about deception and delusion designed to keep us from reaching our full potential by being empowered by our awesome Creator. This includes the false teachings that are thoroughly woven within the more than 1,600 denominations of Christianity. You learned from Chapter Four of this book how falsehood and deception were implanted into the minds of the early believers after the Apostles of the first two centuries passed away. The Messianic Judaism that was established by Yahshua Himself began to be transformed into a Greek-Roman mix of beliefs that surfaced as an entirely new belief system based on a salvation-by-works bureaucracy called the Roman Catholic (universal) Church. As I have taught throughout this book, the belief system that Constantine and his early church fathers established as the Church of Rome was nothing like the first-century congregation of Messianic Nazarenes called "the Way."

Almighty Yahweh desires that human beings, created in His likeness, come out of the ways of the flesh and the ways of mixing false beliefs with His truth. He is a jealous Elohim and requires that His children be on His program and none other. It is written:

> **But know this, that in the last days perilous times will come: For men will be lovers of themselves, lovers of money, boasters, proud, blasphemers, disobedient to parents, unthankful, unholy, unloving, unforgiving, slanderers, without self-control, brutal, despisers of good, traitors, headstrong, haughty, lovers of pleasure rather than lovers of God, having a form of godliness but denying its power. And from such people turn away! For of this sort are those who creep into households and make captives of gullible women loaded down with sins, led away by various lusts, always learning and never able to come to the knowledge of the truth. Now as Jannes and Jambres resisted Moses, so do these also resist the truth: men of corrupt minds, disapproved concerning the faith; but they will progress no further, for their folly will be manifest to all, as theirs also was. ... But evil men and impostors will grow worse and worse, deceiving and being deceived.**
> 2 Timothy 3:1-9, 13 (NKJV)

> **"Now the parable is this: The seed is the word of God. Those by the wayside are the ones who hear; then the devil comes and takes away the word out of their hearts, lest they should believe and be saved. But the ones on the rock are those who, when they hear, receive the word with joy; and these have no root, who believe for a while and in time of temptation fall away. Now the ones that fell among thorns are those**

who, when they have heard, go out and are choked with cares, riches, and pleasures of life, and bring no fruit to maturity. But the ones *that* fell on the good ground are those who, having heard the word with a noble and good heart, keep *it* and bear fruit with patience.

Luke 8:11-15 (NKJV)

What is the condition of the soil of your heart? It is written:

But there were also false prophets among the people, even as there will be false teachers among you, who will secretly bring in destructive heresies, even denying the Lord who bought them, *and* bring on themselves swift destruction. And many will follow their destructive ways, because of whom the way of truth will be blasphemed. By covetousness they will exploit you with deceptive words; for a long time their judgment has not been idle, and their destruction does not slumber. For if God did not spare the angels who sinned, but cast *them* down to hell and delivered *them* into chains of darkness, to be reserved for judgment; and did not spare the ancient world, but saved Noah, *one of* eight *people*, a preacher of righteousness, bringing in the flood on the world of the ungodly; and turning the cities of Sodom and Gomorrah into ashes, condemned *them* to destruction, making *them* an example to those who afterward would live ungodly; and delivered righteous Lot, *who was* oppressed by the filthy conduct of the wicked [for that righteous man, dwelling among them, tormented *his* righteous soul from day to day by seeing and hearing *their* lawless deeds]— *then* the Lord knows how to deliver the godly out of temptations and to reserve the unjust under punishment for the day of judgment, and especially those who walk according to the flesh in the lust of uncleanness and despise authority. *They are* presumptuous, self-willed. They are not afraid to speak evil of dignitaries, whereas angels, who are greater in power and might, do not bring a reviling accusation against them before the Lord. But these, like natural brute beasts made to be caught and destroyed, speak evil of the things they do not understand, and will utterly perish in their own corruption, *and* will receive the wages of unrighteousness, as those who count it pleasure to carouse in the daytime. *They are* spots and blemishes, carousing in their own deceptions while they feast with you, having eyes full of adultery and that cannot cease from sin, enticing unstable souls. *They have* a heart trained in covetous practices, *and are* accursed children.

They have forsaken the right way and gone astray, following the way of Balaam *[remember, Balaam was the prophet who was responsible for recommending the plan for the Israelites to go out and marry women from the tribes that worshipped false gods and as a result the some of the nation of Israel mixed true worship and relationship with Yahweh and that of the false gods that fiercely angered Yahweh]* **the** *son* **of Beor, who loved the wages of unrighteousness; but he was rebuked for his iniquity: a dumb donkey speaking with a man's voice restrained the madness of the prophet. These are wells without water, clouds carried by a tempest, for whom is reserved the blackness of darkness forever. For when they speak great swelling** *words* **of emptiness, they allure through the lusts of the flesh, through lewdness, the ones who have actually escaped from those who live in error. While they promise them liberty, they themselves are slaves of corruption; for by whom a person is overcome, by him also he is brought into bondage. For if, after they have escaped the pollutions of the world through the knowledge of the Lord and Savior Jesus Christ, they are again entangled in them and overcome, the latter end is worse for them than the beginning. For it would have been better for them not to have known the way of righteousness, than having known it, to turn from the holy commandment delivered to them. But it has happened to them according to the true proverb:** *"A dog returns to his own vomit,"* **and, "a sow, having washed, to her wallowing in the mire."**

2 Peter 2 (NKJV). *Bracketed words added for clarity.*

If then you were raised with Christ, seek those things which are above, where Christ is, sitting at the right hand of God. Set your mind on things above, not on things on the earth. For you died, and your life is hidden with Christ in God. When Christ *who is* **our life appears, then you also will appear with Him in glory. Therefore put to death your members which are on the earth: fornication, uncleanness, passion, evil desire, and covetousness, which is idolatry. Because of these things the wrath of God is coming upon the sons of disobedience, in which you yourselves once walked when you lived in them. But now you yourselves are to put off all these: anger, wrath, malice, blasphemy, filthy language out of your mouth. Do not lie to one another, since you have put off the old man with his deeds, and have put on the new** *man* **who is renewed in knowledge according to the image of Him who created him, where there is neither Greek nor Jew, circumcised nor uncircumcised, barbarian, Scythian, slave**

nor free, but Christ *is* all and in all. Therefore, as *the* elect of God, holy and beloved, put on tender mercies, kindness, humility, meekness, long-suffering; bearing with one another, and forgiving one another, if anyone has a complaint against another; even as Christ forgave you, so you also *must do.* But above all these things put on love, which is the bond of perfection. And let the peace of God rule in your hearts, to which also you were called in one body; and be thankful. Let the word of Christ dwell in you richly in all wisdom, teaching and admonishing one another in psalms and hymns and spiritual songs, singing with grace in your hearts to the Lord. And *whatever* you do in word or deed, *do* all in the name of the Lord Jesus, giving thanks to God the Father through Him.

Colossians 3:1-17 (NKJV)

Say to your brethren, 'My people,' and to your sisters, 'Mercy *is shown.'* "Bring charges against your mother, bring charges; for she *is* not My wife, nor *am* I her Husband! Let her put away her harlotries *[spiritual adultery; pursuing falsehood]* from her sight, and her adulteries from between her breasts; lest I strip her naked and expose her, as in the day she was born, and make her like a wilderness, and set her like a dry land, and slay her with thirst. I will not have mercy on her children, for they *are* the children of harlotry. ... She decked herself with her earrings and jewelry, and went after her lovers; but Me she forgot," says the LORD.

Hosea 2:1-4, 13b (NKJV). *Bracketed words added for clarity.*

As you therefore have received Christ Jesus the Lord, so walk in Him, rooted and built up in Him and established in the faith, as you have been taught, abounding in it with thanksgiving. Beware lest anyone cheat you through philosophy and empty deceit, according to the tradition of men, according to the basic principles of the world, and not according to Christ. For in Him dwells all the fullness of the Godhead bodily; and you are complete in Him, who is the head of all principality and power.

Colossians 2:6-10 (NKJV)

I will finish this important run of Scriptures with words from our Master Yahshua's lips that make it crystal clear that we are to remove ourselves from the ways of this world and falsehood.

It is written:

"Enter by the narrow gate; for wide *is* the gate and broad *is* the way that leads to destruction, and there are many who go in by it. Because narrow *is* the gate and difficult *is* the way which leads to life, and there are few who find it. Beware of false prophets, who come to you in sheep's clothing, but inwardly they are ravenous wolves. You will know them by their fruits. Do men gather grapes from thornbushes or figs from thistles? Even so, every good tree bears good fruit, but a bad tree bears bad fruit. A good tree cannot bear bad fruit, nor *can* a bad tree bear good fruit. Every tree that does not bear good fruit is cut down and thrown into the fire. Therefore by their fruits you will know them. Not everyone who says to Me, 'Lord, Lord,' shall enter the kingdom of heaven, but he who does the will of My Father in heaven. Many will say to Me in that day, 'Lord, Lord, have we not prophesied in Your name, cast out demons in Your name, and done many wonders in Your name?' And then I will declare to them, 'I never knew you; depart from Me, you who practice lawlessness!' *[not practicing the laws and instructions found in the Torah.]* Therefore whoever hears these sayings of Mine, and does them, I will liken him to a wise man who built his house on the rock: and the rain descended, the floods came, and the winds blew and beat on that house; and it did not fall, for it was founded on the rock. But everyone who hears these sayings of Mine, and does not do them, will be like a foolish man who built his house on the sand: and the rain descended, the floods came, and the winds blew and beat on that house; and it fell. And great was its fall."

Matthew 7:13-27 (NKJV). *Bracketed words added for clarity.*

From an angel that spoke to the Apostle John during his revelation concerning the second coming of Messiah Yahshua, it is written:

After these things I saw another angel coming down from heaven, having great authority, and the earth was illuminated with his glory. And he cried mightily with a loud voice, saying, "Babylon the great is fallen, is fallen, and has become a dwelling place of demons, a prison for every foul spirit, and a cage for every unclean and hated bird! For all the nations have drunk of the wine of the wrath of her fornication, the kings of the earth have committed fornication with her, and the merchants of the earth have become rich through the abundance of her luxury." And I heard another voice from heaven saying, "Come out of

her, my people, lest you share in her sins, and lest you receive of her plagues. For her sins have reached to heaven, and God has remembered her iniquities. Render to her just as she rendered to you, and repay her double according to her works; in the cup which she has mixed, mix double for her. In the measure that she glorified herself and lived luxuriously, in the same measure give her torment and sorrow; for she says in her heart, 'I sit *as* queen, and am no widow, and will not see sorrow.' Therefore her plagues will come in one day—death and mourning and famine. And she will be utterly burned with fire, for strong *is* the Lord God who judges her.
Revelation 18:1-8 (NKJV)

This run of connecting Scriptures shows the identification of actions that people do in the flesh that are wrong and the reality of people committing spiritual adultery by embracing false belief systems even in what is today known as the Christian church. Remember, all of these seven letters in Revelation were addressed by Master Yahshua to the called-out assemblies of believers who were alive at the time the Apostle John wrote down and sent the letters, but they were also to believers in congregations in each century since, especially in this last generation. The word *church* was not introduced for several hundred years after the New Testament Scriptures were written.

In His letter to the assembly at Laodicea, Yahshua is making it clear that they are not going to make it into His Kingdom unless they do some major repenting and conform to His instructions.

It is written:

"I know your works; you are neither cold nor hot. I wish that you were either cold or hot. So, because you are lukewarm, and neither cold not hot, I am about to spit you out of my mouth."
Revelation 3:15-16 (NRSV)

We are to be red hot in our passion for our Creator, Savior, Master, and coming Judge, set on fire by His indwelling Holy Spirit living in us. If we do not choose to invite Him in so we can be born of His Spirit, so Holy spirit can guide us into all the truth that we are to then live out, then He will have no part with us, and He will separate Himself from us.

"For you say, 'I am rich, I have prospered, and I need nothing.' You do not realize that you are wretched, pitiful, poor, blind, and naked."
Revelation 3:17 (NRSV)

Having health and the ability to work and earn a living in this life is truly a blessing. When we have all that we need and many things that we want, it is easy to look at all we have accomplished and think too highly of ourselves. That can lead us into pride, which will lead us down the road to self destruction. We must always give the credit for accomplishments where the credit due, and that is first and foremost to the One Who created us and blessed us with health and the ability to prosper.

This letter to the Laodicean church is for everyone who has put their trust in themselves, their worldly accomplishments, and other people, and has left the Creator and Savior, Almighty Yah, out of their lives. People with this type of mindset may appear to be true followers of Yahshua Messiah. The judgment and condemnation will be much greater for those who have heard the truth but have not accepted and lived by it than for those who have never heard the truth.

The descriptions in verse 17 of being "wretched, pitiful, poor, blind, and naked" are referring to individuals who are ruled by vices and passions of the flesh, those rich in material processions and money but spiritually bankrupt, deceived by the teachings of deceived teachers who are blind to the truth, and not covered by the holy blood of Yahshua and His righteousness. This is the condition of many in the present day churches of the Christian faith.

People must wake up and repent before it is too late. If they die or if they are alive at His return to this earth, they will be unprepared to meet Him when He comes burning up everyone that is not under His protection. This should be a very sobering warning for you to ponder and act on.

Master Yahshua goes on to give the instructions of what a person in the terrible state described above must do to escape His judgment. Again it is written:

"Therefore I counsel you to buy from me gold refined by fire so that you may be rich; and white robes to clothe you and to keep the shame of your nakedness from being seen; and salve to anoint your eyes so that you may see. I reprove and discipline those whom I love. Be earnest, therefore, and repent. Listen! I am standing at the door, knocking; if you

hear my voice and open the door, I will come in to you and eat with you, and you with me."
Revelation 3:18-20 (NRSV)

All of the symbolism that Master Yahshua has stated in these verses is about having a humble and repentant heart that is ready to surrender to His will and His way. Humans are stubborn, and we think that we can be saved and inherit eternal life on our own, the way that seems right to us. But we can't. There is only one way, and that is the way of kneeling at the foot of Yahshua's cross where He died to pay our sin debt so that we can receive His gift of eternal life. He, by His Holy Spirit, is around each one of us, knocking on the door of our heart, desiring to be invited in so that He can begin a personal relationship and daily fellowship with us. Are you experiencing the wonderful relationship with the Creator of the universe Who is the Savior of your soul? Please don't keep the door of your heart locked. If you haven't already, invite Him in today and begin living for Him, serving Him and others the way He has instructed us in His Holy *Torah* Word.

The awesome promise for those who conquer the adversary in this life and are overcomers to the end is found in this passage:

"To the one who conquers I will give a place with me on my throne, just I myself conquered and sat down with my Father on His throne. Let anyone who has an ear listen to what the Spirit is saying to the churches."
Revelation 3:21-22 (NRSV)

We prepare for the coming of Messiah by understanding that He is preparing people throughout the earth for the second exodus that will be much greater than the first when He sent Moses to lead the Israelites out of Egypt. The second exodus is one in which our deliver, King Yahshua, is even now leading us out of Babylon the Great during these last years before His physical return.

I believe this great exodus will include individuals within two groups. One group will be the chosen 144,000 that will be true bloodline descendants of the twelve tribes listed below, that will know this as Holy Spirit reveals it to them. I believe that many that will make up this elite army of spiritual warriors are receiving that confirmation from Holy Spirit now in this year of 2007.

It is written:

After these things I saw four angels standing at the four corners of the earth, holding the four winds of the earth, that the wind should not blow on the earth, on the sea, or on any tree. Then I saw another angel ascending from the east, having the seal of the living God. And he cried with a loud voice to the four angels to whom it was granted to harm the earth and the sea, Saying, "Do not harm the earth, the sea, or the trees till we have sealed the servants of our God on their foreheads." And I heard the number of those who were sealed. One hundred *and* forty-four thousand of all the tribes of the children of Israel *were* sealed:
of the tribe of Judah twelve thousand *were* sealed;
of the tribe of Reuben twelve thousand *were* sealed;
of the tribe of Gad twelve thousand *were* sealed;
of the tribe of Asher twelve thousand *were* sealed;
of the tribe of Naphtali twelve thousand *were* sealed;
of the tribe of Manasseh twelve thousand *were* sealed;
of the tribe of Simeon twelve thousand *were* sealed;
of the tribe of Levi twelve thousand *were* sealed;
of the tribe of Issachar twelve thousand *were* sealed;
of the tribe of Zebulun twelve thousand *were* sealed;
of the tribe of Joseph twelve thousand *were* sealed;
of the tribe of Benjamin twelve thousand *were* sealed.
After these things I looked, and behold, a great multitude which no one could number, of all nations, tribes, peoples, and tongues, standing before the throne and before the Lamb, clothed with white robes, with palm branches in their hands, And crying out with a loud voice, saying, "Salvation *belongs* to our God who sits on the throne, and to the Lamb!" All the angels stood around the throne and the elders and the four living creatures, and fell on their faces before the throne and worshiped God, saying: "Amen! Blessing and glory and wisdom, thanksgiving and honor and power and might, *be* to our God forever and ever. Amen."
Revelation 7:1-12 (NKJV)

The 144,000 are sealed for complete protection just prior to the beginning of the three and one-half years of the great tribulation. During the great tribulation they minister to people throughout the earth by proclaiming the three messages of the three angles and doing the supernatural works that Master Yahshua did as no other group of individuals have ever done on such a large scale. Angels are messengers that deliver a message(s) from Almighty Yah to individuals or a group of people. It is written:

> **Then I looked, and there was the Lamb, standing on Mount Zion! And with him were one hundred forty-four thousand who had his name and his Father's name written on their foreheads. ... It is these who have not defiled themselves with women, for they are virgins; these follow the Lamb wherever he goes. They have been redeemed from humankind as first fruits for God and the Lamb, and in their mouth no lie was found; they are blameless. Then I saw another angel flying in midheaven, with an eternal gospel to proclaim to those who live on the earth—to every nation and tribe and language and people. He said in a loud voice, "Fear God and give him glory, for the hour of his judgment has come; and worship him who made heaven and earth, the sea and the springs of water." Then another angel, a second, followed, saying, "Fallen, fallen is Babylon the great! She has made all nations drink of the wine of the wrath of her fornication." Then another angel, a third, followed them, crying with a loud voice, "Those who worship the beast and its image, and receive a mark on their foreheads or on their hands, they will also drink the wine of God's wrath, poured unmixed into the cup of his anger, and they will be tormented with fire and sulfur in the presence of the holy angels and in the presence of the Lamb. And the smoke of their torment goes up forever and ever. There is no rest day or night for those who worship the beast and its image and for anyone who receives the mark of its name." Here is a call for the endurance of the saints, those who keep the commandments of God and hold fast to the faith of Jesus. And I heard a voice from heaven saying, "Write this: Blessed are the dead who from now on die in the Lord." "Yes," says the Spirit, "they will rest from their labors, for their deeds follow them."**
> Revelation 14:1, 4-13 (NRSV)

The following Scriptures were originally given to Yahshua's disciples after he was resurrected from the dead and just before He ascended back to His home in heaven. Though King Yahshua's instructions were for His disciples then, I believe He will give the same instructions to the 144,000 when He seals them just prior to the beginning of the great tribulation.

It is written:

> And he said to them, "Go into all the world and proclaim the good news to the whole creation. The one who believes and is baptized will be saved; but the one who does not believe will be condemned. And these signs will accompany those who believe: by using my name they will cast out demons; they will speak in new tongues; they will pick up snakes in their hands *[have authority over Satan]*, and if they drink any deadly thing, it will not hurt them; they will lay their hands on the sick, and they will recover."
>
> Mark 16:15-18 (NRSV)

> "He who hears you hears Me, he who rejects you rejects Me, and he who rejects Me rejects Him who sent Me." Then the seventy returned with joy, saying, "Lord, even the demons are subject to us in Your name." And He said to them, "I saw Satan fall like lightning from heaven. Behold, I give you the authority to trample on serpents and scorpions *[demon spirits]*, and over all the power of the enemy, and nothing shall by any means hurt you. Nevertheless do not rejoice in this, that the spirits are subject to you, but rather rejoice because your names are written in heaven."
>
> Luke 10:16-20 (NKJV). *Bracketed words added for clarity.*

Near the end of the tribulation period, when Yahshua gives the signal, I believe the 144,000 will be supernaturally transported to the wilderness of Mount Horeb, which is the same as Mount Sinai in Saudi Arabia. This is where King Yahshua met with the Israelites and gave the instructions from Father Yahweh to Moses to give to the people for all generations, and that includes you and me. It is written:

> Now when the dragon *[Satan and his host of millions of fallen angels and demons]* saw that he had been cast to the earth, he persecuted *[NRSV states pursued]* the woman who gave birth to the male *Child*. But the woman *[representing many millions of born-again believers from both the House of Ephraim and the House of Judah that make up the "one new man" that worship Almighty Yah in spirit and in truth]* was given two wings of a great eagle *[supernatural transport]*, that she might fly into the wilderness to her place, where she is nourished *[protected and provid-*

ed for just as the Israelites were while in their wilderness journey from Egypt to the promised land], **for a time and times and half a time** [three and one-half years], **from the presence of the serpent. So the serpent spewed water out of his mouth like a flood** [evil vengeance through the international police force of the anti-Messiah] **after the woman, that he might cause her to be carried away by the flood. But the earth helped the woman, and the earth opened its mouth and swallowed up the flood which the dragon had spewed out of his mouth. And the dragon was enraged with the woman, and he went to make war with the rest of her offspring** [the 144,000 and the other protected born-again believers who will not accept the mark of the beast], **who keep the commandments of God and have the testimony of Jesus Christ.**

Revelation 12:13-17 (NKJV). *Bracketed words added for clarity.*

I believe that Mt. Sinai is the same holy place King Yahshua returns to after He first touches down on the Mount of Olives. I believe He and His army of warrior angels will leave the Mount of Olives and go northwest of Jerusalem to the valley of Armageddon where he will slay the army of the anti-Messiah as it is written:

Now I saw heaven opened, and behold, a white horse. And He who sat on him *was* **called Faithful and True, and in righteousness He judges and makes war. His eyes** *were* **like a flame of fire, and on His head** *were* **many crowns. He had a name written that no one knew except Himself. He** *was* **clothed with a robe dipped in blood, and His name is called The Word of God. And the armies** [warrior angels] **in heaven, clothed in fine linen, white and clean, followed Him on white horses. Now out of His mouth goes a sharp sword, that with it He should strike the nations. And He Himself will rule them with a rod of iron. He Himself treads the winepress of the fierceness and wrath of Almighty God. And He has on** *His* **robe and on His thigh** [from the Hebrew, it should be banner or flag not thigh, which would be indecent] **a name written: KING OF KINGS AND LORD OF LORDS. Then I saw an angel standing in the sun; and he cried with a loud voice, saying to all the birds that fly in the midst of heaven, "Come and gather together for the supper of the great God, that you may eat the flesh of kings, the flesh of captains, the flesh of mighty men, the flesh of horses and of those who sit on them, and the flesh of all** *people*, **free and slave, both small and great." And I saw the beast,**

the kings of the earth, and their armies, gathered together to make war against Him who sat on the horse and against His army.
Revelation 19:11-19 (NKJV). *Bracketed words added for clarity.*

I believe that after the destruction of the anti-Messiah's army, King Yahshua and His army of angels will go to the true Mount Sinai, which is southwest of Jerusalem and the Negev Desert to unite with the 144,000 to have a huge celebration. Then I believe King Yahshua, the 144,000, and all of the saved, born again believers, with their new resurrected bodies, will march together north in nearly a direct line through Bozrah and then back to the Mount of Olives for His grand coronation procession through the Eastern Gate into the New Jerusalem. Oh what a joyful, awesome, indescribable event that will be. It is written:

"Who is this that comes from Edom, from Bozrah in garments stained crimson? Who is this so splendidly robed, marching in his great might?" "It is I, announcing vindication, mighty to save." "Why are your robes red, and your garments like theirs who tread the wine press?" "I have trodden the wine press alone, and from the peoples no one was with me; I trod them in my anger and trampled them in my wrath; their juice spattered on my garments, and stained all my robes. For the day of vengeance was in my heart, and the year for my redeeming work had come. I looked, but there was no helper; I stared, but there was no one to sustain me; so my own arm brought me victory, and my wrath sustained me. I trampled down peoples in my anger, I crushed them in my wrath, and I poured out their lifeblood on the earth."
Isaiah 63:1-6 (NRSV)

You who live in the shelter of the Most High, who abide in the shadow of the Almighty, will say to the LORD, "My refuge and my fortress; my God, in whom I trust." For he will deliver you from the snare of the fowler and from the deadly pestilence; he will cover you with his pinions, and under his wings you will find refuge; his faithfulness is a shield and buckler. You will not fear the terror of the night, or the arrow that flies by day, or the pestilence that stalks in darkness, or the destruction that wastes at noonday. A thousand may fall at your side, ten thousand at your right hand, but it will not come near you. You will only look with your eyes and see the punishment of the wicked. Because you have

made the LORD your refuge, the Most High your dwelling place, no evil shall befall you, no scourge come near your tent. For he will command his angels concerning you to guard you in all your ways. On their hands they will bear you up, so that you will not dash your foot against a stone. You will tread on the lion and the adder, the young lion and the serpent you will trample under foot. Those who love me, I will deliver; I will protect those who know my name. When they call to me, I will answer them; I will be with them in trouble, I will rescue them and honor them. With long life I will satisfy them, and show them my salvation.
Psalm 91 (NRSV)

Then I looked, and there was the Lamb, standing on Mount Zion! And with Him were one hundred and forty-four thousand who had his name [Yahshua] and his Father's name [Yahweh] written on their foreheads.
Revelation 14:1 (NRSV). *Bracketed words added for clarity.*

Blessed *are* those who do His commandments, that they may have the right to the tree of life, and may enter through the gates into the city.
Revelation 22:14 (NKJV)

The other of the two groups coming out of Babylon the Great, besides the 144,000, that will be a part of this second great exodus is the great multitude which no one could number of all nations, tribes, peoples, and tongues that the Apostle John described in Chapter Seven. One of the elders states that these are the ones that come out of the great tribulation and have washed their robes and made them white in the blood of the lamb, meaning they have put their complete faith and trust in Yahshua, or Jesus, applied the instructions from the Holy Scriptures, repented of their sins, and lived according to the Scriptures, not being conformed to the world, and certainly not having accepted the mark of the beast. John goes on to state:

After these things I looked, and behold, a great multitude which no one could number, of all nations, tribes, peoples, and tongues, standing before the throne and before the Lamb, clothed with white robes, with palm branches in their hands, and crying out with a loud voice, saying, "Salvation *belongs* to our God who sits on the throne, and to the Lamb!" All the angels stood around the throne and the elders and the four living creatures, and fell on their faces before the throne and worshiped God, Saying: "Amen! Blessing and glory and wisdom, thanksgiving and honor and power and might, *be* to our God forever and ever. Amen." Then one of the elders answered, saying to me, "Who are these arrayed in white robes, and where did they come from?" And I said to him, "Sir, you know." So he said to me, "These are the ones who come out of the great tribulation, and washed their robes and made them white in the blood of the Lamb. Therefore they are before the throne of God, and serve Him day and night in His temple. And He who sits on the throne will dwell among them. They shall neither hunger anymore nor thirst anymore; the sun shall not strike them, nor any heat; for the Lamb who is in the midst of the throne will shepherd them and lead them to living fountains of waters. And God will wipe away every tear from their eyes."

Revelation 7:9-17 (NKJV)

I believe that just prior to the beginning of the great tribulation, a very high percentage of this group of believers will still be in the traditional church that, at that time, will have become affiliated with the United Religions of the World. As a result of not being prepared at the time the anti-Messiah is revealed, many of these dear brothers and sisters will be martyred because of their testimony and faithfulness to Jesus, Yahshua. They will realize that they have been deceived by the popular evangelists, preachers, and authors of books who teach the lie of a pre-tribulation rapture. They will also realize that there is no time to prepare and that they cannot receive the mark of the beast. As sad as this will be, the good news is that the reward for being a martyr for Yahshua is assurance of being a part of His bride. It is written:

Then a third angel followed them, saying with a loud voice, "If anyone worships the beast and his image, and receives *his* mark on his forehead or on his hand, he himself shall also drink of the wine of the wrath of God, which is poured out full strength into the cup of His indignation. He shall be tormented with fire and brimstone in the presence of the holy angels and in the presence of the Lamb. And the smoke of their torment ascends forever and ever; and they have no rest day or night, who worship the beast and his image, and whoever receives the mark of his name." Here is the patience of the saints; here *are* those who keep the commandments of God and the faith of Jesus. Then I heard a voice from

heaven saying to me, "Write: 'Blessed *are* the dead who die in the Lord from now on.'" "Yes," says the Spirit, "that they may rest from their labors, and their works follow them."
Revelation 14:9-13 (NKJV)

When He opened the fifth seal, I saw under the altar the souls of those who had been slain for the word of God and for the testimony which they held. And they cried with a loud voice, saying, "How long, O Lord, holy and true, until You judge and avenge our blood on those who dwell on the earth?" Then a white robe was given to each of them; and it was said to them that they should rest a little while longer, until *both the number of* their fellow servants and their brethren, who would be killed as they *were*, was completed.
Revelation 6:9-11 (NKJV)

This is so very important to remember: we cannot accept the mark of the beast, his number, or his name. The Scriptures reveal to us that there will be a remnant of believers, along with the 144,000 of the restored tribes of Israel, who will make it all the way through the three and one-half years of the great tribulation. It is written:

For the Lord Himself will descend from heaven with a shout, with the voice of an archangel, and with the trumpet of God. And the dead in Christ will rise first. <u>Then we who are alive *and* remain shall be caught up together with them in the clouds to meet the Lord in the air.</u> And thus we shall always be with the Lord. Therefore comfort one another with these words.
1 Thessalonians 4:16-18 (NKJV) *(Emphasis added)*

This remnant of saints, the second-exodus overcomers, will be the born-again believers who are completely sold out to Yahshua and are following Yah's *Torah* instructions, pressing in to Him with all of their hearts. I believe our Comforter, Holy Spirit, along with the coming of the long-prophesied Elijah, will be giving divine instructions and words of knowledge at the right times as to where to go in the wildernesses throughout the earth to prepare for protection and provision. These saints may even be carried away by holy angels to do ministry, as was the Apostle Phillip. It is written:

So he commanded the chariot to stand still. And both Philip and the eunuch went down into the water, and he baptized him. Now when they came up out of the water, the Spirit of the Lord caught Philip away, so that the eunuch saw him no more; and he went on his way rejoicing. But Philip was found at Azotus. And passing through, he preached in all the cities till he came to Caesarea.

Acts 8:38-40 (NKJV)

When the Most High divided their inheritance to the nations, when He separated the sons of Adam, He set the boundaries of the peoples according to the number of the children of Israel. For the LORD's portion *is* His people; Jacob *is* the place of His inheritance. "He found him in a desert land and in the wasteland, a howling wilderness; He encircled him, He instructed him, He kept him as the apple of His eye. As an eagle stirs up its nest, hovers over its young, spreading out its wings, taking them up, carrying them on its wings, so the LORD alone led him, and *there was* no foreign god with him.

Deuteronomy 32:8-12 (NKJV)

Now when the dragon saw that he had been cast to the earth, he persecuted the woman who gave birth to the male *Child.* But the woman was given two wings of a great eagle, that she might fly into the wilderness to her place, where she is nourished for a time and times and half a time, from the presence of the serpent.

Revelation 12:13-14 (NKJV)

The reason I believe in the second greater exodus is because of the many parallels that are found in the plagues the Egyptians experienced before the first Israelite exodus and the very similar plagues that are prophesied to take place during the tribulation period. It is important to make the connection between Almighty Yahweh's awesome power of deliverance when He delivered the Israelites with His mighty outstretched arm, as recorded in the book of Exodus, and His promises to do an even greater deliverance of His remnant bride that takes place at the end of this age. Oh, how incredible it is to ponder.

First, let's begin with an important foundational connection from Father Yahweh's living words that He spoke through His living word, His Son, Yahshua, that are for us today just as they were for the

Israelites who heard them in person at Mount Sinai when they were first given.

> **"All of you stand today before the LORD your God: your leaders and your tribes and your elders and your officers, all the men of Israel, your little ones and your wives—also the stranger who *is* in your camp, from the one who cuts your wood to the one who draws your water—that you may enter into covenant with the LORD your God, and into His oath, which the LORD your God makes with you today, that He may establish you today as a people for Himself, and *that* He may be God to you, just as He has spoken to you, and just as He has sworn to your fathers, to Abraham, Isaac, and Jacob. "I make this covenant and this oath, not with you alone, but with *him* who stands here with us today before the LORD our God, <u>as well as with *him* who *is* not here with us today.</u>**
>
> Deuteronomy 29:10-15 (NKJV). *Emphasis added.*

The underlined words in these two verses are profound indeed because these words from Father Yahweh are speaking to you and me if we are born of His Spirit and in covenant with Him. This great covenant that Almighty Yah initiated with the nation of Israel was His promise to the people that if they chose to follow His instructions, they would be blessed with life and abundance. If they chose not to follow His instructions, they would follow the path that leads to death and curses. The same is true for us today. We are blessed to be able to be independent thinkers who can make decisions, and we do choose throughout every day as we make many decisions. It is imperative that we choose wisely by choosing to accept Yahshua, Jesus, the Messiah, as our Master and Savior. We choose to follow His instructions not out of fear or dread of judgment, but because we love Him with all of our heart, soul, and might.

The Israelites were given instructions under Moses' leadership that would protect them during the Egyptian plagues and would sustain them during their journey to the promised land. In the same way, we are to follow Yahweh's instructions so that we will be protected during the tribulation plagues that will come upon the earth as we make our journey to the same promised land to be united with our Bridegroom at His coming.

The beloved Apostle Peter gave us the straightforward message we need to hear and apply.

Then Peter said to them, "Repent, and let every one of you be baptized in the name of Jesus Christ [In the original Hebrew, Peter said Yahshua Messiah] **for the remission of sins; and you shall receive the gift of the Holy Spirit. For the promise is to you and to your children, and to all who are afar off, as many as the Lord our God will call." And with many other words he testified and exhorted them, saying, "Be saved from this perverse generation."**

Acts 2:38-40 (NKJV). *Bracketed words added for clarity.*

This message has been for each generation since the outpouring of Holy Spirit for every person who would invite Him into their hearts. Have you invited Holy Spirit to live inside of you in the name of our Master Jesus, Yahshua, the Messiah? If you haven't, please stop right now and choose wisely to invite Him in, so you will have the confidence of your salvation and eternal life with our Creator and loved ones who have also chosen wisely. Again, Peter's words have transcended each generation since the day of Pentecost. Peter called people to believe the good news that Messiah Yahshua has come and died for us all, paying our sin debt that we may repent and be set free from sin and eternal death. In the fulfilling of all the prophecies of Yahshua's first coming, He established the beginning of His Kingdom here on earth in the lives of the first believers. Yah's established kingdom has continued on down through the centuries to the present time, as we proclaim and live His kingdom.

I believe the call for people to come out of this perverse generation is more needed now than any other time in the history of mankind. We are to come out of this perverse generation and society that is referred to in the Scriptures as "Babylon the Great." It is written:

After these things I saw another angel coming down from heaven, having great authority, and the earth was illuminated with his glory. And he cried mightily with a loud voice, saying, "Babylon the great is fallen, is fallen, and has become a dwelling place of demons, a prison for every foul spirit, and a cage for every unclean and hated bird! For all the nations have drunk of the wine of the wrath of her fornication, the kings of the earth have committed fornication with her, and the merchants of the earth have become rich through the abundance of her luxury." And I heard another voice from heaven saying, "Come out of her, my people, lest you share in her sins, and lest you receive of her plagues. For her

sins have reached to heaven, and God has remembered her iniquities. Render to her just as she rendered to you, and repay her double according to her works; in the cup which she has mixed, mix double for her. In the measure that she glorified herself and lived luxuriously, in the same measure give her torment and sorrow; for she says in her heart, 'I sit *as* queen, and am no widow, and will not see sorrow.' Therefore her plagues will come in one day—death and mourning and famine. And she will be utterly burned with fire, for strong *is* the Lord God who judges her. The kings of the earth who committed fornication and lived luxuriously with her will weep and lament for her, when they see the smoke of her burning, standing at a distance for fear of her torment, saying, 'Alas, alas, that great city Babylon, that mighty city! For in one hour your judgment has come.'"

Revelation 18:1-10 (NKJV)

The plagues that the Apostle John was referring to here are those found in the trumpets and vials judgments that I covered in Chapter Seven. The important part is that Holy Spirit is drawing people from all over the earth into this last days understanding of the return of Yahshua Messiah and the importance of preparing for the greater second exodus. It is written:

"Therefore behold, the days are coming," says the LORD, "that it shall no more be said, 'The LORD lives who brought up the children of Israel from the land of Egypt,' but, 'The LORD lives who brought up the children of Israel from the land of the north and from all the lands where He had driven them.' For I will bring them back into their land which I gave to their fathers."

Jeremiah 16:14-15 (NKJV)

"Therefore, behold, the days are coming," says the LORD, "that they shall no longer say, 'As the LORD lives who brought up the children of Israel from the land of Egypt,' but, 'As the LORD lives who brought up and led the descendants of the house of Israel from the north country and from all the countries where I had driven them.' And they shall dwell in their own land."

Jeremiah 23:7-8 (NKJV)

When I have brought them back from the peoples and gathered them out of their enemies' lands, and I am hallowed in them in the sight of many nations, then they shall know that I *am* the LORD their God, who sent them into captivity among the nations, but also brought them back to their land, and left none of them captive any longer. And I will not hide My face from them anymore; for I shall have poured out My Spirit on the house of Israel,' says the Lord GOD."
Ezekiel 39:27-29 (NKJV)

These prophecies are definitely referring to the 144,000 and the bridesmaid group that make up the Woman that will be taken into the wilderness and protected, who are being chosen and prepared from many nations of the world where they live. Whether we are part of the 144,000 or the unknown number of those protected in the wilderness who will certainly be in the land of Israel during the tribulation, or wherever Holy Spirit leads us in our place of protection in the many wilderness locations of the earth, we have nothing to fear if we are covered under His wonderful protection.

At the time of the completion of this book (2007), Israel seems to be the scariest place on the earth to be living, with the treat of war on every side and the human bombs exploding and killing innocent people within the cities and neighborhoods. Conversely, the day is quickly coming when living in the land of Israel will be the safest place on the earth because that is where Yahshua is coming to.

As a part of Father Yahweh's great Master Plan, He sent Moses to instruct Pharaoh to allow the nation of Israel to be set free so they could come out from their place of slavery and be able to serve and worship the one true God of Abraham, Isaac, and Jacob in spirit and truth. This applies to us today. When Pharaoh hardened his heart and chose to keep the Israelites in bondage, then Almighty Yah poured out the plagues. The plagues were for the punishment of Pharaoh and the nation of Egypt whose inhabitants had worshiped many false gods that had been initiated over much time, including the hand-made idols for the people to bow down and worship. The plagues were also to reveal to the Egyptians and the people of the world the awesome power of Yahweh, so that the people would have an opportunity to repent and come out of their false belief systems of deception and turn to Yahweh, the one true God. Each of the plagues was a direct attack on the god(s) that the Egyptians had been taught were responsible for a particular provision or protection in their daily lives.

The first plague was turning not only the River Nile into blood, but all water, even drinking water in pots. This was an attack on the Egyptian god Hapi, the father of the Egyptian gods, for life comes from water. Water was also associated with the fertility god, Osiris.

The second plague was frogs, everywhere. This was an attack on Heka, the toad goddess. Heka was also the goddess of the fruitfulness of the land, resurrection, and procreative power. Frogs were very sacred to the Egyptians and to kill one even by accident was punishable by death.

The third plague was gnats and lice. This plague was against the god called Geb, the god of vegetation and father of Osiris, the fertility god.

The fourth plague was that of flies. It was an attack against the god Khepfi, the god of insects, and the beetle god, Scarab, which was the emblem of Ra, the sun god. Something very interesting is revealed to us in the Scriptures in Exodus that give us these accounts. With this fourth plague, Father Yahweh makes a distinction; He sets the people of Israel apart under His protection, while the Egyptians are not.

It is written:

And the LORD said to Moses, "Rise early in the morning and stand before Pharaoh as he comes out to the water. Then say to him, 'Thus says the LORD: "Let My people go, that they may serve Me. Or else, if you will not let My people go, behold, I will send swarms *of flies* on you and your servants, on your people and into your houses. The houses of the Egyptians shall be full of swarms *of flies,* and also the ground on which they *stand.* And in that day I will set apart the land of Goshen, in which My people dwell, that no swarms *of flies* shall be there, in order that you may know that I *am* the LORD in the midst of the land. I will make a difference between My people and your people. Tomorrow this sign shall be."'"
Exodus 8:20-23 (NKJV)

The fifth plague was against the gods of livestock—Apis, the bull god, and Hathor, the cow goddess. Several animals were very sacred to the Egyptians but especially the ox, heifer, and the ram. The Egyptians believed that the soul of their fertility god, Osiris, lived in the body of the bull god, Apis. How weird is that? Again, the protection is over the Hebrew people.

So the LORD did this thing on the next day, and all the livestock of Egypt died; but of the livestock of the children of Israel, not one died. Then Pharaoh sent, and indeed, not even one of the livestock of the Israelites was dead. But the heart of Pharaoh became hard, and he did not let the people go.

Exodus 9:6-7 (NKJV)

The sixth plague was that of festering boils that broke out on the Egyptian priest and all the people. This plague was an attack on the Egyptian god, Thorth, their god of medicine, intelligence, and wisdom. On special occasions, the priest would sacrifice humans that were burnt alive on high altars. The ashes of the murdered victims were scattered into the wind with proclamations that blessings would descend upon the people of Egypt because of the sacrifice to heathen, pagan gods of nothing. The ashes that Moses cast into the air brought more suffering on the priest, the people, and the animals. Moses was instructed to go to Pharaoh once again and say, "Let My people go, that they may serve Me." Almighty Yah warned the Pharaoh. It is written:

But indeed for this *purpose* I have raised you *[Pharaoh]* up, that I may show My power *in* you, and that My name may be declared in all the earth. As yet you exalt yourself against My people in that you will not let them go. Behold, tomorrow about this time I will cause very heavy hail to rain down, such as has not been in Egypt since its founding until now. Therefore send now *and* gather your livestock and all that you have in the field, for the hail shall come down on every man and every animal which is found in the field and is not brought home; and they shall die."'" He who feared the word of the LORD among the servants of Pharaoh made his servants and his livestock flee to the houses. But he who did not regard the word of the LORD left his servants and his livestock in the field. Then the LORD said to Moses, "Stretch out your hand toward heaven, that there may be hail in all the land of Egypt— on man, on beast, and on every herb of the field, throughout the land of Egypt." And Moses stretched out his rod toward heaven; and the LORD sent thunder and hail, and fire darted to the ground. And the LORD rained hail on the land of Egypt. So there was hail, and fire mingled with the hail, so very heavy that there was none like it in all the land of Egypt since it became a nation. And the hail struck throughout

the whole land of Egypt, all that *was* in the field, both man and beast; and the hail struck every herb of the field and broke every tree of the field. Only in the land of Goshen, where the children of Israel *were*, there was no hail. And Pharaoh sent and called for Moses and Aaron, and said to them, "I have sinned this time. The LORD *is* righteous, and my people and I *are* wicked. Entreat the LORD, that there may be no *more* mighty thundering and hail, for *it is* enough. I will let you go, and you shall stay no longer."

Exodus 9:16-28 (NKJV). *Bracketed words added for clarity.*

This seventh plague had to be very humbling and was an attack on Nut, the Egyptian sky goddess and mother of Osiris. The heavy hail destroyed the crops of flax and barley that are harvested in the early spring. The great hail storm from the sky was another attack on Seth, the false god that was supposed to protect the crops, and an attack on Isis, the goddess of life. Notice again that the Israelites in their area were protected. Notice also that Pharaoh spoke of repenting even though he did not mean it. He pleaded for Moses to ask Almighty Yah to stop the devastating hail storm so the later crops that were coming up would be spared. Moses' request was granted again. I believe there will be many people during the time of the great tribulation who will speak of repentance and really mean it.

By the time of the eighth plague, Pharaoh's officials were warning him to let the Israelites go because Egypt was in ruins. Pharaoh's heart was hardened. He lied and would not let the people leave. So, the plague of locusts came. Millions of locusts ate the wheat crop, all plants, and everything else that the hail had not destroyed. Again, Pharaoh had to go to Moses requesting that he ask Almighty Yah to remove the plague. And again, Moses' request was granted. The Scriptures are silent as to whether the Israelites were protected from the plague of the locusts. I believe they were.

The devastating swarm of locusts was an attack on the Egyptian god, Anubis, the god of the fields. And ol' Seth was smacked in the face again. You would think that Pharaoh would have been ready to roll out the carpet for the Israelites to leave. But no, he continued to rebel against the Creator of the universe.

The ninth plague of darkness came without warning to Pharaoh. The darkness was so intense and heavy that it could be felt. It is written:

Then the LORD said to Moses, "Stretch out your hand toward heaven, that there may be darkness over the land of Egypt, darkness *which* may even be felt." So Moses stretched out his hand toward heaven, and there was thick darkness in all the land of Egypt three days. They did not see one another; nor did anyone rise from his place for three days. But all the children of Israel had light in their dwellings.
Exodus 10:21-23 (NKJV)

The Scriptures imply that there was total darkness, with no light from lamps or fires, and that no one was able to move about for three days. This indicates a removal by Almighty Yah of anything resembling light that is from Him, so that He had removed His presence from the land. But notice that the children of Israel had light where they dwelt.

The darkness was an attack on the false god Ra, the famous sun god. Ra was believed by the Egyptians to be the physical father of the Pharaohs, which elevated them to the status of king of the gods. No sunrise meant that the God of the Israelites was completely in control of the god of the king of gods. If you remember back in Chapter Five, I was hammering on Constantine, the Roman emperor of the early fourth century. He proclaimed himself to be the sun god and created a new belief system called the Church of Rome that proceeded to pervert the teaching of Yahshua and His followers. During the later years of the great tribulation, just before Yahshua comes, the anti-Messiah beast will proclaim himself to be god of all gods and require everyone to worship him. We must prepare, for there is a dark time coming like there has never been before in all of history.

All of the nine plagues prior to the tenth were devastating to the Egyptians in their loss of crops, livestock, property, and in the case of the boils, they were physically painful. The tenth plague had to have ripped the hearts out of the Egyptian people because their first-born sons lost their lives as the angel of death passed over their dwellings. This was the last and final plague on Egypt. The death of the firstborn was an attack on Pharaoh, the god-king. Pharaoh was considered a god, as was his first-born son who would succeed him on the throne. In fact, the firstborn of people and animals in general were often worshiped. Pharaoh was considered an incarnation of Ra, the sun god, and Osiris, the giver of life. Because Pharaoh's son was considered a god, when he died it was as if a god of Egypt had actually died.

Moses delivered the final warning of Yahweh's coming judgment to

Pharaoh and left him. It is written:

> Then Moses said, "Thus says the LORD: 'About midnight I will go out into the midst of Egypt; and all the firstborn in the land of Egypt shall die, from the firstborn of Pharaoh who sits on his throne, even to the firstborn of the female servant who is behind the handmill, and all the firstborn of the animals. Then there shall be a great cry throughout all the land of Egypt, such as was not like it before, nor shall be like it again. But against none of the children of Israel shall a dog move its tongue, against man or beast, that you may know that the LORD does make a difference between the Egyptians and Israel.' And all these your servants shall come down to me and bow down to me, saying, 'Get out, and all the people who follow you!' After that I will go out." Then he went out from Pharaoh in great anger.
> Exodus 11:4-8 (NKJV)

Father Yahweh then prepared the Israelites for the devastating final plague by giving the instructions to Moses to convey to the people for their protection before judgment fell upon Pharaoh and the Egyptians. In His judgment of the Egyptians, the Israelites received their redemption and deliverance. The same will be true for the remnant of end-time Israelites who are prepared for the coming of Messiah. They, or we, will be protected and eagerly awaiting our Bridegroom as our redemption comes closer, while the wrath of Almighty Yah is poured out.

It is written:

> "And there will be signs in the sun, in the moon, and in the stars; and on the earth distress of nations, with perplexity, the sea and the waves roaring; men's hearts failing them from fear and the expectation of those things which are coming on the earth, for the powers of heaven will be shaken. *[I believe these signs of catastrophes to be the result of the passing by of Planet X.]* Then they will see the Son of Man coming in a cloud with power and great glory. Now when these things begin to happen, look up and lift up your heads, because your redemption draws near."
> Luke 21:25-28 (NKJV). *Bracketed words added for clarity.*

Just as the Israelites of the first great exodus were given instructions to apply the blood of the Lamb for their redemption and deliverance, so are we as we prepare for the final years of this age. The lamb that they ate and its blood that they applied on the sides and top of the door frame were symbolic of the Lamb of Yahweh that was to come approximately 1,500 years later. We are to apply the blood of the Lamb to our hearts and put our complete faith and trust in Him for our salvation and deliverance.

The Passover is a prophetic picture revealing end-times truth. We are instructed in the Scriptures to celebrate the first Passover as a memorial throughout all of our generations, and learn from it that it is a foreshadow of the second, greater exodus. It is written:

> These are the appointed festivals of the LORD, the holy convocations, which you shall celebrate at the time appointed for them. In the first month, on the fourteenth day of the month, at twilight, there shall be a passover offering to the LORD, and on the fifteenth day of the same month is the festival of unleavened bread to the LORD; seven days you shall eat unleavened bread. On the first day you shall have a holy convocation; you shall not work at your occupations. For seven days you shall present the LORD's offerings by fire; on the seventh day there shall be a holy convocation: you shall not work at your occupations. ... it is a statute forever throughout your generations in all your settlements.
> Leviticus 23:4-8 & 14b (NRSV)

After each of the three seasons when all of the Feasts of Elohim are celebrated, He states, "It is a statute (an established law or rule) forever throughout all of your generations."

As you remember from Chapter Four of this book, in A.D. 325, the leaders of the Church of Rome with the Council of Nicea under the leadership of Constantine, banned Passover, the other six of Father Yahweh's feasts, and the weekly Sabbath. During that time, if individuals were caught keeping the Sabbath and celebrating the Feasts, they could lose their lives, and many did. Passover was replaced with a mixture of the truth of the crucifixion and resurrection of Yahshua and paganized falsehood and nonsense of rabbits, eggs, and the name Easter, which as stated earlier is translated from the name *Ashteroth*, the goddess of fertility.

Today, many people are returning and embracing the richness of truth found in the Feasts of Father Yahweh and His Son, the Living Torah. I encourage you to honor and keep the Sabbath day, the days of the seven annual feasts, and the other instructions of *Torah* that our Creator gave for His people to keep. In your obedience, you will be blessed, set apart, and marked as one of His own special people who make up a remnant of His body, His bride. Whether we live or die, we will be with Him throughout all eternity.

Understand this: I am not teaching that born-again believers who don't keep the biblical Sabbath and feast days and live a *Torah*-observant life aren't saved and guaranteed eternal life with Almighty Yah. I am teaching that according to Scripture, by being Spirit filled and living a *Torah*-observant life, a person will be a part of those described in Revelation 3:8. It is written:

> **"I know your works. Look, I have set before you an open door, which no one is able to shut. I know that you have but little power, and yet you have kept my word and have not denied my name."**
> Revelation 3:8 (NRSV)

There are too many similarities between the plagues recorded in the book of Exodus and the plagues and catastrophes recorded in the book of Revelation for there not to be a connection. There is blood in the water; fire and hail destroying vegetation, livestock and crops, resulting in famine; painful boils; and darkness. As bad as the plagues were for the Egyptians, they pale in comparison to the plagues and wrath that will be poured out on the inhabitants of the earth who accept the mark of the beast.

For all of their similarities, I also see significant differences in these two huge events in human history, one that happened approximately 3,400 years ago and the other that is shaping up to happen sometime during the early part of this the 21st century. In the prophecies from the book of Revelation and other books of the Scriptures, we learn that during the time of the birth pains of the coming of Messiah that we are now in, there will be increased strife and hate manifesting among races of people throughout the world. There will continue to be many natural catastrophes, such as the horrific hurricanes and earthquakes of 2005; increased global warming; and later on, the mass martyrdom of millions of believers who are not prepared for the great deception that is here now and will only increase as we proceed closer to the end. As stated earlier in this book, many are perishing now in the killing fields of Sudan and other Muslim and communist countries because they have committed their lives to Jesus, Yahshua, the Messiah, and will not deny Him.

Toward the end of the prophecies of bad things happening on this earth is the fifth trumpet account of locusts coming upon the earth out of the bottomless pit. I believe John is talking about a swarm of fallen angel demons, not grasshoppers, that come to torment those who accept the mark of the beast. This event seems to take place about the time the 200 million-man army kills one third of the population of the world.

Following that, before we get to the gathering of the armies of the anti-Messiah north of Jerusalem for the battle of HarMegiddo, we have darkness that I believe is the result of a large asteroid from Planet X crashing onto the earth, blasting millions of tons of dirt up into the atmosphere and blocking the sun's light, along with the smoke from volcanoes and fires. That will produce a hail storm raining down hail stones that Revelation 16:21 states will weigh about a talent, which is 70 pounds each.

Are you beginning to understand why it is so important to be prepared for these end-time events and the blessed coming of King Yahshua Messiah? Remember, I have given you the proof from the Scriptures and other sources that the timing of the resurrection of the saved of Yahweh's people is at the time of Messiah Yahshua's coming to pour out His wrath upon Satan's final empire on this earth. I don't believe all of these terrible things will be happening in every area of the earth simultaneously. I do believe that the entire human race will be affected in different degrees depending upon where each person is when these events happen and how well they are prepared.

Today, we watch the evening news and witness terrible devastation and loss of life from earthquakes, hurricanes, and other natural catastrophes that happen in many places on this large earth that we live on. Unless they personally touched us in some way, we sympathize and empathize with the victims, and we may even get involved to help them out the best we can because we are caring people. From a distance, however, we become somewhat desensitized to the reality of it. I believe the more we witness these events from a distance, the more conditioned we become to the events happening to the point that they seem to be part of our normal day-to-day life. The only way to make sense of the prophetic Scriptures that Messiah Yahshua spoke regarding His coming back to earth to physically establish His Kingdom is to see the end-time events that are going to happen on this planet, happening sporadically, not all at one time, and affecting only pockets of people. It is written:

> "So also, when you see all these things, you know that he is near, at the very gates. Truly I tell you, this generation will not pass away until all these things have taken place. Heaven and earth will pass away, but my words will not pass away. But about that day and hour no one knows, neither the angels of heaven, nor the Son, but only the Father. For as the days of Noah were, so will be the coming of the Son of Man. For as in those days before the flood they were eating and drinking, marrying and giving in marriage, until the day Noah entered the ark, and they knew nothing until the flood came and swept them all away, so too will be the coming of the Son of Man."
>
> Matthew 24:33-39 (NRSV)

The elect will see the signs of the end coming as the prophecies are being fulfilled. Remember the road sign events that I stated earlier in this book to watch out for. For people who are lost in this world and have no clue of what is going on, the events, as horrible as they are and will be, will seem normal, and people's lives will go on like normal, as they did in the days of Noah. He preached that the people should repent of their sins and live for Yahweh, and he prophesied the coming of the flood for 120 years as he and his family built the ark. The people mocked him and laughed at him because he was building a huge ship approximately 200 miles from the nearest body of water large enough to float it. They lived in a perfect moisture world where it had never rained before. The same mindset is true today in many skeptical people and will only increase as we draw closer to the end. It is written:

> This is now, beloved, the second letter I am writing to you; in them I am trying to arouse your sincere intention by reminding you that you should remember the words spoken in the past by the holy prophets, and the commandment of the Lord and Savior spoken through your apostles. First of all you must understand this, that in the last days scoffers will come, scoffing and indulging their own lusts and saying, "Where is the promise of his coming? For ever since our ancestors died, all things continue as they were from the beginning of creation!" They deliberately ignore this fact, that by the word of God heavens existed

long ago and an earth was formed out of water and by means of water, through which the world of that time was deluged with water and perished. But by the same word the present heavens and earth have been reserved for fire, being kept until the day of judgment and destruction of the godless.

2 Peter 3:1-7 (NRSV)

The bottom line is this, how prepared are you right now in your relationship with Almighty Yahweh through His Son, Yahshua, and the fellowship of our Comforter, Holy Spirit? We must be willing to lay down our life for the truth just as The Truth laid down His life for us. Yahshua is Truth, and He obeyed His Father, Yahweh, all the way to the end during His life on this earth. He defeated Satan, death, hell, and the grave, and became the first of the firstfruits harvest of humans. HallelluYah, what a Savior, and He has made the way for us.

The Word teaches us that the saved, born-again believers who are living during the last three and a half years of the great tribulation time of persecution and catastrophes will have three destinies. Some will go into captivity, and some will be martyred because they know they cannot accept the mark of the beast. I believe those whose destiny it is to face these two realities will be processed by the controlling government and its military in stealth, undercover, so that the small percentage of society, the true believers, will just drop out of the sight of society. It is written:

Also it was allowed to make war on the saints and to conquer them. It was given authority over every tribe and people and language and nation, and all the inhabitants of the earth will worship it, everyone whose name has not been written from the foundation of the world in the book of life of the Lamb that was slaughtered. Let anyone who has an ear listen: If you are to be taken captive, into captivity you go; if you kill with the sword, with the sword you must be killed. Here is a call for the endurance and faith of the saints.

Revelation 13:7-12 (NRSV)

Then I saw thrones, and those seated on them were given authority to judge. I also saw the souls of those who had been beheaded for their testimony to Jesus and for the word of God. They had not worshiped the beast or its image and had not received its mark on their foreheads or their hands. They

came to life and reigned with Christ a thousand years. (The rest of the dead did not come to life until the thousand years were ended.) This is the first resurrection. Blessed and holy are those who share in the first resurrection. Over these the second death has no power, but they will be priests of God and of Christ, and they will reign with him a thousand years.

Revelation 20:4-6 (NRSV)

I believe the third destiny is that a small percentage of the remnant will survive until the end and will be those who are resurrected at the coming of King Yahshua Messiah and will not experience physical death. It is written:

Then one of the elders addressed me, saying, "Who are these, robed in white, and where have they come from?" I said to him, "Sir, you are the one that knows." Then he said to me, "These are they who have come out of the great ordeal; they have washed their robes and made them white in the blood of the Lamb. For this reason they are before the throne of God, and worship him day and night within his temple, and the one who is seated on the throne will shelter them. They will hunger no more, and thirst no more; the sun will not strike them, nor any scorching heat; for the Lamb at the centre of the throne will be their shepherd, and he will guide them to springs of the water of life, and God will wipe away every tear from their eyes."

Revelation 7:13-17 (NRSV)

It is obvious from these Scriptures that the people with this destiny have endured much hardship by making their exodus and living outside of the beast system of provision. I have to believe that Father Yahweh makes provision for them to be hidden from the soldiers of the beast army, protected from the catastrophes, and provided for even though there will be some suffering. Our Elohim is faithful, and what He did for the Israelites when he delivered them out of Egypt, He will make a way again for the tribulation Israelites who have washed their robes and made them white in the blood of the Lamb.

We prepare for the coming of Messiah by discerning the direction that we should be going when we clearly see the signs and know that we are in the last few years. This is important: Some of you reading this book may be called by Holy Spirit to move to Israel as He reveals to you what tribe you belong to, meaning you will have the incredible destiny of being one of the 144,000 Israelites who will be completely protected and provided for throughout the tribulation. What an awesome experience to ponder, to be alive during the most horrendous time in human history, preaching the truth about accepting the gift of redemption by having faith in Messiah and being born of His Spirit, knowing you are completely protected from Satan and all he can muster against you. The 144,000 are the only ones who can learn the new song to Yahshua. How awesome.

If we are not clearly instructed by Holy Spirit to make that monumental move, or if we are not supernaturally transported by angels to Israel as I covered earlier, which may be the only way for a person(s) to actually be able to get into the country at that time, then we may hear from Holy Spirit to prepare the best we can in whatever wilderness is available to us.

I believe we can learn a lot from the close communities of the ant. It is written:

> **Go to the ant, you lazybones; consider its ways, and be wise. Without having any chief or officer or ruler, it prepares its food in summer, and gathers its sustenance in harvest. How long will you lie there, O lazybones? When will you rise from your sleep? A little sleep, a little slumber, a little folding of the hands to rest, and poverty will come upon you like a robber, and want, like an armed warrior.**
> Proverbs 6:6-11 (NRSV)

I don't know if there is any significance to the fact that these verses are from the sixth chapter of Proverbs, starting with the sixth verse and continuing for six verses (666). Perhaps, as in many cases with Scriptures, this is a hidden message for those of us who are watching for signs and discerning the times. Here is a possible correlation to ponder from the sixth chapter of Revelation starting with the sixth verse and continuing for six verses (666). It is written:

> **... and I heard what seemed to be a voice in the midst of the four living creatures saying, "A quart of wheat for a day's pay, and three quarts of barley for a day's pay, but do not damage the olive oil and the wine!" When he opened the fourth seal, I heard the voice of the fourth living creature call out, "Come!" I looked and there was a pale green horse!**

Its rider's name was Death, and Hades followed with him; they were given authority over a fourth of the earth, to kill with sword, famine, and pestilence, and by the wild animals of the earth. When he opened the fifth seal, I saw under the altar the souls of those who had been slaughtered for the word of God and for the testimony they had given; they cried out with a loud voice, "Sovereign Lord, holy and true, how long will it be before you judge and avenge our blood on the inhabitants of the earth?" They were each given a white robe and told to rest a little longer, until the number would be complete both of their fellow servants and of their brothers and sisters, who were soon to be killed as they themselves had been killed.

Revelation 6:6-11 (NRSV)

My best advice to you is not to worry about anything, but to pray about everything. You must prepare for the coming of our awesome and wonderful Bridegroom, Yahshua, as you are lead by His Spirit. As for me and my house, we will serve our Elohim and be as prepared for the end times as we can be—spiritually, mentally, and physically—without becoming fanatical survivalists. If it is our lot to be martyrs by not denying Yahshua as our Master and King and by not taking the mark of the beast, then so be it. We will leave this life with as much grace and power as Almighty Yah will give us with the words on our lips that the Apostle Stephen had when he was stoned to death. It is written:

And they stoned Stephen as he was calling on *God* and saying, "Lord Jesus, receive my spirit." Then he knelt down and cried out with a loud voice, "Lord, do not charge them with this sin." And when he had said this, he fell asleep.

Acts 7:59-60 (NKJV)

12

THE END TIMES MINISTRY OF THE BODY OF MESSIAH

<hr>

Prior to the death of our mother Dorothy on May 13, 2006, I packed my laptop and traveled the 90 miles to her home every other weekend to care for her in order to give my brother a break. He was her primary caregiver the last two years of her life. Two years before our mother died and went home to be with our Master Yahshua, her gall bladder ruptured. As a result, she nearly died of blood sepsis. She was on full life support with a ventilator and nine IV pumps for three weeks. The doctors did not believe that she would come out of her comatose state or be able to recover. I prayed and heard clearly from Holy Spirit that it was not her time to die and that she would recover enough to return home, and she did. With many prayers and excellent medical care, she recovered enough to leave the hospital and was transferred into a nursing facility for physical therapy. After five weeks, it was clear that mother was not recovering enough to be able to get up and walk on her on and, short of a miracle, would never be able to. We saw her condition deteriorating rapidly and knew the right thing to do was to move her back to her own home. My brother Mark, Yahweh bless him, agreed to leave his job to take care of our mother with my assistance. She recovered enough to walk again and lived to experience my daughter's wedding, a large family reunion, and two more birthday celebrations. We gave our precious Mother the loving care in her own home that she needed and deserved right up until she breathed her last breath and died in my arms.

I have begun this chapter with the above background to convey that the ministry of the Body of Messiah must always be built on a foundation of compassion and true love for others from the foundation of the love that Yahshua has for all of humanity. It is written:

Beloved, let us love one another, because love is from God; everyone who loves is born of God and knows God. Whoever does not love does not know God, for God is love. God's love was revealed among us in this way: God sent his only Son into the world so that we might live through him. In this is love, not that we loved God but that he loved us and sent his Son to be the atoning sacrifice for our sins. Beloved, since God loved us so much, we also ought to love one another. No one has ever seen God; if we love one another, God lives in us, and his love is perfected in us. By this we know that we abide in him and he in us, because he has given us of his Spirit. And we have seen and do testify that the Father has sent his Son as the Savior of the world. God abides in those who confess that Jesus is the Son of God, and they abide in God. So we have known and believe the love that God has for us. God is love, and those who abide in love abide in God, and God abides in them.

1 John 4:7-16 (NRSV)

A Brief Study of the Seven Spirits And the Menorah

The menorah has symbolism that teaches the attributes of the body of Messiah and the application of the different ways of ministry to one another. The menorah of the Holy Scriptures is described as a seven-armed candelabrum that provided light within the holy place of the tabernacle in the wilderness and the first and second temples.

When General Titus and the Roman army destroyed the second temple in A.D. 70, the giant, solid gold menorah was taken as their chief spoil and was transported to Rome. You may have seen pictures of the carved stone relief from the Arch of Titus in Rome showing the very large menorah tied on a horse-drawn wagon.

Exodus 25:31-40 records the complete instructions that Father Yahweh gave to Moses for the handcrafting of the menorah to be like the one that had been shown to Moses when he was with Almighty Yah for forty days on Mount Sinai.

In 1 Samuel 3:1-3, where Samuel ministered unto Yahweh, the menorah in the temple is called the "lamp of God." Almighty Yah designed it and had it constructed from very detailed specifications. This lamp is symbolic of the Word of Yahweh. King David, in Psalm 119:105, referred to Yah's Word as "a lamp unto my feet and a light to my path." This is still true today, if we will study it and apply it to our lives.

The menorah and the Ark of the Covenant are the only articles used in the holy places of the tabernacle and temple that are referenced in the Apostle John's visions recorded in the Book of Revelation. In the first chapter of the Revelation of the coming of Yahshua, verses 12 and 13, John saw in his vision seven golden lamp stands, or menorahs, representing the seven congregations that were covered earlier in this book, and he saw Yahshua walking in the midst of them. A few verses prior to this, John references the seven spirits when he was giving his introduction to the seven congregations. It is written:

John to the seven churches that are in Asia: Grace to you and peace from him who is and who was and who is to come, and from the seven spirits who are before his throne, and from Jesus Christ, the faithful witness, the firstborn of the dead, and the ruler of the kings of the earth.
Revelation 1:4-5 (NRSV)

This reference to the seven spirits is very interesting and important to understand. The only other reference in the Scriptures to a single grouping of seven spirit descriptions is found in Isaiah 11. That is where we find the revelation of what the seven spirits are. It is written:

A shoot shall come out from the stump of Jesse, and a branch shall grow out of his roots. The spirit of the LORD shall rest on him, the spirit of wisdom and understanding, the spirit of counsel and might, the spirit of knowledge and the fear of the LORD. His delight shall be in the fear of the LORD. He shall not judge by what his eyes see, or decide by what his ears hear; but with righteousness he shall judge the poor, and decide with equity for the meek of the earth; he shall strike the earth with the rod of his mouth, and with the breath of his lips he shall kill the wicked. Righteousness shall be the belt around his waist, and faithfulness the belt around his loins.
Isaiah 11:1-5 (NRSV)

This is truly a description of Yahshua and gives understanding of the meaning of each of the seven spirits. The branches of the menorah represent the seven spirits. The description of the seven spirits in the first verses have more to do with Messiah's first coming as the suffering

Servant. He lived and walked out these attributes of Father Yahweh in one way or another in ministering to everyone He came in contact with. Verses four and five clearly refer to Master Yahshua's return to the earth as the great conquering King and Judge of all mankind and the nations. When we accept Yahshua as our Savior and Master and invite Him to live within us, and then seek Him with all of our heart, we begin our faith journey of becoming molded into His likeness, possessing His attributes. It only makes sense that this will happen when He is living within His human tabernacles that He created. HalleluYah, isn't it great? We should aspire to having all of the seven attributes (spirits) operating in each of us. If this is happening, then all of these attributes will be operating in our congregations and fellowships of called-out believers.

When I was praying about a name and logo for the publishing company that would publish this book, I felt led to use the name Menorah Books with a picture of a menorah as the logo. As you can see on the back cover, the logo has Father Yahweh's name on the top level of the base and King Yahshua's name on the bottom level of the base. The menorah represents true light from the Creator of light, truth, and life. I decided to have the center lamp drawn slightly higher than the other six because it represents the Spirit of the Master, Yahshua, for He is the center of life, the Creator of all that was created as was delegated to Him by His and our Almighty Father, Yahweh. He is the root and vine through which life flows in to and out from. It is written:

> **"I am the true vine, and my Father is the vinegrower. He removes every branch in me that bears no fruit. Every branch that bears fruit he prunes to make it bear more fruit. You have already been cleansed by the word that I have spoken to you. Abide in me as I abide in you. Just as the branch cannot bear fruit by itself unless it abides in the vine, neither can you unless you abide in me. I am the vine, you are the branches. Those who abide in me and I in them bear much fruit, because apart from me you can do nothing. Whoever does not abide in me is thrown away like a branch and withers; such branches are gathered, thrown into the fire, and burned. If you abide in me, and my words abide in you, ask for whatever you wish, and it will be done for you. My Father is glorified by this, that you bear much fruit and become my disciples. As the Father has loved me, so I have loved you; abide in my love. If you keep my commandments, you will abide in my love, just as I have kept**

my Father's commandments and abide in his love. I have said these things to you so that my joy may be in you, and that your joy may be complete."

John 15:1-11 (NRSV)

Symbolically, Master Yahshua is the center post of the menorah just as He is the Chief Cornerstone of Father Yahweh's spiritual house. It is written:

Come to him, a living stone, though rejected by mortals yet chosen and precious in God's sight, and like living stones, let yourselves be built into a spiritual house, to be a holy priesthood, to offer spiritual sacrifices acceptable to God through Jesus Christ. For it stands in scripture: "See, I am laying in Zion a stone, a cornerstone chosen and precious; and whoever believes in him will not be put to shame." To you then who believe, he is precious; but for those who do not believe, "The stone that the builders rejected has become the very head of the corner ..."

1 Peter 2:4-7 (NRSV)

Yahshua is the complete and fullest measure of true divine love from the heart of Abba Father Yah. Because He loved us so much, He sent forth His only complete manifestation of Himself from His very heart to become Messiah Yahshua, Who was Almighty Yahweh created from a heavenly seed and egg that was a human likeness. He became our complete redemption by becoming our sin debt for our transgressions of His *Torah* instructions. Like the Scriptures from Genesis One through Revelation Twenty-two, this Book is all about our Creator's love for His human beings created in His likeness. Out from His pure love for us, He has made a way for us to be brought into holy, happy, and secure relationship with Him.

The branches on either side of the center branch of the menorah are symbolic of the other six Spirits, or attributes of Holy Spirit listed in Isaiah 11. They are grouped in pairs that are in harmony and balance: the Spirit of wisdom and understanding, the Spirit of counsel and might, the Spirit of knowledge and the fear of the LORD.

I decided to expound on only one of the Spirits, the Spirit of Might. This Spirit includes the nine manifestation gifts of Holy Spirit that are used in ministry, the seven birth traits, and the five offices or positions of ministry with the body of Yahshua. I am breaking this down for you because it is necessary to clear up some possible confusion.

There are several places in the Scriptures that have references to gifts and positions, or offices, in the body of Messiah. This information should give greater understanding of who you are in Messiah. Knowing that should inspire you to seek Holy Spirit and ask that He reveal to you all that Almighty Yahweh has blessed and empowered you with for the purpose of ministering and being a blessing to others. This brings glory to Him and His Son, Yahshua. Our spiritual gifts can only come from above. It is written:

> **John answered and said, "A man can receive nothing unless it has been given to him from heaven."**
> John 3:27 (NKJV)

This subject matter is very deep and wide. I am providing you with an overview of the three different groupings of the spiritual gifts. There are websites and books that offer much more detail and understanding of these subjects. Two good web sites that I can recommend are:

Plumbline Ministries (www.plumblineministries.com) and
Gift Quest (www.giftquestinc.com).

There are three different sections in the New Covenant Scriptures that teach us about gifts and positions. It is written:

> **Now there are varieties of gifts, but the same Spirit; and there are varieties of services, but the same Lord; and there are varieties of activities, but it is the same God who activates all of them in everyone. To each is given the manifestation of the Spirit for the common good.**
> 1 Corinthians 12:4-7 (NRSV)

I like the *New Revised Standard Version's* translation of these Scriptures because it reveals to us that, first, there are a variety of manifestation gifts that are connected with Holy Spirit; second, there are a variety of services or offices that are connected with our Master Yahshua; third, there are different types of activities, or functions, or motivations of individuality that are connected with Father Yahweh.

The first place in Scripture that a group of gifts are introduced is in Romans. It is written:

For as in one body we have many members, and not all the members have the same function, so we, who are many, are one body in Christ, and individually we are members one of another. We have gifts that differ according to the grace given to us: prophecy, in proportion to faith; ministry, in ministering; the teacher, in teaching; the exhorter, in exhortation; the giver, in generosity; the leader, in diligence; the compassionate, in cheerfulness.
Romans 12:4-8 (NRSV)

I believe these gifts are actually personality traits or attributes from our Heavenly Father Yahweh. We may express several of these traits in our relationships with others, but there will be one main trait that, from birth, we are destined to grow into. Each human being is "hard-wired," so to speak, with one of these specific motivational attributes that make up part of our complex and unique personality. As we mature in our faith journey as followers of Messiah, led by Holy Spirit, the spiritual personality trait that Father Yahweh blessed us with will become more evident in our daily walk as we become involved in ministry to help those around us who are in need. These personality attributes are very basic and foundational to us as individuals and define our function as part of Yahshua's body of believers who are knitted together for His service and ministry.

The functions or descriptions of the activities stated above are:

Prophecy: This is a person who has the ability to hear clearly and consistently from Holy Spirit for the purpose of discerning motives and intentions of specific persons or groups. The person Yahshua chooses for this position will be gifted with the ability to discern which of the positions of elder leadership and service each person has been called into and will work with each person to enable them to mature in their calling for the building up of the congregation and for edification of the body of believers. A person with this motivational activity is able to exercise great perception of what is right and wrong. Along with this comes the ability to be bold and assertive in discerning and addressing issues within the body. All of these gifts are important for the health and success of the congregation, but having one or more people who are born with this ability is vital. People who are born with prophecy in their personality have been identified as the "eyes" of the body of Messiah. This gift is different from the manifestation of prophecy or the office of prophet that will be covered later.

Ministry: This is a person born with the personality attributes to serve and minister assistance to others. This is a person who has the ability to discern the practical needs of others and quickly does whatever it takes to meet those needs. People who have the natural attribute of ministry or service are identified as the "hands" of the body of Messiah.

Teaching: The person born with this personality trait has a burning passion for the truth from Almighty Yah's Word. This individual does research and diligently seeks the depth and width of Yah's Word to find answers to the many questions of life's circumstances in order to be able to effectively teach others to know the truth and not be deceived with falsehood. People who have the natural attribute of teaching are identified as being the "mind" of the body of Messiah. I believe, based on this book that has been a labor of love for the truth from my perspective and is now being presented to the body of Messiah, that teaching is a function attribute that Father Yahweh blessed me with before I was born. For this gift I am truly grateful.

Exhortation: The person born with this personality trait has the ability to be effective in encouraging people as they grow in their faith and relationship with Almighty Yah. An exhorter in the body of Messiah is one who works to comfort others by lifting them up when they are downtrodden, and they are constantly conveying words that establish peace, unity, and harmony in the congregation. Individuals with this function attribute are identified as the "mouth" of the body of Messiah. I believe that many people who are born with this gift become musicians and singers who lead congregations in praise and worship.

Giving: The person born with the personality trait of giving has the ability to give of themselves and of their resources beyond that which is considered normal among the other members of the body. An individual with this activity attribute has a passion to give their whole self in bringing honor to Almighty Yah by giving their time and resources for

Kingdom work. These dedicated individuals are identified as the "arms" of the body of Messiah.

Leading: The person born with this personality trait has the ability to be an administrator with vision to lead a congregation in the areas of organization and pursuing common goals. Individuals with this activity attribute are keen listeners who hear the needs of the congregation and are quick to address those needs. Those with the leader trait are facilitators who are excellent planners and enable ideas for Kingdom building projects to become realities. I believe I was born with the gift of leadership and administration. I currently serve as congregation leader of our fellowship, Beth Yahshua, and for most of my professional career, I have worked as a manager and administrator. Individuals born with the natural ability to be administrators and leaders are identified as the "ears" of the body of Messiah.

Mercy: The person born with this personality trait has the ability to identify with the joys and distresses of others. They are very effective in helping others overcome emotional scars and pain. These individuals minister to hurting people with great empathy and compassion. Individuals born with the natural ability to be merciful and to turn sadness into joy are identified as the "heart" of the body of messiah.

I will cover the second place in the Scriptures that identifies the group of ministry gifts from 1 Corinthians 12 later in this chapter. I will be expounding with more in depth teaching on the manifestations of Holy Spirit in that section.

This next section, the third place in the Scriptures that identifies a group of gifts, is from the book of Ephesians and is actually addressing offices or positions of leadership within the body of Messiah. It is written:

> **But to each one of us grace was given according to the measure of Christ's gift. Therefore He says: *"When He ascended on high, He led captivity captive, and gave gifts to men."* (Now this, *"He ascended"*— what does it mean but that He also first descended into the lower parts of the earth? He who descended is also the One who ascended far above all the heavens, that He might fill all things.) And He Himself gave some *to be* apostles, some prophets, some evangelists, and some pastors and**

teachers, for the equipping of the saints for the work of ministry, for the edifying of the body of Christ, till we all come to the unity of the faith and of the knowledge of the Son of God, to a perfect man, to the measure of the stature of the fullness of Christ.
Ephesians 4:7-13 (NKJV)

Yahshua raised up and trained His apostles to found and establish firmly His Body that through the centuries has been called the church. His original governing body of the first-century groups of believers that was made up of Messianic Jews and Messianic Gentiles was established with the leadership of a five-fold ministry of men and, I believe, women also who were spiritual specialists in their field. It is written:

Where there is no guidance, a nation falls, but in an abundance of counselors there is safety.
Proverbs 11:14 (NRSV)

Our Yahshua is the Spirit and Head of His body, the *ecclesia*, the called-out ones. His headship is manifested physically through the five-fold ministry of apostles, prophets, evangelists, pastors, and teachers. These positions of leadership within a body of born-again believers are honorable offices, and the individuals who fill them are chosen or called into them by our Master Yahshua for service in the building up of the body and bride of Messiah. Through centuries of deception, false teachings, and rampant egos, the five-fold ministry of leadership that King Yahshua originally established for His body has been, in most cases, watered down and changed into a pastor being the head and leader of a congregation. Many denominations have elected elders and deacons who serve and do good, but for the most part, the body of Messiah has strayed away from the original pattern that Yahshua gave for His body to follow. It is important to remember that the words and actions of individuals functioning in any of these positions of service must line up consistently with the Holy Scriptures of Almighty Yah.

Apostle: The word *apostle* is from the Greek language and means "one sent forth." Apostles are sent to raise up congregations and set them in order. This was the main focus and work of the twelve disciples of Yahshua after they were empowered with Holy Spirit during the Feast of

Shavuot (Pentecost). This was also the main focus of the Apostle Paul, Barnabas, Silas, and many others that were chosen for this position of service and ministry. The apostles are a type of "jack of all trades" who are blessed with a measure of the attributes of the other ministry positions in order to discern the elders they are called to ordain to ensure that a new congregation is built on a solid foundation.

Elders are ordained five-fold ministers, not assistants to a pastor. Each of the offices of the five-fold ministry is an elder position. Elders serve together with their traits and gifts as members of the body that is fitted together to bring edification and leadership to the *ecclesia*. The inner functions of ministry and leadership in most of today's Christ-professing congregations are very different from the inner functions, ministry, and leadership of the first-century Messiah-professing congregations. I believe that you can now see why there are over 1,600 denominations within the Protestant faith that operate with their own different set of rules and guidelines.

Prophet: The second elder position of service is that of prophet. The position of prophet requires an individual who flows with the manifestations gifts of discerning of spirits, words of knowledge, and words of wisdom. I believe that most people who are called by Master Yahshua into the position of prophet are also born with the personality trait of prophecy that was covered a few pages back. The position of prophet is key in building up congregations of born-again believers who are in unity and are operating in harmony in their proper traits they are born with, maturing in the office they are called into for service, and flowing in the gifts of Holy Spirit. The position of prophet is vital in the area of discerning of spirits for the safety and spiritual well being of the congregation. Often, Satan, the adversary, through his organizations of witchcraft, will send people into congregations for the purpose of causing as much confusion and problems as possible. The prophet receives spontaneous "words of knowledge" and "words of wisdom" that are true blessings to the hearer whether the words are confirmation the hearer needs for direction, answers to pray, etc., or reproof the hearer needs to hear for something in their life that needs to be changed. The prophet also operates with the manifestation of prophecy—giving a spontaneous word from Holy Spirit that is proclaiming revelation of truth about events, circumstances, etc. Prophecy must always be in line with the Word of Yahweh.

Evangelist: An elder that is chosen for the position of evangelist has the responsibility of going outside of the body of Messiah to the unsaved to proclaim the good news of the kingdom of Yah and to introduce people to the love of Yahshua. Missionaries are evangelists who are commissioned by the Master to go to foreign lands where the good news of redemption through the blood of Jesus, Yahshua, the Messiah, has never been proclaimed. Evangelists are also called to minister to people on street corners and in prisons for the purpose of helping people to understand their need for a Savior and receiving Yahshua into their hearts. Evangelists are to help people fall in love with Messiah and encourage born-again believers to stir up their spiritual gifts and the manifestations from Holy Spirit.

Pastor: Pastors are elders who are to nurture the congregation, often leading them in prayers and worship. Pastors are to encourage the body to study the Scriptures, to be filled with Holy Spirit, and to lead by their example in love. There are not supposed to be assistant pastors. Men and women are either called by Master Yahshua to be a pastor, or any of the other positions, or they are not called. It was never the plan of Almighty Yah to establish a hierarchy of positions in His *ecclesia,* with a pastor as the head, assistant pastors, and a voted-in board of deacons or elders, just as it was never His plan for the nation of Israel to have a king. When the people did not want to trust Yahweh's instructions and ways, He allowed them to have it their way, just as He does today in modern-day Christian churches and Rabbinical Jewish synagogues. A pastor or rabbi operating as the head of a congregation could very well be operating with a spirit of Nicolaitan. If you remember, I covered this in the last chapter, and it deals with those who strive for status and control in the church and teach false doctrines. The office of a pastor as an elder in the body is to teach the truth from the Scriptures and work with the other elders in ministering to the needs of the members of the body.

Teacher: The position of an elder who is called to serve as a teacher is last in the list of the five-fold ministry leaders in the body but is certainly not the least, as none are least or greatest. They are all important positions that are to function together as a body so the whole can function and be healthy and in harmony with the Head, Master Yahshua. The position of teacher means just that—to study the Scriptures, pray for revelation of truth and understanding from Holy Spirit, and then convey the proper truths to the body of believers in a way that all understand. Some people have a special ability to be teachers of young children, or teenagers, or seniors. Proper teaching of the Word of Almighty Yah is so very important. We are greatly indebted to those who are called to write Scripture-based materials, books, teaching and ministry videos, and those who have established teaching ministries on the internet that are reaching people all over the world in these end times.

Remember, the five-fold positions of ministry are appointments given by Yahshua and are different from the seven personality-trait gifts that a person is born with. They are also different from the nine manifestation gifts from Holy Spirit. For example, because of what I see Almighty Yah doing through me with the writing of this book to teach so many of his awesome truths from His Word, I believe that I have been chosen by Yahshua to serve in the elder leadership position of teacher. As I stated earlier, I believe that I was born with the personality trait from Father Yahweh to serve in leadership and administration. Holy Spirit has also blessed me with a few of the manifestations gifts that are used in ministry to help people.

I will finish this section with an excellent example of the first-century elders of the body of believers in Jerusalem working together to resolve some very important issues of the growing *ecclesia*, the called-out assembly. I will keep this brief and not list all 41 verses, only the main ones that apply.

As the "good news" of the Kingdom and redemption through faith in the blood of Yahshua spread from the early Messianic Jews to the Gentiles through the efforts of the Apostle Paul, Barnabas, and others, there were Jews who were influenced with a Pharisaic spirit of legalism demanding that new male Gentile converts have the foreskins of their penises circumcised according to the law that was given to Moses for the Israelites soon after they had departed from Egypt. The law of circumcision was first established by Almighty Yah with Abraham, as recorded in Genesis 17:10; then on to Moses who had forgotten what to do, as recorded in Exodus 4:25; then on to Joshua as he prepared the second generation of Israelites that had made it through the forty-year wilderness trip to go into the promised land, as recorded in Joshua 5: 2-5. Male circumcision certainly promotes healthier hygiene overall, but again, as with so many of His ways, Father Yahweh was doing something in the flesh of the people to prepare them for something that was to come that He would do in the spirit. It is written:

The days are surely coming, says the LORD, when I will make a new covenant with the house of Israel and the house of Judah. It will not be like the covenant that I made with their ancestors when I took them by the hand to bring them out of the land of Egypt—a covenant that they broke, though I was their husband, says the LORD. But this is the covenant that I will make with the house of Israel after those days, says the LORD: I will put my law within them, and I will write it on their hearts; and I will be their God, and they shall be my people. No longer shall they teach one another, or say to each other, "Know the LORD," for they shall all know me, from the least of them to the greatest, says the LORD; for I will forgive their iniquity, and remember their sin no more.
Jeremiah 31:31-34 (NRSV)

For a person is not a Jew who is one outwardly, nor is true circumcision something external and physical. Rather, a person is a Jew who is one inwardly, and real circumcision is a matter of the heart—it is spiritual and not literal. Such a person receives praise not from others but from God.
Romans 2:28-29 (NRSV)

So now we come to the controversy. It is written:

Then certain individuals came down from Judea and were teaching the brothers, "Unless you are circumcised according to the custom of Moses, you cannot be saved." And after Paul and Barnabas had no small dissension and debate with them, Paul and Barnabas and some of the others were appointed to go up to Jerusalem to discuss this question with the apostles and the elders.
Acts 15:1-2 (NRSV)

As you can tell from reading those verses, Paul and Barnabas used prophecy discernment in determining that what had been presented to them was not in line with the words of Yahshua and the revelation they were receiving from Holy Spirit bearing witness with their spirits.

The following is the Apostle Peter's response and testimony by the Apostles Paul and Barnabas. Peter speaks forth as one operating in the office of prophet, spontaneously proclaiming revelation wisdom and knowledge that bubbles up from inside of him and lines up with the truth of Yah's Word. It is written:

The apostles and the elders met together to consider this matter. After there had been much debate, Peter stood up and said to them, "My brothers, you know that in the early days God made a choice among you, that I should be the one through whom the Gentiles would hear the message of the good news and become believers. And God, who knows the human heart, testified to them by giving them the Holy Spirit, just as he did to us; and in cleansing their hearts by faith he has made no distinction between them and us. Now therefore why are you putting God to the test by placing on the neck of the disciples a yoke that neither our ancestors nor we have been able to bear? On the contrary, we believe that we will be saved through the grace of the Lord Jesus, just as they will." The whole assembly kept silence, and listened to Barnabas and Paul as they told of all the signs and wonders that God had done through them among the Gentiles.

Acts 15:6-12 (NRSV)

The fifteenth chapter of the book of Acts is one of the most important sections of Scripture in all of the Holy Bible. In it we learn the foundational teachings that the elders of the Spirit-filled, born-again assembly in Jerusalem established, by way of their letter, as the minimum basics for non-Jews to be accepted into the body of Messiah Yahshua. After the council of the elders of the assembly met and, probably with much prayer and discussion, rendered their response to the legalistic Jewish believers and to all others as the simple requirement for new believers to adhere to after they had accepted Yahshua as their Master and Redeemer, elder James, the half brother of Yahshua, who was also operating in the office of prophet, delivered the response as Holy Spirit gave it to him. It is written:

And after they had become silent, James answered, saying, "Men *and* brethren, listen to me: Simon has declared how God at the first visited the Gentiles to take out of them a people for His name. And with this the words of the prophets agree, just as it is written: '*After this I will return and will rebuild the tabernacle of David, which has fallen down; I will rebuild its ruins, and I will set it up; so that the rest of mankind may seek the LORD, even all the Gentiles who are called by My name, says the LORD who does all these things.*' Known to God from eternity are all His works. Therefore I judge that we should not trouble those from among the Gentiles who are turning to God, but that we write to

them to abstain from things polluted by idols, *from* sexual immorality, *from* things strangled, and *from* blood. For Moses has had throughout many generations those who preach him in every city, being read in the synagogues every Sabbath." Then it pleased the apostles and elders, with the whole church, to send chosen men of their own company to Antioch with Paul and Barnabas, *namely*, Judas who was also named Barsabas, and Silas, leading men among the brethren.
   Acts 15:13-22 (NKJV)

Here we see the example of the elders of the congregation using their spiritual gifts and offices, working together to bring resolve to a very difficult set of circumstances. Not only is this an example of how those first-century congregation's elders worked together using their gifts for our benefit from the recorded word, but also the message of their resolve for the non-Jew believers like most of us who were and are coming into covenant relationship with Almighty Yah.

The elders were instructing Paul, Barnabas, and others in other cities by way of their letter not to hold new believers to the full letter of the law of Judaism, but to require four things.

First, they were to abstain from things polluted by idols, meaning foods that were used in ceremonies of idol worship in the pagan temples and sold in the open markets as regular food. A lot of the meat was that of swine or pigs, which was and still is not considered as food, according to Yah's Word. Abstaining from things polluted by idols also means to stay away from anything that can be an idol to us, which covers about everything in life. Our Creator and Master is a jealous Creator and requires that He and He alone is to be the God we worship and adore.

Second, they were to abstain from sexual immorality. This includes all of the sex sins—adultery, fornication, homosexuality, masturbation, bestiality, and any other type of perverted sex outside of the sanctity of the holy marriage union between a man and a woman.

Third and fourth, abstinence from things strangled and from blood is again referring to dietary rules of the proper Yahweh-instructed way to bleed out slaughter animals, not strangled, and the issues dealing with blood, such as not drinking it, not eating meat that had not been properly prepared with blood drained out, and for men not to have sexual intercourse with their wives during their monthly menstrual cycle. These instructions still apply today.

Lastly James states: "For Moses has had throughout many generations those who preach him in every city, being read in the synagogues every Sabbath."

In this statement, James is indicating that the instructions given to Moses by Almighty Yah that Moses recorded in the first five books of the Bible called the *Torah* are taught each Sabbath for the benefit of all people who desire to have relationship with Yahweh now through relationship with His Son Yahshua. The instructions from the *Torah* regarding how to treat each other, when to worship together as an assembly on the seventh-day Sabbath, on the seven holy feast times of the year, what to eat and not to eat, how to prepare the food, and everything that we need to know about how to please our Creator and Savior would be taught in the synagogues every Sabbath. You can flip back to Chapter Four of this book and see how apostasy came into the early congregations and how the perversion of the truth from the Scriptures began to spread.

In these the last years of the last generation, Almighty Yah is restoring His truths and instructions among His people. Yes, we are saved from our death sentence only by His marvelous grace through the precious shed blood of Yahshua, but in these last years before He returns to establish His kingdom here on this earth as it is in heaven, He is restoring His bride to His likeness in all His ways. Are you part of His Bride that He is restoring in all of His ways, including following His instructions in the *Torah* and ministering in His gifts that He provides to be a blessing to others?

THE MANIFESTATIONS OF HOLY SPIRIT AND MINISTRY

The Spirit of might, as symbolized as one of the branches of the menorah, is referring to the power, force, or energy from Holy Spirit that comes in the name of Yahshua, or Jesus. The Spirit of might is the supernatural anointing from Almighty Yah that makes supernatural things happen. Yahshua presented Himself for forty days to His followers after His resurrection. He instructed them to stay in Jerusalem and wait for the Promise of the Father. The Promise is the birthing within us of the third manifestation of Almighty Yah as His presence, His indwelling, His Holy Spirit within us, Who gives us boldness to speak Almighty Yah's truth and to be a conduit of energy to bring help to others in many ways.

Remember from our study of the seven feasts that Yahshua died from

His crucifixion during the afternoon when the inspected lambs were slain and prepared for the Passover meal. The first day of Unleavened Bread begins after sunset and during the Passover meal, which is symbolic of our repenting of our sins and turning away from everything that separates us from having relationship with our Creator and Master. Yahshua presented Himself before Father Yahweh as the firstfruits offering, was accepted, and became the first of the first ones to be resurrected to eternal life with a new resurrected body. He returned back to His apostles and friends in His new resurrected body to prove that all He had taught them about His death and resurrection was true. He remained with them for forty days and nights teaching and giving them further instructions. It is written:

> ... to whom He also presented Himself alive after His suffering by many infallible proofs, being seen by them during forty days and speaking of the things pertaining to the kingdom of God. And being assembled together with *them*, He commanded them not to depart from Jerusalem, but to wait for the Promise of the Father, "which," *He said*, "you have heard from Me; for John truly baptized with water, but you shall be baptized with the Holy Spirit not many days from now." Therefore, when they had come together, they asked Him, saying, "Lord, will You at this time restore the kingdom to Israel?" And He said to them, "It is not for you to know times or seasons which the Father has put in His own authority. But you shall receive power when the Holy Spirit has come upon you; and you shall be witnesses to Me in Jerusalem, and in all Judea and Samaria, and to the end of the earth."
>
> Acts 1:3-8 (NKJV)

This Holy Spirit power that the Apostles received was the same Holy Spirit power that our Master Yahshua had when He walked the earth and ministered to people He came in contact with. I believe the best summary in all of the Scriptures that best describes and defines the ministry of Yahshua and that of His true followers is in Isaiah. It is written:

> The spirit of the Lord GOD is upon me, because the LORD has anointed me; he has sent me to bring good news to the oppressed, to bind up the broken-hearted, to proclaim liberty to the captives, and release to the prisoners; to proclaim the year of the LORD's favor, and the day of vengeance

of our God; to comfort all who mourn; to provide for those who mourn in Zion—to give them a garland instead of ashes, the oil of gladness instead of mourning, the mantle of praise instead of a faint spirit.
Isaiah 61:1-3a (NRSV)

When we are born of Almighty Yah's Holy Spirit, His very personal presence dwells within us, providing us with His anointing that destroys the yoke (control) that Satan, has over our life. As we grow in our faith journey, the indwelling person of Holy Spirit calls us to free ourselves from all of the strongholds that Satan has placed on us so we can walk as our Master Yahshua walked—in holiness and righteousness (right standing) with Heavenly Father, Yahweh. We are commissioned by Almighty Yah to minister to people by being His ambassadors and by being led and empowered by His Holy Spirit to do the same things that our Master Yahshua did, by boldly bringing the good news of Yah's Kingdom to the oppressed. The good news is that the one true God, the God of Abraham, Isaac, and Jacob, has made a way for all humans to have forgiveness of their sins through the precious blood of His Son, Yahshua, by accepting the gift of salvation, receiving redemption and a restored relationship with the promise of being a part of Yah's Kingdom throughout all eternity. HalleluYah! That is the very best news that any person can receive who is oppressed, depressed, alone, and beaten down by the enemy.

We bind up the broken-hearted by administering the love of Messiah, Who loved us so much that He gave His life freely for us that, by His death, we would have new life in Him. We minister to others by helping them to change their focus from their condition and their problems to the solution, which is to put their complete faith and trust in Yahshua. He has defeated our enemy, the thief who comes to rob us of all the blessings that Almighty Yah has for us, to steal our will to live righteously, to steal our ability to fulfill the purposes that we were created in this life to fulfill for the glory of our Creator, to kill our bodies with disease and accidents before we have lived to the fullest in Yahshua, and to rob us of all that is good and holy, both in this life and in our eternal kingdom home with Almighty Yah and our many saved loved ones. It is written:

So again Jesus said to them, 'Very truly, I tell you, I am the gate for the sheep. All who came before me are thieves and bandits; but the sheep did not listen to them. I am the gate. Whoever enters by me will be

saved, and will come in and go out and find pasture. The thief comes only to steal and kill and destroy. I came that they may have life, and have it abundantly.
John 10:7-10 (NRSV)

We have abundant life in Yahshua when the curses that are on our life have been broken and the demonic spirits have been cast out and are prevented from returning into us. When the curses have been broken and the demons cast out, there is liberty to the captives, and those who are bound in a spiritual prison are set free. Yahshua's ministry was proclaiming that the Kingdom of His Father, Yahweh, had come in Him because of His power to defeat Satan's hold on humanity with sin, demonic oppression, disease, and death. Yahshua proclaimed the truth of the Kingdom and worked the power of the Kingdom with the manifestation of casting out demons and healing all types of human infirmaries. It is written:

After they had gone away, a demoniac who was mute was brought to him. And when the demon had been cast out, the one who had been mute spoke; and the crowds were amazed and said, 'Never has anything like this been seen in Israel.' But the Pharisees said, 'By the ruler of the demons he casts out the demons.' Then Jesus went about all the cities and villages, teaching in their synagogues, and proclaiming the good news of the kingdom, and curing every disease and every sickness. When he saw the crowds, he had compassion for them, because they were harassed and helpless, like sheep without a shepherd. Then he said to his disciples, 'The harvest is plentiful, but the laborers are few; therefore ask the Lord of the harvest to send out laborers into his harvest.'
Matthew 9:32-38 (NRSV)

The body of Messiah is to minister to people the same way that our Master, Yahshua Messiah, ministered to people because the empowerment of Holy Spirit has not changed. It is written:

Jesus Christ is the same yesterday and today and for ever.
Hebrews 13:8 (NRSV)

Yahshua's ministry has continued from the day that Holy Spirit filled the 120 believers during the Feast of *Shavuot* (Pentecost) until now, and will continue until Yahshua returns to the earth, through His true, born-again followers who are ministering to others by His power and in His name.

Yahshua has not changed His ministry. He is still continuing His deliverance and healing ministry today through His faithful body that has washed herself clean from her sins by His blood and His Word and is fulfilling His call upon her life to teach the good news of the Kingdom and to do His mighty works. He equips each member that makes up His body to do different types of ministry. We are individually called by Holy Spirit to different positions and are given different manifestations from Holy Spirit to enable us to do the ministry He has purposed for us to do in this life that will be a blessing to those we minister to and bring glory to Almighty Yah. Amen! It is written:

> **I, therefore, the prisoner of the Lord, beseech you to walk worthy of the calling with which you were called, with all lowliness and gentleness, with longsuffering, bearing with one another in love, endeavoring to keep the unity of the Spirit in the bond of peace.** *There is* **one body and one Spirit, just as you were called in one hope of your calling; one Lord, one faith, one baptism; one God and Father of all, who** *is* **above all, and through all, and in you all. But to each one of us grace was given according to the measure of Christ's gift. ... And He Himself gave some** *to be* **apostles, some prophets, some evangelists, and some pastors and teachers, for the equipping of the saints for the work of ministry, for the edifying of the body of Christ ...**
> Ephesians 4:1-7, 11-12 (NKJV)

These Scriptures describe the different positions or offices in which Yahshua's followers will operate.

One of the best examples I can give you of individuals who received the call upon their lives to operate as evangelists, with gifts of healing to the nations, is that of the great evangelist T. L. Osborn, his daughter LaDonna Osborn, and her son, Tommy O'Dell. Through the faithful work of these three generations of family members over a period of nearly sixty years, many millions of people in nearly 100 countries of the world have heard the good news of the Kingdom preached in their language with evidence of many thousands of people saved, miraculously healed, and demons cast out. I have read only one of the many books that the Osborn family has written. The title is, "Miracles, Proof of God's Love." I encourage you to check out their website at www.OSBORN.ORG.

How awesome is the power of Holy Spirit as He moves in people to bring healing and deliverance from the oppression of the devil. Only a few of Yah's children are chosen for ministries that impact millions of people's lives the way the Osborns have, but we are all called to be faithful to whatever the ministry that Holy Spirit reveals to us that we are to do.

Now for the different manifestations of power from Holy spirit. It is written:

> I [John the Baptist] indeed baptize you with water unto repentance, but He [Yahshua] who is coming after me is mightier than I, whose sandals I am not worthy to carry. He will baptize you with the Holy Spirit and fire.
>
> Matthew 3:11 (NKJV). *Bracketed words added for clarity.*

> And being assembled together with *them*, He commanded them not to depart from Jerusalem, but to wait for the Promise of the Father, "which," *He said,* "you have heard from Me; for John truly baptized with water, but you shall be baptized with the Holy Spirit not many days from now." ... But you shall receive power when the Holy Spirit has come upon you; and you shall be witnesses to Me in Jerusalem, and in all Judea and Samaria, and to the end of the earth."
>
> Acts 1:4-5, 8 (NKJV)

> Now concerning spiritual gifts, brothers and sisters, I do not want you to be uninformed. ... Now there are varieties of gifts, but the same Spirit; and there are varieties of services, but the same Lord; and there are varieties of activities, but it is the same God who activates all of them in everyone. To each is given the manifestation of the Spirit for the common good. To one is given through the Spirit the utterance of wisdom, and to another the utterance of knowledge according to the same Spirit, to another faith by the same Spirit, to another gifts of healing by the one Spirit, to another the working of miracles, to another prophecy, to another the discernment of spirits, to another various kinds of tongues, to another the interpretation of tongues. All these are activated by one and the same Spirit, who allots to each one individually just as the Spirit chooses. For just as the body is one and has many mem-

bers, and all the members of the body, though many, are one body, so it is with Christ. For in the one Spirit we were all baptized into one body—Jews or Greeks, slaves or free—and we were all made to drink of one Spirit.

1 Corinthians 12:1, 4-13 (NRSV)

I truly believe that when we accept Yahshua as our Master and Savior and are born anew with the gift of Holy Spirit from Father Yahweh, that we have His power in us to have some or all nine of the manifestations, or empowerments, available to be used at any given moment. Often, several of the manifestations of Holy Spirit are operating at the same time in ministry. In order for His manifestations of power to work through us, we must seek Him in humility with pure hearts and clean hands. Holy Spirit is faithful and true. Ask Him to reveal to you your purpose in life and the ministry you are to do. You may not receive the answer instantly; it may be gradual, but you will receive your answers and confidence to move forward in ministry to help others.

I have organized the nine manifestation gifts from Holy Spirit into three groups according to functions. This first group of three includes the gifts that help us to know things supernaturally from Holy Spirit.

Word of Wisdom: This is the supernatural revelation from Holy Spirit of Divine purpose; the supernatural declaration of the mind and will of Almighty Yah; the supernatural unfolding of His plans and purposes concerning things, places, peoples, individuals, communities, and even nations. I believe examples from the Scriptures of the word of wisdom are when Yahshua taught with parables and gave teachings of the coming Kingdom and when Paul taught about Gentiles being grafted into the Olive tree, as recorded in Roman 11. I have experienced a word of wisdom coming forth from Holy Spirit within me while teaching different groups. It is an awareness that I was being used as a mouthpiece by the Creator of the universe to proclaim His truths to benefit others. This happens spontaneously without preparation. You may be teaching one direction from your prepared text, and suddenly Holy Spirit delivers through a different divine message that He wants to be given to those in attendance. I have also observed this in the presence of others giving teachings from the Scriptures.

Word of Knowledge: This is the manifestation of divine knowledge that is available from Almighty Yah. A word of knowledge comes in the form of dreams or visions. It is written:

> **And it shall come to pass afterward, that I will pour out my spirit upon all flesh; and your sons and your daughters shall prophesy, your old men shall dream dreams, your young men shall see visions.**
> Joel 2:28 (KJV)

A word of knowledge is information or facts from Yah through Holy Spirit about people, places, things, and events in which the person speaking "the word" could not possibly know unless Holy Spirit revealed it to them. A good example of a word of knowledge is found in Acts Chapter 10 when the Apostle Peter is given a vision of all types of animals and told to eat of them. Peter, being a Jew, was taught from the *Torah* from childhood the meats that Almighty Yah had clearly instructed were clean and unclean. Peter is later given discernment about the dream that is wasn't about what foods to eat but, rather, that Father Yahweh was making His plan of redemption available to the non-Jew Gentiles along with the Jews who had accepted Yahshua as the Messiah and been born of Holy Spirit. Another significant example is that of the Apostle John and the 14 visions he was given of the events of the Day of the Lord and the second coming of King Yahshua. The interpretation of words of knowledge from dreams and visions are a blessing for us in helping us to be able to understand the mysteries of our Creator. We are blessed in our congregation to have a dear brother who receives awesome visions that reveal prophetic things to us that Holy Spirit is doing through Yah's people in the earth in these end times.

Discernment of Spirits: This is the manifestation that Holy Spirit uses in born again individuals that enables them to detect what is true and what is false. The gift of discerning of spirits is not only defensive, it can also be offensive in the sense that once an evil spirit is detected as operating through a person, that person can and should be confronted with compassion and, if they are willing, be delivered from the influence of the demonic spirit. Two examples in Scripture of the discernment of spirits are in the book of Acts. In Chapter Eight, the Apostle Peter is confronting a man named Simon who had a reputation of practicing sorcery.

In verse 23, Peter states that he sees, or discerns, that Simon was poisoned by bitterness (an evil spirit) and bound by iniquity.

The other example is in Chapter 16, verses 16 through 18. Paul and Silas had traveled to Philippi and were confronted by a young woman who was possessed by a spirit of divination that gave her the ability to tell people's fortunes. The demon that was providing her with supernatural information about people spoke through her the truth about Paul and Silas, saying:

"These men are the servants of the Most High God, who proclaim to us the way of salvation."
Acts 16:17b (NKJV)

The Scripture goes on to teach us that Paul grew weary of her relentlessly proclaiming the truth about him and Silas, so he discerned the demonic spirit operating in her and cast it out, which took away her ability to earn lots of money as a fortune teller for her slave owners who were capitalizing on her occult abilities.

I have experienced Holy Spirit giving me discernment about individuals as I was praying over them and ministering to them. One event was when a man came to our congregation for the first time, and several times was trying to take control of the meeting. After the meeting several members came to me saying they discerned that a controlling witchcraft spirit was working through the man. I prayed about it and received confirmation from Holy Spirit that what they said was true. I then prayed and asked Holy Spirit to reveal the root cause of the witchcraft spirit in the man. I heard clearly that when he was a young person, he had played with the Ouija board, and that had opened the door for the demonic spirit to come in. When confronting him about the spirit of witchcraft, he admitted to using the Ouija board, and then he said he had been delivered from the witchcraft spirit. I assured him that he had not been delivered and offered to help, but he did not accept.

Another experience I had was during a service when I was praying over a man and discerned that he had a spirit of falsehood operating through him from Freemasonry. I confronted him, and he admitted to being in the secret organization of the Masons. I explained to him the deception, lies, and curses that men and women come under who are in those types of secret organizations, and that he should renounce all of it and be delivered from the demonic spirits that were working through him. He chose to walk away.

If you, dear reader, are involved in the secret cult organizations of Freemasonry, Shriners, or Eastern Star, resign, get out, and renounce all the oaths that you have sworn and break the curses associated with them in the name of Yahshua or, if you prefer, in the name of Jesus. Most people in those organizations are in them because they are perceived as good fraternities that do good things in our society for children, etc. They do bring blessings to people in need, but at a high cost to those who are swimming in a sea of falsehood and deception. The truth is that the leadership of these cults teaches that the true way of enlightenment is within the lodge. The membership of the lodge is a religion that must be universal, meaning that all belief systems are equal and accepted, and that the initiates put their former beliefs aside to embrace the illumination of deception that the lodge offers as the men and women bow before the altars swearing unspeakable blood oaths that bind the initiates by a spirit of fear. Much of these described cults have to do with progressing through degrees in the pursuit of secret words for rituals, such as in the 17th degree and learning the secret password of Abaddon. Read Revelation 9:11 for a better understanding of how that name connects to Satan.

Another secret name that is sought after in the rituals and progression in the degrees is the blasphemous name Jahbulon. This sickening name is a combination of the three names, Jah-bul-on: *Jah*, the short form of the Hebrew name of Almighty God Yahweh; *Bul,* a rendering of Baal, who from history and the Holy Scriptures, represents a variety of the fertility and nature gods of the ancient Semitic peoples who worshiped idols representing these false gods that Almighty Yah despises; and the last part, *On*, that is used in the Egyptian and Babylonian mysteries to call upon and identify with the false deity of Osiris, the god of fertility.

As born-again believers of the one true God, the God of Abraham, Isaac, and Jacob, and in His Son, Yahshua, our Savior and Messiah, we are to come out of all deception, lies, and falsehood. I recommend two very good books to you on these subjects—"Fast Facts on False Teachings," by Ron Carlson and Ed Decker, and "The Masonic Lodge, What You Need to Know," by Ed Decker. Both can be found in bookstores and at www.HarvestHousePublishers.com

I am sharing these experiences to help you understand the importance of discerning spirits that are operating through people you come in contact with. In most cases, the spirits are operating in very subtle ways so as not to be detected. This is why we need to seek Holy Spirit to give us discernment, which is so important.

I will share one last experience about how Holy Spirit gives discernment to bring forth truth to minister to people. In the spring of 1999, here in my hometown of Greenville, North Carolina, the local Gay Pride organization sponsored a Gay Pride weekend, with speakers, entertainers, and display tables with all types of gay lifestyle books and paraphernalia for sale. I ordered 100 "Dear Robert" tracts from the Exodus International Ministry and had printed the same number of inserts with Scriptures that address homosexuality as being an abomination to Yahweh to hand out to the people who came to the function. At first, I was only allowed to walk on the perimeter of the grounds, but later in the day, I was invited over by some of the people at the function to have dialog with them. They realized that I was not there to judge them and beat them in the head with a Bible. I came to them with compassion in my heart to minister to them with the truth. Two young men who said they had been married to each other for seven years entered into a 30-minute conversation with me. Finally, the one in the husband and headship role asked me a profound question. He said, "I have felt attracted to members of my same sex all my life. This feeling is so deep within me that it has to be normal and right. Why do I feel this way?" I explained to them that the truth was often hard to accept. I said, "You have a demon spirit that entered your body when you were a child, and it became a part of your being and has been the influence of your thinking and decisions, causing you to feel that a same-sex relationship is right for you and that a heterosexual relationship is strange and unacceptable."

Demons enter into people with the goal of perverting their thinking and leading them away from the truth so that Satan can be successful in stealing people away from Almighty Yah. As you can probably imagine, those two young men were dumbfounded, having never before heard anyone give that type of explanation. The sad part is that they looked at each other, joined hands, and turned away. As they were walking away, they said, "Man, I have never heard anything so weird in my life; we have enough Jesus." They had heard the truth, and they did not want any part of it.

In order for a person to be saved by believing that Yahshua is Who He said He is, the Savior, the individual must recognize that they have sin and need to be forgiven, and they must want to be saved. The same is true for deliverance from the full array of conditions that are directly caused by the presence of a demon or demons that are inhabiting a person, causing the person to do things through fleshly desires that do not line up with Yah's Word and are not pleasing or acceptable to Him. And, yes, born-again believers can be under the control and oppression of a demon spirit or spirits living within their body and mind. Holy Spirit draws us to the foot of the cross to accept Yahshua (Jesus) and to help us begin to comprehend all that He has done for us. It is our responsibility to get rid of our spiritual baggage that hinders us and entices us back into our former sins before we applied the blood of Yahshua to wipe away our sins.

Remember this: Satan is a legalist and knows his rights before Almighty Yah. He knows when he can legally send a demon into a person; it is when the person has opened the door to him through sin. We must become submissive to Father Yahweh and committed to allowing the power of Holy Spirit and His holiness to drive out all of the unholiness that is within us.

Will born-again believers who continue to allow themselves to be controlled by demonic spirits make it into Almighty Yah's coming Kingdom? King Yahshua is our judge, and only He can judge the heart and the intentions of our hearts with His righteousness. I leave you with these Scriptures to ponder. It is written:

Then I saw thrones, and those seated on them were given authority to judge. I also saw the souls of those who had been beheaded for their testimony to Jesus and for the word of God. They had not worshipped the beast or its image and had not received its mark on their foreheads or their hands. They came to life and reigned with Christ for a thousand years. (The rest of the dead did not come to life until the thousand years were ended.) This is the first resurrection. Blessed and holy are those who share in the first resurrection. Over these the second death has no power, but they will be priests of God and of Christ, and they will reign with him for a thousand years. ... And the sea gave up the dead that were in it, Death and Hades gave up the dead that were in them, and all were judged according to what they had done. Then Death and Hades were thrown into the lake of fire. This is the second death, the lake of fire; and anyone whose name was not found written in the book of life was thrown into the lake of fire.

Revelation 20:4-6 & 13-15 (NRSV)

"... I will give of the fountain of the water of life freely to him who thirsts. He who overcomes shall inherit all things, and I will be his God and he shall be My son. But the cowardly, unbelieving, abominable, murderers, sexually immoral, sorcerers, idolaters, and all liars shall have their part in the lake which burns with fire and brimstone, which is the second death."

Revelation 21:6b-8 (NKJV)

I encourage you, dear reader, if you are a homosexual, believer or not, seek deliverance from the demon that is binding you to the sin of perverted sexual preference. There is a wonderful ministry that can help. It is Exodus International at www.exodus-international.org. The ministers there have helped many thousands of individuals to be set free from homosexuality.

What applies to homosexuality also applies to all other sex sins— adultery, fornication, pornography, masturbation, bestiality—all such crimes against nature. Be delivered and set free in Yahshua's (Jesus') mighty name. Amen.

The next three gifts are the gifts that help us to act supernaturally by the leading and flow of Holy Spirit's power through us.

Supernatural Faith: This type faith is not the ordinary faith, without which it is impossible to please our Creator. There is saving faith that is a gift from Father Yah as recorded in Ephesians 2:8, but this is a manifestation of supernatural faith that comes by the baptism of fire from Holy Spirit. This empowerment of faith surpasses all reason and sees the impossible as possible by the power of the Creator of the universe. An example of this type faith is found in the book of Acts. It is written:

Now Peter and John went up together to the temple at the hour of prayer, the ninth *hour*. And a certain man lame from his mother's womb was carried, whom they laid daily at the gate of the temple which is called Beautiful, to ask alms from those who entered the temple; who, seeing Peter and John about to go into the temple, asked for alms. And fixing his eyes on him, with John, Peter said, "Look at us." So he gave them his attention, expecting to receive something from them. Then Peter said, "Silver and gold I do not have, but what I do have I give you: In the name of Jesus Christ of Nazareth, rise up and walk." And he took him by the right hand and lifted *him* up, and immediately his feet and ankle bones received strength. So he, leaping up, stood and walked and entered the temple with them—walking, leaping, and praising God. And all the people saw him walking and praising God. ... And His name [*Yahshua, or Jesus*], through faith in His name, has made this man strong, whom you see and know. Yes, the faith which *comes* through Him has given him this perfect soundness in the presence of you all.

   Acts 3:1-9, 16 (NKJV). *Bracketed words added for clarity.*

This is the first recorded miracle in the Scriptures that took place after the outpouring of Holy Spirit on the 120 believers a few hours or days prior during the Feast of *Shavuot*. The poor, lame beggar probably was not a born-again believer, but yet he was miraculously healed, not by his belief and faith, but by the power of Holy Spirit working in Peter and John, who moved in supernatural faith.

   The same supernatural manifestation of faith is in operation in believers today in ministries and all types of day-to-day circumstances. If you need a supernatural miracle in your life, get your life right before Master Yahshua, ask Holy Spirit to bless you with supernatural faith, speak to your mountain (problem), and call things that are not as though they are. Remember, our words are very powerful. Speak the right words that line up with the Scriptures, have faith, and then act on your faith as Abraham did.

   Working of Miracles: This is a supernatural manifestation of Holy Spirit in which supernatural power is released in a person's life to affect an immediate supernatural healing or happening. As I stated earlier, the manifestations of Holy Spirit often work in concert within a person as the power is released for the miracle to happen. An example of the working of miracles is found in the book of Acts. It is written:

God did extraordinary miracles through Paul, so that when the hand-kerchiefs or aprons that had touched his skin were brought to the sick, their diseases left them, and the evil spirits came out of them. ... A young man named Eutychus, who was sitting in the window, began to sink off into a deep sleep while Paul talked still longer. Overcome by sleep, he fell to the ground three floors below and was picked up dead. But Paul went down, and bending over him took him in his arms, and

said, 'Do not be alarmed, for his life is in him.' Then Paul went upstairs, and after he had broken bread and eaten, he continued to converse with them until dawn; then he left. Meanwhile they had taken the boy away alive and were not a little comforted.
Acts 19:11-12; 20:9-12 (NRSV)

These types of miracles are fairly common today, especially in third-world countries. Smith Wigglesworth was an evangelist in the early 1900s in England. There are documented accounts of him, by the power of Holy Spirit in the name of Jesus Christ, having raised twelve people from the dead. HalleluYah, we serve an awesome Creator and Savior.

Gifts of Healings: This supernatural manifestation is given to certain individuals selected by Holy Spirit for the healing ministry. All believers in Yahshua (Jesus) are to minister to those who have infirmaries, as the Scriptures instruct. It is written:

Is anyone among you sick? Let him call for the elders of the church, and let them pray over him, anointing him with oil in the name of the Lord. And the prayer of faith will save the sick, and the Lord will raise him up. And if he has committed sins, he will be forgiven. Confess *your* trespasses to one another, and pray for one another, that you may be healed. The effective, fervent prayer of a righteous man avails much.
James 5:14-16 (NKJV)

Are people with diseases and infirmaries that are prayed for following the instructions above healed 100 percent of the time? No, because sometimes the anointing power of Holy Spirit does not manifest for various reasons, and sometimes in Almighty Yah's supreme wisdom and sovereignty, He chooses for an individual not to receive their healing for His greater purpose in the individual's life to be fulfilled. An example of this in Scripture is the account of the Apostle Paul, who pleaded with our Master three times for his healing. It is written:

But if I wish to boast, I will not be a fool, for I will be speaking the truth. But I refrain from it, so that no one may think better of me than what is seen in me or heard from me, even considering the exceptional character of the revelations. Therefore, to keep me from being too elated, a

thorn was given to me in the flesh, a messenger of Satan to torment me, to keep me from being too elated. Three times I appealed to the Lord about this, that it would leave me, but he said to me, 'My grace is sufficient for you, for power is made perfect in weakness.' So, I will boast all the more gladly of my weaknesses, so that the power of Christ may dwell in me.

2 Corinthians 12:6-9 (NRSV)

I encourage you to read the first five verses of that chapter to gain a better understanding that Paul is teaching about staying humble. What the thorn in Paul's flesh really was has been the subject of much debate among believers who study the Word for deeper meaning. My interpretation is that the thorn was a demonic spirit that Paul was not able to cast away from himself, an instrument of Satan used by Almighty Yah to actually help Paul not to become prideful and not to seek the praise of men. Smith Wigglesworth was responsible for helping many people receive salvation, healings, and deliverances from demonic afflictions, but he endured kidney stones for years, along with other painful conditions. Some things we simply cannot explain or understand. Father Yahweh's thoughts and ways are higher than man's thoughts and ways, and He always knows what is best for us in molding our character. Read Isaiah 55:6-11.

There are many things that can prevent the healing power of Holy Spirit to flow. I will list some that I have learned from the writings of the late Derek Prince, who went on to his heavenly reward in September 2003. Derek Prince, one of the most amazing servants of our Master Yahshua, was born in India and educated in England at Eton College and Cambridge University, where he became a scholar of Greek and Latin. Later, he studied Hebrew and Aramaic at Cambridge and Hebrew University in Jerusalem. He also learned to speak other modern languages. During World War II, while serving in the British Army, he had a life-changing, born-again experience with our Creator and Savior, Jesus, Yahshua, the Messiah, which led him into a life of ministry that began in Jerusalem in 1946. For decades, Mr. Prince has been internationally regarded as one of the world's foremost teachers of the Bible Scriptures. He wrote over forty-five books that have been translated into sixty-plus languages that have impacted millions of people. His ongoing daily radio broadcast reaches more than half of the people on this planet in thirteen languages including Chinese, Russian, Arabic, and Spanish. For many years, he traveled to many countries giving seminars where he would teach on healing and deliverance and then minister healing and deliverance to large groups of people. It would be difficult to identify an individual in modern times whose life and ministry have impacted the lives of more people than that of Mr. Derek Prince.

The book I am referencing that explains the factors that may hinder a person from receiving deliverance is Mr. Prince's "They Shall Expel Demons," published by Chosen Books. This is the very best book I have ever read on the subject of understanding the reality of demons, healing, and deliverance. I highly recommend it to anyone that wants to learn from the great teacher, Derek Prince, how to be delivered and healed. This book and all of his great works can be found in Christian bookstores, or they can be ordered directly from the Derek Prince ministry's web site at http://store.derekprince.ca/us_store.htm.

The ten possible factors that may block the healing flow of Holy Spirit that Mr. Prince lists in his book are: lack of repentance; lack of desperation; wrong motives; self-centeredness—a desire for attention; failure to break with the occult; failure to sever binding, soulish relationships; lack of release from a curse; failure to confess a specific sin; not being "separated" by water baptism; and the individual being part of a larger spiritual battle. I am expounding here only on the lack of release from a curse. I encourage you to order and read this great book that will help you in many ways.

Curses and demonic influence can bring much hurt and misery upon a person. Manipulation by the powers and principalities in the air can cause a person who is bound up and under their influence to commit acts that they know are wrong and sinful because they are defined in Yah's word. The presence of demonic spirits can open the way for many types of diseases and prevent us from receiving the blessings that Almighty Yah has stored up for us. Even when a child is in the womb, demons and curses can, and often do, begin to have influences on the unborn person's life. In order for a demon to be allowed to influence anyone, even the unborn, it must have been given legal access. Legal access can be manifested in many different curses. It is written:

Then God spoke all these words: I am the LORD your God, who brought you out of the land of Egypt, out of the house of slavery; you shall have no other gods before me. You shall not make for yourself an idol,

whether in the form of anything that is in heaven above, or that is on the earth beneath, or that is in the water under the earth. You shall not bow down to them or worship them; for I the LORD your God am a jealous God, punishing children for the iniquity of parents, to the third and the fourth generation of those who reject me, but showing stead-fast love to the thousandth generation of those who love me and keep my commandments.
    Exodus 20:1-6 (NRSV)

As we see clearly in Almighty Yah's Word, He expects us to be in relationship with Him, putting Him above anything and everything else in our lives because, as our Creator and Redeemer, He deserves to be first. He is jealous of anything that we put before Him and makes it clear that we can expect curses by worshiping anything or anyone other that Him. The demons that bring the curses of diseases can come from the words and actions of our parents, grandparents, and up the generational line, by their saying and doing things that give the demons legal access not only to themselves, but to their children and grandchildren, etc. Obliviously, people say and do things out of ignorance, not realizing the effects of what they have done will have on their children and others. I refer to this important Scripture again. It is written:

Death and life are in the power of the tongue: and they that love it shall eat the fruit thereof.
    Proverbs 18:21 (KJV)

A good example of this is someone who is involved with a secret cult organization such as Freemasonry. The oaths the men swear and their allegiance to the god of illumination can and do bring curses of many varieties of diseases on them and their family members. I'm telling you again, dear reader, if you or someone you know is involved in Freemasonry or any type of occult or witchcraft activity, speak the truth to them and encourage them to repent, renounce all they have spoken and done, and get away from anything that is offensive to Almighty Yah.
    Mr. Prince, in his book, "They Shall Expel Demons," states on page 200 how sneaky demons can be. He states, "There is another way demons can be contributory causes of sickness. While not actually causing sick-ness, they can produce an attitude of mind that either opens the door to

sickness or else prevents sick people from receiving their healing by faith. Some examples of such negative spirits are rejection, fear, grief, unforgiveness, discouragement, disappointment, and despair. In such cases, it is usually necessary to expel the negative spirit before seeking to minister physical healing."

This is where the manifestation of words of knowledge provides the person doing the ministering with discernment as to what the person being ministered to has been emotionally expressing and experiencing that unconsciously has produced the infirmity.

On page 210 of Mr. Prince's book, he states: "Over the years I have compiled a list of some of the problems that commonly indicate that a curse is at work: 1) mental or emotional breakdown, 2) repeated or chronic sicknesses (especially if hereditary), 3) barrenness, a tendency to miscarry, or related female problems, 4) breakdown of marriage and family alienation, 5) continuing financial insufficiency, 6) being "accident-prone," 7) a family history of suicides or unnatural or untimely deaths."

When our Master and Redeemer Yahshua, Jesus the Messiah came to this earth that He created, He freely gave His life as the final sacrifice by dying on the cross. With that incredible act of love and allowing the whips to be layed upon His back, He took our death penalty and every curse and disease so that in return we would be able to inherit the blessings of health, happiness, and prosperity that our Heavenly Father intended for us to have from the beginning. We are given the freedom to choose blessings or curses by our words and deeds. It is written:

> **I call heaven and earth to witness against you today that I have set before you life and death, blessings and curses. Choose life so that you and your descendants may live, loving the LORD your God, obeying him, and holding fast to him; for that means life to you and length of days, so that you may live in the land that the LORD swore to give to your ancestors, to Abraham, to Isaac, and to Jacob.**
> Deuteronomy 30:19-20 (KJV)

The blood of Yahshua has defeated Satan and all of his army of demons. I encourage you to plead, or speak, the blood of Yahshua over every area of your life, seeking deliverance from every demon and disease that tries to come against you.

On pages 216 and 217 of Mr. Prince's book, he has provided a model prayer to help any person receive their deliverance and to make the way to also receive their healing. Be fully persuaded in your belief and faith in your Savior, Yahshua. Be completely sincere because Holy Spirit looks even into the intents of our hearts and knows if we are sincere or not. Mr. Prince uses the name *Jesus* and titles *Christ* and *God*. If you feel led to do the same rather than using *Yahshua, Yahweh* and *Messiah*, then you speak as Holy Spirit leads you.

Following is the model prayer.

1. Personally affirm your faith in Christ: "Lord Jesus Christ, I believe You are the Son of God—that You died on the cross for my sins and rose again so that I might be forgiven and receive eternal life."
2. Humble yourself: "I renounce all pride and religious self-righteousness and any dignity that does not come from You. I have no claim on Your mercy except that You died in my place."
3. Confess any known sin: "I confess all my sins before You and hold nothing back. Especially I confess the sin of ..."
4. Repent of all sins: "I repent of all my sins. I turn away from them and I turn to You, Lord, for mercy and forgiveness."
5. Forgive all other people: "By a decision of my free will, I freely forgive all who have ever harmed or wronged me. I lay down all bitterness, all resentment, and all hatred. Specifically, I forgive ..."
6. Break with the occult and all false religion: "I sever all contact I have ever had with the occult or with all false religion—particularly ..."
7. Prepare to be released from every curse over your life: "Lord Jesus, I thank You that on the cross You were made a curse, that I might be redeemed from every curse and inherit God's blessing. On that basis, I ask You to release me and set me free to receive the deliverance I need."
8. Take your stand with God: "I take my stand with You, Lord, against all Satan's demons. I submit to You, Lord, and I resist the devil. Amen!"
9. Expel: "Now I speak to any demons that have control over me (speak directly to them). I command you to go from me now. In the name of Jesus, I expel you!"

I can't leave this section without providing you with some other excellent reference materials from great authors and ministers, who have written on the subjects of healing, deliverance, and breaking curses.

I have been very blessed to have met and experienced my personal deliverance session from a very gifted faith healer and deliverance minister who is a dear sister in Yahshua, Emily Dotson. Emily's testimony is simply amazing. She accepted Jesus as her Savior before the age of nine. She was an unhealthy child, and before reaching age 46, she had experienced eleven surgeries for various conditions. After her first back injury in 1979, she had liver failure. Then she received a diagnosis of advanced lupus. Emily learned to speak God's Word over her diagnosis, and twelve months later, she was healed. Her doctors found her miraculous healing very difficult to believe. They documented her healing as the first ever of someone recovering from the very fatal, chronic, final stages of lupus. This was after they had explained to Emily that there was nothing more they could do and that she should make herself comfortable at home and prepare to die. Now, in the year 2006, after Emily's doctors sent her home to die, she remains healed, well, and strong after speaking God's Word over her diagnosis until her healing manifested. I encourage you to visit her website at www.emilydotson.com and order some of her excellent books and tapes on healing and deliverance. You will be blessed by this amazing lady's work.

I have not met Pastor Larry Huch, but I am impressed with his book, "10 Curses that Block the Blessing," published by Whitaker House. Pastor Huch was given a word of prophesy from Holy Spirit through a pastor's wife while she and her husband were visiting Larry. The next day, the pastor gave confirmation to the word of knowledge as he described a dream. The word of prophesy from the lady was that Almighty had given Pastor Larry the gift of deliverance and the gift to teach it. The dream from her husband revealed that Pastor Larry was to meet Derek Prince, as with the leading of Holy Spirit, the mantle of deliverance ministry was to pass on from Derek Prince to Pastor Larry. This happened, and today Pastor Larry and his wife, Tiz, minister to many people here in America and in other counties. I encourage you to order his book by visiting their website at www.larryhuchministries.com or www.newbeginnings.org.

Each and every time you experience deliverance and healing, praise Father Yahweh and His Son, our master Yahshua, Jesus. Make Him Master and Lord of every area of your life, including your finances. If you have never given a portion of your income away to help ministries and others who are less fortunate than you, start giving with gladness for all that you have been blessed with from our Heavenly Father.

After you have been delivered, healed, and set free from curses, diseases and oppression from the adversary, seek Holy Spirit and inquire what your calling and purpose in life is, so that you can begin the Kingdom work that Almighty Yah has planned for you since before He created the earth. When we truly love our Creator and Master with all of our heart, soul, and strength and are seeking for Him to fulfill His Kingdom purposes in us, Holy Spirit will lead us into the position that is right for us and bless us with the manifestations of power to accomplish the work He desires to do through us as we minister to others. The baptism of fire from Master Yahshua gave the first-century disciples boldness to teach people they encountered the truth about the life of Yahshua, the risen Savior of the human race, and the importance of placing their complete faith in Him. The first-century disciples were instructed by Yahshua to go out and proclaim the Kingdom of Yahweh and do the works that He did. It is written:

> And He said to them, "Go into all the world and preach the gospel to every creature. He who believes and is baptized will be saved; but he who does not believe will be condemned. And these signs will follow those who believe: In My name they will cast out demons; they will speak with new tongues; they will take up serpents; and if they drink anything deadly, it will by no means hurt them; they will lay hands on the sick, and they will recover." So then, after the Lord had spoken to them, He was received up into heaven, and sat down at the right hand of God. And they went out and preached everywhere, the Lord working with *them* and confirming the word through the accompanying signs. Amen.
>
> Mark 16:15-20 (NKJV)

This message of truth was for Messiah's disciples then, every century since, and for His disciples now in this, the last, generation. The reason I state this is because the Holy Scriptures state that our Creator does not change and does not show any greater respect for one person over another. He is looking for whosoever that is willing and desires to walk in His Holy Spirit power in order to be used to minister to others for the building of His kingdom for His glory, and His glory alone.

The last grouping of three manifestation gifts of Holy Spirit is those that are inspirational, in which Holy Spirit spontaneously speaks something through an individual.

Prophecy: An individual that Holy Spirit has blessed with this manifestation will spontaneously speak in his known language a divine oracle that is for the edifying and building up of believers, whether it is spoken to an individual or a body of believers. Speaking prophetic words is not the interpretation of unknown tongues, it is not preaching or teaching from the Scriptures, nor is it any type of prediction of future events about a person or the end times. It will usually happen during or after a time of worship and can come forth as a word of reproof for an individual or a congregation to make changes in lives, to repent from sin, etc., or as words of comfort and confirmation that the hearer is on track, or progressing in the right direction with situations in their life. The main application of this manifestation gift is the receiving of supernatural words from Holy Spirit for the purpose of helping people in the congregation to overcome situations in their lives and to encourage people to mature in their faith journey into the character of our Master Yahshua. A person prophesying must speak words that are in line with the Holy Scriptures, that glorify King Yahshua, that bring clarification and not confusion, and that are liberating rather than bringing bondage. The Apostle Paul teaches us that we should desire spiritual gifts but especially prophesying. It is written:

> **Pursue love and strive for the spiritual gifts, and especially that you may prophesy. For those who speak in a tongue do not speak to other people but to God; for nobody understands them, since they are speaking mysteries in the Spirit. On the other hand, those who prophesy speak to other people for their building up and encouragement and consolation.**
> 1 Corinthians 14:1-3 (NRSV)

Most folks in congregations where Holy Spirit is invited to move freely refer to words of prophecy as words of knowledge, but as I covered earlier, they are different. In my experience, most words of prophecy are given as positive confirmation to the person that the person receiving the word is doing what they should be doing in a certain area of their spiritual growth.

Sometimes, though, I have witnessed a person receiving a word of prophecy that was reproof to bring something to their attention that needed to be dealt with, such as having a spirit of religion.

I had been working very hard on this book in my spare time and was about five years into this project when I went to a local church that had invited a young man who was very gifted in operating in the manifestation of prophesying. He gave words of prophecy that were consistently on the mark. I was the last person in a line of about eighty people that he had been ministering to. The person in front of me received a strong reproof for change that needed to take place in that person's life, so I was expecting that I, too, might receive a reproof to correct something in my life. I was pleasantly surprised when the word came forth and it was such wonderful confirmation that the work that Holy Spirit had purposed for me to do, referring to this book project, was accurate, right on the mark, and that our Heavenly Father was pleased. This is the word of prophecy that the young man spoke to me. "As a laser light beam is straight and hits the mark that it is aimed at, so is the work that you have set forth to accomplish. You are in a category five river, with very difficult rapids ahead. You are capable and will have no problem overcoming them; just continue paddling. Not one hair upon your head will be harmed. You will take risks for the Lord. Many in the Kingdom will come up to you to express gratitude for your acts of kindness."

I wept uncontrollably to know that Almighty Yah was pleased and that the hard work I was putting into this book was what He wanted that would go forth and be a blessing to people who would read this material and apply it. Being in a category five river was a preview of the many events that were about to unfold in my life, and the lives of my mother, father, and brother over the coming three years.

Within two months of the prophesy, my father was in a near fatal car wreck in which it took the rescue workers 30 minutes to cut him out of his vehicle. He received a severe concussion that accelerated his Alzheimer's and Leukemia diseases. My dear brother, Mark, left his job in order to care for our father after he recovered enough to go home.

Eight months later, our mother's gall bladder ruptured and she nearly died of blood sepsis, as I described at the beginning of this chapter.

The prophesy was true and foretold what was, so far, the most stressful time of my life. We prayed a lot. Almighty Yah is faithful, and He gave us the strength and the provisions to persevere and overcome all of the very difficult and challenging circumstances that we had to deal with in providing the very best care that we could for our parents.

Occasionally, while I was working through those three very difficult years, I would re-read the prophecy the young man had spoken to me. Reading the words would give me great comfort in knowing that our all-knowing Creator and Redeemer loves us more that we can comprehend in this life, and that He is faithful to help us through the rough, churning waters of the white water rapids of our lives and bring us to a peaceful shore. Being in a congregation where Holy Spirit is moving and manifesting His gifts through individuals He chooses is truly awesome and a blessing. Sometimes a word of prophecy can be as simple as someone speaking a specific Scripture to you that only you and Holy Spirit would know is your favorite, or just exactly the Scripture you needed to hear at that precise moment.

The Apostle Paul was certainly correct when he stated that we should all pursue to prophesy, for this type ministry truly is a blessing to members individually and to the congregation as a whole. It is written in a different translation than stated earlier:

> **Pursue love, and desire spiritual *gifts*, but especially that you may prophesy. For he who speaks in a tongue does not speak to men but to God, for no one understands *him*; however, in the spirit he speaks mysteries. But he who prophesies speaks edification and exhortation and comfort to men. He who speaks in a tongue edifies himself, but he who prophesies edifies the church. I wish you all spoke with tongues, but even more that you prophesied; for he who prophesies *is* greater than he who speaks with tongues, unless indeed he interprets, that the church may receive edification.**
> 1 Corinthians 14:1-5 (NKJV)

Various Kinds of Tongues: This is certainly another area in which there has been much confusion in the Body of Messiah. In my faith journey, I have had much confusion in seeking to understand the different gifts and manifestations of our Comforter and Teacher, Holy Spirit. The good thing about writing a book that teaches understanding on these topics is that I have had to do a lot of reading and digging for the truth from the Scriptures and other sources in order to provide the very best rendering possible that will benefit all of us in understanding these important truths and to also be able to apply them in ministry to bless others.

The Scriptures of Yah's Holy Word reveal to us that there are three different types of unknown tongues. They are: a known language that is spoken by someone that does not know the different language; an unknown prayer language that a born-again believer exercises in times of supernatural communication with Almighty Yah, and the third is a strong proclamation of an unknown tongue that requires an interpretation.

The example we have in Scripture of the first type that we have stated is in the book of the Acts of the Apostles. It is written:

When the day of Pentecost had come, they were all together in one place. And suddenly from heaven there came a sound like the rush of a violent wind, and it filled the entire house where they were sitting. Divided tongues, as of fire, appeared among them, and a tongue rested on each of them. All of them were filled with the Holy Spirit and began to speak in other languages, as the Spirit gave them ability. Now there were devout Jews from every nation under heaven living in Jerusalem. And at this sound the crowd gathered and was bewildered, because each one heard them speaking in the native language of each. Amazed and astonished, they asked, "Are not all these who are speaking Galileans? And how is it that we hear, each of us, in our own native language? Parthians, Medes, Elamites, and residents of Mesopotamia, Judea and Cappadocia, Pontus and Asia, Phrygia and Pamphylia, Egypt and the parts of Libya belonging to Cyrene, and visitors from Rome, both Jews and proselytes, Cretans and Arabs—in our own languages we hear them speaking about God's deeds of power." All were amazed and perplexed, saying to one another, "What does this mean?" But others sneered and said, "They are filled with new wine."

Acts 2:1-13 (NRSV)

The anointing power and presence of Holy Spirit was poured into the 120 believers so that they were transformed into born-again followers of our Master Yahshua. This event took place in a large room on the side of the great temple in Jerusalem during the Feast of *Shavuot* (Pentecost) when there were many thousands of Jewish pilgrims that had been obedient and gone there to celebrate the great feast. Holy Spirit moved on the 120 followers of Yahshua to empower them to be able to speak the testimony of the crucified and resurrected Messiah to the people around the temple in sixteen different languages as a sign to unbelievers. How awesome. This was the first outpouring of the good news (gospel) of Yahshua and His Kingdom.

Holy Spirit is still performing this great manifestation today in various parts of the world through His servants in order to reach people with the same good news message so that people who don't know the language of the country they are in can hear the truth of the one true God in their native language. I have not personally experienced this, but I know that it is true from the testimonies of very trustworthy friends.

The next type of unknown tongue is manifestation of a born-again believer praying or singing in a supernatural language directly to Almighty Yah. I believe that praying and singing in the spirit is the single most beneficial gift that Almighty Yah blesses a born-again believer with that builds the person up. There are great benefits in communicating supernaturally with our Creator and Master, such as empowering us to have victory over Satan's power. It is written:

Pray in the Spirit at all times in every prayer and supplication. To that end keep alert and always persevere in supplication for all the saints.
Ephesians 6:18 (NRSV)

This Scripture comes on the heels of the Scriptures that Paul wrote describing the defensive armor we are to put on and the one offensive weapon, the Word of Yah, that we are to use against our adversary. Praying in the spirit is having faith in Holy Spirit to bubble up from our inner most being and flow out like a river of living water. Holy Spirit flows in an anointed unction and prays through us so that the supernatural language is pure and has greater application of what we need to pray than we are aware of. Satan hates it when a born-again believer prays in the spirit because it drives his demons out, builds up the believer, helps the believer in worship, refreshes the believer's soul, and enables Holy Spirit to stir the other gifts that are in the believer so they can be used. All of these are for glorifying our Heavenly Father as we place our trust in Him, His Son— our Master and Redeemer, and His Agent—Holy Spirit. When we are led by Almighty Yah's Holy Spirit, we are not concerned with what people think or the traditions of men but only about pleasing our Father Yahweh.

Praying in the Spirit brings unity and harmony to a mature body of believers like nothing else will. It is written:

It is these worldly people, devoid of the Spirit, who are causing divisions. But you, beloved, build yourselves up on your most holy faith; pray in the Holy Spirit; keep yourselves in the love of God; look forward to the mercy of our Lord Jesus Christ that leads to eternal life.
Jude 19-21 (NRSV)

If you are a born-again believer and have never received the manifestation of praying in an unknown tongue and would like to, ask Holy Spirit to bless you with this awesome gift in Yahshua's name and He will. It's like everything else that is part of Yah's Kingdom, you have to seek after it with all of your heart by faith. Relax, take a deep breath, and start repeating HalleluYah, worship your Father and Redeemer, and allow Holy Spirit to speak the unknown anointed utterances through you. You will be amazed and blessed when this happens to you, and you will be thinking to yourself, "Wow, I should have been doing this long ago." I encourage you to pray in the Spirit to Almighty Yah each day. It will help you to mature in your covenant relationship with your Creator like nothing else will.

The third type of unknown tongue is a strong proclamation in an unknown tongue that requires an interpretation. The purpose of this type of supernatural communication from Holy Spirit is for the building up and edification of a body of born-again believers.

It is written:

So with yourselves; since you are eager for spiritual gifts, strive to excel in them for building up the church. Therefore, one who speaks in a tongue should pray for the power to interpret.
1 Corinthians 14:12-13 (NRSV)

I have personally experienced giving the interpretation of a strong proclamation of an unknown tongue among a group of believers only two times in my life. It is a very humbling and powerful experience when Holy Spirit comes upon you to use your vocal cords as His mouthpiece to interpret an unknown tongue that He has just spoken though another individual for the purpose of building up the body of Messiah. In the last part of the next section, I will share the interpretation that came forth as a revelation message for the body of Messiah from one of the two experiences I have had of interpreting an unknown tongue.

Interpretation of Unknown Tongues: The interpretation of tongues is just that—the translation of the supernatural manifestation of the unknown tongue that was boldly proclaimed by one believer and then interpreted by either the same person or a different person who is present. When you are among a mature body of born-again believers and the anointing of Holy Spirit is strong in each person in the midst of the body, sometimes Holy Spirit will communicate through an unknown tongue that will come forth boldly and will be louder than the sounds of all who are praying and singing in the spirit. Then there will be silence with anticipation of the interpretation that is coming forth. Those in attendance will be praying for the interpretation to come forth. Holy Spirit will reveal clearly to the individual who is to give the interpretation. Sometimes it is the same person that spoke the tongue; at other times Holy Spirit will choose someone else. There is no doubt in your mind when you know it is you that is to give the interpretation. Holy Spirit will speak to your mind and heart something like, "It's you. I will give you the words." You must trust and obey without trying to figure out what to say. You just open your mouth, and the words come forth in your native language. These are truly two of the most amazing experiences I have ever had: having Holy Spirit speak through me in the giving of a tongue, and also speaking through me in the interpretation of a tongue. These two experiences were at two different places and times.

In the winter of the year 2003, I had been invited to attend an all-night intercessory prayer watch to pray for America, Israel, and whatever else Holy Spirit placed in hearts. It was approximately four o'clock during that early Sabbath morning, and most of the group were praying and interceding. Suddenly, a lady near the front of the building proclaimed in a loud, bold unknown tongue that went on for about a minute. I was taking a coffee break and was sitting quietly in the back kitchen area. After the lady finished giving the tongue, it became perfectly still and quiet in the room. I took a sip of coffee, and Holy Spirit spoke to me clearly, "You will give the interpretation; I will give you the words." This had never happened to me before, and I was new to attending prayer watches with people who really pressed in and had been intercessors for years. I was sure it would be anyone in the room except me to give the interpretation. However, Holy Spirit chose me.

The interpretation of the supernatural, unknown tongue that Holy Spirit spoke through a woman and then spoke the interpretation through me on that cold morning of February 8, 2003, was this: "Come into Me, My bride. Press into Me, for the days ahead will be difficult. Press into Me, the Living Word, the Living Torah. I am re-building the Tabernacle of David. I am preparing My army—mighty men and women of valor—to go out and do My work. My army will set the captives free. They will lay hands on the sick, and the sick will be healed. Press into Me, My bride. I yearn for you."

One week later, I was attending a worship service at the Church of the Open Door near my home in Greenville, North Carolina, and during a time of prayer, a woman gave a powerful and bold unknown tongue. It became very still among the nearly three hundred people who were there. Then a man stood up and boldly gave the interpretation of the tongue the lady had just spoken.

"I am the God of Abraham, Isaac, and Jacob. Your praise is a sweet savor to Me. Come into Me, My bride. I am preparing you for difficult times. You are part of My army that I am preparing to send out in these last days. I am preparing a table for you. I am with you always, and I will never forsake you."

Being a writer, I always have a pad and pens so I can write down important messages in sermons, teaching, and moves of Holy Spirit. I recorded these two prophetic words for the body of Messiah verbatim.

I pray that what I have shared with you from these prophetic tongue interpretations is a blessing for you. I encourage you to pray and seek Almighty Yah with all of your heart, mind, and being. You could be one of the individuals that He is raising up to be in His great end-time army, His bride, the 144,000 that will be gathered to Jerusalem and sealed for protection just before the last three and one-half years of the great tribulation begins.

BIRTHRIGHT

I conclude this chapter with a short but important teaching on birthright that ties in with the other teachings in this chapter. I was given permission to share this teaching from a dear brother in Yahshua, whose name is Bradley. He accepted Jesus as his Lord and Savior at the age of 13 and began to seek his purpose in life as he continued to struggle with many physical challenges. Almighty Yahweh did a gradual healing of Bradley from cerebral palsy and other birth defects that he endured from childhood into his adult life. In 1982, he received the baptism of fire and was called into a ministry to the nations. Doors were opened for him, and he began to travel and minister to young adults, teaching them about the importance of prayer and how to overcome rejection because, in his life, he had learned to call upon the Lord to help him overcome much rejection and fear. Bradley returned to college after many years of being away and worked hard to receive a Ph.D. in Theology, graduating *summa cum laude*. He has traveled to 39 counties ministering to people and teaching about Yah's goodness and His desire for all people to pursue their birthright. The following is a summary of a teaching he gave to a small prayer group that I was blessed to be a part of.

In teaching in 39 countries, by far the question most often asked by the masses is, "What is God's will for my life?" It is written:

For it was you who formed my inward parts; you knit me together in my mother's womb. I praise you, for I am fearfully and wonderfully made. Wonderful are your works; that I know very well. My frame was not hidden from you, when I was being made in secret, intricately woven in the depths of the earth. Your eyes beheld my unformed substance. In your book were written all the days that were formed for me, when none of them as yet existed.
    Psalm 139:13-16 (NRSV)

Now the word of the LORD came to me saying, "Before I formed you in the womb I knew you, and before you were born I consecrated you; I appointed you a prophet to the nations." Then I said, "Ah, Lord GOD! Truly I do not know how to speak, for I am only a boy." But the LORD said to me, "Do not say, 'I am only a boy'; for you shall go to all to whom I send you, and you shall speak whatever I command you. Do not be afraid of them, for I am with you to deliver you, says the LORD."
    Jeremiah 1:4-8 (NRSV)

I pray that the God of our Lord Jesus Christ, the Father of glory, may give you a spirit of wisdom and revelation as you come to know him, so that, with the eyes of your heart enlightened, you may know what is the hope to which he has called you, what are the riches of his glorious inheritance among the saints, and what is the immeasurable greatness of his power for us who believe, according to the working of his great power.
    Ephesians 1:17-19 (NRSV)

Soon after Bradley received the baptism by fire, Holy Spirit spoke to him and said, "I'm not looking at your ability, I'm looking at your availability." Are you making yourself available to God so He can help you fulfill the birthright purpose that He created you for? The greatest obstacle that keeps us from fulfilling our birthright is fear; fear of failure, fear of the future, and fear of rejection. We must pray fervently and seek Holy Spirit's discernment for what our birthright purpose in life is so that we can be led into it, not driven by our own fleshly egos or pressure from others. We follow our Great Shepherd, Yahshua, as He leads us, and no matter how much ministry and kingdom work we do, we must always remember to keep Him first in our life and to stay in intimate relationship with our Creator, Redeemer, Master and Best Friend. Holy Spirit spoke to Bradley another time and said, "I'm not looking for your performance, I'm looking for you."

I am grateful to have met Brother Bradley. I was blessed by his testimony and teaching. In this last generation before King Yahshua comes to this earth to establish His Kingdom, He is raising up a remnant of men and women who desire to make themselves available to serve Him and work for His Kingdom purposes. They are seeking their birthright destiny. I have sought the Holy One of Israel and found mine in the writing and publishing of this book to bless all who will read it and have ears to hear. How about you, dear reader? Are you seeking Almighty Yah to reveal to you what His will and purpose is for your life?

There is a awesome and great work that Holy Spirit has been doing for a few years that is increasing in momentum in these last years before the beginning of Daniel's 70th week, and that is the restoration of the two houses of Israel to become the "one new man."

CONCLUSION

You are finishing the reading of twelve chapters of teaching from the Scriptures of Almighty Yah's Holy Word and my perspective of current world events that relate to the last generation Bible prophecies. I pray the information in this book has blessed you and helped you to grow as a person and helped in your faith journey.

I know that part of what I have written will be controversial with some readers, and I also know that I, being human, have made some mistakes in this work that will be revealed to me as readers discover them. I assure you I have not made any mistakes intentionally and will be making revisions to this book in future printings as the mistakes are brought to my attention.

I have attempted, with much hard work and diligence, to prepare you by the outpouring of the Spirit of EliYah for the coming catastrophic events of the great tribulation period, which is the last three and one-half years of this the last generation, and more importantly, to prepare you for the coming of King Yahshua Messiah, Who is our Creator, Redeemer, Master, King, High Priest, and the Great Judge Whom every human being that has ever lived will be judged by. These twelve chapters of teaching should have given you what you need from the following five categories, to face the difficult times ahead. If it happens that you are reading this book and the tribulation has already started, it will still be relative and will be a significant blessing to you and your loved ones.

1. To Know That You are Redeemed and That You Are a Member in Almighty Yah's Family.

In Chapters One through Three, you received wonderful knowledge from the Scriptures of Almighty Yah's master plan and of how the human race had to be separated from having relationship with our Creator because our ancient ancestors, Adam and Eve, did not following Father Yah's instructions. Next, you were taught that Father Yah provided in His plan a way to purchase back the souls of His created human race when He established His covenant with His servant Moses by making a provision for the covering of man's sins with the atoning sacrifice of the blood of clean animals. Chapter Two provided the many prophecies written several hundred years before the first coming of Messiah Yahshua by His faithful prophets to prepare people for His coming into the world as the Lamb of Yahweh. Father Yahweh amended and improved His covenant by making a provision for humanity to be forgiven of all sins and to be able to be brought into right standing and relationship with Him, and that was when He gave forth Himself as His own Holy Son, Yahshua.

Chapter Three contains my testimony of how Almighty Yah saved me, a sinner, and set my feet on His solid Rock, so that I would know that I had been redeemed by the blood of Yahshua. I have been blessed by Him to share with others the incredible change He made in my life after I accepted Him and made Him Master of my life. Oh, how wonderful to know that you have been forgiven of all of your sins, that you are a child in Father Yah's Kingdom, and to be blessed with the indwelling of His Holy Spirit Who gives us the peace that surpasses all understanding.

2. *To Understand the Deception That Has Influenced the History of the World Compared to the Truth in Yah's Holy Word and Our Hebraic Roots.*

Chapter Four provided you with the historical account of the attempt and success of Satan in his quest to create many false belief systems, teachings, and traditions throughout the human race in all generations for the purpose of drawing people as far away from Almighty Yah and His truth as possible. As you have read, Satan is the father of all lies and deception and comes forth to rob, kill, and destroy everyone and everything in retaliation to Almighty Yah for removing him from his place of authority when he served as Almighty Yah's highest worshipping angel in heaven.

In that chapter you also learned of the creation of a new belief system by Constantine, the Roman Caesar who instituted the Church of Rome that was responsible for changing the day of rest and worship from Saturday. the last day of the week, the Biblical Sabbath, to Sunday, the first day of the week and the day at that time that was the day to worship the sun god throughout the empire. The belief system of the Church of Rome was designed to turn people away from the Messianic Hebraic roots and doctrines of the first-century congregations and replaced them with new doctrines that were a mix of truth about the life, death, and resurrection of Yahshua and the holiday observances of the former state religion of sun god worship called Mithraism. That new belief system created deception among the people who were accepting Yahshua as their Savior by making the false doctrines punishable by death for those who did not obey them. Many of these false doctrines and traditions are still entrenched within our Christian churches today.

In Chapter Five you were able to understand the significance of the Sabbath day as a memorial to Yah's creation and a foreshadow of the millennial reign of King Yahshua when He returns and establishes His kingdom here on earth. The teaching on the revelation of understanding of the symbolism within the seven feasts should have provided you with much insight of Almighty Yah's timing for the first and second coming of Yahshua.

We are commanded in the *Torah* to keep all of the sanctified, set apart feast times of Yah because He tells us in His Word that these are His appointed times to meet with us and to be intimate with us. Learning about the truth is great, but living His truth and walking it out is what He desires for us in Him so that we can be the bride He desires.

3. *To Have Proof That We Are In the Last Days and to Have Revelation Knowledge of the Prophecies of the Second Coming of Messiah and the Events Prior To and After His Return.*

Chapters Six through Ten provided you with an abundance of information and knowledge relating to the end-times prophecies as to their relationship to current events in Israel and throughout the world. In Chapter Eight, you were given proof that the pre-tribulation rapture doctrine is a false teaching and that the true timing of the resurrection of the redeemed is at the very end of the tribulation when King Yahshua comes in all of His glory to rescue His saved body of overcomers and to pour out

His wrath on Satan's army, along with all those who received the mark of the anti-Messiah beast system. In Chapter Nine, you learned of post resurrection events and how to identify the group within the Body of Messiah that make up His bridesmaids and those that make up His Bride. Chapter Ten should have been a blessing in helping you to identify major events and situations to watch out for and remember as "road signs" as we progress closer to the tribulation years. Remember, as it is written in Luke 21:36, that we are instructed by our Master Yahshua to watch and pray that we may be counted worthy to escape, by His protection, all of the terrible catastrophes that are coming on the earth during the tribulation and to stand without fear and with confidence before the Son of Man.

4. *To Have Practical Information to Help Prepare You for the Coming Tribulation.*

In Chapter Eleven, I provided you with much insight and teaching of the importance of hearing from Holy Spirit and being led by Him in our daily decisions. He is our Teacher, Comforter, and Guide. He helps build up our faith so that if it is our lot to lay down our life for Yahshua's name and sake that we will be prepared to do so and not cave in to the pressure of the beast system to take the mark of the beast. Remember that you cannot take the mark of the beast, whatever it ends up being. Also in that chapter, you were taught that we are to come out of all false teachings and traditions that don't line up with Yah's Word. We will be held accountable for the truth we know from His Word and how well we have applied and lived that truth that we have received. It is written:

> **"Be dressed for action and have your lamps lit; be like those who are waiting for their master to return from the wedding banquet, so that they may open the door for him as soon as he comes and knocks. Blessed are those slaves whom the master finds alert** [*watching*] **when he comes; truly I tell you, he will fasten his belt and have them sit down to eat, and he will come and serve them. If he comes during the middle of the night, or near dawn, and finds them so, blessed are those slaves. But know this: if the owner of the house had known at what hour the thief was coming, he would not have let his house be broken into. You also must be ready, for the Son of Man is coming at an unexpected hour." Peter said, "Lord, are you telling this parable for us or for every-**

one?" And the Lord said, "Who then is the faithful and prudent manager whom his master will put in charge of his slaves, to give them their allowance of food *[physical food and spiritual food by ministering and teaching from the Word]* at the proper time? Blessed is that slave whom his master will find at work when he arrives. Truly I tell you, he will put that one in charge of all his possessions. But if that slave says to himself, 'My master is delayed in coming,' and if he begins to beat the other slaves, men and women, and to eat and drink and get drunk, the master of that slave will come on a day when he does not expect him and at an hour that he does not know, and will cut him in pieces, and put him with the unfaithful. That slave who knew what his master wanted, but did not prepare himself or do what was wanted, will receive a severe beating. But one who did not know and did what deserved a beating will receive a light beating. From everyone to whom much has been given, much will be required; and from one to whom much has been entrusted, even more will be demanded. I came to bring fire to the earth, and how I wish it were already kindled! I have a baptism with which to be baptized, and what stress I am under until it is completed! Do you think that I have come to bring peace to the earth? No, I tell you, but rather division! From now on, five in one household will be divided, three against two and two against three; they will be divided: father against son and son against father, mother against daughter and daughter against mother, mother-in-law against her daughter-in-law and daughter-in-law against mother-in-law."

Luke 12:35-53 (NRSV)

Holy Spirit is leading people all over the earth back to their Hebraic roots to rebuild the Tabernacle of David by worshiping Almighty Yah in spirit and in truth. Holy Spirit is restoring the House of Ephraim, that is made up of born again believers primarily here in America, to know their birthright in Him, which is to pray for and be a blessing to our brothers and sisters of the House of Judah who have not yet accepted Yahshua as their Messiah and Savior. Almighty Yah is returning Ephraim to understanding and living His *Torah*, and He is preparing to take the scales off of Judah's eyes so he will understand and accept Yahshua, so the two can be joined and be the "One New Man" that Almighty Yah has planned from the beginning.

In the latter part of Chapter Eleven, you read practical information about developing a plan for preparing a place of refuge if you hear those instructions from Holy Spirit to do so. Or you may hear from Holy Spirit that you have been chosen to be one of the 144,000 who will be the bride of Messiah or the countless others that make up the woman that is part of the body of Messiah that will be the bridesmaids that will be taken to the places in the wilderness for protection and will be provided for during the tribulation period. There will be many born-again servants of Yahshua who will be protected through the terrible tribulation times and who will be purged and prepared to become Almighty Yah's kings and priests that will rule and reign with King Yahshua throughout the thousand years of His Kingdom here on earth before He creates a new heaven and earth that will endure for all eternity. It is written:

> **... and from Jesus Christ, the faithful witness, the firstborn from the dead, and the ruler over the kings of the earth. To Him who loved us and washed us from our sins in His own blood, and has made us kings and priests to His God and Father, to Him *be* glory and dominion forever and ever. Amen.**
> Revelation 1:5-6 (NKJV)

> **But you are a chosen race, a royal priesthood, a holy nation, God's own people, in order that you may proclaim the mighty acts of him who called you out of darkness into his marvelous light.**
> 1 Peter 2:9 (NRSV)

The important message in the teachings throughout this book has been to seek Almighty Yah with all of your heart, to obey His instructions in His Holy Word, and to worship Him with His spirit and Truth living in you.

5. *To Teach You To Be Empowered By Yah's Holy Spirit To Do His Work Throughout the Earth.*

In Chapter Twelve you were taught the seven different personality traits that we may all have working in our lives. You learned that one of those traits is clearly predominate in each of us and is the ability that Almighty Yah created within us before we were born to mature into for the building of His kingdom and for His glory.

You were also taught about the five different offices of service that are within the Body of Messiah that He establishes as His government within His Body so that His Body works together in unity and harmony. This allows Him to establish His kingdom within his people in preparation of His coming. He will complete the establishment of His Kingdom when He comes with His host of angels and gives us our new resurrected bodies so we will be complete as He is.

In the latter part of the chapter, you were given a breakdown of the nine different manifestation gifts that are provided by Holy Spirit in the name of Yahshua, or Jesus, when you, the-born again believer, prays to be baptized by fire. These nine gifts are used within the body to edify and build up the body of believers in their congregations and fellowships so that Yahshua, the head of His Body, can minister though His members to each other and to the lost, infirmed, and demon possessed, so that they, too, can be set free to become His disciples and part of His Kingdom. Also included was a brief teaching about our birthright and the importance of seeking Holy Spirit to know what our birthright is and fulfilling it. Amen!

If you have not done so before now, I encourage you pray the prayer below as a model, so that Holy Spirit can minister to you to bring you into our Almighty Yah's Kingdom.

PRAYER OF REPENTANCE AND SALVATION

Confession:

"I believe that *Yahshua Ha Moshiach* / the Messiah is the promised Son of Yahweh, the Messiah of Israel. He lived a perfect, sinless life, revealed to humanity the way to have intimate relationship with our Heavenly Father Yah and how to love our fellowman. He was crucified for my sins, was buried, and arose the third day, according to the Scriptures. I believe He has ascended up into the heavens and that all power in heaven and earth is given unto Him. I believe, according to His Word, in the prophecies of the Scriptures, that He will return to this earth, and all who believe in Him, are immersed into His Name, will receive remission of sins, the gift of the *Ruach HaChodesh* / Holy Spirit, new resurrected bodies like His, and citizenship in the restored nation of Israel where we will serve Him as kings and priest through His millennial reign on earth. I receive and confess this day Yahshua of Nazareth as my personal Master and Redeemer.

Prayer:

Almighty Yah, God of Abraham, Isaac, and Jacob, I ask You now to forgive me of my disobedience, iniquities, and transgressions. I ask You to forgive my forefathers for turning their backs on Your *Torah*. I forgive all those who hurt me physically, spiritually, and emotionally. I ask that all evil influences be bound and not permitted to operate in my life according to *Torah*, and that your Spirit be loosed to operate in my life according to *Torah*, to rule and reign in my life, and to help me walk out Your Will. I ask this in the name of my Master and Redeemer, Yahshua Ha Moshiach. Amen."

Once you have prayed this prayer, I encourage you to have a baptism by immersion in water for status change from the unclean to the clean realm as a final cleansing, according to the instructions given in Acts 2:38. The symbolism of baptism is that when we go down into the water, we are repenting of all of our sins; we are being washed by the blood of Yahshua and, by faith, putting to death our former sinful nature. When we rise up out of the water, we are representing a new creation in Messiah Yahshua, born anew with His Holy Spirit and connected with His power to overcome the devil. We are part of His resurrection that we too will one day experience when He gives us our new dwelling places.

I have included our congregation's Statement of Faith that I pieced together from several that I researched that we believed best summarizes what we believe to be the truth and that we hold dear to our hearts in our daily walk. I pray that you will be blessed by it and receive confirmation in what you believe to be the truth to live by from Yahweh's Holy Word.

STATEMENT OF FAITH

Beth Yahshua (House of Jesus) congregation is a non-denominational community of believers with an end-time prophetic messianic message. Beth Yahshua seeks to cooperate with churches and synagogues that have a similar vision. We are a congregation that welcomes people of any race or background. The ministry objectives and biblical doctrines we adhere to are as follows:

• To proclaim Yahshua (Jesus Christ) as Messiah and coming King of the entire universe and, in our proclamation, to use His sacred Hebrew name.

• To teach from all of the Scriptures found in the Bible, including the *Torah*, Prophets, Writings, and New Covenant.

• To call all people to repentance from sin and to walk uprightly before the Lord.

• To administer with love to anyone that requests prayer and ministry as conveyed in Mark 16:17-18.

• To explore our Hebraic roots and heritage.

• To encourage Believers to follow Yahshua's example in faith and practice, and to learn how to live a *Torah*-observant lifestyle led by the Holy Spirit.

1. We believe that the Bible, both the *Tanakh* (Old Covenant) and the *Brit Hadasha* (New Covenant), is the only inspired, infallible, and authoritative Word of YHWH (1 Thess. 2:13; 2 Tim. 3:16; 2 Peter 1:21).
2. We believe in ONE God as He has revealed Himself in the Holy Scriptures (Deut. 6:4; Mark 12:29).
3. We believe that Yahshua is the Son of Almighty Yahweh; the Messiah; the Eternal One in whom all the fullness of deity dwells in bodily form; the Word who became flesh and dwelt among us, and we beheld His glory, the glory of the uniquely begotten Son of Yahweh, full of grace and truth (John 1:1-14; Col. 2:9).

4. We believe in the deity of Yahshua and His virgin birth (Isa. 9:6; Isa. 7:14; Matt. 1:18-25), in His vicarious and atoning death through His shed blood (Isa. 53; Dan. 9:24-27; Rom. 3:21-31; Heb. 9, 10), in His bodily resurrection (Zech. 12:10, Zech. 14; Matt. 28), and in His personal return in power and glory (Dan. 7:9-14; Matt. 26:57-64; Rev. 1:1-18). We believe that Yahshua is the Way, the Truth, and the Life; and that no one comes to the Father except through Him (John 14:6, John 6:29, John 40, John 44; 1 John 5:11).

5. Man is a created being made in the likeness and image of Almighty Yahweh, but through Adam's transgression and fall, sin came into the world, for "all have sinned and come short of the glory of YHWH." As it is written, "There is none righteous, no, not one." Yahshua, the Messiah and the Son of Yahweh, was manifested to undo the work of the devil and gave His life and shed His blood to redeem and restore man back to Yahweh (Rom. 3:10 & 23, 5:14; 1 John 3:8). Salvation is a gift of Yahweh to man, separate from works and the *Torah*, and is made operative by grace through faith in Yahshua, producing works acceptable to YHWH. One may not earn, merit, or keep this eternal salvation by his own efforts. A new creation is the work of Yahweh alone (Eph. 2:8-9; Rom. 5; Rom. 6).

6. We believe that the *Torah* (the five books of Moses) is a comprehensive summary of Yahweh's foundational teachings and instructions as found in both the new and older covenants (Ex. 19 & 20; Deut. 5; Jer. 31:31-34; Matt. 5:17-19; Heb. 8:10). Therefore, we encourage all believers, both Jew and non-Jew, to affirm, embrace, and practice these foundational laws and ways as clarified through the life of Messiah Yahshua (Matt. 5:17-19; 1 Cor. 7:19; Rev. 14:12).

7. The Bible teaches that without holiness no man can see YHWH. We believe in the doctrine of sanctification as a definite, yet progressive, work of grace commencing at the time of regeneration and continuing until the consummation of salvation (1 Thess. 5:23; 2 Pet. 3:18; Heb. 12:14).

8. The baptism with the Holy Spirit and fire is a gift from YHWH promised by Yahshua to all believers and is received subsequent to the new birth (Matt. 3:11; John 14:16-17; Acts 2:38-39). We believe in the operation of and embrace all the gifts of the Holy Spirit as enumerated in Yahweh's Word (Acts 19:1-7; 1 Cor. 12:1-11).

9. We believe that Jewish and non-Jewish people who trust in Yahshua

are grafted into the olive tree of Israel, which grants them the privilege of following the *Torah* (Yahweh's teachings and instructions) having written it upon their hearts as participants of the New Covenant. Thus, all Israel will be saved (Jer. 31:31-34; Rom. 11:11-26).

10. We believe in the resurrection of both the wicked and the righteous. Those who have trusted in Yahshua will be resurrected unto life and those who die without having believed in Yahshua will experience the eternal wrath of YHWH (John 5:19-29; Rom. 1:18; 1 Cor. 15; Rev. 20; Rev. 21).

I leave you with these final words. Seek your Heavenly Father, your Creator, Redeemer, Master, closest Friend, coming King and Judge with all of your heart. Believe in Yahshua as your Redeemer and put your complete faith and trust in His blood that He shed for our sins so that we could be purchased from Satan, the devil and ruler of this world. Repent and turn away from all sin, for this is what our Father Yah requires. Desire intimate relationship with Him, for this is what He desires from all of His children, not religion. Pray often in the language of Holy Spirit. Worship Almighty Yah in spirit and in truth, for He seeks to dwell within those who do this. Pray for Him to reveal to you the purposes that He created for you to fulfill in your life, so that you can be all that He intended for you to be in Him, which includes being a blessing to others. Rejoice, knowing that you are His child, and He loves you as one of His many children who are part of His Kingdom. Treat all people with true compassion and respect, forgiving all who seek to hurt you. Take no offense and be quick to forgive, loving the sinner, but hating the sin.

It is written:

The end of the matter; all has been heard. Fear God, and keep his commandments; for that is the whole duty of everyone. For God will bring every deed into judgment, including every secret thing, whether good or evil.
Ecclesiastes 12:13-14 (NRSV)

Finally, be strong in the Lord and in the strength of his power. Put on the whole armour of God, so that you may be able to stand against the wiles of the devil.
Ephesians 6:10-11 (NRSV)

"Do not let your hearts be troubled. Believe in God, believe also in me. In my Father's house there are many dwelling places. If it were not so, would I have told you that I go to prepare a place for you? And if I go and prepare a place for you, I will come again and will take you to myself, so that where I am, there you may be also. And you know the way to the place where I am going." Thomas said to him, "Lord, we do not know where you are going. How can we know the way?" Jesus said to him, "I am the way, and the truth, and the life. No one comes to the Father except through me. If you know me, you will know my Father also. From now on you do know him and have seen him."

John 14:1-7 (NRSV)

The LORD spoke to Moses, saying: Speak to Aaron and his sons, saying, Thus you shall bless the Israelites: You shall say to them, The LORD bless you and keep you; the LORD make his face to shine upon you, and be gracious to you; the LORD lift up his countenance upon you, and give you peace. So they shall put my name on the Israelites, and I will bless them.

Numbers 6:22-27 (NRSV)

Dear reader, it is my sincere prayer for you that you take to heart what you have received from Almighty Yah's Holy Word and my teachings in this book, that you may be blessed in being obedient to Yah's Word, be in love with your Creator and Master Yahshua and all people that you are in contact with, and that you be prepared for the coming of Messiah. I pray blessings and shalom upon you in Yahshua's name. Amen.

A humble servant of Yahshua,
Perry Ennis

You may contact Perry Ennis at:

MENORAH BOOKS

740 Greenville Blvd., Suite 400-154
Greenville, NC 27858-5135 USA
E-mail: perrye@embarqmail.com

BIBLIOGRAPHY AND WEB SITES

END TIMES PROPHECY AND HEBRAIC ROOTS

- Hebraic Heritage International at: www.hebroots.org/index.htm#Network
- Chumney, Eddie. *Who is the Bride of Christ?* Serenity Books, 1997
- Chumney, Eddie. *Restoring the Two Houses of Israel.* Serenity Books, 1997
- Chumney, Eddie. *The Seven Festivals of the Messiah.* Serenity Books, 1994
- Messianic Israel Alliance at: www.mim.net/front.html
- Wooten, Batya. *Israel Revealed: Ephraim and Judah.* Key of David, 2002
- Wooten, Batya. *Who Is Israel?* Key of David, 2003
- Wooten, Batya. *Israel's Feast and Their Fullness.* Key of David, 2004
- Wooten, Batya. *Passover In All Its Fullness.* Key of David, 2004
- Wooten, Angus. *Take Two Tablets Daily.* Key of David, 2005
- Cavallaro, Gloria. *My Beloved's Israel.* Key of David, 2001
- Tregelles, S.P., LL.D. *The Hope of Christ's Second Coming.* Whitstable Litho Ltd., 1864
- Lion and Lamb Ministries at: www.lionlamb.net
- Judah, Monte. *A Study of the Book of Revelation.*
- End Times Bible Prophecy Made Plain at: www.EscapeAllTheseThings.com
- McHyde, Tim. *Know the Future.* Tim McHyde Publishing, 2003
- Messianic Vision at: www.sidroth.org
- Roth, Sid. *Time is Running Short.* Destiny Image Publishers, 1990
- Battlestein, Baruch. *Covenant, G-d's Plan for Israel in the Last Days.* Destiny Image Europe, 2005
- Stein, David. *Israel, God and America.* Zion Publishers, 2002
- Koch, Robert and Remy. *Christianity: New Religion of Sect of Biblical Judaism?* Messenger Media, 1999
- Weiss, Jeffery. *The Truth of Reformation.* For the Glory of Yahshuah Ministries, 2000

Continued

MINISTRY

- The King of Glory Ministry at: www.yahveh.com/store.asp
- Seedman, Terrye Goldblum. *Holy To YAHVEH*. Goldblum Seedman Foundation, 1996
- Roth, Sid. *They Thought for Themselves*. Messianic Vision Press, 1996
- Roth, Sid. *There Must Be Something More*. Messianic Vision Press, 1994
- Derek Prince Ministries at: www.derekprince.com
- Prince, Derek. *They Shall Expel Demons*. Chosen Books, 1998
- Larry Huch Ministries at: www.larryhuchministries.com
- Huch, Larry. *10 Blessings That Block the Blessing*. Whitaker House, 2006
- Telchin, Stan. *Abandoned*. Chosen Books, 1997
- Osborn, T.L. Ministry at: www.osborn.org/about/tlosborn.html
- Osborn, T.L. Miracles, *Proof of God's Love*. Osborn Publishers, 2003
- Norman Robertson Ministries at: www.normanrobertson.com/index.html
- Robertson, Norman. *Walking in Victory*. NRM Publications, 1996
- Wholeness Ministries: *Learning to do What Jesus Did*. Archer-Ellison Publishing Company, 1997
- Francen, Mike, *A Miracle Settles The Issue*. Francen World Outreach, 1992
- Ed Decker's Personal Bookshelf at: www.saintsalive.com/bookshelf.html
- Decker, Ed. *Fast Facts on False Teachings*. Harvest House, 1994
- Harfouche, Christian. *The Miracle Ministry of the Prophet*. Christian Publications, 1993
- Madden, Peter J. *The Wigglesworth Standard*. Whitaker House, 1993